TEACHING MARITIME STUDIES

Teaching
Maritime Studies

Edited by
Phillip Buckner

Acadiensis Press
Fredericton, New Brunswick

1986

Canadian Cataloguing in Publication Data

Teaching Maritime Studies

(Sources in the history of Atlantic Canada; no. 5)
Papers presented at a conference held in Fredericton, N.B.,
November 1985.
Bibliography: p. 299
ISBN 0-919107-08-7

1. Maritime Provinces - Study and teaching - Congresses.
2. Atlantic Provinces - Study and teaching - Congresses.
I. Buckner, Phillip A. (Phillip Alfred), 1942 -
II. Series.

FC2028.T42 1985   971.5'007   C86-094108-6
F1035.8.T42 1985

This book has been published with the aid of grants from the
Multiculturalism Directorate, Department of the Secretary of
State, and the Social Sciences and Humanities Research Council
of Canada.

Printed by Keystone Printing & Lithographing Ltd., Saint John, N.B.

TEACHING MARITIME STUDIES

Introduction

P.A. Buckner

THE ESSAYS CONTAINED IN THIS book were originally presented at a Conference on "Teaching Maritime Studies", held at the Fredericton campus of the University of New Brunswick from 7-10 November 1985. The purpose of the Conference was a simple one. The organizers were aware that a new course on "Maritime Studies" was to be introduced into the school systems of the three Maritime Provinces in the near future. The history of this course had been somewhat unusual. Its genesis lay in a decision of the Council of Maritime Premiers and to some extent it was introduced over opposition — or at least without much enthusiasm — from those in the various departments of education who were normally responsible for designing the provincial curricula. Moreover, although Maritime Studies were already being taught at many Universities in (and without) the region, it was clear that only a few of those who had been in the forefront of regional scholarship had been involved in the preparation or design of the new course. Since many teachers had also expressed concern over their lack of preparedness in the area of Maritime Studies, it seemed to the organizers that it would be desirable to bring together academic specialists and teachers and administrators from the public schools systems and to attempt to break down some of the artificial institutional barriers which so often seem to inhibit the free exchange of ideas and information between two groups of professionals who in the end do have the same goals.

The primary purpose of the conference, therefore, was to invite a number of the best known academics in the field of Maritime Studies to suggest, from the perspective of their own discipline or scholarly interest, what ought to be included in a course on Maritime Studies. They were asked to give brief presentations outlining what they felt to be the most important topics and themes in their field and assessing the most significant literature on these subjects; in other words to give a kind of state of the art address. They were also asked to focus on issues of content, on the question of what should be included in the curriculum rather than on the question of how the material should be presented in the classroom. Of course, the questions of *what* and *how* are to some extent inseparable and many of the contributors legitimately ignored the latter instruction and focused directly on the methods of introducing a school-aged population to the field of Maritime Studies. In planning the program of the conference the organizers tried to ensure that all of the major disciplines and interdisciplinary approaches were represented at the conference, although partly because of constraints of time and money the conference could not be as all-inclusive as was hoped. For example, such important topics as regional linguistics and the whole area of the performing arts were neglected. An effort was also made to ensure that where there were conflicting views within a discipline, both sides were represented.

As one can see from this volume, the papers reflected a wide diversity of views and approaches toward the teaching of Maritime Studies. Yet certain themes did recur again and again. The first of these was that any course on Maritime Studies must be truly interdisciplinary in nature. In fact, one of the remarkable features of the conference was the degree of unanimity on this point. Indeed, one of the concerns frequently expressed about the proposed content of the new course was that it seemed to be overly committed to a division of the material along disciplinary lines. Second, there was a general consensus that the proposed course ought to be truly regional in approach. Peter Waite's *cri di coeur* for the inclusion of Newfoundland in the proposed course seemed to fall on somewhat stoney ground, but there was a very strong and very negative reaction to the rumour (undoubtedly founded in fact) that those involved in designing the proposed course were under pressure from some of the provincial departments of education (in particular, the Nova Scotia department) to adopt a kind of provincial quota system in allocating the themes and topics to be included in the curriculum. Similarly considerable concern was expressed by the overwhelmingly Anglophone audience over the fact that two separate courses and two separate textbooks were being developed, one for the Anglophone and another for the Francophone students, since this implied that a single course and text could not be developed that would do justice to both the majority and the largest minority in the region. Third, there was also widespread agreement that the decision to focus the proposed course on the period since 1945 was a serious error. It was not just the historians who raised this concern. Speaker after speaker stressed the need for an historical perspective if students were to understand the present condition and the distinctive cultural patterns of the Maritimes.

There was also widespread concern lest the proposed course become a kind of exercise in self-congratulation. No one denied that one of the legitimate purposes of a Maritime Studies course was to instil in those who were born and raised within the region a greater sense of regional pride. In fact, most of the papers stressed the need to avoid glib comparisons with the rest of Canada that were frequently based upon a stereotypical view of Maritime development and society. But the danger is that in accentuating the positive one may adopt what one member of the audience called an "*Atlantic Insight*" approach to Maritime Studies. Although the new publisher of *Atlantic Insight* legitimately objected to this characterization of his publication, it remains true that, partly for political reasons, the course is likely to ignore or gloss over the very real economic and social problems which students of the region must be trained to confront directly. As a number of the papers in the collection show, there is a dark side to Maritime society. Racism, ethnocentricism and sexism have flourished here as elsewhere in Canada and while traditional prejudices may have gone underground they have not disappeared. Moreover, several of the papers point to the weaknesses of imposing upon the region a Whig interpretation which emphasizes the inevitability of progress. Although federal government policies since 1945 have mitigated some of the economic difficulties of the region, they have institutionalized regional dependency and left the region extremely vulnerable to federal policy. Yet, as Colin Howell points out in his perceptive article, there is a danger that by attributing this dependency to outside economic forces over which Maritimers have no control, one may perpetuate a "victimization ideology" which "has operated to preserve existing power relations in the past and the present".

All of those who spoke at the Conference were aware of the constraints — political, ideological and fiscal — under which the Maritime Studies course was being developed. Certainly among some of the teachers (many of whom had been reluctantly coopted into teaching Maritime Studies) there appeared to be considerable concern over the difficulties of mounting an academically respectable and intellectually stimulating course. But as the following papers make clear, there is no academic or intellectual reason why such a course can not be developed. Two requirements seem necessary. First, as many of the participants suggested, a course which focuses on regional studies must involve local materials and a hands-on approach in which the students themselves are encouraged to engage in original research. There are difficulties in this approach, but they are not insurmountable and the rewards, as Sandy Ives so eloquently shows, are great. Second, it is not enough to develop a curriculum and a text-book, however good both may be. In the end what is critical is what happens in the classroom and here the influence of the teacher is critical. Since very few of the teachers who will be involved in introducing the Maritime Studies programme will have been trained in that field, it is essential that they be given proper pre-service and in-service training. We hope that this collection of papers will be of use to them in discovering how various topics might be approached and some idea of the literature available to them. But as Frank McGee persuasively argues, "Words are not Enough". Indeed, there was a general feeling among the participants that more conferences — perhaps focusing on more specialized aspects of the topic — of this kind were necessary.

It is difficult to estimate how much impact the conference will have upon the course when it is introduced into the schools. Certainly it was well attended. Over 200 academics, school teachers, educational administrators and government bureaucrats registered and a much larger number of people attended one or more sessions of the conference. Yet this is, of course, only a small fraction of those who will be involved in designing and teaching the course. It is for this reason that the organizers decided to publish a collection of the papers delivered at the conference. Not all of those who participated in the conference submitted their papers for publication with the result that the disciplines of sociology and economics are underrepresented and there is not as much on Acadian Studies or on Maritime Literature as we had hoped. The authors were given time to revise their papers for publication, but they are presented here with only light copyediting. All of the authors were encouraged to submit short bibliographies, although some preferred to rely on detailed footnotes.

The conference in Fredericton was made possible by grants from the Maritime Provinces Education Foundation, the Social Sciences and Humanities Research Council of Canada, the Multiculturalism Directorate of the Department of Secretary of State, the Government of New Brunswick and the University of New Brunswick. The publication of this book was made possible by subsidies from the Multiculturalism Directorate and the Social Sciences and Humanities Research Council of Canada. Many people assisted in the organization of the conference and the preparation of this book for publication but as always Beckey Daniel's role was indispensable.

We believe that the essays which follow will be of general interest to anyone interested in Maritime Studies and trust that their publication will stimulate greater discussion about the structure and purpose of the proposed course, not only among teachers but among all those who believe that a course on Maritime Studies, if properly conceived, has a positive and important contribution to make in preparing the students of the region to participate actively and energetically as citizens in the public life of the region. As the late David Alexander (who is frequently quoted in the papers which follow) suggested, lack of educational skills and information breeds "an unimaginative and inefficient debate" about the goals of a society and how they are best realized. At no time in their history have the Maritime Provinces been in greater need of such a debate and it is our hope that the Maritime Studies course will be sufficiently stimulating and innovative to produce a generation of students who are prepared to engage in that debate.

1

Maritime Studies: Some Problems in Perspective

Ernest Forbes

THE TOPIC OF THIS SESSION is the study of Maritime history and geography. We are not asked what should be written or how to write it, but rather to suggest how to approach the existing literature to gain maximum understanding of the Maritime Provinces in the last forty years. There are no general histories or other syntheses to take the student by the hand and guide him or her through the material.[1] This presentation will briefly consider three problems which the student may encounter in studying historical and other literature on the region. I call them problems in perspective.

This talk is predicated upon the assumption that an essential ingredient to the understanding of almost any situation involving people is the historical perspective. By way of illustration, imagine a photograph of your grandmother. Since imagination is not yet subject to economic restraint make it a large, glossy colour photograph. What could a stranger learn from such a picture? An informed student might deduce information regarding your grandmother's racial characteristics, and social class and even make precise physical measurements. Now imagine a video cassette which, complete with narrative, presents as a series of flashback episodes of the most significant events from your grandmother's life. Which would contribute more to understanding? It is the cassette which provides the historical perspective through which one might begin to understand your grandmother as a person. The information yielded by the photograph is by comparison speculative, superficial and trivial.

Lest it should seem that this talk is merely a "plug" for one's own discipline, I should point out that historians have had no monopoly in the

---

1   The closest we have come to a comprehensive text on the Maritimes is a collection of articles, P.A. Buckner and David Frank, eds., *The Acadiensis Reader* (Fredericton, 1985), vols. 1 and 2. Verner Smitheram, D. Milne and S. Dasgupta, *The Garden Transformed: Prince Edward Island, 1945-1980* (Charlottetown, 1982) traces several themes through the modern period from an Island perspective. For a survey of modern historical scholarship see William Godfrey, "'A New Golden Age': Recent Historical Writing on the Maritimes", *Queen's Quarterly*, 91/2 (Summer 1984), pp. 350-82.

development of an historical perspective. Indeed, until the last two decades, historians did little work on the Maritimes for the period after Confederation. The compilers of the historical literature include economists, political scientists and sociologists. Moreover, it has become a truism that some of the best historical research on the Maritimes is currently undertaken by geographers.

An obvious problem in developing historical perspective is where to begin. In studying the Maritimes of the last forty years does one start in 1945? Or does one go back to Confederation? Some of you may remember Professor George Wilson at Dalhousie University about two decades ago. Wilson, who had taught history for about half a century, began his course on the French Revolution with the Romans. Some of us in the class became restless when Christmas arrived and the revolution had not yet begun. Wilson was not sympathetic to our queries suggesting that he probably should have begun with the Egyptians! We later came to realize that he had provided us with carefully selected information with which to develop the perspective necessary to understand the events of the revolutionary period.

In studying the modern Maritimes one probably cannot depend on some wise old teacher selecting and boiling down relevant material from earlier periods. We have to go back and survey the literature for ourselves as we require the information to answer specific questions pertinent to the modern period. For example, an obvious query at the outset of any course of study on the Maritimes is "Who are the Maritimers". An answer must address the complexity of a cultural mosaic in the region. The distinctive traditions of Acadians, Scots, Irish, Blacks, Micmacs, Yankees, Loyalists and others have persisted and do exist. Closely intertwined with their cultural traditions have been basic social institutions such as churches and universities. Scholars of the recent past regularly invoke cultural traditions whether explaining the role of the Scottish Catholic Society in the Co-operative movement, the Irish Catholics in analyzing voting patterns in Saint John or the interests of Acadians in the programme for "equal opportunity".[2] One can learn something about the cultural mosaic by analyzing census statistics in the modern period, but one can learn far more by tapping the rich historical literature which offers the equivalent of a video cassette in providing the historical perspective on the cultural mosaic. But most of the literature deals with formative periods of cultural traditions and often predates Confederation. Anyone who attempts to identify Maritimers only within the time frame of the last forty years will

2 Ian MacPherson, *Each For All: A History of the Cooperative Movement in English Canada*, 1900-1945 (Toronto, 1979); Della Stanley, *Louis Robichaud: A Decade of Power* (Halifax, 1984).

produce a picture which is speculative, superficial and trivial.

A second problem in perspective is also susceptible to photographic analogy. One may have noticed that pictures which highlight individuals or objects often leave the background blurred. Cameras employing what is known as a "fisheye" lens usually render peripheral objects so distorted as to be unrecognizable. Canadian historians have tended to present Ontario and Quebec front and centre in their general works with the Maritimes relegated to peripheral status. Inevitably the element of distortion tends to creep in. A blatant example of this phenomenon was pointed out some years ago by Murray Beck as occurring in Donald Creighton's biography of Sir John A. Macdonald.[3] In highlighting his hero's efforts to bring about what was, in Creighton's view, the truly noble concept of Confederation, the author explained Joseph Howe's opposition by portraying him at this time as a tired, bitter and almost senile old man. Here the fisheye lens was employed with a definite purpose.

In most general studies of the post-confederation period blurring and distortion have been quite inadvertent. Scholars in attempting to say something about the Maritimes in the absence of substantial research on that region often resorted to the uncritical repetition of stereotypes and myths. As these have been repeated in one general study after another, they have acquired an orthodoxy accepted even by scholars of the region. In political history patronage and corruption have been almost constant themes for Maritime coverage — as though these were not features of the political process in all regions. Political and social historians have reiterated the theme of Maritime conservatism to suggest and explain supposed differences in Maritime behavior and to deny Maritime participation in common intellectual currents and social movements of the day.[4] In economic history the stereotype too has provided an explanation for Maritime economic difficulties, as "conservative" Maritimers supposedly failed to invest, modernize, or otherwise show entrepreneurial initiative.

In the flowering of historical research on the Maritimes in the last two decades, labour historians, such as David Frank, Ian McKay, Donald Macgillivray and Nolan Reilly, have worked to push back the stereotype to uncover a militant and sometimes radical labour tradition in the region.[5]

---

3 J. Murray Beck, *Joseph Howe: Anti-Confederate*, Canadian Historical Association Booklet No. 17 (Ottawa, 1965), pp. 13-4.

4 E.R. Forbes, "In search of post-confederation Maritime historiography, 1900-1967", D.J. Bercuson and P.A. Buckner, eds. *Eastern and Western Perspectives* (Toronto, 1981), pp. 47-67.

5 For samples of their work see David Frank and Don Macgillivray's "Introduction" to Dawn Fraser's *Echoes from Labour's War* (Toronto, 1976); Macgillivray, "Glace Bay: Images and Impressions" in *Mining and other Pictures* (Glace Bay, 1983), pp. 171-91;

Political works, such as Margaret Conrad's biography of George Nowlan, have surmounted the stereotypes of corruption and patronage to suggest that the Maritimes' voting behavior is often explicable in terms of regional self interest.[6] Historians of women in the region, such as Christina Simmons and John Reid, have uncovered interesting aspects of women's status and behavior beneath the blanket of conservatism which Cleverdon threw over the women of the region.[7] While the stereotypes tend to be revised and corrected in modern literature in which the Maritimes appears front and centre, the student may need to employ the older or more general works for information and, in so doing, must read critically to avoid absorbing the old stereotypes. Moreover one still has to allow for the fisheye lens in some recent general literature. One is pleased to report, however, at least the beginning of the integration of the regional historiography into the national literature. The latest volume of the Centenary History of Canada by John Thompson and Allen Seager offers a panoramic view of Canada in the 1920s and 1930s which includes the Maritimes in realistic proportions.[8]

A third problem in perspective in literature on the Maritimes might be suggested through the analogy of the telescopic lens. The telescope allows an analysis in depth and detail which would otherwise be impossible. Yet it is accompanied by narrowing of perspective, which may conceal the broad patterns. For some scholars a narrowing in perspective may result from disciplinary pre-occupations and specialization.

This problem can be illustrated in the literature on one of the most important themes in Maritime studies — the question of regional disparity or regional underdevelopment. In 1948 B.S. Keirstead, an economist formerly at the University of New Brunswick, attributed the decline in manufacturing in the Maritimes to the free interplay of the forces of the

Frank and Reilly, "The Emergence of the Socialist Movement in the Maritimes, 1899-1916", R.J. Brym and R.J. Sacouman, eds., *Underdevelopment and Social Movements in Atlantic Canada* (Toronto, 1979), pp. 81-106; Ian McKay, "Strikes in the Maritimes, 1901-1914", *Acadiensis* XIII/1 (Autumn 1983), pp. 3-46; and McKay, "Springhill 1958", *New Maritimes* (December 1983-January 1984). Paul MacEwan, *Miners and Steelworkers: Labour in Cape Breton* (Toronto, 1967) is useful as a factual narrative.

6 Margaret Conrad, "George Nowlan and the Conservative Party in the Annapolis Valley" (PhD thesis, University of Toronto, 1979). Her book on this topic is soon to be published by the University of Toronto Press.

7 J.G. Reid, "The Education of Women at Mount Allison, 1954-1914", *Acadiensis*, XII/2 (Spring 1983), pp. 3-33; Christina Simmons, " 'Helping the Poorer Sisters': The Women of the Jost Mission, Halifax, 1905-1945", *Acadiensis*, XIV/2 (Autumn 1984), pp. 3-27; Catherine Cleverdon, *The Woman Suffrage Movement in Canada* (Toronto, 1950).

8 John Herd Thompson with Allen Seager, *Canada, 1922-1939: Decades of Discord* (Toronto, 1985).

marketplace. Closer to the large centres of population, manufacturers in Ontario and Quebec enjoyed advantages of scale and agglomeration which enabled them to draw business away from the Maritimes.[9] Ironically, Keirstead researched and wrote his book at a time when the interplay of economic forces in Canada was anything but free. The Canadian economy was still emerging from the controls imposed by the federal government during the second world war. Moreover, it was during the war that, financed by public funds and under the direction of a federal bureaucracy, Canada's industrial plant more than doubled while the relative decline of that of the Maritimes continued at a greater pace.[10] Keirstead, as an economist, in treating the Maritimes' economic decline stopped short of any serious analysis of political and constitutional factors in the region's difficulties. Meanwhile, historically-minded political scientists such as J.M. Beck, Hugh Thorburn and Frank MacKinnon did find political and constitutional factors adverse to the Maritimes, especially in the area of Dominion-provincial finance. They were, however, unprepared to pursue the economic implications of the weaknesses of the Maritimes' position within Confederation, which their own studies often suggested.[11] Thus we have two traditions of scholarship on regional disparity — one which looked at economic problems and one which looked at constitutional and political problems, but the two seldom if ever came together until the 1970s.

In the last two decades scholars have sought approaches which would allow them to perceive the interrelationships of political, constitutional and economic factors in historical perspective. Some have argued the need for a new discipline or the return to an older one called "political economy". Others have stressed the importance of interdisciplinary approaches. But some Maritime scholars have simply sought broader concepts within their disciplines with which to explore inter-relationships. Metropolitanism, regionalism, and a revised Marxian underdevelopment and dependency theory are a few of the approaches employed by modern historians in their attempt to obtain a better perspective on the development of Maritime regional disparity. (And here I would draw particular attention to the work of the late David Alexander.[12]) The older literature is still useful and

---

9   B.S. Keirstead, *Theory of Economic Change* (Toronto, 1948), pp. 267-310.

10 E.R. Forbes, "Consolidating Disparity: The Maritimes and the Industrialization of Canada during the Second World War", *Acadiensis*, XVI/1 (Spring 1986), pp. 3-27.

11 J.M. Beck, *The Government of Nova Scotia* (Toronto, 1957); Frank MacKinnon, *The Government of Prince Edward Island* (Toronto, 1951); and Hugh Thorburn, *The Politics of New Brunswick* (Toronto, 1961).

12 David G. Alexander, *Atlantic Canada and Confederation: Essays in Canadian Political Economy* (Toronto, 1983).

contains information that is not to be found elsewhere. Yet students would be advised to peruse recent works for concepts and a framework of analysis before immersing themselves in the detailed studies of the earlier specialists.

To recapitulate, in studying the recent Maritimes one should identify topics of interest and go back in time in the literature as far as is necessary to see events in historical perspective. One may wish to view the region in a national context but must be careful to avoid absorbing myths and stereotypes often carried by the so-called "national" literature. And finally one should approach the products of a narrow and specialized expertise armed with the concepts and analytical framework necessary to fit that information into a broader pattern. Or to put it another way, the student should choose the video cassette over the flat photograph, recognize and avoid the distortions of the fisheye lens, and fit products of the telescopic lens into a larger picture.

2

Economism, Ideology, and the Teaching of Maritime History

Colin D. Howell

WHEN PHIL BUCKNER FIRST ASKED ME TO prepare a paper on the teaching of Maritime history, I considered it a reasonably straightforward and uncomplicated request. The new Maritime Studies textbook, I knew, had a contemporary focus, concentrating upon the period since 1945. Surely teachers would want to know what Maritime historians have been working on for the past decade and a half: surely they would want to know the way in which historical research shed light on issues that the new school curriculum was intending to address. There seemed no question that a snappy twenty minute sermon from a member of the historical priesthood would reassure teachers who were anxious about the new Maritime Studies course. The gospel of Clio even contained an appropriate message: if teachers were teaching about transportation, historians have written about it; if teachers were interested in women's issues, historians have been engaged in writing women's history; if teachers wanted to know about the origins of regional disparity, there has been a lively historical debate about this. Salvation was there for all in the message of the Book of *Acadiensis*. "Yea though I wander in the windowless room of the current event, historical scholarship on the Maritimes is both easily rendered and simple to understand".

But the more I reflected upon the relationship of scholarly historical research to the nature of the new curriculum the more my faith was tested. There really are two issues of concern here. The first, as Ernie Forbes has pointed out, involves ways in which recent historical scholarship might help teachers provide a context for the proposed curriculum; the second involves the significance of the decision to dispense with an historical approach in the first place. It seems at least ironic, and at worst perverse, that the new curriculum largely ignores that it was the discipline of history that led the recent renaissance of regional studies that began during the early 1970s. No other discipline has made such a consistent commitment to the region, as is exemplified by the journal *Acadiensis*. And yet the decision to construct a contemporary issues orientation largely vitiates the significance of that work, at least as far as the new textbook is concerned.

Of course, this decision was made in part because there already are historical treatments of the region at other grade levels, and in an age of fiscal responsibility and restraint there is no greater fear than the fear of duplication. But the very nature of this broader school curriculum points to an even more serious problem: the routine fracturing of past and present that goes on in our minds, the tendency to place history in one hermetically sealed container, and contemporary studies in another. In this light, the new textbook and curriculum provides not only a challenge to classroom teachers, but should provoke professional historians working in the field of Maritime history to address more explicitly the ways in which history speaks to the present. What I want to do here is to address the contributions made by historians over the past two decades, but also to inquire into the ways in which the recent historiography of the Maritimes has left itself vulnerable to easy appropriation and ultimate neglect by those whose interests are more clearly contemporary and utilitarian.

It is not long ago that both the history and contemporary concerns of the Maritimes could be ignored with impunity. I remember a night in 1966 at Dalhousie when the economist Scott Gordon told his audience that the solution to the problems of the Maritimes lay in a one-way fare to Montreal of less than $100.00. And not a whimper of protest emerged! I remember Frank Underhill in his collection of essays published in 1964 under the suggestive title *The Image of Confederation* concluding that "as for the Maritimes, of course, nothing much ever happens down there".[1] What is more, I remember that even historians with a research interest in the region had little faith in the possibility of a lively historiography developing here. In the words of one such historian writing in 1969 about the post-Confederation period "further study is rather a discouraging prospect, since Maritime history, in a way, stopped in 1867".[2] But all of that changed in the 1970s. Just as blacks and women had come to recognize that one source of their deprivation was that they had been robbed of their history, so did people in hinterland regions of Canada like the Maritimes recognize the importance of rediscovering and rewriting Canadian history. The result was an assault on "national history" during the 1970s and the fashioning of a vigorous regional historiography.

In Atlantic Canada the historiography of the post-Confederation period has centered largely upon the various structural changes in the regional economy since 1867. These structural changes include the transformation of the Maritimes in the late nineteenth century from a staples based, export oriented community into a more industrially oriented one; the subsequent erosion of Maritime industry or "deindustrialization" that began near the end of the century and was well nigh complete by 1920; and the

---

1 Frank Underhill, *The Image of Confederation* (Toronto, 1964), p. 63.
2 C.M. Wallace, "The Nationalization of the Maritimes, 1867-1914", in J.M. Bumsted, ed., *Documentary Problems in Canadian History* (Georgetown, Ont., 1969), II, p.131.

gradual development of a service oriented economy and welfarism in the wake of our failed industrialism. Without question the single most influential piece of work relating to the development of the regional economy to come out of the 1970s was Bill Acheson's groundbreaking article "The National Policy and the Industrialization of the Maritimes, 1880-1910".[3] Acheson's article drew attention to the significant expansion of industry in the Maritimes during the 1880s, to the gradual loss of local ownership of secondary manufacturing, and to the subsequent dismantling of the region's industrial base. This article prompted a lively debate on the origins of deindustrialization and focussed attention on such issues as entrepreneurial failure, resource deficiency, locational disadvantage, discriminatory government policy, political conservatism, metropolitan weakness, and undercapitalization. Careful studies of banking, outmigration, regional protest, shipping, coal mining, and agriculture, all provided further elaboration upon the process of regional economic development that Acheson had first identified.[4]

The concentration of Maritime scholars on the question of regional development gave the new scholarship on the region a focus and direction. More than anywhere else in the country, scholars in the Maritimes built upon the work of their colleagues in the field. But there was also an unexpected price to pay for this new vitality. The economistic nature of many of the studies done by historians attracted the attention of those in other areas such as sociology and political economy, who were interested in the process of capitalist underdevelopment and largely unconcerned with questions relating to ideology and culture. This tradition, which tends to see men and women as bearers of an historical process rather than as agents who shaped it, appropriates history for its own purposes and ultimately diminishes its significance. What becomes important in the political economy model is the way in which processes of development make themselves evident in the present, in the decline of the family farm, for example, or in the continuing dependency of the Maritimes within a welfare state context. It would not be surprising to me, therefore, if the approach of the new textbook was to blend an underdevelopment analysis with cultural boosterism — mixing victimization and regional patriotism in order to create a more genuine Maritime consciousness. To prevent this from happening it is necessary to fashion a careful history of the region which emphasizes ideology as an important component of social change.

The Maritime economy at the time of Confederation was a staples and sea-based economy, dominated by wholesale shippers, lumber millers, and

---

3 T.W. Acheson, "The National Policy and the Industrialization of the Maritimes, 1880-1910", *Acadiensis*, I/2 (Spring 1971), pp. 3-28.

4 Many of these studies are included in P. Buckner and D. Frank, eds., *Atlantic Canada After Confederation: The Acadiensis Reader, Volume Two* (Fredericton, 1985).

ship manufacturers. In keeping with this export-oriented, maritime economy the prevailing political philosophy was that of laissez-faire, the classic
expression of which is contained in Adam Smith's *Wealth of Nations*
(1776). Smith's ideal marketplace was one made up of individuals competing freely, unrestrained by combinations of any sort. This vision was
anti-monopoly, anti-union, and opposed to government intervention. In
Smith's view, if individuals were allowed to compete to the best of their
ability, a Great Guiding Hand would ensure that optimum economic conditions would ensue.

This laissez-faire vision was particularly appropriate to a community
tied to the sea and to staples production, where the hard work and resourceful-
ness of an individual ship's captain or small farmer could mean the
difference between prosperity or hardship. Yet, even before the decline of
the traditional staples economy and the coming of industrial capitalism to
the region in the last quarter of the nineteenth century, a competing vision
of the marketplace was emerging. The advances in science and technology
that accompanied the industrial revolution were creating a conviction that
the world was not regulated by natural forces (such as Smith's Guiding
Hand), but that it could be organized, regulated, and manipulated by
human beings and the state. The new industrial capitalists (not to mention
professionals in fields such as medicine, psychiatry, and education) tended
to place more faith in the management of society than did their predecessors: on the whole they promised a more organized and state-regulated
economic system freed from destructive and ruthless competition.[5] The
watchwords of the new age were scientific management and efficiency. In
the new age individual autonomy would give way to industrial organization and scientific production, all of this rationalized as necessary for
efficiency, prosperity, and social well-being. Nor was this scientism confined to the factory: it also permeated reform initiatives in public health,
municipal government, conservation and education.

In the first two decades after Confederation these two ideologies — one
populist and the other progressive — revealed themselves in the tariff and
Confederation questions. But with the advance of industrial capitalism,
other issues began to take precedence. The new areas of concern included
the growing antagonism between capital and labour, the increased incidence of strike activity, marked resistance to the extension of managerial
control into the workplace, and most significantly, the emergence of socialism and labour radicalism. David Frank and Nolan Reilly have spent considerable time addressing the growth of socialism in the region during the
first two decades of the century. They point to the development of the

---

5   See Colin D. Howell, "Reform and the Monopolistic Impulse: The Professionalization of
    Medicine in the Maritimes", *Acadiensis*, XI/1 (Autumn 1981), pp. 3-22.

Halifax-based United Labour party in 1898, the Saint John League (1901), the activities of the Socialist Paty of Canada in the region, the success of socialists in municipal elections in industrial towns like Amherst and Springhill, and ultimately, the emergence of the Farmer-Labour party.[6] Unlike populism and progressivism, the socialist or radical political tradition concerned itself with the question of ownership. Socialists were convinced that the concentration of ownership in private hands undermined real democracy, and ensured continuing class conflict. Piecemeal reform might mitigate the intensity of conflict, but as long as some owned the means of production and others sold their labour for a wage, conflict or class struggle would endure.

With the decline of the tariff and the Confederation question as issues of moment, Maritime governments in the first quarter of the twentieth century took on an increasingly progressive profile. Having gone beyond the nineteenth-century populist challenge of *laissez-faire*, the Liberal governments of George F. Murray in Nova Scotia and Peter J. Veniot in New Brunswick believed in humanizing capitalism, protecting workers through reforms such as workmen's compensation or the shortening of the hours of work, encouraging reforms in the area of public health, placing essential services such as electric power under provincial regulatory agencies, and supporting the prohibition of the manufacture and sale of alcoholic beverages. In this way they believed they were serving public rather than private interests. But progressive reform never threatened the hegemony of the dominant class. Reform might improve the lot of working people, but it would come from the top down, rather than from the bottom up. As the slogan of the Murray government during the 1911 election indicated, progressivism was "government for the masses and not the classes".

The extent to which progressive reform was intended to counter the growing influence of socialism was made explicit in the Report of the Nova Scotia Royal Commission on Hours of Work (1910). In it, commission chairman David Robb, President of Robb Engineering, outlined two advantages to the eight hour day. A shorter workday would result in increased productivity, and at the same time would win the allegiance of working people to the existing order. He wrote:

> The shorter day then means as a rule increased product per hour, and the chief cause of this is the improvement of the workers. The shorter day improves the physique, the intelligence, and the morale of the workers; hence they work with more insight and push. There is less time lost in stoppages for accidents, in tying up broken threads, in

---

6 David Frank and Nolan Reilly, "The Emergence of the Socialist Movement in the Maritimes", *Labour/Le Travailleur*, 4 (1979), pp. 85-114.

putting in and taking out work, in doodling, in interruption during the day, in repairing spoiled work, in irregularities of attendance, in drinking and sickness.

In addition, Robb argued, the shorter day would have "citizenship benefits", allowing people to acquire an intelligent grasp of the responsibilities of citizenship and make them "less prone to the unprincipled agitator and revolutionist".[7]

During the 1920s the progressive approach was continued, but in this decade it became wrapped in the language of regional victimization. In a period characterized by the bitter labour struggles in the Cape Breton coal fields and the political successes of the Farmer-Labour coalition, proponents of Maritime Rights urged people of all classes to join in a struggle for a square deal within Confederation. But the limited achievements of the Maritime Rights movement and the continuing depression of the 1930s effectively destroyed the regional protest tradition, and left the Maritimes ready to collapse into the arms of a federal government offering a system of social welfarism. Yet welfarism was no magic solution. In the long run, the social welfare state, while mitigating some of the region's serious economic disabilities, tended to institutionalize regional dependency.

The historiography of the past fifteen years has arisen out of the recognition that welfarism has not meant equitable advantage for the region within Confederation. But the very successes of recent scholarship in elaborating regional dependency in economic ways also explains scholarly inattentiveness to ways in which victimization ideology has operated to preserve existing power relations both in the past and in the present. The late David Alexander had come to realize the weaknesses of economism before his tragic death in 1980. Alexander called for a greater emphasis on intellectual history. Noting the impact of literacy upon the quality of public life and public decision-making both inside and outside of the region, Alexander suggested that a critical analysis of the region's intellectual history was a prerequisite to any meaningful social transformation. He wrote:

> The extent of illiteracy in Newfoundland is not proof that labour productivity was less than it might have been, but it is good reason to suspect a linkage. Far more important, however, are its implications in terms of class social relations and the quality of public life and public decision making. Wide differences in educational skills and information between a governing elite and the mass of the population can breed an unwarranted deference on the one hand and a

---

7 Province of Nova Scotia, *Report of the Royal Commission on Hours of Work* (Halifax, 1910), pp. 10, 15.

selfish *noblesse oblige* on the other. It also breeds a sluggish intellectual life and an unimaginative and inefficient debate about the goals of the society and how they might best be realized. Anyone who surveys the economic and political history of Newfoundland cannot escape the impression of a political culture which was sunk in a mediocrity which the country and its people did not need. Perhaps it was an inescapable adjunct of the county's small size, its relative youth and the conflict of loyalties generated for British people abroad of vicariously participating in the magnificence of the British Empire. We will not know until some scholar produces an intellectual portrait of the country, for in such a work lies more of the answers to the problems of its economic history than its economic historians are ever likely to supply.[8]

Those who knew David well, would not want to ignore his advice.

---

8   David Alexander, "Literacy and Economic Development in Nineteenth Century Newfoundland", *Acadiensis*, X/1 (Autumn 1980), pp. 33-4.

3 Keeping Newfoundland and other Issues: Perspectives on Political History

P.B. Waite

IN FIFTEEN OR TWENTY MINUTES ONE cannot pretend to cover the bibliography of 300 years of the political history of these provinces. Happily the recent edition of the *Reader's Guide to Canadian History* (2 vols., Toronto, 1982) covers the ground sufficiently well; while one can quarrel with some individual judgments we are well served by it. I prefer today to deal with principles, practices, problems, with limited reference to particularities, mainly since 1981.

The chapters in the *Reader's Guide* that deal with the Maritimes are entitled, in both volumes, Atlantic Canada. My argument is that the proper area comprehended by "Maritime studies" ought not to be the old definition — Nova Scotia, New Brunswick, Prince Edward Island — but the new one, Atlantic Canada. Because the Council of Maritime Premiers has decreed there should be Maritime history, it does not follow that what is subsumed under it should be so narrowly conceived. I would argue, indeed, that it must not. We are not to allow Newfoundland and Labrador to be de-confederated by the fiat of Hatfield, Buchanan and Lee. I have written three stanzas of doggerel to clinch my point, perhaps even to immortalize it:

> Great Newfoundland's life is too vital, you see,
> Her coast rugged and gaunt as her long history,
> These Maritime views by our premiers three
> Are too narrow, dear Hatfield, Buchanan and Lee.
>
> *Acadiensis* gives articles by Peter Neary,
> Juxtaposes and contrasts Newfoundland by the sea
> With riches by Buckner, and Rawlyk and Reid,
> Why bother with Hatfield, Buchanan and Lee?
>
> There's no sense in returning, whatever it be,
> It's nonsense alone as colonies three
> We're four on the Gulf of St Lawrence; we're free
> To spurn even Hatfield, Buchanan and Lee.

We must not act like the *Historical Statistics of Canada*, and assume that the history of Newfoundland begins only in 1949. Her history is too rich and vital to be neglected. Indeed, one could go further and argue that the history of Atlantic Canada should not omit the Magdalen Islands, Sable Island, George's Bank, Grand Banks, St. Pierre & Miquelon, or even Maine down to the Penobscot. Let us take the big view, not the little one. There are parochialisms enough in our constituency to satisfy the most avid longings for narrow, local history.

I do not quite mean the full pejorativeness of that. For we are local in origin. We all begin with some rooted sense of localness. That is valuable. Each of our memories is a set of localities; my own is from a childhood in the tight little Protestant towns of eastern Ontario where one never even knew what a Roman Catholic looked like, where one never heard a word of a language that was not English, to an adolescence in the rocky, grimy, delicious old town that Saint John was in the 1930s. My father used to say that he didn't know what a party was till he came from Ontario to Saint John in 1934. The parties on the Kennebecasis (and adjacent headlands) seemed to Father to have at least a fifty-year start on Belleville, Ontario. They did have. I remember Pond Street, Saint John, in the 1930s, where from peeling and unpainted houses leaned peeling and painted ladies. One could not but help be struck with the contrast between the glories of Zane Grey, his heroines still sibilant with longing as their lovers galloped away (for two-thirds of the book) across the purple sage, and the grim reality of Pond Street. I was saved from sin by imagination. Zane Grey and the Saint John Public Library was a metamorphosis of emotion. I could give you similar stories of St. John's, Newfoundland during the war, except I no longer had Zane Grey to help me. Nothing but pride. My point is that we occupy a joint imperialism of these delightful Atlantic localisms. We must have Newfoundland in. Our Maritime geography expands outward, not inward. Champlain never could have controlled the fur trade at Port Royal, not even with a stopper in the bottle at Digby Gut. He needed a real bottle with a real stopper: the St. Lawrence at Quebec. We have no Atlantic analogies to that, unless you want to try stopping the Strait of Belle Isle. The only river with a whiff of monopoly built into it is the Saint John.

Everyone complains of the fundamental weakness of the post-Confederation history of Nova Scotia, New Brunswick and Prince Edward Island. There is no lack of it in Newfoundland, either from 1867 or from 1949. Another reason for keeping hold of Newfoundland history! But in the three Maritime provinces it is as if the big men were creamed off to Ottawa where, diabolically, their papers mostly remain: Howe, Tilley, Tupper, Thompson, Borden, Ilsley, Ralston — only R.B. Bennett remains here. They tended to grow up into a bigger world and keep on going, like the Beaver, who found even Montreal could not contain him. I think Sir

John Thompson, after he had won a federal election in 1895, would have either gone to the Bench or to a law practice in Toronto. He would not have returned to Nova Scotia. So the papers go too. The Thompson Papers were in Toronto within four months of Thompson's death, and they stayed there until the late 1940s. Perhaps part of the weakness of our post-Confederation history may also lie in the paucity of papers, of reminiscences, of the first hand primary stuff that is the very basis of our history. It is thus all very well for our premiers three to call our history to come forth: but will it come? *Can* it come? The weakness of post-Confederation provincial history may thus start with the weaknesses in the men left behind.

It is part of a more deep-seated problem: the attitudes of our men and women to papers. I have an impression — archivists can correct me — that Maritimers tend to fear papers. You're better off without "them things". Who knows what some researcher will turn up if you leave all those letters open and intact? Tupper went through his letters three ways, and didn't miss a trick. There seems to be rooted in our provincial political mentality a decidedly costive attitude to papers. It used to be said of W.S. Fielding that he was so closed-in that he would barely admit to being premier of Nova Scotia, or Minister of Finance in Laurier's government. The man who wrote Fielding's biography was in this respect well qualified: if there was anyone more costive than W.S. Fielding it was C. Bruce Fergusson. But *de mortuis nil nisi bene!* Nor is costiveness confined to Nova Scotia. Sir Louis Davies' daughter, the wife of a justice of the Supreme Court of Canada, burnt all her father's papers after she moved to Ottawa. And there is a delicious example from right here in New Brunswick.

In 1952 I was looking for the Executive Council records of New Brunswick for the 1860s, and it seemed sensible to go to the Clerk of the Council in Fredericton. When I announced politely what I was looking for, a look of slight panic appeared in his eyes. Why would anyone want to see the records of the New Brunswick Cabinet for the 1860s? And what would anyone do with them? But he swallowed his reluctance and took me to a steel-lined vault. On the upper shelves lay the records of the Executive Council of New Brunswick, starting from the present indicative and stretching back into the past indefinite, and the imperfect subjunctive. We found the 1865 and 1866 minutes. I was placed at a desk next to a stern lady secretary, whose proportions and physiognomy reminded one of Stephen Leacock's definition of a landlady, "a parallelogram square on all sides and equal to anything". She eyed me with infinite suspicion. Now you don't read such minutes for long without discovering a Maritime political art, refined by us here over the years to infinite subtleties and variations: the art of patronage. It began in Nova Scotia in 1758, Prince

Edward Island in 1769, New Brunswick in 1784 and Newfoundland in 1832. In the Atlantic provinces we have had a two centuries' running start at it. It makes even hardened central Canadians blanch. So it was inevitable that in a little while I would encounter it, and made the mistake of producing an audible chuckle. The lady secretary was very unamused. Ready to consign me and the Minutes back to the vault, she said disgustedly — I can still hear her — "I knew no good would come of lettin' the public into them Minutes". It is right to add that the Minutes are easily and happily available in 1985 at the New Brunswick Archives. Yes, Julia, progress *is* possible.

We have also new riches since the last edition of the *Reader's Guide.* I think of D.G. Bell's new book *Early Loyalist Saint John* (Fredericton, 1983), Harry Bruce's new biography of Frank Sobey (Toronto, 1985), and Murray Beck's biography of Howe (Montreal/Kingston, 1982-3). Murray Beck's 2-volumes on Howe are too well known to need much comment from me. There was after all a whole conference about it, and Phil Buckner has given an analysis in *Acadiensis.* There is also a new book by Vincent Durant on Sir Charles Tupper, entitled *War Horse of Cumberland: the life and times of Sir Charles Tupper* (Windsor, N.S., 1985). The book was lit into by George Rawlyk in the Kingston *Whig-Standard* (15 June 1985), I think wrongly. The main thing wrong with the book is the misleading title. We do need a comprehensive new book on Sir Charles Tupper, but Durant never set out to offer one. What he intended to do, and did, was to write a brief 102-page résumé of Tupper's career. It is not bad, and without too many mistakes.

In many ways the most spectacular biography on Atlantic province history in recent years is Joseph Smallwood's book on that subject of infinite fascination to him, Joey Smallwood (Toronto, 1973). In some ways it is the most appalling book ever published by a responsible Canadian publisher. Macmillan's editor, John Gray, told me what happened. Macmillan's did not know Smallwood very well and recklessly commissioned him to write his autobiography. It duly came: some 2000 or more pages of manuscript. It was like the ghastly manuscript of Donald Fleming that McClelland & Stewart got hooked on. Each man had a monumental ego and each manuscript was an ego trip. But there was a fundamental difference: Smallwood could write, Fleming could not. No matter that Smallwood could write, Macmillan's had the devil of a time getting the manuscript even down to its present size. And certain things Joey could not be prevailed upon to part with: the great list of Smallwood ancestors is just one. But for growing up in Newfoundland after 1900 I know of few better sources, and on the Confederation movement 1946-9 it has some marvellous stories, some indeed that surpass whatever I found out about that lesser, earlier, Confederation movement of 1864-1867!

Marc Milner's new book, *The North Atlantic Run: the Royal Canadian Navy and the Battle for the Convoys* (Toronto, 1985), is an important Atlantic provinces book, dealing with Halifax, St. John's, the Gulf of St. Lawrence and the North Atlantic. It has an elegant complement, Michael Hadley's *U-Boats against Canada: German submarines in Canadian Waters* (Montreal, 1985). In this 75th year of the founding of the Canadian Navy, these two fine books need come as no surprise, but their elegance and control of strategic considerations is invigorating. They supplement my argument that Maritime history is not, and cannot be, confined to the land.

One of the most needed books in the Centenary series is now out, after two authors — F.W. Gibson and Roger Graham — had tried, and for one reason or another, had to give up. The book is written by John H. Thompson of McGill with Allen Seager's help: *Canada 1922-1939: Decades of Discord* (Toronto, 1985). (In the Centenary History of Canada we seem to have had a penchant for anguished sub-titles, like *Arduous Destiny, The Forked Road*, and now *Decades of Discord*. Cook and Brown escape with *A Nation Transformed*!) Thompson and Seager seem to have made a genuine effort to get at provincial history, and readers will find the overview of Maritime province history refreshing. There is brief but solid coverage of Cape Breton labour troubles, 1921-5. There is also a list of all the provincial ministries, across Canada, 1920-1940. The Maritime Rights movement is covered and the attendant swing to the Conservatives, in the provincial elections in Prince Edward Island (1923), Nova Scotia and New Brunswick (1925), is made to lead up to the federal election of late October, 1925. I have not read the book completely yet, but my initial impression is decidedly favourable. I have one big complaint. It is sad to record that Newfoundland is not even in the index. Poor Newfoundland! She is an orphan here when her history is so needed to round out the story. She is excluded from the statistics as well.

I would like to put in a word for the *Atlantic Provinces Book Review*, out of St. Mary's University, a quarterly that tries with some success to cover the ground of Atlantic province books, especially the little books that are so important to us, and that are so apt to get by unnoticed in the *Globe and Mail*, or for that matter the Halifax *Chronicle-Herald*. For the future of Atlantic province history may not lie only in the worthy pages of *Acadiensis*, the *Nova Scotia Historical Review*, or the new *Newfoundland Studies*, it may also lie in the little books from the little presses. Admittedly often their proofing is bad and their editorial control negligible, but for all that, the little books may represent the growing edge of versatility, the celebration of our localness and our localities that is so important in the absence of any discernible new big, biographies, based upon fat archives, like Beck's *Howe*. A good new one about Angus L. Macdonald, or John B. McNair, would be very welcome. Will we get it? Perhaps not. Probably the papers aren't there. So on Angus L. we may have to be satisfied with Hawkins' ghastly, and plagiarized, book. On the other hand, Alison Mitcham's new little book, *Three Remarkable Maritimers* (Hantsport, 1985) on Moses Perley, Silas Rand and William Ganong is thin but useful.

Still more, toward the growing edge of history, is David Bell's *Manners, Morals and Mayhem* (Fredericton, 1985) published this year by the Law Society of New Brunswick. Law is the place where politics and society meet; I would suggest that the role of Attorneys-General, the one end of the scale, and Justices of the Peace at the other, are too important to be so neglected as they are. (I do feel compelled to say, however, that while the New Brunswick Justices of the Peace may have been just as conscientious as David Bell says they were, Sir John Thompson's long experience in Nova Scotia was anything but corroborative.) The New Brunswick Law Foundation has thus published a version of what in Nova Scotia we have published under a title rather more staid, *Law in a Colonial Society: the Nova Scotia Experience* (Toronto, 1984), produced under the auspices of the Canadian Institute for the Administration of Justice.

The hinge of politics and society is fundamentally law, and I should like to think that our history in the future will be more developed in its consciousness of law and legal administration and how both work, than the history has been up to now. It is too important to be left to the lawyers, most of whom are far too preoccupied with the paying present, to worry about how the present came to be what it is. Legal precedents are historical all right, but they are relevant only to the here and now. Few lawyers could accept the premise that all generations are equidistant from eternity, whereas historians can, and perhaps should.

I would like to put in a plea for two more things. Let us have good indexes. Abominations in this line are legion and not confined to Atlantic Canada. Have a look at the index in Sandra Gwyn's *The Private Capital* (Toronto, 1984), if you want to contemplate a bad one; look at Murray Beck's *Howe* if you want to emulate a good one. Do not give us nominal indexes: they are cheap substitutes for the real thing. Indexing is not hard; it is rewarding to do a good one, and best of all it is useful. And could we, finally, have only annotated bibliographies? What use is a list of books without a critical opinion to go with it?

4 Regional Geography and Maritime Studies: An Interdisciplinary Perspective

L.D. McCann

WHEN LISTENING TO CONVERSATIONS about geography, it is still possible to hear students, and even some teachers, argue that geographic study emphasizes merely "capes and bays", the capitals of provinces, or the products of countries. But for many, there is honest recognition that geography is much more: it is an exciting, vital, and meaningful subject that helps us explain much of what we see and encounter in our daily experience. For this very reason, when I begin teaching a geography course, a field trip is a first priority, because observing and explaining the ordinary landscapes that support our daily experiences introduces students to the rewarding possibilities of geographic study. Quite obviously, a field trip is impossible here and now, but my remarks will offer a perspective for integrating the approach of the regional geographer with those of the historian, sociologist, economist, and others. After all, the approach to a Maritime studies programme is meant to be interdisciplinary.

Within the traditions of geography, three time-honoured questions command our attention. First, what are the characteristics of the feature we are interested in studying, be it a soil type, an ethnic group, or an economic activity? Second, where is this feature located on the landscape? And third, a more challenging question, why is it located where it is? To this trilogy, many of us now go a step further and ask, what is the meaning of the landscape so shaped or characterized by this feature?[1] Landscapes are, in fact, symbolic: they represent the cumulative agency of the human experience. Anybody who has read Ernest Buckler's *The Mountain and The Valley*, or Charles Bruce's *The Channel Shore*, cannot help but recognize how the pattern of landscape is a mirror of regional society and economy.

It is one thing to pose these time-honoured questions, quite another to answer them from an interdisciplinary perspective. All disciplines have their particular vocabularies, including geography. Some geographers hide behind jargonistic expressions, rendering impossible the conversion of their listeners or readers to the field. Most would agree there is need for at least a moderate use of a spatial vocabulary. In this connection, the "geo-

---

1   D.W. Meinig, ed., *The Interpretation of Ordinary Landscapes* (New York, 1979).

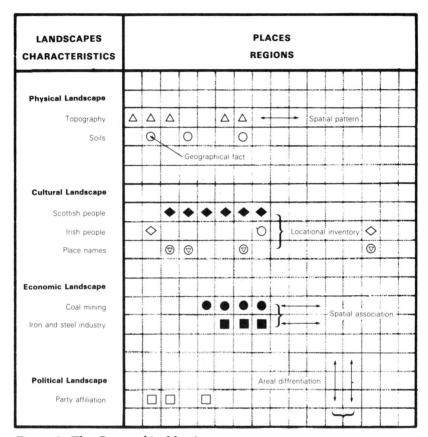

Figure 1: The Geographic Matrix

graphic matrix" is a useful pedogogic device (Figure 1).[2] A row of this matrix presents the place-to-place variation of some characteristic, or the spatial pattern on the landscape of the feature thus mapped. Each column contains the locational inventory of the many characteristics of some place. Every cell of the matrix therefore contains a "geographic fact": the value assumed by some characteristic at some place. Comparison of complete columns is the study of areal differentiation in its holistic sense, and thus regional geography. Comparison of rows implies the study of spatial associations, and leads to topical or systematic geography.

The uniform or homogeneous distribution of a characteristic (characteristics) across space defines a region. A region, therefore, is a homo-

2 A fuller discussion of the geographic matrix can be found in Brian J.L. Berry, "Approaches to Regional Analysis: A Synthesis", *Annals of the Association of American Geographers*, 54 (1964), pp. 2-11.

geneous segment of the earth's surface with physical and human characteristics distinct from those of neighbouring areas. The component
regional landscapes — physical, cultural, social, political — when viewed
in association with each other, that is, when synthesized in a holistic sense,
yield a region that is sufficiently unified for the people to be conscious of
its geographic character. A region therefore possesses an identity distinct
from those of other regions.[3]

The term regionalism applies to a society's identification with a
territorial unit. Regionalism is shaped and given expression by the interplay of land, economy and society; by the emergence of a group's consciousness that voices regional grievances and demands; and by the behaviour of society as expressed most commonly through political actions.
Clearly, as the references to politics, economy and other key features
suggest, no geographer can rightly ignore the contribution of economics,
sociology, political science — to name only a few disciplines — in the
study of regional geography. Conversely, can a course in Maritime studies
ignore the perspective of geography?

So synthesized, the essence of a region's character stands boldly in the
landscape, to be interpreted by the regional geographer. Interpretation is
critical. Description of characteristics is important; so is the discussion of
location and the analysis of why features are located where they are on the
landscape. But of greater importance are the questions: What is the
significance of the regional landscape? How do we interpret regional landscapes?

The latter question forces us to consider a theoretical framework for
regional analysis and interpretation. An entirely realistic and relevant
framework, given the basic structure of core and hinterland regions that
distinguish Canada and each of the Maritime provinces, is the heartland-
hinterland paradigm.[4] Indeed, it is in the Maritime scholarly tradition, be
it from an historical, social, cultural, political, even economic perspective,
to speak of the role of metropolis and hinterland in shaping our daily
experience.

Much about the Maritimes and its landscapes can be explained and
interpreted by reference to the heartland-hinterland approach. The
approach accurately defines the status and geographical role of the Maritimes in the Canadian federation; it accounts for the significant shaping

3   The standard discussion of regional geography remains Derwent Whittlesey, "The
    Regional Concept and the Regional Method", in P.E. James and C.F. Jones, eds.,
    American Geography: Inventory and Prospect (Syracuse, 1954), pp. 19-69. See also R.C.
    Harris, "Regionalism", in *The Canadian Encyclopedia* (Edmonton, 1985), III, pp.
    1561-2.

4   L.D. McCann, ed., *Heartland and Hinterland: A Geography of Canada* (Toronto, 1982).

forces of regional growth and development; and it focuses attention on the issues of regionalism — to cite only several of its explanatory and interpretive powers. Clearly, the Maritimes is a hinterland region; it has long been subject to the forces of concentration and centralization associated with industrial and corporate capitalism, and its people are the criers of "Maritime Rights".[5]

If we could take a field trip to illustrate the regional approach, where might we go? To the Saint John River Valley? The Miramichi? Cape Breton? The Annapolis Valley? Each of these places is really a region unto itself, supporting Graeme Wynn's contention that a distinguishing feature of the Maritime whole is fragmentation.[6] All these regions and others have been touched by the heartland-hinterland process. The movement of people, goods and services, investment capital, and technology between these and core regions have shaped the essence of their regional landscapes. Regional patterns of economic livelihood and well-being, of political and social organization, and of attachment to place all owe much, perhaps most, to the heartland-hinterland process.

Let us, with the aid of descriptive images, take an armchair geographer's field trip through the landscapes of Pictou County.[7] Our purpose is to illustrate not only the interpretive power of the heartland-hinterland approach, but also to review its interdisciplinary perspective. Located in north-central Nova Scotia, Pictou County focuses upon the harbour that empties the rivers that drain the surrounding hills, which in turn separate the County from its neighbouring regions (Plate 1). These geographic features — the physical landscape of harbour, rivers and hills — comprise a unified whole. So, too, does the imprint of Scottish settlers, migrants from a European cultural hearth. The Scottish fact is everywhere present in the cultural landscape — in field patterns, stone houses, Presbyterian churches

5   Ernest R. Forbes, *The Maritimes Rights Movement, 1919-1927: A Study in Canadian Regionalism* (Montreal, 1979).

6   Graeme Wynn, "The Maritimes: The Geography of Fragmentation and Underdevelopment", in McCann, *Heartland and Hinterland*, pp. 156-213. The Maritimes is also treated in the following texts on Canada's geography: D.F. Putnam and R.G. Putnam, *Canada: A Regional Analysis* (2nd ed., Toronto, 1979); J. Lewis Robinson, *Concepts and Themes in the Regional Geography of Canada* (Vancouver, 1983); and John Warkentin, ed., *Canada: A Geographical Interpretation* (Toronto, 1968).

7   The following references provide useful information on the regional character of Pictou County: James M. Cameron, *Industrial History of New Glasgow* (New Glasgow, 1961); Donald MacKay, *Scotland Farewell: The People of the Hector* (Toronto, 1980); L.D. McCann, "The Mercantile-Industrial Transition in the Metals Towns of Pictou County, 1857-1931", *Acadiensis*, X/2 (1981), pp. 29-64; Rev. George Paterson, *A History of the County of Pictou* (Montreal, 1877); and Roland Sherwood, *Pictou Pioneers* (Windsor, 1973).

Plate 1: Pictou Harbour from Green Hill

Plate 2: Scottish Houses c.1840, Pictou Town

and the nomenclature of place (Plate 2). To this region we can add the economic landscape of the nineteenth-century industrial revolution in coal mining, steel processing, and other industries, now in decline, the victim of the centralizing tendencies of the Canadian economy (Plates 3 and 4). The

Plate 3: *An advertisement for steel products, Trenton Works*

Plate 4: *The railway car operations of Hawker-Siddley depend upon government contracts*

political appeasement of place can be read, for example, from the failed efforts of Robert Stanfield to establish an electronics industry near Stellarton, now the home of a Sears distribution depot. More recently, recalling television images, we might remember Brian Mulroney "roughing it" in the $100 per day Pictou log cabin he used as headquarters when selling Central Nova the virtues of his political designs. Even though Brian Mulroney failed to stay, his one-time presence nonetheless added something to the political landscape.

Given these images, what is the essence of Pictou County's regional character? To read the landscape closely is to interpret a hinterland region of considerable industrial decline, but a region also marked by an unmistakable Scottish heritage. To read it properly, we must draw upon the perspectives of an interdisciplinary approach. Spatial analysis provides certain tools and results, but regional study is richer when we share perspectives with other disciplines.

Geography can be viewed as synthetic discipline, one that examines various factors from a spatial perspective to arrive at an holistic understanding of the essence of regional character. As such, it can certainly play a meaningful role in a programme of Maritime Studies. When practiced properly and to its fullest potential, the landscape approach couples well with other disciplinary objectives. Interpretation of the regional landscape by using a theoretical and interdisciplinary framework like the heartland-hinterland paradigm can only enhance our understanding of the Maritimes.

5

Beyond Capes
and Bays

Graeme Wynn

THIS PAPER ARGUES, AND ATTEMPTS to demonstrate, that modern Geography offers an enormously useful set of perspectives on a wide range of matters of central interest in a Maritime Studies programme, and that the subject could serve to integrate teaching on various facets of the region. Central to these arguments is the recognition that Geography is no longer concerned simply with the names and locations of capitals, countries and physical features on the earth's surface, and the contention that geographical perspectives are relevant to the search for an integrated understanding of our world as well as to an issue-based approach to teaching.

Probably the most unfortunate thing about modern Geography is its reputation among the lay public. If few of us have been accosted by a latter-day Mrs. Malaprop, anxious for geographical instruction in hope of discovering "something of the contagious countries", many of us have encountered a view of the subject (to borrow from Dickens again), as learning "about all the water sheds of all the world...and all the names of all the rivers and mountains, and all the productions, manners, and customs of all the countries, and all their boundaries and bearings on the two-and-thirty points of the compass".[1] In days of yore teachers charged with imparting such information often sought to ease the burden of memorization. Thus classes were assembled in front of a map to sing the song of the lakes — which ran:

> Oh Winnipeg, dear Winnipeg, if you
> will be my Bride
> I'll take you down to Athabask and be
> your Slave, he sighed.
> This so displeased Miss Winnipeg, she
> called him a Great Bear —[2]

1 Dickens, *Hard Times* cited by Kennard W. Rummage and Leslie Cummings, "Introduction to Geography — A Spatial Approach", in Association of American Geographers, *New Approaches in Introductory College Geography Courses* (Washington, D.C., 1967), p. 114.

2 Quoted in W. Warntz, *Geography Now and Then; some notes on the history of academic*

and children learned well the heights of mountains. Now I have no wish to deny that the basic knowledge about the configuration of the continents conveyed by such exercises remains useful.[3] But I do contend that it does not lead anywhere, and that it is more fittingly treated as one aspect of primary instruction than as a focus of high school education.

This point bears emphasis, because even in relatively recent times the regional geography taught in secondary schools and universities as the complex capstone of geographical education was often little more than inventory and description, a more elaborate form of factual ingestion than those to which I have alluded.[4] As one commentator observed, a generation ago "geographers were pre-occupied with fixed boundaries, fixed principles, and fixed explanations. Their attitudes toward the discipline were reflected in the didactic teaching of geographical facts to students whose main task was to accept and remember them". Not surprisingly, common perceptions of geography made it a recitation of capes and bays and capitals, a venerable form of intellectual stamp-collecting that found its belated purpose with the invention of *Trivial Pursuit*. But lists and mnemonic rhymes are no longer the geographer's stock in trade. If we are to believe a recent curriculum manual, geographers have moved far beyond such concerns: "More restless, more curious, more dissatisfied" than his predecessors, the modern geographer surveys wider horizons, "considers more factors . . . thinks in terms of the past and peers into the future, in addition to evaluating the present", is "ever conscious of the flux, the movement, the change, the growth" of today's world and "appreciates the constant interaction of forces, people [and] places".[5] By this account, today's geographers are vigorous, insatiable explorers, quick and flexible thinkers with all the complex world their oyster, scholars whose diverse and dynamic discipline is a far cry from the image enshrined in Abbot's and Haney's board game.

Geography in the United States (New York, 1964), p. 139. Further background can be found in D.M. Stowers Jr., "Geography in American Schools 1892-1935: Text books and Reports of National Committees" (Ed.D. dissertation, Duke University, 1962).

3   As evidenced by the following "encounter from life". Scene: A Montreal restaurant, 7:30 a.m. on a November morning, 1985. Four young men at a table, the letters CAPERS emblazoned on their green track suits. The waitress enters, offering coffee, and engages the quartet in conversation. "Where you boys from?" First youth: "Cape Breton". Waitress: "Cape Breton! Where's that?" Second youth: "You don't know where Cape Breton is?" First youth (simultaneously): "Down Nova Scotia". Waitress: "Ah, Nova Scotia, I'm from New Brunswick".

4   See Tudor David, "Against Geography", *Universities Quarterly*, 13 (1957/8), pp. 261-73.

5   John M. Ball, "Introducing New Concepts of Geography in the Social Studies Curriculum", *Geography Curriculum Project Occasional Papers*, no. 1 (Athens, University of Georgia, 1970), pp. 26-7.

For all its vigour and breadth, modern geography echoes recurrent emphases within the subject and may be treated, conveniently, as an amalgam of four central traditions: the earth science (or physical geography) tradition; the spatial tradition; the area studies tradition; and the man-land tradition.[6] None of these can be fully described here, but each warrants a few brief words of explanation. *Physical Geography* is the study of the earth, its waters, its atmosphere and the interrelations between them. Landforms, climate, vegetation, and soils are its essential subject matter; at one level they are classified and considered as composite elements of an interacting system, at another they are seen as the results of the physical processes operating at several scales and the processes themselves are subject to detailed scientific investigation.[7] In recent times, the *spatial tradition* has focussed upon the quantitative analysis and mathematical description of location patterns; it has sought models or theories of spatial behaviour, depended upon simplifying assumptions, prized abstraction and employed the methodology of positivistic social science. Yet perhaps we can think of it more broadly here as a concern with basic questions of location and distribution.[8] *Area studies* characterize places. They can be conducted at a variety of scales, from the neighborhood to the sub-continental, and they serve to illustrate the diversity of the earth's surface. By most reckonings such inquiries are more akin to art than science; their success depends upon the judicious selection and intelligent interpretation of information. They are "subjective" and they depend upon an intimate familiarity with the study area. Thus they are usually grounded in local knowledge or field experience.[9] Geographers working in the *man-land*

---

6 W.D. Pattison, "The Four Traditions of Geography", *Journal of Geography*, 63 (1964), pp. 211-16, and J.L. Robinson, "A New Look at the Four Traditions of Geography", *Journal of Geography*, 75 (1976), pp. 520-30. For a more contextual, chronological view see J.E. Spencer, "The Evolution of the Discipline of Geography in the Twentieth Century", *Geographical Perspectives*, 33 (1974), pp. 20-36. Several books purport to distill the essence of geography; perhaps the best known, cited in the attached bibliography, are by S.W. Wooldridge and W.G. East, and J.O.M. Broek. Note that the terms man-land and man-environment are entrenched in the geographical literature. They should be seen as shorthands for the cumbersome "humankind-land" or "humankind-environment" rather than as denials of the roles of women and children in shaping and giving character to earth-spaces.

7 For example, see A.N. Strahler and A.H. Strahler, *Modern Physical Geography* (New York, 1983).

8 See P. Haggett, *Locational Analysis in Human Geography* (London, 1965).

9 See R. Minshull, *Regional Geography. Theory and Practice* (Chicago, 1967); J.F. Hart, "The Highest Form of the Geographer's Art", *Annals, Association of American Geographers*, 72 (1982), pp. 1-29; B. Wallach "The Potato Landscape, Aroostook County Maine", *Landscape*, 23 (1979), pp.15-22 and "Logging in Maine's empty Quarter", *Annals, Association of American Geographers*, 70 (1980), pp. 542-52.

tradition no longer insist that people and their actions are irresistibly moulded by their physical surroundings; environmental determinism has given way to a broad concern with *Man's role in Changing the Face of the Earth.* Under this rubric geographers investigate the development of human[ized] landscapes and address questions of resource use and conservation. Their inquiries frequently rest on cultural and ecological foundations.[10]

In sum, modern geography is a multi-faceted enterprise employing a variety of approaches to order and understand information about people and their world. This is important, because however the subject may appear to sprawl (and the philosophical and methodological distances between climatologists and historical geographers are vast), it allows local studies to be an integral part of a broader liberal education intended to foster independent, logical, and critical thought, provide the basis of sensible judgements, heighten ethical understanding, and demonstrate that people can shape their settings. The subject's embrace of physical science, social science, and the humanities exposes students to different modes of inquiry, and introduces them to a range of methodologies, research questions, and types of data. Because geography also allows various approaches to be focussed on understanding particular problems or places, the subject encourages an integrated view of the world, while revealing the complexity of the human habitat. And finally, in its concern with the world around us, geography is ideally fitted for the implementation of a problem-solving approach to teaching which should encourage sound habits of inquiry and foster the testing of generalizations against experience.[11]

But enough of this arcane puffery. Let us, in a manner entirely congenial to the geographical spirit, climb down from these abstract plateaus of intellectual self-justification to explore the more tangible ground of actual practice. In preparation, we need to arm ourselves with a few basic precepts: i) that the local and familiar scene will provide a basis for our investigations; ii) that we are concerned with people *and* places, with the actors and their dialogue as well as the props on the stage; iii) that our emphasis will be on developing ways of knowing rather than on conveying established information — on doing rather than telling; and iv) that "field work" will be an integral part of our endeavours. We must also realise that we are embarked on an open-ended exploration, full of promise, but more

---

10 W.L. Thomas, Jr., *Man's Role in Changing the Face of the Earth* (Chicago, 1956); P. Wagner, *The Human Use of the Earth* (London, 1960).

11 Graeme Wynn, "Human Geography in a Changing World", *New Zealand Geographer*, 39 (October 1983), pp. 64-9; M. Storm, "Schools and the Community: An Issue Based Approach", in J.Bale, N. Graves, and R. Walford, eds., *Perspectives in Geographical Education* (London, 1973), pp. 289-304.

likely to resemble a Boy Scout's first cook-out than a gourmet's repast: elegance, clarity and delicate complimentarity are all less probable than that the fire will sputter, that the potatoes will turn to mush, and that soup will follow dessert.[12]

At least, two very different approaches are possible. Aiming for a relatively comprehensive and integrated understanding of area and region we might investigate the local scene from the several perspectives embodied in the four traditions of Geography. For coherence and economy of time, the nature of the physical environment and the impact of humans upon it might be considered in tandem. Here a simple conceptual model will serve to clarify our discussion (Figure 1). First proposed by Carl Sauer some sixty years ago, it has been the basis of much subsequent human geography.[13] At its heart was the "natural landscape" made up of the climatic, vegetational, and land forms that together constitute a "habitat complex".

FIGURE 1

In considering this landscape one comes to understand the stage on which people have acted and which they have inevitably altered. Depending upon the extent to which such enquiries are pursued, much can be achieved in expanding the students' grasp of their world, introducing new concepts (of scale, of the earth as a dynamic system), demonstrating new methods of inquiry (sampling, induction, testing alternative hypotheses), and revealing the diversity of evidence upon which understanding of the physical world is based. Moreover, any consideration of the local "habitat complex" is an obvious springboard for comparisons that reveal both the diversity of the regional environment and some of the foundations of the region's distinctiveness in Canada.

12 Compare Association of American Geographers, *New Approaches in Introductory College Geography Courses*, Commission on College Geography, Publication no. 4 (Washington, D.C., 1967), p. 3.

13 C.O. Sauer, "The morphology of landscape", in J. Leighly, ed., *Land and Life* (Berkeley, 1967), pp. 315-50.

The remainder of Sauer's conceptual model directs attention to the "cultural landscape". This is the product of human actions on earth. It is delineated in part, by the distribution of population, and differentiated by the patterns of land use people established over area. "Its forms are all the works of man that characterize the landscape" — the assemblage of roads and bridges, farms and fields, towns and villages, fences and gardens that reflects human endeavour.[14] Each and every such landscape is shaped from the natural landscape, but its precise character is determined by the culture (broadly defined) of those who create it. Essential to this view is the fact that natural resources are cultural appraisals. Different groups perceive the potential of the environment in different ways and make use of it accordingly. In part, these decisions are shaped by economic and technological contexts — but they also reflect learned habits and values, the "cultural baggage" of individuals and peoples. This is to say that the landscape will reflect, more or less clearly, the imprint of different ethnic or cultural groups, as well as the impact of changing technologies and market circumstances.

Whether one encourages pupils to uncover past landscapes by mapping, interviewing, and examining old maps, photographs, and documents; takes a comparative view of areas occupied by different groups or at different times; or illustrates the changing face of the local environment in the manner suggested by the elaborate 3-dimensional models of the Harvard Forest diorama (Figure 2), this perspective can render local studies both relevant and revealing.[15] Through it, pupils should appreciate the impact of people on places, realize that change occurs at a variety of rates, recognize that some human modifications of the earth are irreversible (at least in the medium term), and understand that modern societies have far greater power to alter their environments, for good or ill, than did their predecessors. Furthermore it should be clear that there is considerable scope for integration of this approach with the concerns of other disciplines: of the sessions scheduled in the Teaching Maritime Studies Conference the foci of those treating the regional environment, native peoples, ethnic groups, the economy, and native culture might all be considered in relation to the cultural landscape, or *vice versa*.

Many geographers regard questions about the organization of space — about location, interconnection, patterns, and distribution — as fundamental. Their focus is on the arrangement and interaction of goods and people, on why things are where they are. One obvious emphasis here is upon the geography of production and consumption. The topic might be broached in countless ways to take advantage of local circumstances. Thus

14 *Ibid.*, p. 342.

15 *The Harvard Forest Models* (Petersham, Mass., 1941).

Height of Cultivation, 1830

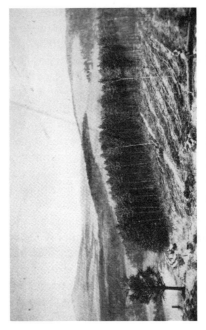

Abandoned Farm Produces White Pine Crop, 1910

Early Homestead Clearing, 1740

Farm Abandonment, 1850

FIGURE 2

we might begin with the pattern of retail stores and large supermarkets as well as the characteristic journeys-to-stop of the customers who patronize these places. From local survey and analyses it is a short step to the introduction of such concepts as the *range* of a particular good and the *threshold* of demand which underpin models of central place location that posit a normative arrangement of service centres across space.[16] Once this is recognized, the distribution of towns in the Maritimes might be compared with the "expectations" of the "model" to suggest the importance of context in shaping the region, and to demonstrate a good deal of its uniqueness while providing an introduction to the methods and models of social science.

At a different scale, the locational perspective is also germane to understanding the important issue of regional development, or underdevelopment, and the economic circumstances of the maritime region. Here too, questions of scale economies, agglomeration, market access, resource endowment, and inter-regional competition — all of which have a spatial dimension and have been treated in the framework of locational analysis — can be broached as attention is focussed on the regional economy. Here too, students might be encouraged to investigate how and how far the local area (or region) is, and has been, integrated into the wider Canadian/ North American/Atlantic economy by examining such sources as newspapers, shipping lists, and so on.

Finally, this catalogue brings us to the perspectives of regional geography. These are surely important in a programme of Maritime studies, not least because many conceive of the Maritimes as a distinctive region within the Canadian mosaic. But on what, we might ask, are such perceptions based? How useful are they? How accurate are they? The diversity of these provinces is, after all, something of a cliché. To those who know them they hardly qualify as a "formal region", exhibiting uniformity over area. Nor in any strict sense do they constitute a functional region integrated about a single important centre. But if it is only from afar that the three provinces are recognizable as a region in the formal sense — because their clocks keep a time of their own, because they are "down east" — there is no denying the importance of regional consciousness or regionalism in the area.[17] About this I will say little, because Ernest Forbes' fine book treats its brightest moments so well.[18] But I would simply allude to the special quality of life within the provinces that is shaped by and re-

16 For a summary see Haggett, *Locational Analysis*, pp. 120-22.

17 I have endeavoured to summarize some of this material in "The Mark of the Maritimes", in J. Acheson and R. Berry, eds., *Regionalism and National Identity* (Christchurch, forthcoming).

18 E.R. Forbes, *The Maritime Rights Movement 1919-1927* (Montreal, 1979).

flected in its people to make two points: that this region and others, cannot be measured by tangible and concrete indicators alone; and that the geographer's sensitivity to questions of scale and the meaning of area can go a long way to sharpening and clarifying any discussion of the Maritimes as a distinctive place.

Alternatively, we might adopt an issue-based approach, to examine change and conflict through a broadly geographical lens. This has much to commend it. It involves pupils directly in the affairs of their community; and it should catch their attention, allow them to employ a range of geographical skills, and hone their sense of citizenship. Of course, the issues examined, and the nature of student involvement in them will vary from place to place and year by year; no standard approach can be identified. But a few possibilities are worth mentioning to suggest the utility of a geographical perspective on many conflict situations.

Regional development issues are an obvious focus. As geographers Ralph Krueger and John Koegler have demonstrated in their study of northeastern New Brunswick, patterns of regional disparity rest on complex foundations; to grapple with them we need to understand the nature of the resource base, "the pattern of development, the social and cultural history, and the present social and economic structure of the region" as well as the wider context in which it is located.[19] Perspectives on such matters can be developed through simulations based upon role-playing in which students participate as representatives of the various interests involved, and consider the impact of different strategies, or compromise positions, on land use, environment, and population (or social) change. Similarly, questions of importance to the region in general might be broached by considering the environmental impact (broadly defined) of the introduction of a hypothetical industry to the local community. Students might also consider how local patterns of land-use, manufacturing activity, population distribution, employment, and consumer-consumption would be affected by a dramatic increase or decline in the costs of transportation.

Environmental issues are also worth considering from a geographical viewpoint. Beginning with the debate over budworm spraying or the use of herbicides in the forest brings us directly to questions of ecology and cost-benefit that require some consideration of both the physical environment (e.g. the hydrological cycle) and economic systems in space. It also raises important considerations about the human use of the earth, about whether its resources are given to us for exploitation or "for usufruct alone".[20] And

19 R.R. Krueger and J. Koegler, *Regional Development in Northeast New Brunswick* (Toronto, 1975), p. 9.

20 G.P. Marsh, *Man and Nature* (Cambridge, Mass., 1965), p. 36.

thus, it involves students in a concern of enormous local consequence, while placing it, and their understanding of it in a wider context.

In sum, this paper has argued that Geographers are concerned with more than simply locating capes and bays and cropping patterns on maps. Their diverse discipline offers a distinctive vantage point from which to consider the human condition; its focus on the nature of the physical environment, on the evolving character of places, on the organization of space, and on the interrelationships of people and their settings provides an important window on our world. And because Geography marries, to some degree, the humanities, the natural, and the social sciences it offers an enormously useful integrative perspective on a wide range of matters of central interest to our concern with Maritime studies. Here indeed it is of little moment if the borders between Geography and other disciplines sometimes seem blurred. This is as it is. Knowledge is a seamless web and should be treated as such in a comprehensive regional studies programme.

SELECTED BIBLIOGRAPHY

A. *Works defining geography as a field.*

Broek, J.O.M., *Geography, its scope and spirit* (Columbus, Ohio, 1965).

Hartshorne, R., *The Nature of Geography* (Ann Arbor, Michigan, 1939).

——————, *Perspective on the Nature of Geography* (Chicago, 1959).

Holt-Jensen, A., *Geography: Its History and Concepts* (London, 1980).

Johnston, R.J., *Geography and Geographers: Anglo-American Human Geography Since 1945* (London, 1979).

——————, *Philosophy and Human Geography* (London, 1983).

Wooldridge, S.W. and East, W.G., *The Spirit and Purpose of Geography* (London, 1951).

B. *Works useful in developing a geographical perspective on the Maritimes.*

Ennals, P.M. and Holdsworth, D.W., "Vernacular Architecture and the Cultural Landscape of the Maritime Provinces — A Reconnaissance", *Acadiensis*, X/2 (1981), pp. 86-106.

Erskine, David, "The Atlantic Region" in J. Warkentin, ed., *Canada. A Geographical Interpretation* (Toronto, 1968), pp. 231-80.

Hornsby, Stephen and Wynn, Graeme, "Walking through the past", *Acadiensis*, X/2 (1981), pp. 152-9.

Mannion, J.J., *Irish Settlements in Eastern Canada* (Toronto, 1974).

McCann, L.D., "The mercantile-industrial transition in the Metal Towns of Pictou County, 1857-1931", *Acadiensis*, X/2 (1981), pp. 29-64.

Millward, H., *Regional Patterns of Ethnicity in Nova Scotia: A Geographical Study* (Halifax, 1981).

——————, "A model of coalfield development. Six stages exemplified by the Sydney field", *Canadian Geographer*, 29/3 (1985), pp. 234-48.

Robinson, J.L., *Concepts and Themes in the Regional Geography of Canada* (Vancouver, 1983), pp. 69-104.

Ross, E., "The Atlantic Provinces in Recent Studies in Canadian Historical Geography", *Acadiensis*, V/1 (1975), pp. 108-17.

Wynn, Graeme, "W.F. Ganong, A.H. Clark and the Historical Geography of Maritime Canada", *Acadiensis*, X/2 (1981), pp. 5-28.

——————, "The Maritimes: The Geography of Fragmentation and Underdevelopment", in L.D. McCann, ed., *Heartland and Hinterland. A Geography of Canada* (Scarborough, 1982), pp. 156-213.

——————, "Ethnic Migrations and Atlantic Canada: Geographical Perspectives", *Canadian Ethnic Studies/Études Ethniques au Canada*, XVIII (1986), pp. 1-15.

C. *Works relevant to geographical teaching.*

Archer, J.E. and Dalton,T.H., *Fieldwork in Geography* (London, 1968).

Boardman, D., *Geography and Geography Teaching* (London, 1983).

Chorley, R.J., and Haggett, P., eds., *Frontiers in Geographical Teaching* (London, 1965).

Durrenberger, R.W., *Geographical Research and Writing* (New York, 1971).

Graves, N.J., *Curriculum\ Planning in Geography* (London, 1979).

D. *Periodicals.*

Canadian Geographic, published bimonthly by the Royal Canadian Geographic Society and devoted to all aspects of geography, carries well-illustrated articles intended to make Canada better known to Canadians and the world.

The Canadian Geographer, the quarterly publication of the Canadian Association of Geographers, contains scholarly articles by Canadian geographers and on Canadian topics, as well as book reviews and "Geographica" a forum for topics of current importance.

Geography, the journal of the British Geographical Association includes articles on the means and ends of teaching as well as on substantive topics.

Journal of Geography, published by the American National Council for Geographic Education six times a year is probably the most diverse and useful journal for teachers developing geographical perspectives in their courses.

6 *Indian Education Issues in the Maritime Provinces*

W.D. Hamilton

WE ALL FIND IT DIFFICULT TO admit that our perceptions, beliefs, and values have no universal or eternal validity, but are bounded by the culture to which we happen to belong and the time in which we happen to live. For this reason it is not easy for us to rationalize the existence of a truly different minority cultural tradition in our midst or to assign any particular importance to that tradition. Yet, in the case of the Native Indians, we are assuredly faced with a very different kind of cultural tradition which has refused to go away and which, in fact, is now gaining rapidly in size and strength throughout North America. Whether we like it or not, the Indian people have a lengthy and growing list of grievances to lodge against North American society, and an increasingly better-articulated set of demands to make of our governments and institutions.

We may try to comfort ourselves by supposing that most of what we are hearing and seeing from Indian spokesmen is merely political rhetoric or empty theatrics, but even after all of the suspect portions of the Indian agenda have been stripped away we are left with such stark facts as the following:

a) The Indian people believe that they have been the victims of systematic injustice over the centuries and that the problems of their present condition are largely an outgrowth and reflection of this.

b) In the area of education, specifically, Indian parents are almost universally unhappy with the performance of their children in school, and thus with the whole school system.

c) Even the most sensitive and accommodating of Indian educators believe that the school curriculum has been seriously biased against the Indians in two respects: i) by the stereotypical depiction of them as heathen savages without redeeming virtues, and ii) by the ignoring of their contribution to the larger society and their rightful place in the scheme of things.

Responses to the educational concerns and allegations mentioned above have come from both sides. The Indians themselves, through the National Indian Brotherhood's call in 1972 for "Indian control of Indian education", have set in motion a process of devolution by means of which control over the federal schools on Canadian Indian reserves is rapidly passing into the hands of the Indian bands themselves. At the same time, Indian educators and other leaders have been far more energetic and effective during the past decade than previously in getting their concerns over secondary and higher education expressed, in helping to get new programs and courses in place (especially in universities), and in obtaining a serious hearing at all levels.

On the side of the governments and institutions, equally important steps have been taken. There is no provincial department of education today, for example, which is not actively concerned, to one degree or another, with the Indian question, and a number of universities (including my own) have both responded to specific Indian pressures for higher education and seen fit to take initiatives of their own in accordance with changing perceptions of needs and responsibilities. Curriculum concerns at the school level are of two kinds: i) appropriate curriculum for the reserve schools, which are coming increasingly under Indian control, and ii) curriculum modifications for the public schools, to eliminate textbook bias and to give better balance to the curriculum through the recognition of the accomplishments and contributions of the Indian people.

The Micmac-Maliseet Institute at the University of New Brunswick is very much involved in responding to the whole spectrum of educational needs articulated by the Indian people of the region. Most of you will be aware of our degree program for Indian students, from which we have graduated approximately 60 Indian teachers since 1981. Curriculum development for both the Indian schools and the public schools has also been a major concern of ours. Unfortunately, I cannot go into detail on this more than to alert you to one project which I feel will be beneficial to all junior/senior high schools of the region, Indian and non-Indian alike. The project is funded by a $70,000 grant from Multiculturalism Canada for the creation of curriculum units concerning the Indians, and focusing, in particular, on inter-relationships, historical and contemporary, between the Indian people and the other ethnic populations of this region during the historical period.

The challenge of the project is to depict Indian life and Indian-white relations in these units as objectively as possible, given the fact that most of the records are documents written by white men, and that we ourselves (the writers) inevitably bring our own cultural biases to bear. To allow these facts to prevent the project from being undertaken, however, would be no service to anyone. We have had the benefit of Indian advice on the committee on the project. We shall be consulting with Indian educators at later stages as well. And we think that, through the project, we can make a contribution towards, first, simply making usable materials available and, second, bringing more balance into the picture than was present previously. The units on which we are working are as follows (all in terms of the Micmac and Maliseet cultures of this region):

a) the archaeological record of the region
b) Indian-white relations historically
c) the Indian land question
d) a case study of a Micmac community (18th/19th century)
e) Indian spirituality relative to Christianity
f) Indian technology/arts/crafts
g) the Indian languages
h) the Indian in contemporary society

Before we reach the point of preparing these units for publication as curriculum, we will be consulting extensively with the New Brunswick, Nova Scotia and Prince Edward Island schools before they are released for general use.

In the end, of course, any curriculum will be only as good and effective, as well balanced and free from bias, as the teachers who teach it. Thus there is a need also for the faculties and departments of education of the region to offer pre-service and in-service courses, course components, or training sessions which would have the effect of increasing teacher awareness and sensitivity to contemporary Indian education issues.

7   *Words Are Not Enough*

Harold Franklin McGee, Jr.

TO ALLOW MAXIMUM TIME FOR discussion I shall keep my comments relatively short and introductory in nature. Accounts of two personal experiences are relevant here.

The first occurred when I was in graduate school. A fellow student was showing his three-year old son a library and asked him "what are these", expecting to hear "books". The child looked around for a bit, then said, "a bunch of words".

The second happened a number of years ago when I was involved as a consultant in the assembling of the native peoples section of the Atlantic Canada Museumobile. At the time of the invitation, I saw this as an opportunity to alter the negative image of Micmacs that prevailed in textbooks of the day — and of native people generally. Consequently, in consultation with the designer, I chose to emphasize an aspect of life that focused upon leisure activities, demonstrating that the aboriginal technology was sufficient to provide for the restful pursuit of recreational activity in a domestic atmosphere that suggested peace and tranquility. The designer agreed. I also suggested that the interpreters be given a series of lectures about the various displays in the museumobile so that they could knowledgeably answer questions that the general public might put to them. That idea was rejected, apparently for fiscal reasons.

A year or so later, the five trailers of the Atlantic Canada display began their tour of the country in Victoria. A local television station featured the travelling museum on its news programme by having an interpreter give the reporter a tour of the display. When they approached the diarama of the interior of a pre-contact wigwam depicting a trio of men playing *waltes* (a form of dice game), a woman preparing food, and children frolicking, the interpreter said something like the following: "This is a scene showing Micmac men playing *waltes*, a type of dice game in which they would bet everything they owned — including their wives. The outcome of the game was also used to predict a warrior's fortunes in battle".

In the past few years, there have been a number of books developed for use in the schools or written for school-aged children. I had planned to provide an evaluation of these. However, there are two reasons for my not doing so. The first is that I have been involved with the writing, production, or evaluation of most of them and therefore cannot provide an unbiased assessment. The second reason is that there is a more fundamental issue at hand than the development of texts or curriculum. As the second story demonstrates, there is no guarantee that well-intentioned authors or conscientious curriculum development committees will have the desired consequences in the classroom. The question becomes not can we develop accurate, sensitive, and attractive texts and classroom materials; but rather, what can we do to keep these materials from becoming just a "bunch of words"?

Some conceptual tools of a theoretical orientation within anthropology known as transactionalism are useful in examining what happens to ideas as they are transmitted from a source to a recipient. These are patron, client, and broker. For our purposes a *patron* is one who creates value and dispenses it; in this case, an author who wishes to portray some aspect of the history and culture of native peoples of the Maritimes. A *client* is the target of the message containing the value; this is the individual the patron wishes to influence. In our situation, the client is the student. A *broker* is one who transmits the message from the patron to the client but who alters the value in the process. The alteration may be an enhancement, but, as we saw with the museum interpreter, it may be a negation of the intended value. Obviously, teachers are brokers. It would seem that the production of texts and curriculae are insufficient; words are not enough. We must be involved with teacher education.

The cooperation of local school boards, provincial departments of education, and universities is required at the institutional level. At the interpersonal level, there has to be understanding and accommodation between university instructors and classroom instructors. When a text is finally adopted — hopefully with the cooperative involvement of all concerned — it will be necessary to have a series of in-service workshops and longer summer school workshops devoted to the implementation of the new materials. Ideally universities which offer courses concerned with Maritime native peoples will make them available during the academic year at times convenient to teachers.

To conclude, and to open for discussion, I suggest that in addition to the development of a first-rate textbook dealing with contemporary and historic issues concerning the Malecite and Micmac peoples which are integrated with the socio-economic environment of the region, the details of a teacher re-education programme should be a part of the plan for the development of curriculum materials for the teaching of native studies to primary and secondary school children.

SELECTED BIBLIOGRAPHY

Anger, Dorothy C., "The Micmacs of Newfoundland: a resurgent culture", *Culture*, I (1981), pp. 78-81.

Bailey, Alfred G., *The conflict of European and eastern Algonkian cultures, 1504-1700* (2nd ed., Toronto, 1969).

Bock, Philip K., *The Micmac Indians of Restigouche* (Ottawa, 1966).

_____, "Micmac", in *Handbook of North American Indians, Volume 15: Northeast* (Washington, 1978).

Daughterty, W.E., *Maritime Indian treaties in historical perspective* (Ottawa, 1983).

Erickson, Vincent O., "Maliseet-Passamaquoddy", in *Handbook of North American Indians, Volume 15: Northeast* (Washington, 1978).

Gonzalez, Ellice B., *Changing economic roles for Micmac men and women*, (Ottawa, 1981).

Gould, G.P. and Semple, A.J., *Our land: the Maritimes* (Fredericton, 1980).

Guillemin, Jeanne, *Urban Renegades: The cultural strategy of American Indians* (New York, 1975).

Hamilton, W.D., *The Julian tribe* (Fredericton, 1984).

_____ and Spray, William, *Source material relating to the New Brunswick Indian* (Fredericton, 1977).

Jaenen, Cornelius J., *The French relationship with the native peoples of New France and Acadia* (Ottawa, 1984).

Larsen, Tord, "Negotiating identity: the Micmac of Nova Scotia" in A. Tanner, ed., *The politics of Indianness* (St. John's, 1983).

Leavitt, Robert M., *The Micmacs* (Toronto, 1985).

McGee, Harold F., "White encroachment on Micmac reserve lands in Nova Scotia, 1830-1867", *Man in the Northeast*, 8 (1974), 57-64.

_____, "The Micmac Indians: the earliest migrants" in D. Campbell, ed., *Banked fires — the ethnics of Nova Scotia* (Port Credit, Ont., 1978).

_____, *The native peoples of Atlantic Canada* (2nd ed., Ottawa, 1983).

Mechling, W.H., "The Malecite Indians, with notes on the Micmac", *Anthropologica (Old Series)* 7/8 (1958-59).

Upton, Leslie F.S., *Micmacs and colonists: Indian-White relations in the Maritimes, 1713-1867* (Vancouver, 1979).

Wallis, Wilson D. and Wallis, Ruth S., *Micmac Indians of eastern Canada* (Minneappolis, 1955).

——————, *The Malecite Indians of New Brunswick* (Ottawa, 1957).

Whitehead, Ruth Holmes, *Elitekey: Micmac material culture from 1600 A.D. to the present* (Halifax, 1980).

——————, *Micmac quillwork* (Halifax, 1982).

—————— and McGee, Harold, *The Micmac: how their ancestors lived five hundred years ago* (Halifax, 1983).

8

Teaching Acadian History

Naomi Griffiths

THE OBVIOUS STARTING PLACE for me, when I consider the question of teaching Acadian history, is the need to be clear about the nature of teaching "the other". I am not of Acadian descent, and the question has immediately to be faced of the extent to which someone of one set of traditions and cultural habits can understand and interpret those whose lives have been formed in a different mold. While I am fully convinced of the ability of one human being to understand another, I am also aware that the ability demands a considerable exercise of analytical imagination and intelligence. I do not believe that only women can understand the lives of women but I think that men must exercise considerable effort if they wish to see the world from the point of view of their opposite sex. Similarly, those of us whose primary allegiance is to groups other than Acadian have to make a conscious decision to discover and appreciate the norms of Acadian life.

In some ways, of course, there is no difference between the teaching of Acadian studies and teaching anything else. The old bromide remains true: move from the known to the unknown. The beginning should not be "here are Acadians: they are not as we", but "here are men and women, teachers, lawyers, doctors, farmers or fishermen. Their lives are based on the demands of these pursuits, as are ours". Only when common ground has been established should the next step be taken: the delineation of the difference, the extent to which the solution of problems posed has been found in other ways than those selected by one's own kin and kith.

In working along these line it is particularly important not only to build a clear picture of the characteristics that define the majority of this different community but also to indicate the significant variations within the community. It is not enough to present the Acadians as French-speaking, Catholics, basically rural rather than urban, with considerable attachment to family and traditions of their ancestors. The subtle shifts between what is a "true enough generalisation" and the every-day reality of individual lives has to be conveyed. In the attempt which follows at the elucidation of this idea, the bias of a professional historian will be apparent but it is hoped that, as usual, the discipline of history has a universal application.

If one begins with the attribute of French-speaking, for example, as a major part of Acadian identity, something must be said about the way in which the French spoken in Quebec, in Martinique, in France and among the Acadians varies. Further, when that is done, something must also be told about the way in which Acadian writers of the nineteenth century, Pascal Poirier say, or Placide Gaudet, used the language in distinction to the styles of later scholars, such as Guy Arsenault and Regis Lebrun.[1] And, of course, the variation between the writings of contemporary authors whose vision is Acadie itself, people such as Antonine Maillet, Herménégilde Chiasson, Léonard Forest and Laurier Melanson also needs exposition and explanation.[2]

Similarly, the designation of the Acadian as Catholic really says very little about the nature of Acadian religious belief and the place of religion in Acadian life. In the context of Maritime experience it seems particularly important to note that the Acadians deliberately chose a patron saint, Mary, Mother of God, other than the saint selected by Quebec, St. Jean-Baptiste.[3] Further the fact that the religious orders that so formed and shaped Acadian lives in the nineteenth and twentieth centuries were as often centered in France as in Quebec added an interesting flavour to the development of Acadian Catholicism in Nova Scotia and New Brunswick. The experience of the Eudiste fathers, whose work in establishing College St. Anne, Nova Scotia, has yet to be given its due in the history of Acadians in the twentieth century, was that of people pressured to leave by an anti-clerical state, the French Third Republic. The way in which these men structured their pastoral duties, their college curricula and their cultural activities was shaped as much by the legacy of a bitter past as by the experience of a tolerant present. Their ideas of their vocation varied from those held by the Holy Cross Fathers who built St. Joseph's, the parent of Moncton University. One can cite similar evidence to show that the rich heritage brought by the sisters and nuns was equally diverse. Members of orders such as the Filles de la Sagesse, the Hospitalières, and the Congregation of Notre Dame, built a heritage which was rich and complex and produced a ùnique cultural life for many of the Acadian youth.

Once one has outlined what particular Acadian flavour has been given

1 Pascal Poirier, *Origine des Acadians* (Montreal, 1874); Placide Gaudet, *Le grand dérangement* (Shediac, 1922); Bona Arsenault, *L'Acadie des Ancêtres avec la généologie* (Laval, 1955); Regis Brun, *Pionnier de la nouvelle Acadie Joseph Gueguen, 1741-1800* (nouvelle édition, Moncton, 1984).

2 Antonine Maillet, *La Sagouine* (Grasset, 1976); Herménégilde Chiasson, *Mourir à Scoudouc* (Moncton, 1974); Léonard Forest, *Saisons Anterieures* (Moncton, 1973); Laurier Melanson, *Zélika à cochon vert* (Moncton, 1981).

3 See Ferdinand J. Robidoux, *Conventions Nationales des Acadiens* (Shédiac, 1907).

to the qualities of "French-speaking" and "Catholic", one can turn to broader questions of the distinctive nature of Acadian history. The presentation of material needs not only to emphasize the development of the Acadian community, but also to disentangle the complex interpretations that have been placed at different times by the Acadians on that very past. The varying emphasis which has been placed upon the events of 1755 by, for example, Michel Roy in his work *L'Acadie Perdue*, as opposed to the interpretation of Léon Thériault in *La Question du Pouvoir en Acadie*, needs to be considered.[4] The former follows the path of earlier historians such as Lauvrière, and depicts the Acadians as the hapless and helpless victims of events utterly beyond their control. The latter turns from interpretations of the past and emphasises the reality of the Acadian presence in the Maritimes today. My own work, especially the essay that serves as the introduction to Volume IV of the *Dictionary of Canadian Biography* (Toronto, 1979), is an attempt to return the Acadians from puppets to human beings and to highlight some of the events that live in Acadian memory as centre-pieces of the lives of their ancestors. Unquestionably, however, for those teaching any aspect of Acadian experience, the reference work to have at hand, is that edited by Jean Daigle, *Les Acadiens des Maritimes* (Moncton, 1983), now available in English.

Space and time preclude any exhaustive analysis of the challenges to be faced in weaving the Acadian experience into its rightful place in Maritime studies. The task is to present the reality of human experience to the student. It is at this point that I would urge on you the usefulness of two particular works of Canadian scholarship. Firstly, the *Dictionary of Canadian Biography* encloses in its multi-volumed pages sufficient detail about a crowd of individuals whose lives built so much of the past. It is too easy to forget that biography is still one of the most effective methods of illuminating theory and analysis. Secondly, the collection of essays published as *The Acadiensis Reader*, Volumes I and II (Fredericton, 1985), has made readily accessible much recent thought about Maritime life. Even if the bias of both sources is historical, history is, after all, the context for almost every aspect of Maritime studies.

---

4 Michel Roy, *L'Acadie Perdue* (Quebec, 1978); Léon Thériault, *La Question du Pouvoir en Acadie* (Moncton, n.d.).

9   *Some Important Features of Contemporary Acadia*

Léon Thériault

THERE WAS A TIME, NOT TOO long past, when Acadians would refer primarily to history in order to express themselves collectively and to convince themselves and others that they were indeed a distinct people with particular aspirations and needs. History is still part of the arguments the Acadians use to support their case but it has lost some of its importance. For reasons that probably relate more to substance than to style, the contemporary Acadian leadership uses arguments and facts that have more to do with what is going on in present day Acadia than what occurred in the past. Hence, an overview of present-day Acadia, of its people, of its institutions, of the diversity of its endeavours, cannot be eliminated from any serious study on the Acadians without indulging in a very incomplete and somewhat biased account. And it is some of those contemporary aspects of Acadia that I would like to present for further discussion, without pretending to be thorough or complete.

A fundamental characteristic of present-day Acadia is the diversity of its origins. If, during the French Regime, the number of Acadians of non-French origin was negligible, it is not so now.[1] And that is a very important aspect of the kind of Acadia that was recreated in the Maritime provinces after the Treaty of Paris in 1763. Indeed, the Acadian communities assimilated more "foreign" elements than is generally realized. People of Irish origin, but also of Scottish and English stock, particularly in northeastern New Brunswick, account for a sizable, but yet undetermined, number of Francophones. Although these descendants have names like McGraw, Finn, McLaughlin, Ferguson and Kerry, their mother tongue is French and they consider themselves Acadians. Their ancestors arrived in the latter part of the eighteenth century or at the beginning of the nineteenth and married Acadian women. There are also Acadians whose paternal ancestors came from the island of Jersey (a British possession off the coast of France) like the LeGresleys and the Duvals, who were Pro-

---

1   For an interesting study of the Acadian population from 1603 to the present, see Muriel K. Roy, "Settlement and Population Growth", in Jean Daigle, ed., *The Acadians of the Maritimes. Thematic Studies* (Moncton, 1982), pp. 125-96.

testant but who themselves, once in the Maritimes, or their sons after-wards, became Catholic before marrying Acadian women. Still more numerous are those Acadians, both in northwestern and northeastern New Brunswick, whose ancestors came from Québec after 1763. They have names like Losier, Brideau, Allard, Beaulieu, Jean, Lepage, Ouellet, Des-jardins, and Saint-Onge. Even immigration from France was not entirely stopped at the Treaty of Paris as can be ascertained by Acadians bearing names like Lanteigne, Gionet, Parisé and Renaud.

It is true that the Acadian communities of Nova Scotia, Prince Edward Island and of southeastern New Brunswick have not experienced this diver-sity to the same degree, but because these elements have become so impor-tant in all of northern New Brunswick, a region which accounts for a large percentage of New Brunswick Francophones, researchers should give more attention to this phenomenon. This would not dilute Acadian history into something that would resemble a "pot-pourri": the main line of acadi-anity does go back to 1604 and there is a continuity of themes from that date on. But modern Acadia has very diverse roots which have to be taken into account. Of course, there is an on-going debate within the Acadian community as to who is and who is not an Acadian. Some people will say that an Acadian is a person whose ancestors resided in the Maritime pro-vinces *before* the Deportation, although that interpretation is more common in northwestern and southwestern New Brunswick, in Nova Scotia and in Prince Edward Island than in northeastern New Brunswick. Nevertheless, an in-depth study, using both demographic and historical techniques, would contribute greatly to the comprehension of the "new" Acadia.

Another aspect of the problem, which is one of terminology, is the too liberal use of the concept of *French origin* to define and count Acadians. It is as if there were some kind of an indelible ethnicity mark attached to the idea of acadianity. In that case, the descendants of an Acadian would always be Acadians no matter what their mother tongue came to be in the future generations. Indeed, a lot of studies count as Acadians all those of French origin, particularly when they have names like LeBlanc, Gallant, Thériault, and Cormier, even if they do not speak French any longer. Would not the concept of mother tongue be more useful here? Hence, there would be Maritimers of Acadian origin, but not Acadian any longer (having become Anglophones); on the other hand, there would be Acadians of English, German (like the Raiches), Irish, and, of course, French origin (these last the more numerous).[2] But that concept may

2 Elsewhere, I have argued against a definition of "acadianity" that would be exclusively based upon the idea that an Acadian is necessarily someone whose ancestors came here before the Deportation. I personally favor a definition that would also take into account

become widely accepted only when the history of the French Regime, particularly the Deportation, has been "exorcised".

Another important aspect of present-day Acadia is that its population is unequally divided amongst the three Maritime provinces. Not only is the population unequally distributed, but it is more widely scattered than at the time of the French Regime. These are aspects that probably would not be overlooked by any analyst. But what could be overlooked is that French New Brunswick has become a very special group not only within the three Maritime provinces but within French Canada as a whole. In all the other provinces except Quebec the French population is less than six per cent, while in New Brunswick it is around 33 per cent. The rate of assimilation is also slower in New Brunswick than elsewhere and there are more French institutions and structures in this province than elsewhere in Canada except Quebec. There are also legal and constitutional guarantees pertaining to the French language in New Brunswick that do not exist outside Quebec.[3] There is even a political discourse quite particular to French New Brunswick. The idea of *equality*, for example, is very seldom discussed in the other eight provinces with an English majority. Indeed, acadianity, in New Brunswick, comprises a political dimension that is not expressed elsewhere, at least not in the same terms or with the same intensity.[4] French New Brunswick is therefore in a category all by itself within French Canada and that point should be stressed in any study relating to contemporary Acadia.

The organization of Acadian society should constitute another theme in studying contemporary Acadia. I am not hinting at themes like the idea of family which may or may not be more important in Acadia than with any other group, nor am I alluding to the impact of tradition. I do not think the Acadian community is very much different from others in Canada in these respects. But the "official" Acadian society, if I may use the expression, is organized around certain institutions which are very visible, at least to certain of us. These institutions exist in various fields, but particularly in the economic, cultural and the pressure group areas. Some-

those immigrants of various origins who came after the Deportation and who assimilated into our group. See my *La question du pouvoir en Acadie* (Moncton, 1982), pp. 54-62.

3 New Brunswick is the only bilingual province in Canada and linguistic rights have been enshrined into the Canadian constitution in 1982. Furthermore, a provincial law, passed in 1981, decreed equality of status for Francophone and Anglophone communities in New Brunswick.

4 In New Brunswick, Acadians think more and more in terms of sharing power with the Anglophones, while in the other provinces the questions debated concern chiefly linguistic aspects as such. For a comparison of the various Francophone communities outside Quebec, see Fédération des francophones hors Québec, *The Heirs of Lord Durham* (2 vols., Ottawa, 1977).

thing of their history, of their mandate, of their failures and realizations should be included in the theme.

It is not my purpose here to go over all those associations but I should like to mention a few. First, there is the *Société Nationale des Acadiens*. Founded in 1881 under the name of *Société Nationale l'Assomption* (it acquired its present name in 1956 in order to distinguish it from the Assomption insurance company), that pressure group was for a long time the only such cultural association. Under its auspices the various Acadian symbols were chosen in the last part of the nineteenth century and requests were made from time to time regarding school and ecclesiastical matters.[5] In this century, provincial associations were founded which dealt with the needs of the Acadians in a given province. The *Société Saint-Thomas-d'Aquin* was founded for the P.E.I. Acadians in 1919. The *Fédération acadienne de la Nouvelle-Ecosse* followed in 1967. Lastly, the *Société des Acadiens du Nouveau-Brunswick* appeared in 1974; up to 1974 the Acadians of that province had used the *Société Nationale des Acadiens* as their own vehicle. Now the latter looks after problems which are common to the three groups, like the media and external relations. Each provincial association has a membership, an Executive, a couple of employees and a head office. They debate all kinds of questions; they write briefs to governments; they publish various reports of some concern to the Acadians.[6] They are pivotal elements among those that chart the course of cultural development in the French regions of the Maritimes. These associations, in turn, are members of the *Fédération des francophones hors Québec*, established in 1970, whose head office is in Ottawa. The FFHQ deals primarily with matters that are under federal jurisdiction.

Besides those structures, there is a host of other associations and institutions whose mission is more specific and which are too numerous to mention here. The spectrum encompasses associations as varied as the Association of Acadian Writers and the credit unions. Furthermore, a

---

5 The speeches, resolutions and conclusions of the first three Acadian national conventions (1881, 1884, 1890) were printed in Ferdinand J. Robidoux, *Conventions nationales des Acadiens: recueil des travaux et délibérations des six premières conventions compilé par Ferdinand J. Robidoux* (Shédiac, 1907). Only one volume was ever published. Material on the other conventions can be found in the Acadian newspapers of the day.

6 See for example *The Heirs of Lord Durham*. Of particular interest is *Pour un nouveau contrat social: plan d'action* (Moncton, 1984), which outlined its objectives for the next five years. The SANB is now (1985) in the process of releasing its findings regarding Francophones and health care in New Brunswick. The SANB has its head office in Petit-Rocher (the question of the head office is to be reexamined in 1986); the SSTA is based in Summerside and the FANE is in Halifax. The head office of the FFHQ is in Ottawa. From time to time, it organizes symposia pertaining to language rights, communications, etc.

number of semi-official anglophone associations have their French equivalent. For example, there is a Human Rights Awareness Association in
New Brunswick; there is also an *Association francophone pour la promo-
tion des droits de la personne* with the same mandate. There are two school
teachers' unions in this province — one French and one English — though
federated at the top. There are two school councillors' associations, etc.,
etc. The French electronic media (radio and television) and the French
newspapers and periodicals are also important features of present-day
Acadia.[7] All this, then, should be part, in one way or another, of any
serious presentation of the Acadians to the general public or to the school
population.

An interesting recent development within Acadian society and worth
mentioning is the concerted effort to establish links with the rest of the
Francophone world. In some cases, these links are rather formal and
official, that is to say through government channels, like those that exist
between New Brunswick and Québec, France and Belgium; in other cases,
they are promoted through less official channels like the contacts recently
developed between the Association of Acadian writers and certain groups
in Francophone Africa, or with *Les Amitiés Acadiennes* of Paris.[8]

There are, of course, important questions debated within the Acadian
community, but these include quite a few outside the specific domain of
culture or of acadianity. Urban development, natural resource management, unemployment, issues like abortion and the death penalty, all this is
part of the total picture of Acadian society. Acadians discuss educational
problems, for example, but not only from the point of view of French education. They also debate these problems from a general educational perspective, for the sake of education, like everyone else does. Though specific,

---

7 There is one French-language television in Moncton (CBAFT); that station may be
   picked up in almost all Acadian communities throughout the Maritime provinces. In
   northern New Brunswick, Quebec stations can be also picked up. There are three French
   radio stations: Radio-Canada (CBAF) in Moncton; CJVA, a private station, in Caraquet
   and CJEM, a private station, in Edmundston. The only French language daily newspaper
   is *L'Acadie Nouvelle*, published in Caraquet since 1984, entirely privately financed. A
   replacement for *L'Evangeline*, a daily which folded in Moncton in 1982 is contemplated
   by a Moncton group through a trust fund that has been set up with a grant of $4,000,000
   from the provincial government and one of $2,000,000 from Ottawa. The name of this
   paper would be *Le Matin* and should appear at the end of the summer of 1986. Needless
   to say, the issue has generated a great deal of controversy among Acadians. There are
   also six weekly newspapers: four in New Brunswick, one each in P.E.I. and N.S.; one
   monthly, published in Bathurst. There are three major periodicals, all published in New
   Brunswick.

8 See Léon Thériault, "L'évolution des relations extérieures de l'Acadie (1603-1978)",
   Egalité, revue acadienne d'analyse politique, no. 12 (Printemps 1984), pp. 19-47. That
   issue of *Egalité* was devoted entirely to the international dimension of Acadia.

because of its French culture, that society is nevertheless faced with the same problems and realities found elsewhere in the world and it reacts in a not too different manner from societies faced with similar problems elsewhere.

Since the creation of the Université de Moncton in 1964, Acadian studies have received an impetus unknown till then. There was a time, not too long ago, when the publication of a book by an Acadian would be quite an event. Not quite so now. The *Centre d'études acadiennes* at the Université de Moncton serves as a kind of central archives and as a repository for published material concerning the Acadians. A good survey of what is available in the field of Acadian studies can be found in the *Inventaire général des sources documentaires sur les Acadiens*. This three volume research tool is a must for any serious researcher in Acadian studies. The first volume deals with the archival material; the second, with studies published in book form; the third volume lists articles. The three volumes have excellent author/subject indexes.[9] Once in a while a plea is made to update this work. Nevertheless, the Center is well advanced in the inventorying of its many collections.

The problems faced by Acadian researchers are the very same problems we hear about elsewhere, namely, the lack of grants and the teaching load. Still, the Acadian researchers hold their own symposia in many fields: history, folklore, economics, political science, gerontology, and literature. Acadian researchers themselves may not be great in numbers, given what remains to be done, but they are fortunately helped and shouldered by quite a sizable number of non-Acadians from other parts of Canada or of the world. The latter contribute greatly to the advancement of our knowledge, whether they write in French or not.

Recent research, at least at the Université de Moncton, concerns both traditional and new fields. Local history, for example, is certainly part of that new preoccupation, with a special interest in the social and economic aspects.[10] Economic history is slowly emerging as a distinct field but while the coop movement, land acquisition and industries like the fisheries and

---

9 Centre d'études acadiennes, Université de Moncton, *Inventaire général des sources documentaires sur les Acadiens*, Tome I (no sub-title) (Moncton, 1975); Tome II: *Bibliographie acadienne. Liste des volumes, brochures et thèses concernant l'Acadie et les Acadiens des débuts à 1975* (Moncton, 1975); Tome III: *Bibliographie acadienne. Liste des articles de périodiques concernant l'Acadie et les Acadiens des débuts à 1976* (Moncton, 1977).

10 Of course, quality varies greatly. But a good example of that type of research would be Donat Robichaud's *Le Grand Chipagan: Histoire de Shippagan* (n.p., 1976). Commerce, communications, industry, politics are some of the themes presented in that study, and some of the information concerns not only Shippagan but also certain localities from Bathurst to Newcastle.

the forestry are now being researched by historians, the field still lies fallow. Political history has received notable contributions, especially in the form of biographies of politicians and in the study of the voting pattern of the Acadians.[11] Religious history and educational history are now being examined in a more detached manner than in the past.[12] But a lot remains to be done. Taking the history of education as an example, we know fairly well the institutional part of it (the circumstances surrounding the foundation of schools and colleges, and the establishment of French in the curriculum, for example), but very little about the content of programmes, teachers' academic background, school attendance, or illiteracy. The history of Acadian literature, on the other hand, is fairly well taken care of. At least, it has been put on firmer ground with the publication of both an anthology and a history of that literature.[13] Folklore is also among the research fields where great progress has been made recently, especially under the auspices of the *Centre d'études folkloriques* at the Université de Moncton. Books and recordings related to that specialty are now available on the market.[14] Genealogy, an ancient but respectable, preoccupation of quite a few amateur researchers, is now being studied by specialists.[15] At

---

11 Biographies remain popular in Acadian political studies, probably because isolating the Acadian factor from the rest would prove too difficult a task and this field, more than others, interests greatly non-Acadian scholars. Della M. Stanley, for example, has published two interesting biographies of Acadian politicians: *Au service de deux peuples. Pierre-Amand Landry* (Moncton, 1977); *Louis-J. Robichaud: a Decade of Power* (Halifax, 1984).

12 On religion, see, for example, Léon Thériault, "The Acadianization of the Catholic Church in Acadia (1763-1953)" in *The Acadians of the Maritimes. Thematic Studies*, pp. 271-339. An excellent recent biography is Bertha Plourde, *Mgr L.-J. Arthur Melanson, 1879-1941* (Montréal, 1985). On education, see Alexandre J. Savoie, *Un siècle de revendications scolaires au Nouveau-Brunswick: 1871-1971* (The Author, 1978). For a brief survey in English, see the same author, "Education in Acadia: 1604-1970", in Jean Daigle, *The Acadians of the Maritimes. Thematic Studies* (Moncton, 1982), pp. 383-427.

13 Marguerite Maillet, Gerald LeBlanc and Bernard Emont, *Anthologie de textes littéraires acadiens* (Moncton, 1979); Marguerite Maillet, *Histoire de la littérature acadienne: De rêve en rêve* (Moncton, 1983).

14 See Ronald Labelle, *Inventaire des sources en folklore acadien* (Moncton, 1984). An interesting monograph in folklore is Anselme Chiasson's *Chéticamp: histoire et traditions acadiennes* (Moncton, 1961). For examples of the type of research being done, see Ronald Labelle and Lauraine Léger, eds., *En r'montant la tradition. Hommage au père Anselme Chiasson* (Moncton, 1982). Acadian material culture, on the other hand, has been studied by Jean-Claude Dupont in two works: *Héritage d'Acadie* (Montréal, 1977), and *Histoire populaire de l'Acadie* (Montréal, 1979).

15 A fine example of that research can be found in Fidèle Thériault's *Les familles de Caraquet: Dictionnaire généalogique* (n.p., 1985). Information on the first Acadian generations can be gathered in Adrien Bergeron's genealogical study of the Acadians who took refuge in Quebec in the mid-eighteenth century: *Le grand arrangement des Acadiens au Québec* (8 vols., Montréal, 1981).

least, there is one employed full time at the *Centre d'études acadiennes* and its first volume of genealogy, comprising the Acadian population of the 1604-1713 period, should be available sometime in 1986 or 1987.

I will not close my comments without underlining the very important role played by our local historical societies. Not only do their members show zeal for the study of the history of their region, but most of them do so with a special regard towards scientific methods as can be ascertained through an examination of their regular publications. I would mention three in particular: the *Société historique acadienne* of Moncton, the *Société historique Nicolas-Denys* of Shippagan, and the *Société historique du Madawaska* of Edmundston. Besides the regular publication of their periodicals, these societies have saved a great deal of archival material that would have been lost without their determined intervention. Thanks to their efforts the future holds out the promise of even greater progress in our understanding of both the past and future of the Acadian community.

10   *Ethnicity and Culture in Maritime Canada*

J.M. Bumsted

AS WE ALL REALIZE AND APPRECIATE, the study of ethnicity has been one of the major growth industries of contemporary scholarship in Canada. There are several reasons for the flourishing of ethnic studies. In the first place, it represents a scholarly subject which touches on many disciplines and conceptual perspectives, thus raising a host of fascinating questions for research and enquiry. In the second place, it represents a scholarly subject which has broad popular appeal from at least two constituencies: the "roots" people interested in tracing their ancestry and family origins, and the ethnic politicians and activists who employ ethnicity as a political lever by which — as one commentator has observed — "the symbols of a common culture . . . lend themselves to appropriate strategies for securing resources collectively".[1] Finally, ethnicity represents a force which governments and politicians find it important to be seen supporting. On the federal level, the policy of Multiculturalism has emerged out of the debate over Bilingualism and Biculturalism, and there has been substantial public funding for research, conferences, and publication in ethnic studies, mainly by the Office of the Secretary of State, Multiculturalism Branch.[2] On the provincial level as well, ethnic studies have been subsidized, often in ways little different than grants for other community projects.

Despite this burgeoning interest in ethnic studies by scholars, politicians, and public alike, there remains no commonly-accepted definition of ethnicity and no really satisfactory theoretical frameworks into which ethnicity can be placed. Laments from specialists about the conceptual vagueness of the term "ethnic" abound in the scholarly journals and published conference proceedings.[3] In the literature of sociology, for example,

---

1   Kogila Moodley, "Canadian Ethnicity in Comparative Perspective: Issues in the Literature", in J. Dahlie and T. Fernando, eds., *Ethnicity, Power and Politics in Canada* (Toronto, 1981), pp. 6-21, esp. p. 9.

2   See for example, the "Generations Series" of monographs on ethnic groups commissioned by the Department of the Secretary of State; the journal *Ethnic Studies*; and the collections of papers from the annual conference of the Canadian Ethnic Studies Association.

3   Roberto Perin, "Clio as an Ethnic: The Third Force in Canadian Historiography",

one study in 1970 found that in 65 commonly-cited studies of ethnicity, only 13 attempted some explicit definition and those definitions diverged greatly from one another.[4] The situation has not changed appreciably in the ensuing fifteen years. Thus the literature of ethnicity tends to be descriptive, conceptually imprecise, and extremely confusing to the reader. Most studies focus on particular ethnic groups in particular historical and/or geographical contexts, and certain groups tend to be neglected.

In Canada there appears to be a direct correlation between the status of an ethnic group, the degree or extent of its perceived distinctiveness from Canadian society, and the focus upon it by students of ethnicity. Ethnic groups with low statuses and/or perceived high resistance to acculturation or assimilation — the two are often but not necessarily linked — are typically studied far more regularly than are ethnic groups with high statuses and low resistances to assimilation. A good deal of work has been done on the Black communities in the Maritimes. But as James Morrison's recently published bibliography of ethnic groups in Nova Scotia demonstrates, the literature on such groups as the English or the Americans is very sparse, particularly after initial settlement.[5] Few scholars would deny, at least in principle, that such groups are ethnic.[6] But the assumption is that they rapidly merge into the majority and lose their special ethnic quality, although such assumptions have never really been thoroughly tested. In any event, the tendency is to approach ethnicity either from the perspective of the immigrant experience or from the perspective of the minority experience, in either case with acculturation the major if often unspoken conceptual framework. At least one American textbook defines ethnicity as "those cultural traits retained by immigrant groups . . . from their home culture".[7] Whatever perspective is employed, there are conceptual problems which lead to a tendency on the one hand, to eschew theory altogether, or to be unable to relate existing theory to the complex realities of the local, regional, or even national, experience.

In a brief presentation one can hardly hope to offer a fully-articulated reconceptualization of a phenomenon as complex as ethnicity. But perhaps some of the dimensions of one of the major aspects of ethnicity — culture — can be suggested. For basic to most definitions of ethnicity is the notion

Canadian Historical Review, LXIV (1983), p. 443.

4   Wserolod W. Isajiw, "Definitions of Ethnicity", in Jay E. Goldstein and Rita M. Bienvenue, eds., *Ethnicity and Ethnic Relations in Canada* (Toronto, 1980), pp. 13-26.

5   James H. Morrison, ed., *Common Heritage: An Annotated Bibliography of Ethnic Groups in Nova Scotia* (Halifax, 1984).

6   Ross McCormack, "Cloth Caps and Jobs: The Ethnicity of English Immigrants in Canada 1900-1914", in Dahlie and Fernando, *Ethnicity, Power and Politics in Canada,* pp. 38-55.

7   P.L. and B. Berger, *Sociology: A Biographical Approach* (New York, 1972), p. 119.

that it involves a shared common culture. Of course, culture is another one of those concepts which is slippery and difficult to pin down, less because it is undefined than because it is used in so many different ways. One team of American scholars has identified over 300 separate usages for the term culture.[8] For our purposes, I will use the term in its anthropological sense as referring to the manifold behavioural patterns, conscious and unconscious, of a particular society.

The typical conception of culture implicit in most ethnic studies is a continuum which posits a complete culture distinctive from that of the host society on the one extreme and a culture totally assimilated or acculturated to the host society on the other extreme. In between are various stages of cultural retention and cultural assimilation, but usually starting from the premise that ideal cultures are monolithic and static rather than complex and dynamic. This cultural model, however prevalent and appealing, bears little relationship either to recent work on the nature of culture or to the realities of the experience in the Maritimes.

An examination of the cultural background of early Atlantic Canada, focusing particularly on the American and British immigrants of the pre-industrial eighteenth and nineteenth centuries, suggests the complexities of the problem. In the first place, neither Great Britain (much less any of its constituent "nations") nor the United States were culturally homogeneous or complete at the time they were throwing off the bulk of the emigrants who settled in the Atlantic region. Ireland was an early subject of colonization by the English and Scots and was divided in a variety of ways: Northern Protestants largely of Scottish background; Catholics in North and South; and the Anglo-Irish, each with their own language and traditions. Scotland was divided into Highland and Lowland, the former containing a Gaelic-speaking population which shared linguistic characteristics and origins with the Irish, the Welsh, and the Bretons in France, the latter holding a people speaking a dialect of English which did not so much copy the English spoken to the south as come from the same root language. The Welsh were also linguistically and culturally divided along a north-south axis, and within England itself there were regional dialects and even some lingering ancient tongues such as Cornish. Assuming some relationship among language, traditions, and culture, the extent of English homogeneity within the British Isles in the seventeenth and eighteenth centuries is really quite debatable.[9]

---

8 A.L. Kroebner and Clyde Kluckhohn, *Culture: A Critical Review of Concepts and Definitions* (New York, 1963).

9 According to one American scholar, "Our presentist concern with ethnic groups as political or social forces in nineteenth- and twentieth-century American history has perhaps obscured the existence of subcultures within groups such as the English". David

While the linguistic differences were clearly being reduced in the period of great emigration — the formalization of the Celtic languages in the eighteenth century can probably be viewed as a desperate effort to save them — two points must be emphasized. On the one hand, efforts to resist cultural homogenization were a principal factor in decisions to emigrate to North America by many members of the cultural fringes, and, on the other hand, many of those who came to America were effectively bilingual and bicultural (and in some cases multilingual and multicultural), able to operate in the larger Anglo world of business, commerce, and government at the same time that they maintained the traditional ways among their own people. This ability to live in more than one world simultaneously is perhaps most readily apparent among the leaders of the Scots Highlanders, but they were not unique in this regard.

Moreover, if the American colonies of Great Britain were not settled by a culturally homogeneous British population, they in addition had both their own non-British elements among the population and considerable regional differences with which to contend. New England had developed the most homogeneity, but the Middle Colonies of New York, New Jersey, and Pennsylvania were a rich cultural and linguistic mixture even at the time of the American Rebellion. Indeed, in Pennsylvania leaders like Benjamin Franklin feared that German would supplant English as the major language. In the Southern colonies, with their plantation economies, many thousands of their inhabitants — albeit in a position of inferiority and enslavement — had a culture which bore virtually no relationship to that of the Europeans. American scholars are still debating the impact of the African on American culture, but no one would today argue that the blacks simply took on the cultural characteristics of their masters.[10] If the Americans achieved a cultural homogeneity, it was by blending the various cultural traditions of several peoples and colonies into something quite distinctive, and although derivative mainly from Britain and Europe, much influenced by the American environment. Moreover, the achievement of an American culture did not occur overnight, and was still in process until well into the nineteenth century. Further complicating matters from our standpoint, those Americans who settled in the Atlantic region may have migrated to evade the process of homogenization, both by the act of resettlement and in terms of the motivations behind it. Loyalists came because in some profound if unidentifiable way they were out of

Grayson Allen, *In English Ways: The Movement of Societies and the Transferal of English Local Law and Custom to Massachusetts Bay in the Seventeenth Century* (Chapel Hill, 1981), p. 8.

10 See, for example, Lawrence W. Levine, *Black Culture and Black Consciousness: Afro-American Folk Thought from Slavery to Freedom* (Oxford, 1977).

sympathy with the American Dream, and many of those loyalists were members of distinct cultural groups which had either resisted assimilation or been unable to enjoy it. We have come to appreciate the heterogeneity of the Loyalists, and if they were a representative cross-section of the American population, that fact only underlines the point.[11]

Thus, although at first glance the Atlantic region would appear to have been settled in the post-Acadian period initially by people who had much in common, culturally and linguistically, the Americans were not British and the British were not necessarily English. Moreover, as the case of Newfoundland makes abundantly plain, regional factors played an important role in adapting these incoming cultures to local conditions. The real problem in comprehending all these complexities is our difficulty in conceiving of people who are capable of operating culturally on a variety of different levels, not necessarily simultaneously but certainly without noticeable trauma. The concept of sub-cultures is not a rich enough one to suggest the situation. Dualities or even Multi-alities of cultural experience and expression were, I would again suggest, more common than one might imagine, particularly in the formative years of the region.

One test of cultural homogeneity has been language, but language specialists have become increasingly aware of the existence of simultaneous levels or layers of language usage, even within the supposed unity of a single tongue. Thus there is a vehicular language of politics, business, and work; a vernacular language of home and family; and a mythic language of literature and tradition.[12] While modern states exert strong pressures to reduce language distinctions, including the development of public education, many people throughout the world have had experience of living with the levels of language in situations where different tongues are employed vehicularly and vernacularly. This experience was particularly common for the Acadians and for many of those who emigrated from the British Isles in the eighteenth and early nineteenth centuries. Historically, therefore, the Maritime region has always been characterized by cultural and linguistic complexity.

In post-industrial society there have been new and different cultural distinctions emerging beyond the geographical ones common in the earlier period. These new distinctions have been reflected in various attempts to produce a taxonomy of cultures within a society speaking the same language based on delivery systems or class differences and employing such concepts as mass or popular culture, working-class culture and folk culture. Such efforts have not yet born much fruit because of the number

---

11 One finds heterogeneity emphasized even in the entry on Loyalists by Bruce Wilson in *The Canadian Encyclopedia* (Edmonton, 1985), II, pp. 1041-2.

12 Henri Gobard, *L'Aliénation linguistique: Analyse tetraglossique* (Paris, 1976).

of variables involved, including national differences within common language groups, but obviously a farmer in P.E.I. or a miner in Cape Breton watching American television programmes is observing a culture far removed from his own experiences, however much it may be transmitted in a common language. The ideal of a complete and distinctive ethnic culture fits, therefore, neither with historical nor contemporary realities in Maritime Canada.

If no culture has ever been complete in the Maritimes, no culture has ever remained static either. Culture is a dynamic entity quite apart from the question of a cultural continuum ranging from distinctive to assimilated. Whether or not one accepts Marxist cultural theory as advanced by scholars like Raymond Williams, the distinction Williams makes between residual culture and emergent culture seems to me important.[13] There is no reason to assume that any culture ought to be, can be, or is frozen in time, whether that culture is an ethnic one or not. Too often ethnic studies in Canada, especially on the popular level, exhibit the "Brigadoon" syndrome, a loving emphasis upon certain observable vestiges of residual ethnic culture as if their presence somehow authenticates ethnicity. The significant feature of Brigadoon, of course, was that it was a *fantasy* in which a community came to life for one day every hundred years. Real communities exist under too many pressures on a daily basis to emulate Brigadoon.

Moreover, cultural change in the "Brigadoon" approach to ethnicity is usually treated as undesirable because it is imposed from without upon a victimized population. The concept of emergent culture does not simply refer to cultural assimilation, but to cultural adaptation — even regeneration — from within. There are many illustrations of emergent culture in a regenerative sense relevant to Maritime experience, particularly the Acadian renaissance and the resurgence of black culture in Nova Scotia. Such emergent cultures build upon the past, but represent something quite new, adapted to modern circumstances and conditions.

Culture in Maritime Canada, whether that of component ethnic populations or of the majority society, has always been complex, fluid, and dynamic. Culture is only one part of that phenomenon known as ethnicity, although clearly a central part. In dealing with the region's ethnic groups, we must take care to avoid concentrating on snapshots of Brigadoons, but rather to approach ethnicity as an important variable in a constantly evolving cultural kaleidoscope, which tells us far more about the region than merely its ethnic composition.

---

13 Raymond Williams, "Base and Superstructure in Marxist Cultural Theory", *Studies on the Left*, no. 22 (1973), pp. 3-16.

11 Mosaic to Kaleidoscope: Ethnic Culture in the Maritimes

James Morrison

DEFINING ETHNICITY IN THE Maritimes has until recently been a matter of identifying the shadow of reality not the substance: "What ethnic groups? We've got some British types (Scots, Irish, English), some Acadians, a few Blacks and a handful of Native People. End of discussion!" The reality is that there are over 80 different nationalities represented in this region and the size of the ethnic populations is surprising. For example, if a series of ethnic villages were set up in Nova Scotia, there would be enough Ukrainians to populate Pugwash, enough Chinese to occupy Shubenacadie, or Italians to populate Mahone Bay. By this example it can be observed that the population figures are not insignificant.

The ethnic impact in the Maritimes is variable — sometimes permanent — at times transitory. In a photograph discovered recently in the Public Archives of Canada, I noted Sikh labourers working on the Valley Railway in New Brunswick in 1910. The interviews I carried out in Queens County, Nova Scotia, a few years ago mentioned the Italian railroad workers who constructed the Central line in North Queens County in 1902. In both cases, when the labour was completed, the labourer departed and there was no long term impact. Initially, then, we have to establish an ethnic context for our region. In this way, a better understanding of our ethnic separateness and/or ethnic pluralism can be fashioned.

A better understanding of the ethnic mix in the Maritimes must include some basic assumptions. The first is that we are all "boat people" of some description or other. An immigrant in Canada can be defined as the person who got off the boat most recently. The second assumption is that "visible" immigrants (read non-white) have had and continue to have considerable difficulty advancing socially and economically in Maritime society. They may be adjudged as culturally acceptable in language or dress but not "structurally acceptable", that is, jobs and housing may not be available to them. The third and final assertion is that we live in a plural society in which individuals can and do cross racial, religious and economic lines to socialize, to work, and to marry. The popular Canadian term to describe our ethnic context is a mosaic. I suggest to you that our ethnic context is that of a kaleidoscope — constantly moving, adjusting and never still as each individual comes to terms with ethnicity and its place in their world view.

What is ethnic? Although sociologists, anthropologists, and historians usually have a difficult time finding *their* definitions, the Concise Oxford dictionary simply defines ethnic as "a group of people recognized as a type on the basis of certain distinctive characteristics such as religion, language, ancestry, culture and national origin". As each ethnic group is examined in turn, it will quickly be seen that many "groups of people", especially those who have been in the Maritimes for more than one generation, are no longer of a "type". Some "distinctive characteristics" are no longer evident; new characteristics gleaned from popular, urban or industrial culture have taken their place. Yet old characteristics may also return with each new generation. Ethnicity in a plural society like the Maritimes is like the amoeba: its definitive characteristic is its indefinite and changeable form.

An examination of the history of the Maritime region leads to the conclusion that various ethnic groups can be analyzed in four stages, although none of these stages is independent or mutually exclusive of the other. The first stage involves the indigenous Amerindian population in the region — the Micmac and the Malicite presence that goes back thousands of years. Without the technical skills of the Micmac — so well suited to our environment — and their readiness to share those skills, the early French and English settlers would not have survived. As long as the native peoples were a force to be reckoned with militarily, their presence was recognized. However, once a lasting peace with the English had been made in 1760, the Native Peoples "disappeared" for over 200 years. They were not to be seen between the covers of our history books until recently. Their return to prominence in the 1960s is not unrelated to the non-European migration to Canada in the 1960s and 1970s.

The second stage, the Anglo-French period of settlement, military destruction of settlements and then re-settlement, is a familiar litany. If this were Africa, it would be called tribal warfare. We, however, dignify the mutual blood letting by calling it a struggle between two nationalisms for an empire. This ethnic/military struggle was waged for over 150 years — until 1760 when English sovereignity was established. Halifax had been founded in 1749 to ensure that the English presence was maintained. A number of New England settlers arrived in the region a few years after the Acadians had been deported. It soon became apparent that English language, law and commercial practice would be supreme in the region.

Even before 1760, there were some ethnic cracks in the Anglo-French monolith. At a time when a common belief system was the basis of many alliances — alliances which overstepped ethnic bounds — it was important that the Germans who were brought to Nova Scotia in 1751 were Protestant and not Catholic. The good burghers settled in the Lunenburg coastal area by 1753 and soon turned to the sea for their livelihood. Long before their arrival, the Maritimes had imported service labour from non-European sources. The French Governor of Port Royal had kept a Black servant in 1608. In the 1690s, a Black man was abducted from Massachusetts and brought to New Brunswick. With the defeat of the French, the Treaty of Paris was signed in 1763. This peace treaty signed between the French and the English placed the Maritimes under the English crown but did not free this black labour. In fact, it stated that the Blacks and Indians who were slaves under the French would continue to be slaves under the English. Thus, the ethnicity of these groups defined their position in society.

In 1760, our Maritime region consisted of a number of ethnic groups: English both old and new, Acadians who had survived the expulsion, Native Peoples, Germans, a few Scots and Irish and some Blacks. The next half century would in essence consolidate the perceived ethnic make-up and prevailing cultural perspective of the Maritime region up to the 1970s. The New England Planters arrived in New Brunswick and Nova Scotia in the 1760s. By the late 1760s and early 1770s, the Scots had established themselves in the Gulf region, in the Pictou area, northeastern New Brunswick and Prince Edward Island. The dawn of the nineteenth century would bring many more to Cape Breton Island. The Irish had migrated to Halifax in the 1750s and continued to trickle into the interior of the eastern shore of Nova Scotia and also to northeastern New Brunswick in the 1790s.

The most significant migration was, of course, the much celebrated movement of the Loyalists who arrived in their thousands after 1783 from the newly formed United States of America. The Maritime region was affected politically, economically and not least of all culturally by this influx. A fact which we often fail to note is that 10 percent of these migrants were Black. In Saint John, for example, there were 500 slaves in 1784. It should also be noted that 75 percent of these Black Loyalists were free. In the 1790s, many Black Nova Scotians migrated to Sierra Leone, as did the Jamaican Maroons who sojourned briefly in Halifax. The last large Black immigration was the movement of Black Refugees from the United States in 1815-16 after the War of 1812. In toto, the Black population of the Maritime region was probably the largest in Canada until well into the twentieth century.

In the mid-nineteenth century then, the Maritimes perceived itself as predominantly British, although there were some Acadians, mostly in New Brunswick, and a smattering of "others" — visible and less visible minorities. Today, over 100 years later, many Maritimers perceive the region exactly the same way. The reality is somewhat different. In the last century there have been a number of ethnic additions to the region. The majority of the additions have come from European sources: Italians, Ukrainians, Jews, Poles, to name a few. These peoples were attracted by industry or trade or had been displaced by the wars in Europe. In addition, there were immigrants from the Middle East (most notably the Lebanese) to all three provinces, as merchants; West Indians who settled in Whitney Pier, Cape Breton, as steel workers; and the Chinese family which set up a laundry in Halifax in 1910. But they were exceptions for the bulk of the immigrants were from European countries. After World War II, agricultural schemes attracted German and Dutch settlers. By the 1950s and 1960s, European migration to the Maritimes declined, while the number of non-European immigrants from economically depressed or war racked Third World countries increased. Since 1960, peoples from India, Uganda, Pakistan, the West Indies, and Indo-China have settled in the region. For the most part they have established themselves in the urban centres, as the majority of them are well-trained professionals who have passed through an immigration system that looks for youth and education as prerequisites for entering Canada.

This fourth and last stage has meant that today we are a region of many ethnic groups and the members of these groups are at various cultural stages. Some first generation immigrants are clinging to the culture of their homeland for stability, while trying to choose what is best in the new culture. Others are second generation immigrants rejecting all the old ways in order to be truly "Canadian". Then there are third, fourth or fifth generation immigrants who may maintain those aspects of their ethnic culture which are of most value to them — perhaps music, literature or language.

Given the above survey, it is clear that many teachers will be teaching in an ethnically mixed classroom. This will not be an easy task. The resources are scarce, the students' perspectives are diverse, and given the ethnic mix, the teaching goals must include more than simply conveying information. In the standard histories of the Maritimes or those that include the Maritime region, the concentration has been on political, economic and military matters. If ethnic/national groups are mentioned, they are usually the British (Scots, Irish, English), French Acadians, Micmacs and maybe the Germans. Written materials about other ethnic groups are spotty.

The Black community especially in New Brunswick and Nova Scotia has stimulated the largest amount of research material. James Walker's *Black Loyalists 1783-1870*, and William Spray's *Blacks in New Brunswick* are both excellent starters. *Blacks in Canada* by Robin Winks, although 15 years in print, is still the favoured overview. Other groups like the Chinese, Italians or Indian communities have not been as well served. The Chinese community has yet to be thoroughly studied, although Anthony Chan's

Gold Mountain: The Chinese in the New World does refer to the Chinese population in Halifax. The Germans in Nova Scotia have been examined by historians like Winthrop Bell and folklorists like Helen Creighton.

Articles and monographs have been written on the Indo-Canadians by Sukhdev Sandhu, Italians by Maria Razzolini, Jews by Sheva Medjuck and M.M. Lazer and Syrians/Lebanese by Nancy and Joseph Jabbra. The recent volume *Ethnicity in Atlantic Canada* included articles on Ethnicity and Regionalism in the Maritimes, the Lebanese, Acadian neo-nationalism and racial minorities. Nonetheless, published sources are not abundant and certainly not easily accessible and many teachers will find they have to fall back on their own resources to "create" material. Create is an appropriate word, for teachers will have to look at each new situation, each lack of resources as an opportunity to adopt a new approach. In addition, teachers must remember that teaching about ethnicity is not something that occurs only at a particular moment in the curriculum; it should permeate the curriculum in such subjects as Mathematics, Home Economics and Science. To the Arabs we owe the concept of the zero in math. Credit for the development of the potato and corn must go to the Indians of the Americas and their advanced agricultural methods. Gunpowder, paper and the ship's compass are all Chinese inventions. We have lived and are living in a constant state of borrowings from somewhere else at some other time — borrowings from people of very different cultures. An international perspective is obviously important in teaching about ethnicity.

In any consideration of ethnicity, teachers must also be conscious of bias, stereotyping and racism. The classic literature, Uncle Tom's Cabin or Huckleberry Finn, has to be handled with considerable care. Even the immortal *Sam Slick* from the Father of Canadian humourists Thomas Haliburton was not above what we would interpret today as a racist comment. A close look at such popular children's books as Mary Poppins shows that non-white people are consistently used to symbolize improper or unruly behaviour. When Mary Poppins reprimands Michael in this classic she admonishes him with "You will not behave like a Red Indian". A keen sensitivity therefore to the context and application of this material is vital. In our profession very often there are no good books or bad books — only badly taught or well taught books. The textbook analysis of the Nova Scotia Human Rights Commission carried out in 1974 puts the matter more succinctly: "You know you can get an ideal textbook which everyone is in agreement about — male, female, the majority race, the lingo problems — everybody is saying this is an ideal textbook; and, put it into the hands of a bad teacher and bang! — it's a bad book".[1]

1 Nova Scotia Human Rights Commission, *Textbook Analysis Nova Scotia* (Halifax, 1974), p. 12.

Books, however, are only a small part of the resources available. In all three provinces, there are many cultural organizations and multicultural councils which would be quite prepared to share their written and human resources with the school classroom. Perhaps an interview with a recent immigrant would be a useful class project, or interviews with immigrants from two or three countries and a comparison made. This may also be an excellent opportunity to introduce spoken languages other than French and English. How does one write Chinese characters or pronounce Sallam Aleikum in Arabic properly? Language is a window on culture for it shapes how we think about things, why we think about them and what is important to the culture in which we live. We say snow or *la neige* but the Eskimos have dozens of words for snow — each with a specific meaning and a particular message about its relative importance in their environment.

A student's personal genealogy, if handled carefully, is sometimes a useful method to show by example the pluralistic nature of our society. Slide programs and films from resource centres on ethnicity are also readily available, although those materials have to be used after some background research has been done by the teacher for they become dated very quickly.[2] Even a visit to a Museum or historic site like Caraquet, Louisbourg, or the Halifax Citadel may be seen as an opportunity to teach about ethnicity. For example, the British army was stationed in many parts of the Maritimes in the eighteenth, nineteenth and early twentieth centuries. Almost half of the troops were Irish and the vast majority of those in the lower ranks. Questions of ethnicity, religion and class can be raised in this context.

What is the purpose of all these efforts, aside from the accumulation of more knowledge on ethnic groups in the Maritimes? First, it is to recognize and to appreciate the cultural diversity around us. Second, it is to understand why these cultural differences exist. Third, it is to encourage positive attitudes towards people from other cultures. Fourth, for a number of students in your classes it is to enhance a feeling of self worth. In the last instance, it is a proven fact that a minority student's sense of self can be damaged by a curriculum which fails to give recognition to the contribution and history of certain groups, that fails to provide appropriate models to emulate, and that presents members of certain groups in inaccurate or demeaning ways. A curriculum that is blind to cultural diversity may be

2 In the Department of Education, Nova Scotia the film "You Laugh Like a Duck" is a film which is produced in the region and examines a Black child's life experience in New Glasgow. Other films or videos the department holds are "Black Youth in Halifax", "Men of Lunenburg", "Micmac" and "Acadia, Acadia". Interested teachers should write to: Film Library/Video Library, Department of Education, Education Media Services, 6955 Bayers Road, Halifax, N.S. B3L 4S4.

reinforcing prejudice and nurturing ethnocentrism rather than preparing students to live in a multicultural world. As Bharati Mukherjee writes in her recent book, "Instead of seeing my Indianess as a fragile identity to be preserved against obliteration (or worse, a "visible" disfigurement to be hidden) I see it now as a set of fluid identities to be celebrated".[3]

Teachers must examine this ethnic mosaic or ethnic kaleidoscope of ours without romanticism and without condescension. Teachers also must ensure that it does not become a wonderland trivialization of culture or the first step towards a "tribal" system of our own — based on one's ethnic culture. Teaching about ethnicity and ethnic groups is not an attempt to divide — for our cultural diversity does not mean that we are intrinsically different from each other. World history cannot be seen as a constant progression towards speaking English, drinking Coca Cola, and eating at a take out. It is our task as teachers to recognize the differences, attempt to understand them and communicate this understanding to our students. This differentness is a positive part of the world in which we live. As former Justice Thomas Berger wrote in 1981: "to know ourselves, to discover who we are and what we may become, to realize the uses of diversity and dissent. This is what the Canadian experience is all about; to see if people who are different can live together, to learn to regard diversity not with suspicion, but as a cause of celebration".[4]

3   Bharati Mukherjee, *Darkness* (Markham, 1985), p. 3.
4   Thomas Berger, *Fragile Freedoms; Human Rights and Dissent in Canada* (Toronto, 1981), p. 262.

SELECTED BIBLIOGRAPHY

Ethnic Bibliographies:

Mallea, John R. and Shea, E.A. , *Multiculturalism and Education: A Select Bibliography* (Toronto, 1979).

McGee, Harold F., Davis, Stephen A. and Taft, Michael, *Three Atlantic Bibliographies* (Halifax, 1975).

Miller, Virginia P., *A Survey of Ethnohistorical Materials in Nova Scotia* (Ottawa, 1974).

Morrison, James H., *Common Heritage: An Annotated Bibliography of Ethnic Groups in Nova Scotia* (Halifax, 1984).

Peterson, Jean, *The Loyalist Guide: Nova Scotian Loyalists and their Documents* (Halifax, 1984).

Ray, Roger B., *The Indians of Maine and the Atlantic Provinces: A Bibliographic Guide* (Portland, Maine, 1977).

General:

Bailey, Alfred G., *Culture and Nationality* (Toronto, 1972).

Berger, Thomas, *Fragile Freedoms: Human Rights and Dissent in Canada* (Toronto, 1981).

Campbell, Douglas, *Banked Fires — Ethnics of Nova Scotia* (Port Credit, Ontario, 1978).

Toner, Peter *et al.*, *Ethnicity in Atlantic Canada* (Saint John, 1985).

Cosper, Ronald L., *Ethnicity and Occupation in Atlantic Canada* (Halifax, 1984).

Goldstein, Joy E. and Bienvenue, R.M., *Ethnicity and Ethnic Relations in Canada: A Book of Readings* (Toronto, 1980).

McCreath, Peter L., ed., *Multiculturalism: A Handbook for Teachers* (Halifax, 1981).

Multiculturalism Directorate, Department of the Secretary of State, *The Canadian Family Tree: Canadian People* (Don Mills, 1979).

Nova Scotia Human Rights Commission, *Textbook Analysis: Nova Scotia* (Halifax, 1974).

Palmer, H., *Immigration and the Rise of Multiculturalism* (Toronto, 1975).

Sheffe, Norman, ed., *Many Cultures, Many Heritages* (Toronto, 1975).

Sullivan, Keith C., *Minority Group Perceptions of the Goals of Education for Nova Scotia Schools* (Halifax, 1982).

Ethnic Groups:

Bell, Winthrop, *The 'Foreign Protestants' and the Settlement of Nova Scotia* (Toronto, 1961).

Chan, Anthony B., *Gold Mountain: The Chinese in the New World* (Vancouver, 1983).

Creighton, Helen, *Folklore of Lunenburg County* (Ottawa, 1950).

Jabbra, Nancy and Joseph, *Rocky Shore: Lebanese and Syrians in Nova Scotia* (Halifax, 1984).

Medjuk, Sheva and Lazar, M.M., *The Jews of Atlantic Canada* (Halifax, 1986).

Razzolini, E. Martha, *All our Fathers: The North Italian Colony of Industrial Cape Britain* (Halifax, 1983).

Sandhu, Sukhdev Singh, *"The Second Generation" Culture and the East Indian Community in Nova Scotia* (Halifax, 1981).

Spray, William, *The Blacks in New Brunswick* (Fredericton, 1972).

Walker, James, *A History of Blacks in Canada: A Study Guide for Teachers and Students* (Hull, 1980).

Winks, Robin, *Blacks in Canada* (Montreal, 1971).

12 *Blackness and Maritime Studies*

J.A. Mannette

B LACKS HAVE NOT BEEN NUMEROUS in the province of Nova Scotia; nor have they been visible in the mainstream of Nova Scotian social life. Although they have been a part of the province's history since colonial times, we know little about their history and their place in modern Nova Scotian society. What we do know often reflects distortions rather than reality. This is due primarily to our methods of doing history and sociology. Given dominant socio-cultural assumptions, Blacks have been especially vulnerable to the invidious characterizations of 'other' that conventional social science has tended to produce. The transmission of perjorative assessments of Blacks through the education process tends to ensure their reproduction over time, and thus helps to maintain Black Nova Scotians as oppressed social outcasts. Therefore, this paper addresses these two related aspects of knowledge production: social definitions and their reproduction. As A. Inkeles has argued, "insofar as ... actions reflect a mutual adjustment between ideology and social realities, an understanding of ideology becomes a necessary condition for an understanding of the action".[1] The point here is that what comes to be known about Nova Scotian blackness has real consequences for Black and white life. In the teaching of Maritime studies, we must be sensitive to the ways in which we may contribute to the perpetuation of existing ethnic relations.

The position of schools and of classroom teachers, in the processes of social life, has been explored in a variety of contexts. M. Apple and L. Weiss, eds., *Ideology and Practice in Schooling* (Philadelphia, 1983), as well as studies by Porter and Harp focussing on Canada, can be used to determine how Canada's "vertical mosaic" is produced, and held in place over time, in the education process. Such work suggests the implications of class-structured education for the ways in which people make a living, fit into an existing labour market, and live out their lives. More recently, a number of studies have specifically addressed the ethnic variable in the education process.[2] These studies have examined how ethnic relations are

---

1 A. Inkeles, *Public Opinion in Soviet Russia* (Cambridge, 1950), p. 21.

2 L. Weiss, *Between Two Worlds* (London, 1985); S. Tomlinson, "Black Women in Higher

socially constructed and what these power relations mean for the life chances of ethnic youth. Recent conceptualization on relations of class and ethnicity in Canada has compellingly documented the "institutional barriers and bureaucratic impediments" to ethnic 'progress' in Canadian society.[3]

In two unpublished theses, S.L. Pratt and P. Fleming have shown that even when access to education was possible, apparently it did not translate into upward mobility for Black Nova Scotians. This finding is echoed in F. Wien and J. Browne's conclusion that, although Black Nova Scotians generally reached higher educational levels, they were (in the 1970s) still concentrated in low status and low wage work, in comparison with other minorities in the province. B. Moreau has argued that, in the face of institutional barriers, Black Nova Scotians became increasingly dependent on community-based informal education to learn skills necessary for individual and collective, economic and social survival. In a comparative study of Black Nova Scotian communities, J. Browne points out that the relative security of men's wage labour in the Sydney area, coupled with education values the Sydney Blacks brought with them from Barbados, have resulted in higher than national average educational levels since the 1920s; she suggests that employment, consistent with their education, often was achieved by Sydney Blacks elsewhere (e.g. in central Canada). Overall, these studies emphasize the role played by the education process in maintaining Black Nova Scotians as a deskilled, oppressed population over time.

Since the mid-1970s, discussions have also emerged concerning how a gender system gets transmitted through both the form and content of the education process. The gender system in contemporary western societies, like Canada, "delineates the authoritative versions of masculinity and femininity, the socially legitimated opportunities for living one's life as a male or a female".[4] It also posits relations of difference and inequality between men and women in social life. However, many studies have demonstrated that gendered education is shaped by ethnicity. L. Weiss has examined the particular problems encountered by young Black women and men in an American community college, while S. Tomlinson has suggested that educational achievement and upward mobility were more possible for middle-class Black daughters who are brought up outside of

---

Education" and B. Carrington, "Sport as a Side Track" in L. Barton and S. Walker, eds., *Race, Class and Education* (London 1983).

3 J. Dahlie and T. Fernando, "Reflections on Ethnicity and the Exercise of Power: An Introductory Note", *Ethnicity, Power and Politics in Canada* (Toronto, 1981), p. 1.

4 E. Fox-Genovese, "Placing Women's History in History", *New Left Review*, 133 (May-June, 1982), p. 15.

the Black community, and that both 'successes' were more accessible to Black *daughters* than to Black *sons*. In the Nova Scotian context, even when formal education was an option for Black children, it was sex-typed. Recent affirmative action policies for Black education in Nova Scotia have directed Black university women into the nurturing arena of social work, or perhaps teaching. For young Black men, the avenues for social standing tend to be outside the mainstream due to "institutional barriers".

Despite the sociological proclivity for isolating and examining only one variable at a time, what the lived experiences of Black Nova Scotians, past and present, show us is that the structures of inequality overlap. Black Nova Scotians are men or women, members of an oppressed ethnic group in a depressed Canadian region, and usually part of the working or under-class *all at the same moment*. Many studies have not been particularly good at dealing with this complexity of lived experience. In Nova Scotia, E. Beaton-Planetta's work-in-progress on the Whitney Pier area of Sydney increasingly points to the playing out of class/region, ethnic and gender relations in the periods of industrialization and economic decline there. And a key component of Whitney Pier is its Black population. B. Moreau has examined the different roles played by women and men in Black Nova Scotian communities in ensuring that future generations would have sufficient skills to cope with, and perhaps overcome, their subordinate situation. And elsewhere, I have pointed to the importance of Black Nova Scotia female and male cultural producers in the 1980s. These women and men are (re)defining blackness, blackmanness, and black-womanness, within Black communities and in the larger white society. All of these studies show that our society renders different and unequal treatment to people, based on their gender, their ethnicity, and their social class. For Black Nova Scotians this entails a lived experience of layers of marginality. What I will seek to determine now is: how do differences and inequalities occur, and get carried forward in time, in the education process? And, secondly, what implications does this have for the lived experience of Nova Scotian blackness and our knowledge of it?[5]

Social phenomena arise through a process of interaction between human activity and the pressures of social structures. Together these give shape to social life. Lived experience is essentially an active process: people enter into social interaction. Through social interaction our lives are given expression. Through our activities, our lives and social life in general, are carried forward in time. Our social lives have mental, as well

---

5 However, it is important to stress that while the education process reproduces powerful definitions and social relations, it may also (under certain circumstances) serve as an arena for struggle against them. The focus of this paper, however, is on social reproduction of inequalities in the schools, not on the structures of resistance which develop there.

as material manifestations. That is, we rely on socially acquired maps of meaning to make sense of our social lives. However, people tend to have a limited horizon of conceptual and material possibilities from which they 'choose' certain understandings and certain activities. This is one way of understanding structural pressures on human thought and activity.

If social production is about what we do, and what factors influence what we do, social reproduction is about how certain patterns of human thought and activity get carried forward in time. The mechanisms for social production are not the same as those for social reproduction. Sociologists tend to look to social institutions, like media and the education process, to explain how certain kinds of human thought and activity, and not others, get transmitted to present and future generations. We can point to certain things which are generally 'known' about Canadian social life. We tend to believe that freedom and equality of all is guaranteed, that racism is an anomoly to the norm of intergroup behaviour, and that all can get ahead if they work hard. In reality, Canadian society is structured unequally. Gender, ethnicity, and class are key social structures which shape the range of human activities available to us as, for example, white working class men, or as native middle class women. In this sense, Canadian society is sexist, racist, and classist.

The relative subordination of Black Nova Scotians has been held in place for over 200 years. The *forms* of Black subordination have, of course, changed. But the *fact* of their structured and experienced inequalities has not altered. This argument, however, flies in the face of received wisdom that suggests racism is a thing of the past, that 'progress' has been made in the Black communities of Nova Scotia. Certainly, progress has been made. But this has been due more to a conjuncture of historical circumstances in the last 20 years. And in this conjuncture, Black Nova Scotians have creatively and determinedly seized an advantage. Such developments should not be confused with an abatement of white racism.

Although Black Nova Scotians have been a subordinate group in the social fabric of Nova Scotian life, they have always challenged mainstream definitions of them. Given historic circumstances, they have been, more or less, successful in these struggles. Since the mid-1970s, there have been particularly significant alternate views of blackness produced by indigenous Black Nova Scotians. Elsewhere, I referred to these developments as part of what Nova Scotia media has termed a "Black Renaissance". The multicultural ideological climate, the international rise of minorities, an expanding state sector, and a prescient Black population, have made it possible for these cultural producers to be heard — sometimes accommodated, sometimes co-opted. However, regardless of their reception, and the use to which their work is put, Nova Scotia's Black communities have thrown up a resistant population of thinkers of, and reflectors upon, the Black experience. Concentrated in the apparently non-threatening cultural realm, as poets, playwrights, singers/composers, these Black Nova Scotians are winning space for themselves, and perhaps for their people. They reflect to whites and to Blacks a different conception of blackness in Nova Scotia.

A. James has argued that the construction of the word "black" in English language discourse, has perjorative "associations with darkness and death, dirt and sin, evil and taboo(s)".[6] The implications of these constructions for the bearers of blackness are clear. But the work of Nova Scotian Black cultural producers can turn these constructions on their head. It can potentially engender Black self-pride, and can potentially rupture white social understandings of what blackness (and whiteness) entails. Although it appears that such developments are occurring, particularly among Black youth and some white liberals, emphasis must be placed on such work's *potential*. An excellent case study of both the value and limits of using such material can be found by examining the ways in which the work of Black cultural producer, Maxine Tynes, has been included in the projected Maritime Studies textbook.[7] At this moment, at least, it seems to be a case of co-optation, a reconstitution of alternate, oppositional views of blackness in dominant terms.

Applying S. Hall *et al.*'s analysis of mechanisms of social reproduction, one can see that the education process is a crucial site of social reproduction; that is, in the education process social meaning is generated and passed on. Social meanings in the education process are considered legitimate knowledge; they are seen and are presented, as the 'truth' about social phenomena, as opposed to the partial view which they constitute. Since, in the education process, information is often transmitted about occurrences outside of the realm of many people's existence, education process knowledge often emerges as a crucial definer of events. Given the persistent institutional segregation of the dominant and subordinate ethnic groups in Canada, it is likely that dominant ethnics will come to know

6   A. James, "'Black': An Inquiry Into The Perjorative Associations of An English Word", *New Community*, 9/1 (1981), p. 19.

7   From September to December, 1985, I worked with Maritext publishers Jim Lorimer and Carolyn McGregor, in the preparation of the sociology chapter of the Maritime Studies text. McGregor and Lorimer were particularly concerned that text content reflect disciplinary developments. Thus, early drafts included a fairly critical orientation to society and social life. My comments on the inclusion and 'reading' of Tynes' *In Service* are derived from my experiences in this process. It is important to note that the Maritime Studies text is still *in process*. Thus, in this negotiated process, it is possible that there will be further mediation of dominant ideologies. Also, although I identify a likely scenario for its classroom use, only further investigation when the book (and course) is in place will determine if my predicted outcome of *In Service* will emerge.

'others' through knowledge of this kind. The 'others', however, as B. Hooks argues, "developed a particular way of seeing reality. They looked both from the outside in and from the inside out".[8] Standardization of curricula and curriculum materials in the education process tends to ensure that, there, alternate versions of social phenomena, while they may be included, are necessarily reconstituted in dominant terms, or are rendered as outside the mainstream. Thus, we can discover a line of fit between curriculum in the schools and dominant societal beliefs (e.g. all ethnic groups are 'free' to participate in, and to contribute to, Canadian society which exists independently of ethnics; ethnicity is about "colourful" things like singing, dancing, and eating, not about power and inequality; racism in Canada is largely a thing of the past). Maxine Tynes' *In Service*, in itself, is an alternate and oppositional account of Nova Scotia blackness. In the Maritext volume, it seems to be reconstituted in dominant terms.

In 1983, Black Nova Scotian poet and schoolteacher, Maxine Tynes, wrote and aired *In Service* on CBC's 'Atlantic Airwaves'. The short story reflects her adult reconstruction of childish understandings. She re-examines the live-in domestic labour which Black women, from her family and the Black community, did in white homes:

> My little girl mind imagined shiny, wonderful things, not clearly defined. Not knees sore from years on hardwood floors. Not hands cracked, dry and painful, calloused and scrub-worn. Not early morning walking miles into town to start the day off right with morning labours for some family. Not always going to and coming from the back door. Not 'speak when you're spoken to; see and don't see; hear and don't hear'; in case you anger them and they let you go. Not eating their leftovers in the kitchen alone. Not one dollar a day for back-breaking floors, walls, dishes, furniture, windows, washing, ironing, sweat-soaked labour. In Service.

As Maxine wrote it, and meant it, *In Service* is a powerful indictment of our kind of social system, and of those of us who hold it in place. At the same moment, Tynes turns the tables on understandings of domestic work. It becomes a noble endeavour and those who did it emerge as strong just for doing it. These "armies of Black women in that sea of domestic service" battled not only for the immediate survival of themselves and their families. They struggled, too, for a better future for their daughters, keeping the "dark and female mystery" of in-service from Maxine. They hid from her the 'shame' of in-service and propelled her towards a different life. As K. McNeil wrote, "we rise again in the faces of our children"; so

---

8   B. Hooks, *Feminist Theory from margin to center* (Boston, 1984), preface.

did these Black women rise again in young Black women, like Maxine.[9] Yet Maxine turns their shame to triumph and points to the nobility of their work, in itself, and in the face of such 'choices'. For Maxine has found out "the awful mystery of In Service un-ravelled now from the whispers of Lady-talk, found now in the voice of these words". And *In-Service* can potentially force us to find out, as well.[10]

Part of the strategy of the Maritext publishers was to organize the sociology chapter around Maritime literary pieces. Thus, *In Service* was included in the chapter. The point is to demonstrate that the study of Maritime life is a legitimate undertaking. The publishers are reinforced in their overall aim by the support, the co-operation, and the financial assistance of the Departments of Education and teachers' groups in New Brunswick, Prince Edward Island, and Nova Scotia. Thus inserted into the state process, the Maritext project is imbued with social authority. It is able to delineate what Maritime life is about and how we can best understand it (e.g. through subject disciplines).

The Editorial Review Board for the Maritext project is comprised of representatives from provincial teachers' groups, and Departments of Education. However, the structural relevancies and proclivities of the various contributors, of the publishers, and of the Editorial Review Board 'disappear' as the accounts of Maritime life are presented to students and teachers. By this I mean that the social construction of the text is not apparent. The Maritime Studies text will be used (variously) by grades 9 and 10 Maritime students. Many of the examples cited (e.g. *In Service*) speak to experiences, events outside of the lived reality of many students and teachers. Thus, in the case of Tynes' *In Service*, this view of blackness, and how it is dealt with, may be a key definer to students of ethnic relations. Since there has been historically persistent Black/white segregation in Nova Scotian society (as elsewhere), there is an increased likelihood that authoritative versions of blackness will come to be known, by whites, largely through what is encountered in education process knowledge, like the Maritime studies text. Standardization of the Maritime Studies curriculum ensures that this is the education process version of Nova Scotian blackness available. Yet this standardized curriculum is constituted in terms of dominant societal beliefs about blackness. What is addressed here is how blackness is included in the text. Of equal importance are the 'sins of omission' — where discussion of blackness is excluded (e.g. in terms of the labour market, in terms of communities, in terms of societal contributions).

9   K. McNeil, "Rise Again", song from *The Rise and Follies of Cape Breton Island, 1785-1985* (Sydney, 1985).

10 M. Tynes, *In Service* (Halifax, 1983).

Education process knowledge makes what is socially problematic (e.g. Black/white relations) comprehensible. Thus, Tynes' *In Service* can be seen to explain Black/white relations in Nova Scotia. The reader, though, decodes its message — its version of reality — in terms of what is already *potentially* known about the situation. Thus: Blacks are poor; Black families are large; whites own and control; Blacks serve. In the maps of meaning through which dominant society makes sense of *In Service* a discussion of the social practices of racism, which enable Black poverty and subservience, are absent. But these dominant assessments of blackness are not Tynes'. According to her, how can we make sense of the events/issues she introduces? Tynes produces an alternate version of blackness. As a middle-class Black woman and teacher, she writes about the experience of women of her mother's generation. Tynes suggests that white racism and sexism meant that Black women did domestic work to get wages. She points out that there were few 'choices' for Black women. The option of domestic service was shaped by white understandings of Black womanness, and its class implications. In Tynes' view, in order for Black women to enter wage labour, they had to do *Black women's* work. And they hid the stigma of this work from daughters whom they struggled to direct away from what they knew as a degrading work ghetto. However, *In Service* can be 'read' differently to demonstrate an understanding more in keeping with dominant ideologies. *In Service* can be seen as 'proof' that racism is a thing of the past. Maxine Tynes is a schoolteacher and poet; unlike her mother's generation, she does not work "in-service". One member of the Maritext Editorial Review Board argued that it was important to point out that Maxine had 'made it', that menial work for Black women is a thing of the past. In such a view, Maxine has worked hard (e.g. studied, perfected her art); she has gotten ahead. Thus, *In Service* can be read to suggest that 'successes', like Maxine's, are now possible for Black Nova Scotians. However, Maxine knows what an exception to the rule her life demonstrates, and she points to the ongoing practices of white racism which pervert and blight Black progress. Heedlessly, the dominant view sees that in writing *In Service* Maxine is an author. She is a Black writer whose work has been included in a textbook about Maritime society. She is seen to make a contribution to society, both artistically through her writing, and practically, through her teaching. The dominant view holds that Maxine, as a Black woman, though potentially 'exotic' (e.g. outside of Canadian society), has, through her work, joined in/contributed.

In the Maritime Studies text, Maxine and her work stand in the place of Nova Scotian blackness. The dominant reading suggests that if they work hard, Blacks can get ahead; they can contribute to Canadian society. (The reverse of this is that if Blacks don't get ahead, they haven't worked hard enough.) Blackness in the dominant reading is about: bad things in the past, potentially good things in the present, the virtue of hard work to achieve goals, the possibility of upward mobility for all. Blackness is not about structural powerlessness and inequality, which can be experienced as both psychically and physically painful. These readings are possible because they correspond to what is already potentially known about the course of social events in Canadian life; that is, they correspond to dominant Canadian ideologies. Also, they serve to prevent the naming of the problem; this saccharine version does not allow discussion of the dimensions of Canadian racism. Living in Nova Scotia society, we learn to make sense of our lives in particular ways. This results in what S. Hall calls a "preferred" reading of an account.[11] Other readings are possible. We could, perhaps, 'see' (as Tynes does) the racist and sexist relations which relegated a previous generation of Black women to live-in domestic work. We could also make connections between the previous generation's work and what is usually available to Black Nova Scotian women today. We could then understand the necessary historical connections between "Helen's" in-service and contemporary Black women working for Modern Cleaners in Halifax. This reading of *In Service* would allow us to understand that the form, not the fact, of racism and sexism has changed over time. However, this reading would not 'fit' with what the ideological horizon of Canadian society emphasizes as preferred readings of work like Tynes'. And it is no accident that the reading of *In Service*, by the Maritext Editorial Review Board was outlined in dominant terms, not in alternate and oppositional. This is an essential feature of the process of social reproduction. Change is possible but only within a range of possibilities.

P. Braham has argued that, even if they are offered to audiences, alternate accounts seldom fall on fertile ground. Thus, perjorative social understandings of blackness are so powerful and so entrenched that readers of *In Service* may discredit, or dismiss, the more 'positive' images it offers. Alternate accounts do not fit with what is potentially known. And what the media reinforce about blackness is its violent problem (criminal) status. 'Evidence' from stereotypical thinking is drummed up from real life to support preferred readings. And in many ways, the triumphs of *In Service* can be seen to point to the exception which proves the rule: Blacks are lazy, etc. Once more dominant society blames the victim. In these ways, a partial, dominantly-structured image of blackness prevails.

Why is it that Maritime students are likely to give the preferred reading of *In Service*, which I suggest? A key feature of the education process is its bureaucratic, and thus hierarchical, organization. Within this bureaucratic form, there is a hierarchy of knowledge values. The curriculum consul-

---

11 S. Hall, "Culture, the Media and the 'Ideological Effect'" in J. Curran, M. Gurevitch, and J. Woollacott, eds., *Mass Communication and Society* (London, 1977), p. 341.

tants, and in the Maritext project, teacher 'representatives', are the arbiters of what the Maritime Studies curriculum is to consist. Thus, the Editorial Review Board, given its vetting function, shapes the content and the form of the text. However, and this is crucial to our understanding of social reproduction, the Editorial Review Board are *bearers of social values*; they are not individual actors. They air but do not take up alternate understandings. Further, social emphasis on consensus and majority rule reinforces the perpetuation of dominant versions of reality. The power of the Editorial Review Board is determined by its position in the education process hierarchy. The unfocused unease and resentment of some classroom teachers to the introduction of the Maritime Studies course, are relatively mute testimonies to teachers' awareness of their inability to influence this process.

But while more powerful factions judge curriculum content, so are certain social values placed on various curricula. This results in a ranking of disciplinary knowledge. In the Maritext project, high standing is accorded to (mainstream) history. In today's schools, pride of place is given over to science and maths, with the arts, humanities, and social sciences trailing in their wake. This involves considerations not only of status, but also for budgeting. The ranking of disciplinary knowledge also has resulted in an emphasis on *technical*, as opposed to *reflective*, learning. We teach, and children learn the 'how' of things, largely ignoring the 'why' questions. Thus, in the Maritext sociology chapter, students also learn that sociologists have ranked ethnic groups in the Maritimes. They do not learn why the kind of social organization we have produced is hierarchical, nor what this means for the Black Nova Scotians of *In Service*. They further do not learn why sociologists have ranked peoples on the basis of certain social characteristics, like ethnicity, or why sociologists have often been content to imply "that's just the way it is". This orientation in the education process has real consequences for the status of social studies courses in the curriculum (and for Maritime Studies courses within Social Studies). It results in a particular orientation to social inquiry. Thus, we often have passive, unreflective students who are unable in, terms of skills, and unwilling, in terms of attitudes, beliefs, to be much more than receptacles for knowledge which is given to be received.

Is it possible that some students and some teachers will challenge both these dominant definitions and dominant learning processes? Possibly, but this requires a conjuncture of factors. Black Nova Scotians and their teacher advisors in the Cultural Awareness Youth Groups at various Halifax metro schools have learned to 'see' differently; they are organized enough to feel secure in seeing differently. They confront the powerful practices and ideas, and have had some successes in altering them. However, the learning which goes on in these groups is outside the mainstream curriculum; these groups have been defined in the education process as extra-curricular. Generally, both the form and content of learning in the education process are more oriented towards social control and conformity — both ideological and practical — than geared towards a spirit of inquiry. Such a spirit would be difficult to regulate and would posit a distinct challenge to the received sense of knowledge.

In the construction of the Maritime Studies text, a form/content collision actually emerged. The Editorial Review Board stressed the form of learning, what is known as teaching methods. This was what they saw as a particular problem. How to interest and motivate students were priorities in their efforts. Laudable as this may be, it tended to obscure the shaping of meaning in the text. The currently preferred teaching method which inspires the Maritext project is known as the inquiry method. In practical terms, what this means is that teachers are given privileged information in the teachers' guide, which is not included in the students' text. The teachers' guide provides frameworks through which sense can be made of stories like *In Service*. Through socratic questioning and direction, teachers channel students into preferred readings of the text, like the ones I outlined for *In Service*. 'Right answers', or more appropriately, one right answer, or way to understand a situation, can be arrived at. (And evaluation strategies drill home the point.) In the overall view of the Editorial Review Board, this teaching method allows students to discover meaning in the text, for themselves.

In terms of content, the position of the Editorial Review Board seemed to be that the 'facts spoke for themselves'. However, I found that those facts which did not 'fit' with dominant ideologies were not often taken up. The position of the Editorial Review Board, that form was more important than content, obscured the shaping of content in which they engaged. It eliminated alternate versions of reality and posited that knowledge about social life was unproblematic. Thus, the 'consensus' about *In Service* among the Editorial Review Board was that it was a story about family relationships. This micro emphasis necessarily meant that macro questions of the intersections among race and class and gender were not raised. One Board member argued that "the sensitive issue of race" should not be raised in the classroom context. Such a position reinforces a consensual view of Canadian society — no major divisions or fissures. It also whitewashes reality. And, as I have previously indicated, another Board member stressed the importance of pointing out that such things, as raised by *In Service*, are a thing of the past.[12] 'Readings' of chapter content thus

---

12 In a similar line of 'liberal' reasoning, the inherited wealth and power of Halifax's Dennis family were excluded from the chapter by the Board. Inherited wealth and poverty are inconsistent with working hard and getting ahead.

reflected dominant social understandings.

Generally, classroom teachers played a small role in the actual construction of the Maritime Studies text, or in decisions concerning how, and if, it would be implemented in the schools. (Representative, rather than participatory democracy in action.) For classroom teachers, curriculum is received to be given. But teachers are also understood to be professionals; they are seen to be legitimate transmitters of knowledge. They are certified by universities, and by the state, to do so. However, as the Maritext example demonstrates, classroom teachers are usually not the primary definers of social phenomena. Classroom teachers could more appropriately be called secondary definers of social situations, amplifying accounts of social phenomena generated by academics, curriculum planners, etc. The Maritext project demonstrates this process, as the raw materials socially produced by artists, journalists, and publishers, were given shape by the relevancies of the Editorial Review Board (e.g. dominant ideologies, equal provincial representation, etc.). And the teachers receive this partial version of reality to transmit to students as the 'truth'.

There are many pressures on teachers to reproduce these accounts as received. In a time of increasing cutbacks teachers are not secure in their employment. They are evaluated on the basis of their prowess in transmitting received curriculum, in both form and context, to often unresponsive and resistant audiences. The curriculum dictates a selective content of certain items within discrete subject areas. Thus, connections among family life in *In Service*, the organization of the Nova Scotian economy, and racism in the Maritimes, are not made. The teacher labour force is organized into subject specialties which reinforce these categorizations. However, inter-disciplinary competence is being expected of teachers of Maritime Studies, and this can be threatening to them. Inter-disciplinary work is also seen by many teachers to erode the tenuous job security offered by being a subject specialist.

The form of learning is determined by the structure of the learning process. It is contingent on students progressing in an orderly fashion through a daily timetable. This further fragments learning through time slots, personnel changes, and physical movement from room to room. In the midst of this, teachers are expected to do more, in less time, using fewer resources. Couple these structural pressures with a received sense that there is a 'right answer', and that teachers must have it, and it is not difficult to understand how some versions of *In Service*, and not others, will prevail. Good education, then, entails a systematic sorting and selecting of events, topics, and understandings, according to a socially-constructed set of categories of what is, and is not, good education. It tends to stress the form of the education process, not its content. And great emphasis in both is placed on hierarchical arrangements, on order, on conformity, on deference. Some researchers have chosen to call this part of the "hidden curriculum". The education process structurally reproduces, relatively faithfully, existing social relations of inequality, and teachers tend to find themselves caught in this process. This is why many new, and not-so-new teachers struggle with the realities of the social organization of the education process, which facilitate some readings of accounts like *In Service* and not others. The "how it's s'posed to be" relevancies of teacher training yield to the realities of actual practices in a racist, sexist, classist system. At the same moment that their labour process places time, ideological, and organizational pressures on them, teachers are also products of varying levels of educative processes which reproduce dominant understandings of social life. Like the members of the Maritext Editorial Review Board, classroom teachers have absorbed, and bear, the definitions of social reality which enable them to 'see' Maxine Tynes, and *In Service*, as personal triumphs over past adversities. It is also the case, that the precariousness and constraints of their labour process tend to ensure that teachers do not have the time, nor the energy, to seek out or introduce alternative views. And, as some teachers have learned, there is dubious reward in the education process for deviation from the norm. Pressure is often exerted by superiors, colleagues, and students, to conform to received patterns of thinking and acting. After all, education process rewards, for all constituents, are utilitarian (e.g. salary, promotions, passing, etc.), rather than philosophical. Thus, it is in teachers' interests, as they are articulated in the education process, to receive a certain dominant version of *In Service*, and to transmit it in a specified manner.

I have not explored in this paper the alternate and potentially oppositional meanings which can be generated in the education process about blackness (and ethnic relations in general). Such things do happen, but they are not the norm. At the beginning of this paper, I argued that we must be sensitive to the fact that, through our teaching, we may serve to hold in place existing ethnic relations. As a teacher, a secondary definer, this possibility concerns me greatly. As an academic, one of the primary definers (albeit not mainstream) of Nova Scotian blackness, I also struggle against producing racist accounts of Black Nova Scotian life. In 1981, Black Dartmouth High School student Cherrie Woods articulated compellingly why it is necessary for me and for you to confront dominant beliefs about Nova Scotian Blacks, and to stop their reproduction. In closing, I quote at length from this strong Black woman since she points a direction through which Maxine Tynes and *In Service* can be reclaimed for blackness:

The Black Youth Organization

We the black students of Dartmouth High have come together to make things easier for the black students at Dartmouth High School. We are reaching out to form a unity through the bonding of our minds, possibly create solutions.

The black student in Dartmouth High School (as) of any other high school faces many unique problems such as: name calling, being unfairly treated because of their colour, or *by having to listen to their race being degraded in classrooms.*

Through this newspaper "Black Voice" *we want to reach out to not only the blacks but also the whites and to inject a portion of our culture;* through poetry, stories, fashions, etc., *into the school system.* Our most important objective, however, is to make the plight of black students an easier one through one of the most important period(s) in their lives.

BLACKNESS

I sat in class today
Trapped
I sat and heard my people
Being
Degraded
Put down
And I thought
Wasn't slavery enough?
Haven't we suffered already?

They have destroyed and mutilated
Our history
We have no heritage
Even our names aren't our own
Why won't they let us be?

All we want is to be equal.[13]

---

13 C. Woods, "The Black Youth Organization" and "Blackness" in *Black Voice* (Dartmouth, 1981). (emphasis mine)

SELECTED BIBLIOGRAPHY

Acker, S., "Women and Teaching: A Semi-Detached Sociology of Semi-Profession", in S. Walker and L. Burton, eds., *Gender, Class and Education* (Barcombe Lewes, 1983).

Brittan, A. and Maynard, M., *Sexism, Racism and Oppression* (Oxford, 1984).

Braham, P., "How media report race", in M. Gurevitch, T. Bennett, J. Curan, and J. Woollocott, eds., *Culture, society and the media* (London, 1982).

Browne, J.A., "A comparative study of socio-economic patterns in black Nova Scotia communities" (MA thesis, Dalhousie University, 1982).

Carby, H.V., "Schooling in Babylon", in The Centre for Contemporary Cultural Studies, *The Empire Strikes Back* (London, 1982).

Carrington, B., "Sport as a Side-Track: An Analysis of West Indian Involvement in Extra-Curricular Sport", in L. Barton and S. Walker, eds., *Race, Class and Education* (London, 1983).

Clarke, J., Hall, S., Jefferson, T., and Roberts, B., "Subcultures, cultures and class: a theoretical overview", in S. Hall and T. Jefferson, eds., *Resistance Through Rituals* (London, 1976).

Dahlie, J. and Fernando, T., eds. *Ethnicity, Power and Politics in Canada* (Toronto, 1981).

Fleming, P., "Education and Inequality: The Case of Blacks in Nova Scotia" (BA thesis, Saint Mary's University, 1980).

Fox-Genovese, E., "Placing Women's History in History", *New Left Review*, 133 (May-June, 1982), pp. 5-29.

Hall, S., "Culture, the Media and the 'Ideological Effect'", in J. Curran, M. Gurevitch, and J. Woollacott, eds., *Mass Communication and Society* (London, 1977).

Hall, S., Critcher, C., Jefferson, T., Clarke, J., and Roberts, B., *Policing The Crisis* (London, 1981).

Harp J., "Social Inequalities and the Transmission of Knowledge" in J. Harp and J.R. Hofley, eds., *Structured Inequality in Canada* (Scarborough, 1980).

James, A., "'Black': An Inquiry Into the Perjorative Associations of an English Word", *New Community*, 9/1 (1981), pp. 19-30.

McNeil, K., "Rise Again", song from recording *The Rise and Follies of Cape Breton Island, 1785-1985* (Sydney, 1985).

McRobbie, A. and McCabe, T., *Feminism for Girls* (London, 1982).

Mannette, J.A., "Black in A Black Voice? Understanding the Race Margin on the Atlantic Periphery", paper prepared for the Sixth Conference on Workers and Their Communities, Université d'Ottawa, May 1986.

——————, "Conceptual and Social Marginality: The Recovery of Black Women in Nova Scotian Social Life, 1780-1900", in C. deRoche and J. deRoche, eds., *Notes From The Margin* (forthcoming).

——————, "Nova Scotia's Black Renaissance: A Social Construction of Blackness in the 1980s", paper prepared for the Atlantic Workshop, Sydney, September 1985.

——————, "Setting The Record Straight: The Experiences of Black People in Nova Scotia, 1780-1900" (MA thesis, Carleton University, 1983).

——————, "Social Constructions of Black Nova Scotians: The Weymouth Falls Case", paper prepared for the Atlantic Association of Sociologists and Anthropologists, Annual Meeting, Acadia University, March 1986.

——————, "'Stark Remnants of Blackpast': Thinking on Gender, Ethnicity, and Class in 1780s Nova Scotia", *Alternate Routes,* 7 (1984), pp. 102-33.

Marchak, M.P., *Ideological Perspectives on Canada* (Toronto, 1980).

Moreau, B., "The Role Played by Adult Education in the Struggle of Black Nova Scotians for Survival: 1750-1945", paper prepared for the Atlantic Association of Sociologists and Anthropologists, Annual Meeting, Acadia University, March 1986.

Porter, J., *The Measure of Canadian Society: Education, Equality and Opportunity* (Toronto, 1979).

Pratt, S.L., "Black Education in Nova Scotia" (MA thesis, Dalhousie University, 1973).

Saracho, O.N. and Spodek, B., eds., *Understanding the Multicultural Experience in Early Childhood Education* (Washington, 1983).

Spender, D., ed., *Men's Studies Modified* (Oxford, 1981).

Stanworth, M., *Gender and Schooling* (London, 1983).

Tomlinson, S., "Black Women in Higher Education — Case Studies of University Women in Britain", in L. Barton and S. Walker, eds., *Race, Class and Education* (London, 1983).

Walker, James W. St.G., *A History of Blacks in Canada: A Study Guide for Teachers and Students* (Toronto, 1980).

Weiss, L., *Between Two Worlds: Black Students in an Urban Community College* (London, 1985).

Wien, F. and Browne, J., "A Report on Employment Patterns in the Black Communities of Nova Scotia" (unpublished report, Institute of Public Affairs, Dalhousie University, 1981).

Williams, R., *Culture* (London, 1981).

Willis, P., *Learning To Labour: How Working Class Kids Get Working Class Jobs* (New York, 1977).

13 Black History in the Maritimes: Major Themes and Teaching Strategies

James W. St.G. Walker

BLACKS HAVE BEEN A PART OF the Maritimes' population since the beginnings of trans-Atlantic settlement, and have therefore participated in the history of the region as a whole. There are however certain features and episodes in the history of blacks in the Maritimes which remain unique, setting them apart from other identifiable groups and providing illustrations, through their own experiences, which lend a peculiar and valuable insight into the nature of Maritime society. The many events and trends which characterize black history in the Maritimes can be understood, for purposes of study, within two thematic "clusters": one concerns the growth and nature of Canadian racism, and the other traces the development of a distinct black community and identity. The two "clusters" overlap to produce a culturally self-sufficient but economically dependent black enclave, or more accurately a series of such enclaves, within a mainstream society which has throughout most of its history been unwilling to accept blacks as full and equal members.

Black history in all three Maritime provinces begins inauspiciously, in the institution of slavery. By definition a slave occupies a subordinate role in society; his or her function is to serve others. Despite the presence of skilled craftsmen among the slaves who helped establish both Louisbourg and Halifax, and, later, virtually all the Loyalist settlements, still the service function prevailed and blacks gained an image and were accorded a role which placed them beneath the white population. Even when slavery died out in the Maritimes, shortly after 1800, the image was nourished by the continued enslavement of blacks in the British Empire until 1834 and the United States until 1865. Through slavery, patterns were established into which later free black migrants were forced to fit.

The earliest of these free black settlers were the black Loyalists, formerly American slaves who joined the British during the Revolutionary War in response to a series of proclamations which led them to expect full equality and the rewards of loyalty to the Crown, including the grants of land and provisions offered to all Loyalists. They were motivated not just by the promise of individual freedom but by the additonal prospect of independence, that is, the means of economic self-sufficiency; furthermore,

British statements during the War appeared to mean that a Loyalist victory would result in the eradication of slavery for all blacks in America, thus encouraging blacks to engage in what they believed was a war of black liberation. Though the war ended in defeat, the 3,500 black Loyalists who joined the exodus to the Maritimes in 1783-84 carried with them the attitudes and expectations which had first attracted them to the British side.

In Nova Scotia and New Brunswick, officials were incapable of managing the settlement of over 30,000 Loyalists; priorities had to be set, and the group of former slaves was relegated to the bottom of the list, taking their position from the slaves whose colour they shared rather than from the Loyalists whose status they had earned. Located on the outskirts of such centres as Halifax, Shelburne, Digby and Saint John, often landless or at best with farms inadequate for full self-support, the blacks were a desperate and therefore exploitable reserve of labour. With most white Loyalists engaged in establishing their own farms and businesses, the blacks supplied the chief part of the labor required for the construction of public works. The legacy of slavery was in this way perpetuated as blacks continued to be perceived, even in freedom, as a service and labouring caste serving the needs of white society.

Physically segregated and economically deprived, blacks were also denied the vote, could not serve on juries or claim a jury trial, and were prevented from holding public office. They were not, however, passive victims. They sent a flow of petitions to Halifax and Fredericton demanding their land grants, insisting on their rights, and condemning the continued existence of black slavery in the Maritimes. When local officials failed to respond they looked directly to London, sending a delegate there in 1790 to advise the king that they were being treated unjustly. The British cabinet reacted with an offer to accept the black Loyalists as free British subjects with grants of land and full political participation in the new colony of Sierra Leone in West Africa. In response about 1,200 blacks, or one-third the total number in the Maritimes, sailed from Halifax to Freetown in 1792. Those who remained behind had been led to expect an improvement, for the British government had ordered an inquiry into conditions for blacks in the Maritimes, but in fact no improvements occurred. The black remnant tended to withdraw into their own settlements, their own churches, societies and schools, to territory which they themselves controlled. This was not a surrender but a tactic, not an end but a means, for the blacks retained a faith that once their merits were recognized, white Maritimers would accept them.

Meanwhile, another black migration occurred which was dramatic but temporary. In 1796 over 500 Maroons in Jamaica were tricked into surrendering their arms during a war against the British colonial authorities, and once rendered vulnerable they were dispatched to exile in Nova Scotia. Incensed by their betrayal, discomforted by the climate, frustrated by the loss of their former freedom to roam the Jamaican forests at will, the Maroons refused to settle quietly in Nova Scotia. After repeated appeals to London, they were finally allowed in 1800 to proceed to Sierra Leone. Only four Maroon deserters are known to have remained behind in Nova Scotia, presumably for personal reasons, but the Maroon episode lent a greater significance than this through the example of pride and independence which they reinforced upon the emerging community of free blacks in the provice.

The 1792 Sierra Leone exodus seriously depopulated the black settlements, and the opportunities for a vibrant community life were more limited. This situation was changed by the arrival of over 2,000 black Refugees during the War of 1812. Attracted by the promise of complete freedom and settlement on lands in British territory, these former American slaves shared many of the attitudes and aspirations of their Loyalist predecessors. Unfortunately they also had in common the treatment received at the hands of local whites. At first both the Nova Scotia and New Brunswick governments welcomed the Refugees as a valuable addition to the supply of labour, but a post-war depression and an influx of white immigrant labour reduced their significance to the regional economy. With farms too small to provide support and with few opportunities for employment, the Refugees slipped into a state of poverty and economic dependence upon white society, forced to accept any job for any wage. In a vicious circle, their image of dependence fed white stereotypes and encouraged the notion that blacks were suited only for the meanest kinds of employment. Discrimination fulfilled its own expectations. More positively, the Refugees re-established the population base to facilitate a black community revival. Scattered black Loyalists and their descendants were inclined to migrate to the new concentrations of black settlement, helping to create conditions favourable to the development of institutions tailored to the needs of a local black community and effecting a merger between Loyalists and Refugees which produced a combined people and a combined culture within a generation.

Migration and settlement patterns placed a relatively large number of blacks in one location, isolated from whites and from other black settlements. This physical separation encouraged the perpetuation of cultural characteristics brought from slavery, and it enabled the evolution of cultural features appropriate to the new Maritime environment. Family structure, for example, demonstrated both these influences. Kinship was defined more broadly than in white society, reflecting the plantation experience, and women were full participants in the family's economic support. In the Maritimes employment opportunities were defined by sex as well as by race, so that in times of limited male employment the women would be the chief bread-winners. Children were necessarily the responsibility of a broader range of relationships, and women were far more independent, than in the nuclear structure of white families. Churches, schools, recreational practices and community identities were similarly developed to respond to the needs of the population they served. An attitude of non-confrontation was fostered by the sense of a small and unique group offering refuge in a sea of hostility or, at best, indifference. A high degree of communal unity was demanded and mutual cooperation was valued over individual achievement.

Collective survival was undoubtedly a strong motivation for the maintenance of a separate community existence, but the eventual goal of full integration was not abandoned. This was revealed in the 1840s by the Anglo-African Mutual Improvement and Aid Association of Nova Scotia, which overtly sought to demonstrate black abilities to a skeptical white population in order to overcome the barriers of racist stereotypes. In a programme designed to present a good example, members could be fined for public drunkenness or tardiness, and they were instructed to let no insult go unanswered and to accept no limitations on their rights. In the 1841 provincial election the Association required members to exercise their vote, contrary to the prevailing convention, since no actual law disallowed black voters. In 1854 there was established the African Baptist Association of Nova Scotia, similarly intended to lend collective institutional strength to the black churches and to represent their interests more forcefully to the white society. Ironically, however, the blacks' tactics of group strength and collective activity enabled racist whites to conclude that blacks were endorsing their own segregation and that they lacked individual ambition; even sympathetic whites could be misled into believing that all was well.

Confederation gave British North America a westward frontier and emphasis; Ontarians and Maritimers were encouraged to seek their fortunes in the new west. Black Maritimers intent upon improving their circumstances, however, tended rather to migrate to the United States. In the Maritimes, where racial disadvantage was not generally upheld by the law, the most damaging disabilities were economic. The barriers of stereotype and racism made it virtually impossible for blacks to move into the economic mainstream; a "place" had been established for blacks, and it was limited to the lowest paid and least secure fields of employment. In the United States, on the other hand, where segregation was legally sanctioned, there existed a full range of educational institutions, professional opportunities and community functions offering immeasurably greater scope to the ambitious individual. Contrary to Canadian myth, therefore, the flow of disadvantaged blacks occasionally operated in a southerly direction.

In Nova Scotia separate black schools could be established under the law, but this was rarely necessary as residential segregation throughout the Maritimes produced "de facto" separation in schools, churches and services. Whites did not encourage blacks to integrate, for by the late nineteenth century "scientific" racist beliefs taught that blacks were genetically inferior and were incapable of assimilating into white society or even of participating in institutions designed by and for the Northern races. Immigration policies which sought to prevent any non-whites from entering Canada were reflected in domestic attitudes and practices. A most dramatic example of white exclusion occurred during the First World War, when black volunteers anxious to do their part for the defence of Canada were rejected by the military. According to the racist beliefs of the time, blacks were not considered to be good soldier material. When the blacks persisted, despite the insults, the decision was made in 1916 to create the Nova Scotia No. 2 Construction Battalion, not to fight Germans but to perform auxiliary labour service for white troops. At a time when French Canadians were being coerced into the army, racist stereotypes succeeded in preventing or restricting the contribution of willing black volunteers.

The period between the wars witnessed an even further deterioration in the blacks' relative position in Maritime society. Black men were concentrated in increasingly specialized corners of the economy as waiters, janitors, barbers and labourers, and black women as domestic servants, laundresses and waitresses. The elite among the men became railway waiters and porters. This range shrank, especially during the Depression, so that waiting jobs and other personal contact positions passed increasingly to whites. Blacks were required to rely more than ever upon mutual cooperation within their own families and communities for economic survival, and upon black institutions and cultural activities for their social lives. No institution was more significant than the church, for it lent a sense of dignity and sanctification as well as an outlet for collective activity both secular and religious. Those disinclined to the intimacies of communal sharing, often including the most personally ambitious, tended to leave the community entirely for better perceived opportunities in Montreal or Toronto. The result was smaller, more compact and more united local black communities bonded by ties of family, religion and interdependence.

The Second World War set a momentum for direct confrontation with restrictive conditions. There was a global reaction against the excesses of Nazi racism, which in turn influenced white Canadian attitudes. Researchers meanwhile were discrediting any "scientific" foundations for racist beliefs and practices. A much more receptive white population created an opportunity for blacks to press for reforms. In 1945 the Nova Scotia Association for the Advancement of Coloured People was founded to strive for greater opportunities in employment, housing and education, including the education of adults long deprived in their inadequate segregated schools. The black community, ironically reinforced by the historical experience of racism, became itself the chief instrument to confront racist barriers. Subtle approaches were made to businesses, hospitals and government agencies seeking training or employment positions for blacks. Delegates visited provincial legislatures, calling for legislation to achieve fair employment and accommodation practices. Information was compiled illustrating black disadvantage for presentation to sympathetic audiences. Occasionally more dramatic demonstrations occurred, as in the legal controversy surrounding the 1947 case of Mrs. Viola Desmond who was denied admission to the downstairs section of a New Glasgow cinema because she was black.

Increasing white awareness was followed by legislative reforms. Nova Scotia introduced a fair employment practices act in 1955, followed by New Brunswick in 1956, and in 1959 both provinces passed fair accommodations practices acts. Nova Scotia took the next step with a comprehensive Human Rights Act in 1963, and with a full Human Rights Commission in 1967. That same year New Brunswick passed a Human Rights Act including a Commission; Prince Edward Island's Human Rights Act came in 1968, with the Commission following in 1975. Meanwhile, municipalities passed by-laws against discrimination and eliminated long-standing regulations which had supported racially distinctive facilities. At the federal level, immigration regulations changed in 1962 and 1967 which removed race as a legitimate factor in immigrant selection. Instead, immigrants were to be admitted according to their individual qualifications as measured by a "points system" which ignored race, colour or country of origin.

A review of Canadian laws in the 1960s would reveal a situation which was technically egalitarian: overt discrimination had been made illegal. But ancient syndromes remained largely unaffected. Data from that same decade showed that blacks earned lower wages, experienced more unemployment, inhabited distinctly inferior accommodations, and enjoyed fewer educational opportunities than whites in neighbouring communities. From the mid-1940s to the 1960s black Maritimers had tended to attack specific areas of complaint; general attitudes were usually not the target, so that although the laws were adjusted the most damaging stereotypes survived. By the later 1960s there was a recognition that case-by-case victories were not eliminating the underlying causes of racial disadvantage, and that a much broader strategy must be adopted. Inspired not only by their own experience but by the example of American blacks and the new assertiveness of many Canadian groups, blacks became much more confrontationist, insisting upon positive intervention to break the syndrome which kept them unequal. In Nova Scotia the Black United Front was organized to seek out instances of racism, to unite people of all Nova Scotia's black settlements into a conscious community for public action, and to conduct programmes for black education, employment and cultural awareness. For many whites this was a new experience, and they attributed the black complaints to outside agitators such as the Black Panthers who visited Halifax in 1968. In fact, of course, blacks had recognized their disadvantages from the very outset and had taken steps in every generation to overcome them: petitions to government officials; migration to Sierra Leone, to the United States, to Toronto; self-improvement schemes to earn recognition; efforts to participate in mainstream political and social activities; lobbying for jobs, for schools, for training programmes; court cases to challenge overt barriers; urging legislative reforms. What was new was not black disadvantage or black dissatisfaction, but white awareness of a situation long accepted as "normal".

During this same period profound demographic changes have been affecting the black communities. As a result of the immigration policy reforms a new black influx occurred, chiefly composed of West Indians, for the first time since the War of 1812. Nationally, the West Indians captured the public's imagination, outnumbering indigenous black Canadians ten-fold and diverting attention from specifically black to more generally immigrant concerns. Within the Maritime region West Indians are still a numerical minority, but their educational levels and upward mobility have given them an impact beyond their numbers. Many institutions initially designed to serve the existing black communities now have West Indians among their leadership. Meanwhile internal developments have been occurring, as younger people leave the isolated settlements now that residential barriers are being lifted, moving to Halifax or other urban centres. Even within the outlying settlements direct government and social welfare activity has interrupted old communal relationships of interdependence; the preacher is no longer the chief arbiter and dispenser, the church is no longer the exclusive organization offering cultural or recreational outlets. This is, clearly, a transitional phase in the history of blacks in the Maritimes, calling for sincere and serious adjustments from both blacks and whites.

There are many ways in which these various messages could be presented in the classroom, some more effective than others. Black history has often been presented as a story of degradation, as a series of wrongs inflicted upon blacks by whites. To give discrimination exclusive place is to deny the internal dynamics of the black communities, and in effect to reinforce the notion that all historical trends of any significance have been established by whites. A frequent alternative format has been the presentation of black success stories, those individuals who have "made it" according to the standards of white society. This approach similarly tends to underemphasize the community existence and collective endeavour which has characterized so much of black history, highlighting exceptional individuals who rarely represent the black experience generally, and it could minimize the impact of racism. Clearly the two thematic areas incorporating race relations and the community identity are so closely related as to require their treatment in tandem.

Black history does not require an exclusive course, or even an exclusive segment in a sequence of ethnic minicourses. To follow this option would at the very least confuse students and could lead to the false impression that Maritime history is a patchwork of group histories with no organic relationship to each other. Ethnic history and Canadian history are one and the same thing: they are divided only by textbooks and by teachers. It is therefore quite accurate, and no doubt pedagogically preferable, to integrate the themes and episodes of black history into a general account of the Maritimes' story. A genuine integration, of course, would not mean the simple insertion of black material at suitable chronological intervals, but an analysis of the implications of that material for our understanding of mainstream Maritime history. A few examples will serve to illustrate this point.

How different is our picture of pioneer life when the existence of slavery is acknowledged. Simply to mention it is to adjust the image, and it helps to bring into clearer focus the problems of labour shortage on the frontier, the social divisions, the relationships between status and economic function. The addition of the racial issue to slavery will help students to understand that racial stereotypes have an historical origin, that connections between colour and behaviour can be explained in terms of a specific time and conjunction of events. To understand stereotypes is the first essential step toward their destruction. The black Loyalists can be introduced to similar effect. Their inclusion changes fundamentally the impression of Loyalist society, the nature of work in the settlement period, the dedication to freedom and British justice, the origins and applications of British institutions in the wilderness. The circumstances through which slavery-derived stereotypes were applied to free blacks can be extremely enlightening, and may provoke discussion on the phenomenon whereby discrimination can produce its own justification. If a gender analogy does not arise spontaneously, the teacher might choose to introduce it.

The imaginative teacher will find numerous instructive examples from black history to challenge or enhance the "received view" of Maritime history. In the period of reform leading up to Responsible Government, why were blacks not voting? What can we learn about the black community from the methods adopted by the Anglo-African Mutual Improvement and Aid Association? What type of democracy were Canadian soldiers fighting for in the First World War? Does the Nova Scotia No. 2 Construction Battalion offer any clues? Why did the blacks persist in volunteering? Why was human rights legislation passed in the 1960s, and upon whose initiative? What conditions made it necessary?

Such testings will be fruitful and should provide stimulation for the history teacher's favourite pedagogical technique, the classroom discussion. Yet all these examples continue to reflect the existing "touchstones" in Maritime history, the dates, events, wars, elections and government acts which constitute the record of the white, educated, male minority. If black history is to make a thorough contribution to our understanding of the Maritime past then it must supply alternative touchstones and alternative heroes. The year 1792 could be added to the standard string of dates, the year in which 1,200 black Loyalists left Nova Scotia and New Brunswick for a better life in Africa. Why did they go? Why were they not treated like other Loyalists? Did they make the right choice? In 1839 blacks declined an offer to move to larger, more fertile farms, scattered throughout Nova Scotia, because to accept would have exposed them to white racism as isolated individuals, and it would have destroyed their communities and institutions. Were they wise to foresake the prospect of individual economic advance in order to retain their communities? How did they arrive at such a choice? What made their communities so valuable, or life outside them so frightening? The formation of the African Baptist Association in 1854, to use one final example, supplies another opportunity for enrichment. What role did the church play in black community life? Why was it difficult to produce institutions and loyalties beyond the local community level? Is there any significance to the use of the term "African" in several important black organizations? There is no shortage of alternative events capable of supplying an entrance to a new vision of Maritime history. Similarly, heroes abound who can, when taken in context, provide further insight into the most important historical themes while offering human interest to the story: Catherine Abernathy, leader of Preston's black Anglicans and founder of that community's first school; Thomas Peters, the Revolutionary War veteran who went to London to present black grievances before the king; Richard Preston, who created and led the African Baptist Association.

Obviously if any of these objectives are to be accomplished, a great deal of information is required both for teachers to use as lesson preparation and for students to read themselves. In the accompanying bibliography those items deemed most suitable for student use have been identified with an asterisk. Only materials relating directly to the Maritimes, and which are reasonably accessible to the public, are included. For more titles, and to gain a Canada-wide perspective on events in the Maritimes, readers can consult James Walker, *A History of Blacks in Canada: A Study Guide for*

Teachers and Students (Ottawa, 1980), and Robin Winks, *The Blacks in Canada: A History* (New Haven and Montreal, 1971). Also useful for discovering additional sources are Elizabeth Beaton-Planetta, *Ethnic Resources Inventory: Nova Scotia* (Sydney, 1985), and James Morrison, *Common Heritage: An Annotated Bibliography of Ethnic Groups in Nova Scotia* (Halifax, 1984).

SELECTED BIBLIOGRAPHY

Section A: *Biographical Works*

Best, Carrie M., *That Lonesome Road: The Autobiography of Carrie M. Best* (New Glasgow, 1977).

Blakeley, Phyllis, "Boston King: A Negro Loyalist Who Sought Refuge in Nova Scotia", *Dalhousie Review*, XLVIII (1968), pp. 347-56.*

Blakeley, Phyllis, "William Hall: Canada's First Naval V.C.", *Dalhousie Review*, XXXVII (1957-8), pp. 250-58.*

Fyfe, Christopher, "Thomas Peters: History and Legend", *Sierra Leone Studies*, IX (1953), pp. 4-13.

Kirk-Greene, Anthony, "David George: The Nova Scotian Experience", *Sierra Leone Studies*, XIV (1960), pp. 93-120.

Morrison, Alan, "Amazing Career of Sam Langford", *Ebony*, XI (April 1956), pp. 97-105.*

Pachai, Bridglal, "The Search for a Black Self-Identity in Nova Scotia", *Journal of Education*, V (1978), pp. 18-34.

Tudor, Kathleen, "David George: Black Loyalist", *Nova Scotia Historical Review*, III (1983), pp. 71-82.*

Young, Alexander, "The Boston Tarbaby", *Nova Scotia Historical Quarterly*, IV (1974), pp. 277-98.*

Section B: *Books on Blacks in the Maritimes*

Boyd, Frank, ed., *McKerrow, A Brief History of Blacks in Nova Scotia, 1783-1895* (Halifax, 1976).

Clairmont, Donald and Magill, Dennis, *Africville: The Life and Death of a Canadian Black Community* (Toronto, 1974).

Clairmont, D.H. and Magill, D.W., *Nova Scotia Blacks: An Historical and Structural Overview* (Halifax, 1971).

D'Oyley, Vincent, ed., *Black Presence in Multi-Ethnic Canada* (Toronto, 1978).

Fergusson, C.B., ed., *A Documentary Study of the Establishment of the Negroes in Nova Scotia Between The War of 1812 and the Winning of Responsible Government* (Halifax, 1948).

Grant, John N., *Black Nova Scotians* (Halifax, 1980).*

Henry, Frances, *Forgotten Canadians: The Blacks of Nova Scotia* (Toronto, 1973).

Oliver, Pearleen, *A Brief History of the Colored Baptists of Nova Scotia, 1782-1953* (Halifax, 1953).

Pachai, Bridglal, *Canadian Black Studies* (Halifax, 1979).

Spray, William, *The Blacks in New Brunswick* (Fredericton, 1972).*

Walker, James W. St.G., *The Black Loyalists: The Search for a Promised Land in Nova Scotia and Sierra Leone, 1783-1870* (London and New York, 1976).

Walker, James W. St.G., *Racial Discrimination in Canada: The Black Experience* (Ottawa, 1985).*

Section C: *Articles on Blacks in the Maritimes*

Bell, David G., "Slavery and the Judges of Loyalist New Brunswick", *University of New Brunswick Law Journal*, XXXI (1982), pp. 9-42.

Clairmont, Donald and Wien, Fred, "Blacks and Whites: The Nova Scotia Race Relations Experience", in Douglas Campbell, ed., *Banked Fires: The Ethnics of Nova Scotia* (Port Credit, 1978).

Clairmont, D.H. and Magill, D.W., "Nova Scotia Blacks: Marginal People in a Depressed Region", in J.E. Gallagher and R.D. Lambert, eds., *Social Process and Institutions: The Canadian Case* (Toronto, 1971).

Grant, John, "Black Immigrants into Nova Scotia 1776-1815", *Journal of Negro History*, LVIII (1973), pp. 253-70.*

Grant, John, "The 1821 Emigration of Black Nova Scotians to Trinidad", *Nova Scotia Historical Quarterly*, II (1972), pp. 283-92.*

Holman, H.T., "Slaves and Servants on Prince Edward Island: The Case of Jupiter Wise", *Acadiensis*, XII (1982), pp. 100-104.

How, Douglas, "The Holy Town Will Have To Take Its Halo Down", *Weekend Magazine*, 7 October 1972.*

Lubka, Nancy, "Ferment in Nova Scotia", *Queen's Quarterly*, LXXVI (1969), pp. 213-228.*

MacKay, W.A., "Equality of Opportunity: Recent Developments in the Field of Human Rights in Nova Scotia", *University of Toronto Law Journal*, XVII (1967), pp. 176-186.

Milner, J.B., "Civil Liberties — Theatre Refusing to Admit Negro Person to Orchestra Seat", *Canadian Bar Review*, XXV (1947), pp. 915-924.

"Nova Scotia: Model in Race Relations", *Saturday Night*, 6 June 1959.

McClain-Tatum, Paula D., "Political Alienation: Some Social/Psychological Aspects of the Political Culture of Afro-Canadians", *Ethnicity*, VI (1979), pp. 358-372.

Oliver, W.P., "Cultural Progress of the Negro in Nova Scotia", *Dalhousie Review*, XXIX (1949), pp. 293-300.

Quig, James, "Walking Black Through Halifax", *Weekend Magazine*, 19 June 1976.*

Rawlyk, George A., "The Guysborough Negroes: A Study in Isolation", *Dalhousie Review*, XLVIII (1968), pp. 24-36.

Reid, A.D., "The New Brunswick Human Rights Act", *University of Toronto Law Journal*, XVIII (1968), pp. 394-400.

Riddell, W.R., "The Slave in Canada", *Journal of Negro History*, V (1920), pp. 261-377.*

Smith, T. Watson, "The Slave in Canada", *Collections of the Nova Scotia Historical Society*, X (1899).*

Spray, William, "The Settlement of the Black Refugees in New Brunswick, 1815-1836", *Acadiensis*, VI (1977), pp. 64-79.

"The Blacks of Canada — A Special Survey", *Globe Magazine*, 15 January 1969.*

"The New Blacks in Canada", *Saturday Night*, January 1970.*

Walker, James W. St.G., "The Establishment of a Free Black Community in Nova Scotia, 1783-1840", in M. Kilson and R. Rotberg, eds., *African Diaspora, Interpretive Essays* (Cambridge, Mass., 1976).

Williams, Savanah E., "Two Hundred Years in the Development of the Afro-Canadians in Nova Scotia, 1782-1982", in Jean L. Elliott, ed., *Two Nations, Many Cultures. Ethnic Groups in Canada* (2nd ed., Toronto, 1983).

Winks, Robin, "Negroes in the Maritimes: An Introductory Survey", *Dalhousie Review*, XLVIII (1968), pp. 453-471.

Winks, Robin, "Negro School Segregation in Ontario and Nova Scotia", *Canadian Historical Review*, L (1969), pp. 164-91.

14 Out of the Kitchen and into the Curriculum: Women's Studies in Maritime Canada

Margaret Conrad

THE SOCIETY OF THE MARITIME Provinces consists of 50 per cent women, the student population is half female, and this audience, while falling somewhat short of the halfway mark, could conceivably include a majority of women. In contrast, our schools are controlled by male administrators, teachers' unions are dominated by men, and our textbooks, despite recent reforms, still portray the frontiers of human activity in male, never female, terms. In a society where power structures systematically exclude women, where sexist jokes still bring a hearty laugh in polite society, and where the media serves up erotic fantasies from an exclusively male perspective, the inclusion of women in our textbooks becomes not only an issue of fair play; it is important to the mental and physical health of the next generation of Maritime women.

Even as I am writing this, I can sense the disbelief written on the faces of the reader. Does not the human story encompass both men and women? Is gender really relevant? Obviously, I would not be here if I did not answer that question in the affirmative. And, I recently was confirmed in my conviction by an incident which occurred in Annapolis Royal where Margaret Atwood was reading a piece about her mother, who grew up in Annapolis Valley.[1] Speaking to an audience that was mixed in more ways than one, she sensibly did not approach her feminist politics directly. Instead, Atwood remarked on how in her mother's world, women clustered in kitchens and talked in hushed tones about men who beat their wives, women who had abortions, and girls molested by their fathers. Of course, she said, when men entered the kitchen all such discussions ceased. Men, she concluded, liked to be left alone to play in their own sandbox. Talk about such disturbing issues as wife battery, abortion and child abuse would upset them. They might, she suggested, become cranky and refuse to eat their suppers. At this point, the women, young and old, most of whom would eschew the label feminist, burst into wild applause, bringing Atwood's reading to an abrupt halt. Even the men, their eyes glazed by a joke made at their expense, were forced to concede the central role played

---

1   Annapolis Festival, 29 September 1985.

by food in the power relationship between the women who prepare it and the men who consume it.

As Atwood's anecdote suggests, the process of writing women into the curriculum requires more than adding a few "women worthies" to the rostrum of male achievers who have built empires, led governments and waged wars. It even requires more than mention of the fact that women as a group have been discriminated against in patriarchal society. It requires us to recognize that women historically have been socialized to different roles from men; that women in the Maritimes, as elsewhere, have had a separate culture, or more exactly separate cultures; and that women's culture is, in itself, an appropriate topic for inclusion in our textbooks.[2] Only when women's talk and women's work are taken out of the kitchen and into the curriculum will education meet the needs of all our students.

I will not pretend that it is always easy to introduce women's culture into the classroom. The silence shrouding women's sphere has been such as to make even women uncomfortable when it is brought out of the kitchen and placed in the curriculum. As anthropologist Helga Jacobson has noted when discussing kitchen culture with her students:

> The polite tolerance of the topic, when I present it, only lasts as long as the asking of the question. Most discussions of women's work and women's culture are given to the tune of shuffling notebooks and snapping ringbinders. In these responses is made visible the rule that defines the subject matter as inappropriate to the classroom setting.[3]

My experience has not always been as negative as that of Professor Jacobson, in part because I teach a course labelled 'women's history', which automatically excludes those who are embarrassed or offended by 'women's talk'. Moreover, I find that issues such as sexuality, reproduction and personal relationships, which are traditionally relegated to the private sphere of women, are absolutely riveting to the teenagers who fill my classroom. A teacher who is prepared to discuss such topics — that is, prepared to raise such topics from the level of innuendo, trivia or moralism — will be able to hear a pin drop when women's culture is introduced in

---

2   Marilyn Schuster and Susan Van Dyne, "Placing Women in the Liberal Arts: Stages of Curriculum Transformation", *Harvard Education Review*, 54/4 (November 1984), pp. 413-28.

3   Helga E. Jacobson, "Women's Work and Women's Culture: Some Further Considerations", *Women's Culture: Selected Papers From the Halifax Conference* (Ottawa, 1982), pp. 47-61. On sexism in traditional research see Margrit Eichler, "Sexism in Research and Its Policy Implications", in Jill McCalla Vickers, ed., *Taking Sex Into Account* (Ottawa, 1984), pp. 17-39.

the classroom. (For a starter, try offering a historical perspective on teenage pregnancy.)

A decade ago it would have been difficult to suggest sources for helping teachers approach the history of women and gender relations in Maritime society.[4] This is no longer the case. While there are still fewer books, articles and artifacts specifically relating to Maritime women than we would like, the raw material is there and the literature on North American women to help us to interpret our own experience is accumulating so rapidly that it is difficult to keep up with it. This research has revealed significant findings in the areas of: (1) the changing nature of fertility and the family; (2) women's domestic and paid labour; (3) women's creativity and culture; (4) the structures by which women are excluded from the public sphere; and (5) the means by which women resist dehumanization and subordination. By looking at the experience of women in the Maritime Provinces in relationship to developments in other cultures, the similarities and differences immediately give us ample material for our curriculum and enough questions to keep us indefinitely in the archives.

It is impossible here to indicate all the ways in which women's culture can be integrated into the curriculum of a course on the Maritime Provinces since 1945. A few examples will suffice.

Most surveys of Maritime society include a discussion of urbanization and outmigration. Teachers would do well to consider these phenomena in relation to gender. Historically, women in the Maritime Provinces were among the first in the world to be influenced by the industrial revolution. They flocked to jobs in the Boston states, Saint John and Halifax, while men gravitated to the resource industries of mining, lumbering, fishing and, eventually, off-shore oil exploration.[5] The success of women in making their own living led a significant proportion to adopt the single life and late marriage. Population movements meant that there were more men than women in Cape Breton County and more women than men in

4   Ruth Pierson's review essay, "Woman's History: The State of the Art in Atlantic Canada", *Acadiensis*, VII/1 (Autumn 1977), pp. 121-31, gives some idea of the 'progress' of women's history in the region in 1977. See also Margaret Conrad, "The Rebirth of Canada's Past: A Decade of Women's History", *Acadiensis*, XII/2 (Spring 1983), pp. 140-62, and Atlantic Provinces Library Association, *Bulletin* (January 1982), for later discussions of sources for the study of women in Atlantic Canada. Also useful for teachers is Carol Mazur and Sheila Pepper, *Women in Canada* (Toronto, 1984).

5   See Patricia Thornton, "Some Preliminary Comments on the Extent and Consequences of Out-Migration from the Atlantic Region, 1870-1920", in Lewis R. Fischer and Eric W. Sager, eds., *Merchant Shipping and Economic Development in Atlantic Canada* (St. John's, 1982), pp. 187-218; Alan A. Brookes, "The Golden Age and the Exodus: The Case of Canning, Kings County", *Acadiensis*, XI/1 (Autumn 1981), pp. 57-82; Georges Arsenault, "Chanter son Acadie", in Claire Quintal, ed., *L'émigrant acadien vers les Etats-Unis: 1842-1950* (Quebec, 1984), pp. 101-19.

most other urban centres. Anglophone Protestant women were more likely to take up the new working girl lifestyle than were francophone and Catholic women. Middle class women had more opportunities than their working class sisters. All women in the Maritime Provinces experienced a wider range of options than did women in Latin America or South Africa in the same period. Students in Maritime classrooms come from families with a long history of migration in search of work. A discussion of gender differences in mobility would help young people to understand past trends and to gain a perspective on their own options in a rapidly changing work world.

In the post-war years, Maritime society has witnessed a drastic reduction in fertility and increased divorce rates.[6] Women have helped to precipitate these trends and, in turn, their lives have significantly altered by the trend to smaller and single parent families. Inclusion of this topic in the curriculum will help students to understand the growing plurality in family arrangements among themselves and their friends. It will also give the teacher a chance to discuss such demographic information in the context of changing values and economic conditions in the post-war period.

The most notable change in the lives of married women in the post-war years has been the addition of paid labour to their domestic duties.[7] Students should be aware of the vast transformation in the nature of women's domestic labour. Food preparation, clothing production, laundry and general housework has changed profoundly over the past 40 years, even if the time that women devote to such tasks has not been appreciably reduced.[8] Technological innovations, such as refrigerators, hot and cold running water and telephones, have influenced the domestic workplace as much as they have the factory and office. Books such as Meg Luxton's *Not a Labour of Love* suggest how teachers might aproach the treatment of women's domestic labour in the twentieth century.[9] While it deals with the experience of women in the resource town of Flin Flon, Manitoba, our mothers and grandmothers in the Maritimes would almost certainly recognize the washday tasks, family crisis management and isolation experienced by these women.

---

6   For a discussion of marriage patterns in one Maritime Province see Douglas F. Campbell and David C. Neice, *Ties That Bind — Structure and Marriage in Nova Scotia* (Port Credit, Ont., 1979).

7   For a general discussion of women's work in Canada since the Second World War see Pat and Hugh Armstrong, *The Double Ghetto: Canadian Women and Their Segregated Work* (rev. ed., Toronto, 1985).

8   Susan Clark and Andrew S. Harvey, "The Sexual Division of Labour: The Use of Time", *Atlantis*, 2/1 (Fall 1976), pp. 46-66.

9   Meg Luxton, *More Than A Labour of Love: Three Generations of Women's Work in the Home* (Toronto, 1980).

Accompanying the transformation of the domestic sphere was a movement of married women into the paid labour force. Prior to the Second World War, women entered the paid labour force between leaving school and marriage. On the eve of the Second World War few married women held wage paying jobs in the Maritimes or elsewhere in North America. Now nearly 50 per cent of married women earn a wage. It is important to explain to students the way in which the division of labour in the public sphere reflects those tasks assigned to women in the private sphere and how differential wages for women and men were justified prior to the 1970s.[10] Women still face a job market where they can expect to earn wages which are one-third less than those paid to men and they share with Maritime men the problems associated with high regional unemployment rates. Students should be aware that equal pay laws are only a recent reform and that equal pay for work of equal value is as yet an elusive ideal.

Women's creativity, like that of men, has long been closely associated with productive work. In the curious evolution of the market economy, women's creativity has been called a 'craft' while men's efforts have been elevated to the status of an 'art'. If we ignore labels and received canons, we quickly come to appreciate the artistic merit of Micmac quillwork, Acadian hooked rugs and the magnificent quilts made by women all over the region.[11] In more formal areas of creativity, Maritime women have long been an even match for their male counterparts. Women visual artists are too numerous to mention. The names of Lucy Maud Montgomery, Margaret Marshall Saunders and Antonine Maillet are only the most obvious of an impressive list of female creative writers from the region. Literature written by both men and women is, of course, a useful barometer of the role and status of women in a society, a topic which can profitably be raised whenever regional literature is under discussion.

Women's culture is obviously more than art, crafts and literature.

10 Several useful articles on women's labour force participation in the Maritime Provinces include: Patricia M. Connelly and Martha MacDonald, "Women's Work: Domestic and Wage Labour in a Nova Scotia Community", *Studies in Political Economy*, 10 (Winter 1983), pp. 45-72: Gina Vance and Anne Bishop, "No Lobster for Lizmore" in Jennifer Penney, ed., *Hard Earned Wages: Women Fighting For Better Work* (Toronto, 1983), pp. 41-73; Joan McFarland, "Changing Modes of Social Control in a New Brunswick Fish Packing Town", *Studies in Political Economy*, 4 (Autumn 1980), pp. 99-113. Nanciellen Davis, "Women's Work and Worth in an Acadian Maritime Village" in Naomi Black and Baker Cottrell, eds., *Women and World Change; Equity Issues in Development* (Beverly Hills, 1981), pp. 97-118.

11 Ruth Holmes Whitehead, *Micmac Quillwork: Micmac Indian Techniques of Porcupine Quill Decoration, 1600-1950* (Halifax, 1982); Carter Houck, *Nova Scotia Patchwork Patterns, instructions and full size templates for 12 quilts* (New York, 1981); Joleen Gordon, *With Baskets, Traps and Brooms: traditional crafts in Nova Scotia* (Halifax, 1984).

Women, in fact, have a kind of dual citizenship. They function, as Eliane Silverman has stated, both in a male culture where they are controlled by "tradition, fear, loyalty and love" and in a parallel society of women where actions can range from "intimacy to power".[12] Women in the Maritimes have forged female networks of relatives and friends which serve as a source of comfort and power. These networks and their functions need to be better understood by students and teachers alike.[13] Women have also traditionally been responsible for the socialization of children. The impact of formal education on this process bears scrutiny as does the means by which women transmit values and concerns to their daughters. Women have been the nurturers and nurses in our society as well as the keepers of kinship networks, the letter writers, the compilers of genealogies and the authors of local histories. It is high time that the role of women as scribes, bards and social housekeepers receives the public analysis it deserves.

In the area of formal politics, all the women who have sat in regional and federal legislatures have done so in the period since 1945. Gladys Porter of Kings County, Nova Scotia, claims the distinction of being the first woman in the region to hold provincial office. Women, of course, have less formal ways of effecting political change and a discussion of the avenues of power for the dispossessed should not be excluded from our textbooks. Voluntary organizations, women's auxiliaries, public protest, the vote itself give women the means, albeit limited ones, of exercising influence. Maritime women were among the first in the world to break down the doors of higher education;[14] they were the initiators of social welfare measures;[15] they were among the first Canadian voices to be heard in the call for a peaceful end to cold war politics;[16] and they are leaders in the debate on the issues of human life. Women's roles in these movements, indeed the very movements themselves, are often omitted from official histories. There is no obvious reason why this should be so. That we have excluded such political matters from our texts says more about the gate-

---

12 Eliane Leslau Silverman, "Writing Canadian Women's History 1970-82: an Historiographical Analysis", *Canadian Historical Review*, LXIII (1982), p. 521.

13 For a general discussion of women's culture in the Maritime context see Margaret Conrad, "'Sundays Always Make Me Think of Home': Time and Place in Canadian Women's History" in Barbara K. Latham and Roberta J. Pazdro, eds., *Not Just Pin Money: Selected Essays on the History of Women's Work in British Columbia* (Victoria, 1984), pp. 1-14.

14 John G. Reid, "Education of Women at Mount Allison, 1854-1914", *Acadiensis*, XII/2 (Spring 1983), pp. 3-33.

15 Christina Simmons, "'Helping the Poorer Sisters': The Women of the Jost Mission, Halifax, 1905-1945", *Acadiensis*, XIV/1 (Autumn 1984), pp. 3-27.

16 "Voice of Women Dialogue", *Atlantis*, 6/2 (Spring 1981), pp. 168-76.

keeping function of the educational system than it does about women.[17]

It is important that the structures which serve to exclude women from equality in Maritime society be recognized and analyzed. There is no better place to start than with Helen Creighton's research on the region's folklore.[18] There we find that women and pigs are not welcome on board ship and that women who attempt to transcend their 'proper sphere' are accused of being in league with the devil. The survival of ribald jokes about old maids and difficult wives testifies to a misogyny deeply rooted in our culture. Students also need to be introduced to the whole issue of language.[19] It never ceases to amaze me to hear students and colleagues stumbling over the word 'girl', 'women' and 'lady' while they have no difficulty talking about men — young men, old men, dirty men, handsome men or just plain men. Gentlemen and boys never inspire their tongues. The 'generic' he/ him does not include women and never did. These are not trivial matters. We no longer consider it appropriate to talk of 'niggers', 'savages', and 'frogs' when discussing Blacks, Indians and French Canadians. It is, quite simply, inappropriate to call grown women, 'girls' and working women, 'ladies'. The interchangeability of such terms indicates a confusion about women that is reflected even in the language we use. Other ways of excluding women are less subtle. Until the 1960s professional schools in the region had a quota of 7 per cent for women permitted to study law, medicine and dentistry. Prior to the 1970s women were paid less than men for doing the same job and various laws not only sanctioned but even encouraged the exploitation of women in marriage and in the labour force.[20] Violence against women went unacknowledged and unpunished.

The evidence of women's second class status and their anguish in the face of a systematic discrimination is found in our public records and private papers. We only have to learn to recognize it when we see it. Consider, for instance, this letter written in 1952 to George Nowlan, the Member of Parliament of Digby-Annapolis-Kings:

As a married school teacher for Kings County I would like to ask your advice on a very important matter. We the married teachers of

---

17 Dale Spender, "The Gatekeepers: a feminist critique of academic publishing", in Helen Roberts, ed., *Doing Feminist Research* (London, 1981), pp. 186-202.

18 See, for instance, *Bluenose Ghosts* (Toronto, 1957); *Bluenose Magic: Popular Beliefs and Superstitions in Nova Scotia* (Toronto, 1968); *Folklore of Lunenburg County Nova Scotia* (Ottawa, 1950). A useful bibliography can be found in Herbert Halpert, ed., *A Folklore Sampler from the Maritimes* (St. John's, 1982).

19 See Wendy R. Katz, *Her and His: Language of Equal Value* (Halifax, 1981); Dale Spender, *Man Made Language* (London, 1980).

20 See, for example, Susan Perley, *Women and the Law in Nova Scotia* (Halifax, 1976).

Kings thought that probably you could help us, that is give us some advice.

Probably you knew that the municipality of Kings had $16,000 to give to the teachers of Kings as a bonus for the coming year. It is distributed in this way: $300 for each married male teacher, $150 for each single teacher and $60 for each permissive teacher. The married women teachers get nothing because the counsellers said they did not need it. What other occupation is paid according to their needs? I thought in this democratic country of ours it was equal pay for equal work and license.

If our present government could only recognize the fact the teachers are under paid at present it would save a lot of trouble in the future. When once we are affiliated with labor then they will say what is wanted and will get it.

We realize you have nothing to do with this matter but wish you did.

Kindly reply and advise us what you think we should do to try to get our equal share of this money alloted to the teachers of Kings. Many of the married teachers needs the raise as well as the single and married men.

Thanking you for your interest in the school teachers of Kings Co.[21]

In the light of such evidence, it is imperative that our textbooks include a discussion of discrimination against women and the steps taken by women to oppose it. The regional debate over the status of women has been long and harrowing, borrowing when appropriate from the global women's movement. Teachers seriously interested in making women part of the curriculum should keep up to date on the literature in the field of women's studies as well as regional developments. In particular they should have access to the journal *Canadian Women's Studies* published since 1978. A bilingual journal aimed specifically at high school teachers and students, *Canadian Women's Studies* publishes thematic issues four times a year. The Fall 1982 issue, "Growing into Womanhood", is of value to all teachers who have teenage women in their classrooms. The article by Peter McLaren, "Being Tough: Rituals of Resistance in the Culture of Working Class Schoolgirls" is particularly relevant to Maritime schools, which often perpetuate a culture of sexism, racism, violence and failure. Other articles discuss teenage pregnancy and suicide, sexism in rock and roll music, positive peer culture and that perennial red herring: sex-linked

21 _____ to Nowlan, 2 June 1952, George Nowlan Papers, Acadia University Archives.

learning differences. Other issues focus on everything from women and development to literature and art. Also useful is *Resources for Feminist Research*, published since 1972.

Two recent issues on "Women and Education" provide useful information on films for classroom use and where to get ready-made curriculum ideas. *RFR* also publishes bibliographies of international materials on gender issues relevant to the classroom. More specialized sources include the periodicals *Atlantis*, *The International Journal of Women's Studies*, *Room at the Top*, and *Fireweed*, the latter of which devoted a special issue in the Spring of 1984 to "Atlantic" Women. *The History and Social Science Teacher* also occasionally publishes on topics relevant to women's studies. In addition, teachers should have their schools take out a membership in Canadian Research Institute for the Advancement of Women so that they will be on the mailing list for CRIAW's many useful monographs. Similarly, they will benefit from the literature which comes from the Canadian Advisory Council on the Status of Women and from the various provincial women's bureaus. All teachers will find useful the NFB's fine films on women, many of them produced in Studio D which has a special mandate to produce films on women's issues.

A new alternative publication, *Pandora*, published in Halifax, focuses on contemporary issues relating to women. The *Atlantic Voice of Women Peace Letter* and *Common Ground: A Journal for Island Women* also offer valuable regional perspectives. The persevering teacher can check for new historical material in "Recent Publications Relating to the History of Atlantic Canada" found in each issue of *Acadiensis*. Eric Swanick and his colleagues are adept at tracking down even the most obscure references. Regional journals such as *Acadiensis*, *The Nova Scotia Historical Quarterly*, *Les Cahiers*, *Egalité*, *Cape Breton's Magazine*, *The New Maritimes* and *The Island Magazine*, provide occasional evidence of women's voice in the region's development. Organizations such as the Société Saint-Thomas d'Aquin, the Nova Scotia Museum, Parks Canada and the Centre d'Etudes Acadiennes in Moncton publish monographs on the history and culture of Maritime women. Sadly, there is nothing in the Maritimes equivalent to Memorial University's Centre for the Study of Folklore and Culture which has inspired so many useful studies of women. The lack of a centre or a journal to focus historical research on Maritime women means that the teacher must scramble for evidence. It can be found in David Frank's article on "The Miner's Financier", [22] Sylvia Hamilton's piece on Black women of Nova Scotia,[23] Isabelle McKee-Allain and Huguette

---

22 *Atlantis*, 8/2 (Spring 1983), pp. 137-43.
23 Sylvia Hamilton, "Our Mothers Grand and Great: Black Women of Nova Scotia", *Canadian Women's Studies*, 4/2 (Winter 1982), pp. 32-7.

Clavette on Acadian women in New Brunswick,[24] Ron Caplan's interview with a World War I war bride,[25] Ernest Forbes' work on Maritime suffragists,[26] the study of Ellice B. Gonzalez on the economic roles of Micmac women and men,[27] and the analyses of diary literature by Toni Laidlaw, Donna Smyth and myself.[28] Many of these publications refer to the pre-1945 period but together they offer useful models for studying the lives of Maritime Women in the twentieth century.

The underdeveloped state of Maritime history as it relates to women requires that teachers be particularly creative in developing class projects. For senior students, a comparison of L.M. Montgomery's public and private life highlights the problems of a woman pursuing a career in the early twentiety century.[29] A project which can be geared to any level is an oral history of older women in the family or community. By developing interview questions around women's life cycle and work patterns, students will learn to sense change over time in education, courtship patterns, family size, domestic and paid labour. A project developed around the role of women as portrayed on television, in movies and in rock music would offer scope for discussion of gender roles and how they are defined and reproduced in our culture.[30] For a particularly mature class, a discussion of 'jokes' could bring students to the understanding of how humour and ridi-

---

24 Isabelle McKee-Allain and Huguette Clavette, "Les femmes acadiennes du Nouveau-Brunswick: feminité, sous-developpement et ethnicité", *Egalité*, 10 (automne 1983), pp. 19-35. See also Betty Dugas-Leblanc, *Etude sur les besoins des femmes francophones en Nouvelle-Ecosse* (Halifax, 1981); Edith Commeau Tufts, *Acadiennes de Clare* (n.p., 1977); Thérèse Lemieux and Gemma Caron, *Silhouettes Acadiennes* (Campbellton, 1981).

25 "Gwen Lefort, War Bride in WWI", *Cape Breton's Magazine*, 35, pp. 47-52.

26 Ernest Forbes, "The Ideas of Carol Bacchi and The Suffragists of Halifax: A Review Essay", *Atlantis*, 10/2 (Spring 1985), pp. 119-25.

27 Ellice B. Gonzalez, *Changing Economic Roles for Micmac Men and Women: an Ethnohistorical Analysis* (Ottawa, 1981).

28 Margaret Conrad, "Recording Angels: The Private Chronicles of Women from the Maritime Provinces of Canada, 1750-1950", in Alison Prentice and Susan Mann Trofimenkoff, eds., *The Neglected Majority, Vol II* (Toronto, 1985), pp. 41-60. This essay was originally published by the Canadian Research Institute for the Advancement of Women as #4 in the series The CRIAW Papers.

29 The sources on L.M. Montgomery's life are many and varied. Readers would do well to begin with Mollie Gillen, *The Wheel of Things: A Biography of L.M. Montgomery* (Toronto, 1975); F.W.P. Bolger and Elizabeth R. Epperly, eds., *My Dear Mr. M.: Letters to G.B. MacMullen from L.M. Montgomery* (Toronto, 1980); Mary Rubio and Elizabeth Waterston, eds., *The Selected Journals of L.M. Montgomery* (Toronto, 1985).

30 Molly Haskell, *From Reverence to Rape: The Treatment of Women in the Movies* (New York, 1974); Deborah Harding and Emily Nett, "Women and Rock Music", *Atlantis*, 10/1 (Autumn 1984), pp. 60-76.

cule are used to keep subordinate groups in their places. Asking students to voice 'swear words' frequently elicits a list of chauvinist epithets which can be used to point out some obvious features in our culture.

Those wanting to offer public role models, both conventional and otherwise, for their students will find no lack of worthy candidates. Students can be sent a-sleuthing for information about the region's female politicians, professionals, writers, artists, community pillars and activists. People such as Alexa MacDonough, Muriel Duckworth, Anna Mae Asquash, Portia White, Edith Butler, Angele Arsenault, Rita MacNeil, Margaret Perry, Muriel Fergusson come immediately to mind. There are many others. A discussion of women's life choices in light of the changing conditions of women in the post-war period could be very important in equipping them to face the world of the 1980s in which 1 in 3 marriages ends in divorce, 1 in 10 women will be a battered wife, 1 in 5 will live below the poverty line, and the life expectancy is approaching 80 years. Though a study of the past offers no solution to our present dilemmas, it does provide a useful perspective on them.

15 Studying Maritime Women's Work: Underpaid, Unpaid, Invisible, Invaluable

Martha MacDonald

YOUNG WOMEN ENTERING UNIVERSITY today display a shocking naivite about the socio-economic role and status of women in our society. Their ideas are a confused mixture of youthful idealism, girlish romanticism, advertising images and political rhetoric that mostly assures us that we've "come a long way, baby". Their ideal seems to be personified by television images of attractive women with successful careers, loving, handsome husbands and smart kids, and very shiny kitchen floors. These images seem to obscure the reality they may have observed in their own families and communities. They want careers, though few of their mothers had careers; they expect to be lawyers and accountants, though there are few examples of women in these roles in their communities; they expect to live happily ever after with a man, despite evidence about divorce rates; and they expect to be able to rely on a male income if their own efforts fail, despite evidence that the majority of women spend part of their lives in poverty when marriages fail or husbands die. They seem to accept that they will bear the ultimate responsibility for childcare and housework, without considering how that will affect their careers.

These young women are extremely reluctant to deal with any of the evidence indicating inequality or discrimination. They mostly accept the view that women have separate but equal roles, or else they see inequality as something of the past — pre-dating women's liberation. If women earn less than men, it must mean they are less educated or diligent or committed to work. If women work in a few low-paying occupations, that is their choice. If many of their high school friends dropped out of school, went to work in the fish plant, took hairdressing courses, or got pregnant, that is simply their own fault — bad choice, bad luck, or bad planning.

I realize that my sample is somewhat biased in favour of ambitious, intelligent, privileged women — women entering non-traditional careers in business. But these women have learned nothing in school to help them critically analyze their own prospects, constraints, choices — and to appreciate the constrained choices of others. It is crucial that a knowledge of the economic and social position of women be gained at an earlier age. I begin to hit home with my students when I show them evidence that female graduates with commerce degrees are already making $3,000 per year less than their male counterparts, two years after graduation. Can this be true nowadays? They are amazed when we study the early formal restrictions on women's access to education and paid work — and they are surprised to see remnants of those restrictions today. They have little knowledge of how gains have been made by the struggles of individuals and groups of women. They also have little knowledge or appreciation of the *economic* content of the role women play as wives and mothers and craftspeople and community volunteers. That work is invisible to them, as it is to society in general, and they undervalue it. Romantic notions of marriage and child rearing naturally dominate at this age, but we could sorely use some *informed* romanticism.

The need is there for many and varied courses on Maritime women — and the materials and research are there to support such programs. My focus in this paper is how a junior high school curriculum on Maritime Studies could serve the needs of young people to understand the role women play in our economy, and the complex interrelationships of work and non-work gender roles.

I will discuss four related aspects of studying Maritime women and their work. First, in any study of work in the Maritimes there must be explicit inclusion of the paid work of women and an examination of inequalities in the labour market. Students must learn the evidence and begin to question *why* the inequalities exist. Second, the work women do *outside* the labour market needs to be examined and its economic contribution recognized. Women's work in the home stretches the pay cheques of male workers, supports the unemployed, disabled and elderly, produces goods and services, contributes to the incomes of male farmers and fishermen, and educates the future labour force, to name just a few of the unpaid services rendered. Students will quickly recognize that though these activities are important and have economic value, they are not generally rewarded or valued in our economy. The only pay comes from the voluntary sharing by individual men of *their* pay cheques — a sharing which has proven extremely unreliable, contributing to the tremendous economic insecurity as well as dependence of women. Students will very quickly move to the third aspect of analysing women's work in our economy, and that is to examine the relationship between paid and unpaid work, social and economic roles, or domestic and wage labour, as it is referred to in the literature. They need to understand how the economy as a whole may benefit from this dual labour of women and how at the same time it involves the real subordination of women. The fourth aspect involves moving from an understanding of what has been, or is, the economic situation of women to issues of altering that situation. Policy issues such as day care, affirmative action and equal pay can be discussed. The role of unions and women's groups in making gains for women can be examined.

With each of these four aspects, it is essential that a historical approach be taken, so that students will have a knowledge of past struggles and accomplishments, the origin of current obstacles, and the deep-seated nature of the inequalities. Finally, it is important that local material be incorporated into the program. A course on Maritime women must be a hands-on project, with teachers and students gathering evidence from their own communities.

There has been a lot of work done in the last fifteen years in Canada examining the situation of women in the labour market. Excellent statistical summaries are published by Labour Canada Women's Bureau and by Statistics Canada. In these publications there are also some breakdowns by province. Unfortunately, the situation of women is equally bad across the country; so national data provides a picture which applies fairly well to the Maritimes. If anything, the Maritime situation is slightly worse than the Canadian average. Teachers can use Statistics Canada publications such as *The Labour Force* (monthly) and the Census, or provincial Department of Labour publications for provincial data related to women and work. A very useful resource in Nova Scotia is the *Women and Work Kit*, prepared in 1982 with a grant from Secretary of State. This kit has separate study programs on *Women and the Economy*, *Women and Unions*, *Equal Value*, and *Childcare*. Each program summarizes data and research on the topic and includes suggested course outlines and handouts. It was aimed at a general audience and should be well-suited for use at the high school level.[1]

The statistical evidence has focussed on three dimensions of women's labour market experience compared with men's. First, aspects of labour force participation are examined. What proportion of women are in the labour force, either employed or unemployed? How does this vary by marital status, and by number and age of children, and by husband's income? How has it changed over the years? The changes have obviously been dramatic, with participation rates now over 50 percent in Canada (and approaching 50 percent in the Maritimes), compared with 14 percent in 1901 and 38 percent as late as 1970. Recent Canadian figures show that the participation rate is well over 50 percent for women of all ages up to age 55. Young women today can thus expect to spend a great part of their lives in the workforce. Even the majority of women with preschool children and intact marriages are in the labour force.

1 The *Women and Work Kit* is available through the Secretary of State Women's Program (Halifax), Canadian Union of Public Employees (Halifax), Nova Scotia Federation of Labour (Halifax), Women's Employment Outreach (Halifax), Lunenburg County Women's Group, Cape Breton College Resource Centre (Sydney), St. Francis Xavier Extension Department (Antigonish) and the Counselling Centre, Acadia University.

The second focus of statistical evidence is on what kinds of jobs women hold. Approximately one-quarter of employed women across Canada (and in the Maritimes) work part-time, a figure that has been increasing rapidly in the last decade. Nonetheless, two-thirds of employed women with pre-school children and intact marriages still work full-time. Furthermore, fully one-quarter of married women who work part-time do so because that was the only job they could find. The single most important characteristic of the jobs women hold in the labour market is their concentration in a narrow range of occupations and industries. Despite the dramatic changes in *numbers* of working women, what most women do has changed very little. More than two-thirds of women are still clerical workers, saleswomen, service workers (waitresses, cleaners), nurses or teachers. Despite the attention given to women entering non-traditional fields, the reality of where *most* women work has not changed.

The final area of emphasis in statistical evidence is on the earnings of women relative to men. Again, there has been remarkably little progress made in closing the wage gap. The average annual earnings of full-time female workers have been in the order of 60 percent of those of their male counterparts since the turn of the century. For Canada, in 1982, the ratio was 64 percent; it was 78 percent for those in their mid-twenties and declined to 62 percent for those age 55-64. The ratio ranged from 54 percent in product fabrication, to 68 percent in professional occupations. A study done by Statistics Canada in 1976 of university graduates showed that wages of women were below those of men in virtually *every* narrowly defined field, two years after graduation.

There is other evidence to draw on in studying the paid work of women in the Maritimes. McFarland and Connelly and MacDonald have done case studies of fish plant work and Osberg and Wein of clerical work. The Marginal Work World Research Programme at Dalhousie's Institute of Public Affairs, conducted in the late 1970s, produced many papers on work in the Maritimes which have good information and analysis of women's employment patterns, wages and working conditions.[2] Lois Stevenson, at Acadia, has done research on women and small business in the Maritimes. The Institute for the Study of Women at Mount Saint Vincent is also doing considerable research related to women and work in the Maritimes. There are also historical accounts of women's work in the Maritimes. Magazines such as *Cape Breton's Magazine* often publish stories of working women in the past. A recent article in *Acadiensis* by Christina Simmons portrays poor working women in Halifax in the early

2   A complete list of publications from the Marginal Work World Research Programme may be obtained by writing to the MWW Research Programme, Insititue of Public Affairs, Dalhousie University, Halifax, N.S.

twentieth century, and the social attitudes towards these women. Some information can also be found in the more general Canadian historical accounts of working women, and the journals *Labour/Le Travailleur*, *Atlantis* and *Acadiensis* are good sources for teachers. The index to periodical articles on women published by the Canadian Research Institute for the Advancement of Women will be a great help in keeping up with the literature.

An examination of the record of women's paid work and the inequalities that exist today raises many, many questions. Students must be encouraged to begin searching for explanations. Why are women crowded into a few occupations? Students will recognize the similarity of some of these occupations to work women do in the home and to traditional notions of women's proper place. Why is women's work low paying? Women's earnings are lower than men's both when jobs are virtually the same and when jobs are different, but of similar skill. Lower wages are related to both crowding and wage discrimination. How can we explain women's increased labour force participation? How has the economy been changing so that more women are needed in the workforce and more women need to work? Students should understand that economic need has forced both single and married women to seek paid work, and that the paid work of women keeps many families out of poverty. Students should understand that the expansion of jobs in recent years has been in the service sector — an expansion of the traditional female job ghettos.

There are many easily accessible sources of more detailed explanations of the inequalities, which can be used by teachers to improve their own understanding. These authors focus on the way the inequalities are deeply imbedded in our economy, and are quite resistant to change. *The Double Ghetto* provides a good overview of explanations of gender inequality and there are useful sources by Connelly, MacDonald, and Phillips. Since women are not the only low-wage workers in the Maritmes, it is important to examine the causes and functions of low-wage work in general. The Marginal Work World Programme is a good resource on all aspects of low-wage work in the Maritimes. Furthermore, students must examine how women's experiences in the labour market are also related to their class, racial and ethnic status.

As soon as one begins to explain the position of women in the paid labour force, one starts talking about their role *outside* the labour force. Most explanations reduce in one way or another to the primacy of women's role as wife/mother. Housework and childcare are seen as women's responsibility in our society, and this has limited — and continues to limit — the conditions under which they participate in the work force.

The work of women in the home is isolated, often invisible, and generally unrecognized as real work. It is something private, but as the title of Meg Luxton's excellent book suggests, this work is *More Than a Labour of Love*. A course on Maritime Studies, particularly with a focus on work, must examine this unpaid work of women. Childbearing and housework support the economy and corporations, not just serve individual children and individual husbands. Why is this work not recognized or valued, in any other than a condescending "motherhood and apple pie" way? How has the work done in the home changed over the years? How does it differ by class, or by occupation of the husband? Many of the jobs women used to do for free are now part of the paid economy, with mass-produced food, clothes and so on. Care of old people, sick people and education of children have been taken over by the state. However, cutbacks in these service areas are putting the work back on women who will do for free what was recently done for pay by other women. Learning to *recognize* the work is important. Students can estimate what it would cost to buy all the services that their mothers typically provide. Research has been done using Halifax data measuring the amount of work in terms of *time*, by Clark and Harvey. Another area to examine is the way women's work contributes in sectors such as farming and fishing, where we think of independent fishermen and farmers. Not only are they not very independent in the Maritimes, in terms of real control over their prices or their lives, they are *especially* not very independent from their wives. The work of farm wives and fishermen's wives is essential to the business, yet until recently their contributions were not recognized when the assets were divided. Case studies are being done in the Maritimes of the economic contributions of women in these rural communities. The work of fishermen's wives, for example, is being researched in Prince Edward Island and Nova Scotia.

Another way women contribute to the economy is through volunteer activities — doing for free work that otherwise would go undone or have to be paid for. Students can undertake projects to try to measure all of this unpaid output in their communities and how it changes over time.

Having examined women as paid workers, and women as unpaid workers in the home, the linkages start to become obvious. Women's experience in the labour market is closely related to their role in the home. Many traditional female jobs are extensions of work women do in the home — nurses, teachers, waitresses, cooks, cleaners, textile workers and food processors, for example. Perhaps their low pay reflects in part the low respect accorded women's work in the home. Women have always been paid less, and this has often been justified by their dependence on other (male) earners. They have been perceived as working for "pin money", even though that perception has been wrong for most women workers since the earliest days. Other explanations of women's lower wages stress that they lack a long term commitment to work, so that everyone from employers to unions has systematically bypassed them. Today, when the female business graduate competes for a management job with a male, she may be turned down because the employer fears she will not stay in the workforce long, or will not be mobile.

Changes in women's labour force participation rates reflect changes in the economy and its effects on the household. It is often argued that women have been a convenient reserve labour force, drawn into the labour force when there is need, as in wartime, or when male workers become too demanding. It is also clear that many jobs women once did in the home are now in the market and women have followed that work out of the home. Also, the development of a service economy requires families to have more cash income. Women have always made ends meet in households, only now they must do this by earning wages, for the options of home production are increasingly unable to meet today's household needs.

A final link between paid and unpaid work is that even as more and more women try to participate equally with men in the labour force, the fact remains that the majority of housework and childcare is still the responsibility of women. Women have a double day, a double burden, a double shift, a double ghetto. The resistance women meet when they try to change this, and the *slowness* of it to change, are indications of how the economy as a whole, and men in particular may benefit from this dual labour of women. The structure subordinates women, giving them unequal power, status and incomes. As long as women must do the unpaid household work they will be unable to compete equally in the labour market, and vice versa. It is a vicious circle for women which cannot easily be broken.

The final component of a study of women in Maritime society, or a study of Maritime society that includes women, must be to examine steps taken or needed to achieve greater equality. The list of current work-related policy issues in the Maritimes includes maternity/paternity leave provisions and the need for good daycare services. These policies recognize the effect that household responsibilities have on women's ability to compete equally in the workplace. The *Women and Work Kit* contains good information on the daycare issue in Nova Scotia. A related issue is cutbacks in government spending on social programs, which shift extra burdens onto women in the home. Other policy issues concern the conditions women face in the labour market. Students need to know how much legally sanctioned discrimination has existed in the Maritimes — everything from paying married women less, to denying jobs to married women, to having different pay rates for men and women, to restricting access of women to educational programs. Students need to know the existing laws prohibiting discriminatory hiring or the paying of unequal wages for equal work. They also need to know why many Maritime women think these laws do not go far enough, and are arguing for Equal Pay for Work of Equal Value and affirmative action policies. Only by these means can deep seated systematic patterns of discrimination be altered. One of the best discussions of the Equal Pay issue is in the *Women and Work Kit*, a whole section of which is devoted to this issue and related legislative means of reducing inequality. Other important concerns include health and safety, particularly the use of video display terminals, benefits for part-time workers, and the effects of technological change on women in the labour force. The likely effects on women of the recently declared Charter of Rights should also be discussed. A useful resource on legal questions relevant for women in Nova Scotia is the pamphlet *Understanding the Law.*

Legislation is not the only avenue used by women to improve their situation. Unions in recent years have been a means for working women to make gains, and an arena of struggle. There have been several recent attempts by working women in the Maritimes to organize, particularly in the retail trade and service industries. For example, the recent Keddy's Nursing Home strike mainly involved women, and the Union of Bank Employees has had some small success organizing bank workers in the Maritimes, against aggressive opposition by the banks. Hospital workers, grocery store clerks, hotel workers, building cleaners and fish plant workers are all trying to improve their situations through unionization. I am sure many local union members would be happy to speak to classes, or provide information. Many of these union efforts are documented in the newspaper *New Maritimes*. Unions have also produced some of the best educational materials on women and work — from movies to slide tape shows to course outlines. The provincial Federations of Labour have women's committees which can be contacted for more information. The *Women and Work Kit* also has a section on "Women and Unions", with suggested audio-visual resources.

Finally, no discussion of efforts for change for women in the Maritimes would be complete without crediting the work of innumerable women's groups organizing on a broad range of issues throughout our history. Current examples include the Voice of Women, Women's Health Education Network (WHEN), Canadian Council on Learning Opportunities for Women (CCLOW), Canadian Research Institute for the Advancement of Women (CRIAW), women's centres, rape crisis centres and transition houses, to name only a few. A recent publication by the International Education Centre at Saint Mary's University tries to list all women's organizations in the region. These groups are important agents of change, and they provide useful resources for the classroom. Speakers can be brought in and pamphlets and briefs can be collected and discussed. Too often these types of groups are overlooked in accounts of political activity in the region. The new women's newspaper, *Pandora*, will help us keep up with the organizations, and the struggles. It should be subscribed to by all school libraries in the region.

It is impossible to adequately cover in one short paper all the important questions, issues and resources related to the study of women in the Maritimes. I have only sketched the bare bones of studying the work of women and analysing their economic position. This economic aspect must be combined with the social and cultural aspects of women's lives. There is a pressing need for an integrated study of women in the Maritimes at the junior high school level. The need is not just an academic one. It is a need in terms of the personal development of a generation of young women and men. By the time they reach university, life plans and prejudices are already well in place. If knowledge is power, we need to provide that knowledge early on.

There are two essential components to that knowledge, in terms of curriculum development. First, there must be an explicit examination of the interrelated economic and social roles of women and an analysis of the subordination of women in our society. Just as students are taught mathematics because it will help them in later life, so students deserve a serious analysis of gender to equip them for life in the non-romantic real world. Second, information on women must be integrated into *all* aspects of Maritime Studies, whether it is history, English, ethnic studies, politics, or economics. Women must be made visible. Such curriculum development will be no easy task, I am sure, but resources are there and they are developing at an increasing rate. I firmly believe that in this matter demand will create its own supply. I look forward to the day when my students at university have graduated from such a program.

SELECTED BIBLIOGRAPHY

A. *References on Maritime (or Atlantic) Women and Work*

Antler, Ellen, "Women's Work in Newfoundland Fishing Families", *Atlantis*, 2/2 (Spring 1977), pp. 106-13.

Clark, Susan and Harvey, Andrew, "The Sexual Division of Labour: The Use of Time", *Atlantis*, 2/1 (Fall 1976), pp. 46-65.

Connelly, M.P. and MacDonald, Martha, "Women's Work: Domestic and Wage Labour in a Nova Scotia Community", *Studies in Political Economy*, No. 10 (1983), pp. 45-72.

International Education Centre, *The Atlantic Catalogue of Development Groups and Organizations for Women* (Halifax, 1985).

McFarland, Joan, "Changing Modes of Social Control in a New Brunswick Fish Packing Town", *Studies in Political Economy*, No. 4 (1980), pp. 99-114.

Nova Scotia Association of Women and the Law, *Understanding the Law: A Guide for Women in Nova Scotia* (Halifax, 1981).

Osberg, Lars and Wein, Fred, "Intra-Occupational Stratification and the Allocation of Individuals to Training Programs: The Case of Office Employment", Paper presented to the Canadian Sociology and Anthropology Association, Saskatoon, June 1979 (available from the IPA, Dalhousie University).

Porter, Marilyn, "'A Tangly Bunch': The Political Culture of Outport Women in Newfoundland", *Labour/Le Travail,* No. 15 (1985), pp. 105-24.

Simmons, Christina, "'Helping the Poorer Sisters': The Women of the Jost Mission, Halifax, 1905-1945", *Acadiensis*, XIV/1 (Autumn 1984), pp. 3-27.

Stevenson, Lois, "The Study of Entrepreneurship", *Journal of Small Business Canada*, 2/4 (Spring 1985), pp. 40-9.

Reid, John G., "The Education of Women at Mount Allison, 1854-1914", *Acadiensis*, XII/2 (Spring 1983), pp. 3-33.

Wein, Fred, *Socio-Economic Characteristics of the Micmac in Nova Scotia* (Halifax, 1983).

B. *References on Women and Work in Canada*

Abella, Roaslie Silberman, *Report of the Royal Commission on Equality in Employment* (Ottawa, 1984).

Acton, Janice and Shepard, Bonnie, eds., *Women at Work: Ontario 1850-1930* (Toronto, 1974).

Armstrong, Pat, "Women and Unemployment", *Atlantis*, 5/1 (Autumn 1980), pp. 1-16.

Armstrong, Pat and Armstrong, Hugh, *A Working Majority: What Women Must Do for Pay* (Ottawa, 1983).

_____, *The Double Ghetto: Canadian Women and Their Segregated Work* (Toronto, 1984).

Atlantis, "Special Issue on Domestic Labour and Wage Labour", 7/1 (Fall 1981).

Boulet, Jac-Andre and Lavalee, Level, *The Changing Economic Status of Women* (Ottawa, 1984).

Briskin, Linda and Yanz, Lynda, eds., *Union Sisters* (Toronto, 1983).

Canadian Research Institute for the Advancement of Women, *Canadian Women's Periodicals: Kwic Index* (Toronto, October 1984, March 1985, May 1985).

Conrad, Margaret, "The Re-Birth of Canada's Past: A Decade of Women's History", *Acadiensis*, XII/2 (Spring 1983), pp. 140-61.

Devereaux, M.S. and Rechnitzer, Edith, *Higher Education — Hired?* (Ottawa, 1980).

Economic Council of Canada, *Towards Equity* (Ottawa, 1985).

Labour Canada, Women's Bureau, *Women in the Labour Force* (Ottawa, 1983).

_____, *Part-Time Work in Canada* (Ottawa, 1983a).

Luxton, Meg, *More than a Labour of Love: Three Generations of Women's Work in the Home* (Toronto, 1980).

MacDonald, Martha, "Economics and Feminism: The Dismal Science?", *Studies in Political Economy*, No. 15 (Fall 1984), pp. 151-78.

McFarland, Joan, "Economics and Women: A Critique of the Scope of Traditional Analysis and Research", *Atlantis*, 1/2 (Spring 1976), pp. 26-41.

_____, "Women and Unions: Help or Hindrance", *Atlantis*, 4/2 (Spring 1979), pp. 48-70.

Menzies, Heather, *Women and the Chip: Case Studies of the Effects of Informatics on Employment in Canada* (Montreal, 1981).

National Film Board, *Beyond the Image: A Guide to Films About Women* (Ottawa, 1981).

Phillips, Paul, and Phillips, Erin, *Women and Work* (Toronto, 1983).

Public Services International, *Women in the Public Services* (France, 1985).

Pelletier, Jacqueline, *The Future is Now: Women and the Impact of Microtechnology* (Ottawa, 1983).

Secretary of State Women's Program, *Women's Resource Catalogue* (Ottawa, 1982).

Statistics Canada, *Women in Canada: A Statistical Report* (Ottawa, 1985).

Strong-Boag, Veronica, "Canada's Early Experience with Income Supplements: The Introduction of Mother's Allowances", *Atlantis*, 4/2 Part II (Spring 1979), pp. 35-43.

_____, "Working Women and the State: The Case of Canada, 1889-1945", *Atlantis*, 6/2 (Spring 1981), pp. 1-9.

Weeks, Wendy, "Part-time Work: The Business View on Second-Class Jobs for Housewives and Women", *Atlantis*, 5/2 (Spring, 1980), pp. 69-88.

White, Julie, *Women and Unions* (Ottawa, 1980).

_____, *Women and Part-time Work* (Ottawa, 1983).

16 Discovering Maritime Women: New Developments in the Social Sciences

Sheva Medjuck

IT IS A DIFFICULT TASK TO DETERMINE what should be included under the title "Studying Maritime Women". Indeed, many researchers have argued that in the ideal situation there would be no need for such a separate discussion because women would be fully and completely a part of all aspects of Maritime study and not a unique case to be set aside for "special" treatment. Alas, like the real world, such an ideal state does not exist.

My own experience in teaching courses on women in Canadian society suggests two complementary strategies. One is the historical method whereby we begin to understand ourselves and our contemporary situation first by grasping the experience and lives of our forebearers. While it is a truism that we can better understand the present by understanding the past, nowhere do I think this is more critical than in understanding the role of women in history. Unfortunately, the social sciences have historically not seen or heard women and, with the exception of a growing number of feminist scholars, have treated women as invisible. This is not simple maliciousness on the part of social scientists but rather a model of science which sees its ultimate purpose as understanding the human experience in universal terms. To understand the reality of women's lives and women's experiences contradicts this need for universality. In fact, what has been considered universal has been male science and scholarship. Research that leaves out women clearly does not contribute to our search for universal knowledge.

This recognition may seem obvious. Nevertheless, it is difficult to make the transition from the rigid traditions of social science and to think somewhat differently about our purposes as educators and researchers. An example from my own research on nineteenth-century New Brunswick may serve to clarify this. I conducted a large scale quantitative research project which examined the nineteenth-century census records in order to try to understand the lives of the ordinary people of Moncton Parish in the last century. In this project, a great deal of my energy was expended to gain a clearer understanding of the lives of nineteenth-century men and little energy was spent on understanding women. Following the models of earlier research (many of which totally ignore females altogether), my women remained largely anonymous. In order to rationalize this exclusion from study clear methodological reasons were developed. First, I argued that what I was interested in was an understanding of the development of class as a consequence of industrial expansion. Therefore, I focused on the nature of the labour force: the changing composition of the labour force as a consequence of industrialization, occupational mobility, class consciousness, and so forth. Since women's participation in the paid labour force was limited in the nineteenth-century, women were of only passing interest. This justification was reinforced by other research. For example, Miller argues that because males are "the major breadwinners and carriers of the family's hopes and life chances", females are not included in studies of social stratification.[1] Thernstrom provides a similar rationale for his exclusion of women in his studies of Boston and Newburyport.[2] Although he suggests that while it may perhaps be less true today, he concurs with Miller that the family's hopes and life chances were in the hands of men. This phenomenon is not unique. Women's contribution to history is rarely recorded in the history books. Women have virtually been excluded. Their lives, works, and struggles are inconsequential to historical science.

Second, since women experience a name change upon marriage, they are much more difficult to trace from census to census. Because of this methodological problem, most studies to which I referred simply abandon any extensive discussion of the female experience over time. In additon, those studies which have chosen to focus on women in history have often concentrated their efforts on "notable women". This approach, however, provides us with little information about most women. As Lerner notes:

> The resulting history of "notable women" does not tell us much about those activities in which most women engaged, nor does it tell us about the significance of women's activities to society as a whole. The history of notable women is the history of exceptional, even deviant, women and does not describe the experience and history of the mass of women. This insight is a refinement of an awareness of class differences in history: women of different classes have different historical experiences.[3]

1 S.M. Miller, "Comparative Social Mobility: A Trend Report and Bibliography", *Current Sociology*, 9 (1960), p. 9.

2 Stephen Thernstrom, *Poverty and Progress. Social Mobility in a Nineteenth-Century City* (Cambridge, Mass., 1964) and *The Other Bostonians* (Cambridge, Mass., 1973).

3 Gerda Lerner, "Placing Women in History: Definition and Challenges", *Feminist Studies*, 3/1 (Fall 1975), p. 5.

In subsequent analyses, I have spent a great deal of energy examining the records of nineteenth-century women in order to gain insights into what industrial change meant for their lives.[4] How did they adapt to boom and bust economic cycles? How were their lives transformed and how did they act upon these circumstances? These findings indicate that it is erroneous to assume that the experiences of nineteenth-century women paralleled those of men. Women do not simply fit the empty spaces left in socio-historical analyses. My research on nineteenth-century Moncton provided me with evidence of the role of women as important actors in the unfolding of history. The image that "women were largely passive or that, at the most, they reacted to male pressures or to the restraints of patriarchal society" ignores the importance of women's active functioning in society.[5] The more crucial historical question is no longer the simple debate as to whether women were active or passive but how women have affected the historical conditions.

Having taught a course on the Sociology of Women and also having taught almost exclusively female students at Mount Saint Vincent University, I still am always caught somewhat aback when students seem so totally unaware of the life experiences of their mothers and grandmothers and their active participation in Maritime society. When we talk about women's union activities in the 1930s or women's participation in the war effort, they come back to me to tell me that they talked to their grandmother and "Can you believe it, grandma was a test pilot in the war!" or "Grandma ran the farm all by herself while grandad was overseas!" It is imperative that they see these women as active participants in their society.

I have spent considerable time looking at Maritime women historically. However, the current situation of women in Canada generally and in the Maritimes specifically must be addressed. I am greatly concerned over the complacency of the 1980s, especially among our young people, and the sense that women are no longer unequal. After all we now have the vote!! There is insufficient recognition of the current crisis facing women today in the paid labour force, in the home, and in the culture as a whole.

Increasingly women in our society are finding themselves in the paid labour force. We must impress on young women that most of them for most of their lives will have to work out of economic necessity. They will be responsible for themselves for a good part of their lives. Marriage no longer means leaving the paid labour force forever. Over half of all married women in Canada work. While married women's participation in the paid labour force is slightly below the national average in the Mari-

---

4   Sheva Medjuck, "Women and the Nineteenth-Century Economy, 1851 to 1871", *Atlantis* 10/1 (Fall 1985), pp. 7-21.

5   Lerner, "Placing Women in History", p. 6.

times (for example, 44.8 per cent of married New Brunswick women work compared to 51.9 per cent of all married Canadian women in 1981), this can largely be attributed to the unavailability of jobs rather than attitudinal factors. (Only 72 per cent of New Brunswick married men work as compared to 83.6 per cent of all married Canadian men.) Most women are working out of economic necessity. At least in terms of economics, our young women will not have "men who will take care of them completely". While this increase in the paid labour force participation of women should be heralded as increasing economic independence, many factors mitigate against any enthusiasm for this phenomenon. For while there is increased participation, there is also increased occupational ghettoization. Women are entering "women's" fields, jobs that are usually low pay, low status, low security, often part-time and dead-end. Wage differentials between men and women are large, even within the same occupation. For example, department clerks, largely female, are more poorly paid than liquor store clerks, who are largely male. Ironically, many young people do not recognize that this may occur to them. Things will be different for them. They will not be underpaid, underemployed and squeezed out of their jobs as happens to many women today.

We have looked to the educational institutions to help overcome sexist discrimination, and we have made significant progress. For example, in New Brunswick in 1981 9.2 per cent of all males and 8.9 per cent of all females had university degrees. Indeed, while 11 per cent of males had high school diplomas, 16.9 per cent of females had finished high school in New Brunswick in 1981. Nonetheless, women have been unable to translate their educational advancement into reducing the economic differentials in the labour force. To a great extent this failure can be attributed to the fact that women are still discouraged from so-called non-traditional studies, even at the post-secondary level. Where are the women scientists, the women engineers, the women corporate executives? Our young women are as intelligent, as well or better educated, but undervalued, underemployed and underpaid.

On the home front, we must redefine domestic work as real work and also recognize that it is not the exclusive domain of women. Women who have entered the paid labour force now have two jobs, one outside the home and one inside the home. Men's participation in domestic labour has barely changed despite the dramatic increase in women's labour force participation. It appears that all that is different about men's participation in domestic labour is that women expect more help and men *think* they do more. We must learn to recognize that children have two parents, both of whom can learn caretaking skills.

The culture as a whole compounds this problem. Its influence ranges from the portrayal of women in the media to the language we use. We must recognize the pervasive influence that our culture has over our lives. I am sure that there are millions of women who sit in their living-rooms as they watch the "ring-around-the-collar" commercial and scream at the husband in this commercial "Why don't you ever wash your own shirts? or at least your neck". Are women to be full of self loathing because their family's clothes are not "whiter than white"; are women whose children do not become ecstatic at the wonderful smell of their clothes unfit mothers? Is this what our culture teaches our young people about women's work and men's work?

Finally, culture is expressed through language and our language is an excellent example of how we teach women that they are less than full participants in our society. Throughout my academic career I wondered why I pursued a Bachelor of Arts degree, not a Spinster of Arts; why a Master of Arts not a Mistress of Arts; why I received a fellowship and not a sistership. Closer to home is the whole controversy over the use of he/she and him/her. While such phrasing, it has been argued, sounds awkward, it seems to me more awkward to exclude over 50 per cent of the population in order to conform to archaic grammatical conventions.

In sum, there has been an absence of knowledge about women from either an historical or contemporary perspective. Knowledge has been and is now being created but that is only a first step. It is crucial that we not only make ourselves aware of such knowledge but regard it as important and significant. There is little point in continuing our efforts if our efforts are considered of no consequence. As educators we must work not only to raise consciousness about the position of women in our society but also direct our efforts to work for structural change so that women will be treated equally in all spheres of activity.

SELECTED BIBLIOGRAPHY

Armstrong, Pat and Armstrong, Hugh, *The Double Ghetto* (Toronto, 1978).

—————, *A Working Majority — What Women Must Do For Pay* (Ottawa, 1983).

Armstrong, Pat, *Labour Pains: Women's Work in Crisis* (Toronto, 1984).

Bassett, Isabel, *The Bassett Report: Career Success and Canadian Women* (Toronto, 1985).

Briskin, Linda and Yanz, Lynda, *Union Sisters, Women in the Labour Movement* (Toronto, 1983).

Canadian Advisory Council on the Status of Women, *10 Years Later: An assessment of the Federal Government's Implementation of the Recommendations made by the Royal Commission on the Status of Women* (Ottawa, 1979).

——————, *Women and Unions* (Ottawa, 1980).

Connelly, Patricia, *Last Hired, First Fired: Women and the Canadian Work Force* (Toronto, 1978).

Cook, Gail, ed., *Opportunity for Choice: A Goal for Women in Canada* (Ottawa 1976).

Clark, Lorene and Lewis, Debra, *Rape: The Price of Coercive Sexuality* (Toronto, 1977).

Collins, Kevin, *Women and Pensions* (Ottawa, 1978).

Fox, Bonnie, ed., *Hidden in the Household: Women's Domestic Labour Under Capitalism* (Toronto, 1980).

Henshel, Anne-Marie, *Sex-Structure* (Don Mills, 1973).

Kome, Penny, *Somebody Has To Do It* (Toronto, 1982).

Luxton, Meg, *More Than a Labour of Love — Three Generations of Women's Work in the Home* (Toronto, 1980).

Marchak, Patricia, ed., *The Working Sexes* (Vancouver, 1977).

McClain, J., *Women and Housing* (Toronto, 1982).

Menzies, Heather, *Computer on the Job* (Toronto, 1982).

——————, *Women and the Chip* (Montreal, 1980).

Miles, Angela R. and Finn, Geraldine, *Feminism in Canada: From Pressure to Politics* (Montreal, 1982).

Phillips, Paul and Phillips, Erin, *Women and Work — Inequality in the Labour Market* (Toronto, 1983).

Proulx, Monique, *Five Million Women — A Study of the Canadian Housewife* (Ottawa, 1978).

Stephenson, Marylee, ed., *Women in Canada* (Don Mills, 1977).

Trofimenkoff, Susan Mann and Prentice, Alison, eds., *The Neglected Majority* (Toronto, 1977).

Wilson, S.J., *Women, the Family and the Economy* (Toronto, 1982).

JOURNALS: *Atlantis; Canadian Women's Studies; Fireweed; Health Sharing; Resources for Feminist Research.*

17 *Studying Maritime Politics*

Ian Stewart

A LEADING CANADIAN POLITICAL scientist once concluded that "there are gaps in our ignorance, but not many".[1] Unfortunately, this blunt assessment is particularly applicable to the sub-field of Maritime political studies. Theories about political life in Nova Scotia, New Brunswick, and Prince Edward Island which possess an intuitive plausibility have been accepted on this basis alone; they have not, in general, been subjected to rigorous scrutiny. As a result, what passes for knowledge in Maritime political studies is often little more than an assortment of unsubstantiated suppositions.

Yet one should not necessarily despair at this conclusion. Theories of politics cannot be tested until they have been hypothesized, and observers of Maritime politics have focused our attention on three particularly promising avenues of research. First, to what extent do patterns of political activity cut across provincial boundaries in the Maritime region? Do the similarities between the politics of Nova Scotia, New Brunswick, and Prince Edward Island significantly outweigh the differences? Second, to what degree can political behaviour in the Maritime provinces be differentiated from that which occurs in the rest of Canada and, indeed, elsewhere in the liberal-democratic world? Are Maritime politics idiosyncratic and, if so, what is the essence of this uniqueness? Third, will the politics of Nova Scotia, New Brunswick, and Prince Edward Island continue to exhibit the characteristics with which we are familiar, or will we witness their evolution into altogether different configurations? Each of these questions deserves detailed scrutiny.

Most observers of Maritime politics have little difficulty with the first question and would agree that the politics of the three Maritime provinces are essentially similar. Mildred Schwartz, for example, declared in her study of Canadian regionalism that "in the Atlantic provinces there were no major differences in orientations to the political process", and in a like vein, J. Murray Beck asserted that "because of the similarity of political

---

1   Alan C. Cairns, "National Influences on the Study of Politics", *Queen's Quarterly*, 81 (Autumn, 1974), pp. 333-4.

cultures, Prince Edward Island's elections resemble those in the other Maritime provinces".[2] Is this a valid assessment of the region's politics? Certainly, the list of alleged commonalities between the three provinces is imposing. All have party systems in which only the Liberals and Progressive Conservatives are serious contenders for office. All have elections which are contested on grounds other than political ideology. All have a tradition that "anything goes", that petty electoral corruption and political patronage have either been acceptable or inevitable features of the political process.[3] All have been slow to accept women and ethnic minorities into the political realm, and all have been policy followers, rather than policy innovators. All have voters who tend to be intensely loyal to their party and intensely hostile to political opponents. In the Maritimes, as one longstanding aphorism reminds us, a "mixed marriage" refers to a Tory marrying a Grit.[4] All have governments which, in vain attempts to counter market forces, have spent inordinate sums on economic development programmes. All have electorates which are resentful of Central Canada, suspicious of campaign promises, and generally cynical of all things political. Small wonder, then, that political scientists have been disposed to treat Nova Scotia, New Brunswick and Prince Edward Island as a single political region.

Yet one should be exceedingly cautious about pushing this conception too far. Although there is an impressive catalogue of similarities between the politics of the three provinces, this should not blind us to the substantial and, as yet, largely unexplained, divergences that clearly exist within the Maritime region. New Brunswick, for example, is idiosyncratic in a number of ways. New Brunswickers tend to be less optimistic, less participatory, and less politically interested than their Nova Scotia and Prince Edward Island counterparts.[5] Moreover, New Brunswickers are much less prone to perceive themselves as belonging to an Atlantic political region and much more likely to have stable provincial party identifications.[6] With respect to P.E.I., its voters have historically displayed a unique concern with keeping the two levels of government "in line", with electing provin-

2   Mildred A. Schwartz, *Politics and Territory: The Sociology of Regional Persistence in Canada* (Montreal, 1974), p. 243; J. Murray Beck, "Elections", in David J. Bellamy, Jon H. Pammett, and Donald C. Rowat, eds., *The Provincial Political Systems: Comparative Essays* (Toronto, 1976).

3   J. Murray Beck, *The Government of Nova Scotia* (Toronto, 1957), pp. 265-6.

4   D. Campbell and R.A. MacLean, *Beyond the Atlantic Roar: A Study of the Nova Scotia Scots* (Toronto, 1974), p. 244.

5   Marsha A. Chandler and William M. Chandler, *Public Policy and Provincial Politics* (Toronto, 1979), pp. 76-9.

6   Harold D. Clarke, Jane Jenson, Lawrence LeDuc, and Jon H. Pammett, *Political Choice in Canada* (abridged ed., Toronto, 1980), pp. 41,100.

cial administrations of the same partisan stripe as the contemporary federal government.[7] Unlike Nova Scotians and New Brunswickers, Prince Edward Islanders have never elected third party candidates to the provincial or federal legislature and they have also been shown to have higher levels of political trust than their Maritime neighbours.[8] Moreover, contrary to the regional norm, those Islanders who are of the Protestant faith tend to support the Liberals rather than the Progressive Conservatives.[9] As for Nova Scotia, its electorate is both less politically disaffected and more politically efficacious than that of both New Brunswick and Prince Edward Island.[10] When measured in real per capita terms, Nova Scotia has dramatically lower gross general revenues and gross general expenditures than its Maritime neighbours.[11] Finally, one study of the impact of social cleavages on voting behaviour concluded, first, that Prince Edward Islanders divide most clearly along lines of class, second, that New Brunswickers cleave along lines of religion and ethnicity, and third, that the voting preferences of Nova Scotians cannot be linked to any of the major social cleavages.[12]

Such findings should discourage us from assuming that homogeneity characterizes the politics of Maritime Canada. Too often, survey researchers have automatically aggregated Nova Scotians, New Brunswickers, and Prince Edward Islanders into a single sample large enough to permit a sophisticated treatment of the data. Yet empirical relevance, rather than methodological ease, should be the rationale behind any such grouping. There *are* major similarities between the politics of the three Maritime provinces; there are also substantial and irreducible differences.

Most scholars also do not hesitate to conclude that Maritime politics are genuinely idiosyncratic and that Maritime political practices differ significantly from those in the rest of the country. Two arguments, in particular, are employed in support of this position. First, it is contended that, unlike the rest of Canada, petty electoral corruption continues to flourish in the provinces of Nova Scotia, New Brunswick and Prince

---

7   Ian Stewart, "Friends At Court: Federalism and Provincial Elections on Prince Edward Island", *Canadian Journal of Political Science*, 19 (1986), pp. 127-50.

8   Allan Kornberg, William Mishler and Harold D. Clarke, *Representative Democracy in the Canadian Provinces* (Scarborough, 1982), p. 67.

9   Jane Jenson, "Party Systems", in Bellamy *et al.*, *The Provincial Political Systems*, p. 123.

10 David J. Bellamy, "The Atlantic Provinces", in *ibid.*, p. 16; Clark *et al.*, *Political Choice in Canada*, p. 31. See also Richard Simeon and David J. Elkins, "Provincial Political Cultures in Canada", in David J. Elkins and Richard Simeon, eds., *Small Worlds: Provinces and Parties in Canadian Political Life* (Agincourt, 1980), p. 51.

11 Richard Simeon and E. Robert Miller, "Regional Variations in Public Policy", in Elkins and Simeon, *Small Worlds*, pp. 242-84.

12 Jenson, "Party Systems", p. 121.

Edward Island. Second, it is observed that, again in contrast to the remainder of the country, third parties have had remarkably little electoral success in the Maritime region. Yet we actually know much less about both of these suppositions than is generally admitted.

With respect to petty electoral corruption, we are hamstrung by the very nature of the phenomenon under scrutiny. The popular methods of political research (such as the personal interview or the survey questionnaire) are obviously of little use here. People do not freely admit that they have either given or received flasks of whiskey, boxes of chocolates, five dollar bills, or any of the other forms of treating which are allegedly exchanged on election day for votes. Accordingly, political scientists have simply assumed, on the basis of anecdotal evidence and the occasional charge of electoral irregularities, that those corrupt practices which ostensibly prevailed thirty or forty years ago continue to exist in contemporary Maritime Canada.[13] This may, of course, be a valid assumption, but we should recognize that it is being accepted largely on faith.

Prince Edward Island, for example, is notorious for its petty electoral corruption, and recent references to "Shalegate" have done nothing to alter this reputation. Yet there is some countervailing evidence. If election "treating" were actually on the decline, one would expect a lower voting turnout (since one can assume that at least some members of the electorate would not vote without a material incentive). In fact, the turnout for Island elections has recently been dropping. Similarly, a decline in petty electoral corruption would lead one to expect a decrease in the proportion of spoiled ballots (since the politically illiterate would be less likely to vote and the politically spiteful would no longer be able to derive pleasure from frustrating the will of their electoral patron). In fact, the percentage of Islanders who spoil their ballots in provincial elections has recently been dropping. Given Prince Edward Island's idiosyncratic retention of dual-member constituencies, moreover, one would also expect a growing spread in the voting totals received by candidates of the same party in the same constituency (since party agents would no longer bribe voters to back the party "slate"). In fact, this spread has been widening in recent years. Of course, there may be alternative explanations for each of these phenomena. But if one were also to discover that provincial liquor store sales are no longer perceptibly higher before elections and perceptibly lower after the vote, that withdrawals from Island banks no longer are significantly lower after election day, and that Islanders no longer increase their con-

---

13 See, for example, Frank MacKinnon, "Prince Edward Island: Big Engine, Little Body", in Martin Robin, ed., *Canadian Provincial Politics: The Party Systems of the Ten Provinces* (Scarborough, 1978), pp. 230, 239; and *The Toronto Globe and Mail*, 27 November 1984.

sumption of goods and services immediately subsequent to elections, than one would have strong inferential evidence that the incidence of electoral corruption was actually decreasing. In this and other instances, Maritime political scientists must bring more ingenious methodologies to bear on heretofore untested assumptions.

The gaps in our understanding of Maritime third parties are less obvious. Clearly, the historical record which chronicles the electoral misadventures of new parties in Maritime Canada is there for all to see. Admittedly, the Reconstruction Party of H.H. Stevens gained a higher percentage of the 1935 popular vote in Nova Scotia than in any other province. Moreover, the CCF-NDP's electoral misfortunes in Nova Scotia, New Brunswick, and Prince Edward Island are not dissimilar to those the party has experienced in Newfoundland, Quebec, and Alberta. Nevertheless, the failure of third parties to make significant incursions into Liberal and Progressive Conservative voting strength does, in general, differentiate this region from the rest of the country.

What we do not know, unfortunately, is why Maritime voters have manifested this relatively idiosyncratic pattern. Certainly, there is no shortage of hypotheses. To account for the frustrations of the CCF-NDP in this region, for example, scholars have advanced at least fourteen different explanations:

1. The traditional parties have stolen the more attractive planks in the CCF-NDP's programme.[14]

2. The gap in support between the Liberals and Progressive Conservatives has generally been small and, hence, both traditional parties have been able to retain their electoral credibility.[15]

3. The original party system has always incorporated Maritime feelings of regional discontent.[16]

4. The CCF-NDP has elected unattractive leaders.[17]

5. The CCF-NDP has nominated unattractive candidates.[18]

---

14 Hugh G. Thorburn, *Politics in New Brunswick* (Toronto, 1961), p. 105.

15 Maurice Pinard, *The Rise of a Third Party: A Study in Crisis Politics* (Montreal, 1975), pp. 54-9.

16 Peter Regenstreif, *The Diefenbaker Interlude: Parties and Voting in Canada* (Toronto, 1965), p. 164.

17 This charge might effectively be levied against the New Brunswick branch of the New Democratic Party. See, for example, Calvin A. Woodward, *The History of New Brunswick Provincial Election Campaigns and Platforms, 1866-1974* (Fredericton, 1976), pp. 79, 81 for evidence of leadership incompetence.

18 Thorburn, *Politics in New Brunswick*, p. 104.

6. The CCF-NDP has not had enough money to get its message across to the electorate.[19]

7. The CCF-NDP has not worked hard enough at attracting new supporters.[20]

8. The CCF-NDP's electoral credibility has been sapped by dissension.[21]

9. Maritime voters have been too conservative to support the CCF-NDP.[22]

10. Maritime voters have been insufficiently efficacious to support the CCF-NDP.[23]

11. The CCF-NDP has been unable to gather support outside of working class constituencies.[24]

12. The CCF-NDP has lacked a working class base.[25]

13. Maritime voters have been too traditionalist to support the CCF-NDP.[26]

14. Patronage practices have inhibited the growth of the CCF-NDP.[27]

While each of these theories, taken separately, is intuitively plausible, they do not form an internally consistent aggregate. Even if we can reconcile these contradictions, the dependent variable of the CCF-NDP's electoral failure in the Maritimes has clearly been over-determined. In other words, if all fourteen of these theories actually possessed some measure of

19 Len Russo, "Can Jim Mayne Lead the NDP Out of Limbo?", *Atlantic Insight* (May 1983), p. 1.

20 Paul MacEwan, *The Akerman Years* (Antigonish, 1980), p. xiii.

21 See, for example, Desmond Morton, *NDP: The Dream of Power* (Toronto, 1974), p. 110; and Agar Adamson, "Does MacEwan's Real Ale Give the NDP Heartburn?", paper delivered to the Annual Meeting of the Atlantic Provinces Political Studies Association, Wolfville, October 1985.

22 Thorburn, *Politics in New Brunswick*, p. 103.

23 Simeon and Elkins, *Small Worlds*, p. 71.

24 Beck, *The Government of Nova Scotia*, p. 169. See, also, John Meisel, "The Party System and the 1974 Election", in Howard Penniman, ed., *Canada At The Polls: The General Election of 1974* (Washington, 1975), p. 17.

25 P.J. Fitzpatrick, "New Brunswick: The Politics of Pragmatism", in Robin, *Canadian Provincial Politics*, p. 121.

26 Bellamy, *The Atlantic Provinces*, p. 13.

27 N.H. Chi and G.C. Perlin, "The New Democratic Party: A Party In Transition", in Hugh G. Thorburn, ed., *Party Politics in Canada* (third ed., Scarborough, 1972), p. 182.

explanatory value, it is quite likely that the CCF-NDP would never have received even a single vote in the region.

Until scholars of Maritime politics undertake a rigorous scrutiny of these competing theories, we will continue to know much less than we realize about the failure of third parties in the region.[28] In essence, therefore, any conclusions about the distinctiveness of Maritime politics must be tempered with the awareness that substantial questions about both the nature and source of this distinctiveness remain unanswered.[29]

Most students of Nova Scotia, New Brunswick, and Prince Edward Island politics assume that the regional patterns of political behaviour with which we are familiar will continue for the foreseeable future. Hence, J. Murray Beck has declared that the conditions necessary to bring a third party to power in Nova Scotia "would have be be altogether catastrophic in nature", while Agar Adamson has asserted that "obviously, we are looking at a two-party system in Prince Edward Island, a fact which will remain true for many years to come".[30] Indeed, one analyst has actually celebrated the traditional and static nature of Nova Scotian politics; in such an environment, he noted, the political scientist can successfully analyze voting behaviour without engaging in survey research.[31]

Yet, once again, we must approach these assumptions with caution. While Maritime political norms and practices are manifestly not undergoing a revolutionary transformation, they seem to be gradually converging with those in other parts of the country. After decades of being notorious welfare state laggards, for example, the Maritime provinces now offer a representative range of social services to their citizens, and after a similarly lengthy experience with clientelist politics, some observers have detected Maritime Canada's entry into the "post-clientelist" age.[32] Yet con-

---

28 See Ian Stewart, "Strangers in a Strange Land: The Failure of Social Democracy in the Maritimes", paper presented to the Annual Meeting of the Atlantic Provinces Political Studies Association, Wolfville, October 1985.

29 See Roger Gibbins, *Prairie Politics and Society: Regionalism In Decline* (Scarborough, 1980), pp. 65-121 for an attempt to argue that prairie politics are becoming less regionally distinctive.

30 J. Murray Beck, "Nova Scotia: Tradition and Conservatism", in Robin, *Canadian Provincial Politics*, p. 201; Agar Adamson, "The 1982 Prince Edward Island General Election: An Innocent's Comment", paper presented to the Annual Meeting of the Canadian Political Science Association, Vancouver, 1983, p. 4.

31 Peter Aucoin, "The 1970 Nova Scotia Provincial Election: Some Observations on Recent Party Performance and Electoral Support", *Journal of Canadian Studies*, 7 (August 1972), p. 25.

32 The gap between those services provided in the Maritimes and those available elsewhere in the country has narrowed; it has not, however, entirely disappeared. See Richard Simeon and E. Robert Miller, "Regional Variations in Public Policy", in Simeon and Elkins, *Small Worlds*, pp. 242-84, and Patrick J. Smith and Marshall W. Conley, "Post-

trary to our linear notions of political development,[33] the politics of other parts of the country are also moving towards the Maritime norm. Hence, because other Canadians are now both less politically efficacious and more politically conservative than they once were, this has served to render Maritime values and assumptions less idiosyncratic than in the past.[34]

What underlies this evolutionary convergence? The answer would seem to be the rise of bureaucratic politics. Bureaucratic values of equality and routinization have driven the move to "national standards" in social security. The need for bureaucratic efficiency engendered by an increasingly complex society has overruled the short-term political advantages of clientelist politics. The technocratic nature of bureaucratic policy-making has dampened the optimism of previously efficacious individuals and the backlash against bureaucratic power has buttressed the apparent resurgence of conservatism (or right-wing liberal) values.

If this concluding analysis of recent and future changes in Maritime politics is correct, it will not be long before the answers to our first two questions will have to be reconsidered. In other words, we may soon be even more certain than at present that the politics of the three Maritime provinces are essentially similar. We may soon search in vain, however, for evidence that Maritime political practices differ significantly from those in the rest of the country.

Clientelist Perspectives on Atlantic Canada: Changing Mid-Elite Structures", paper presented to the Annual Meeting of the Canadian Political Science Association , Guelph, 1984.

33 John Wilson, "The Canadian Political Cultures: Towards A Redefinition of the Nature of the Canadian Political System", *Canadian Journal of Political Science*, 7 (1974), pp. 438-83.

34 Kornberg, Mishler, and Clarke, p. 82; Roger Gibbins, *Regionalism: Territorial Politics in Canada and the United States* (Toronto, 1982), pp. 184-6.

SELECTED BIBLIOGRAPHY

A. *General*

Adamson, Agar and Stewart, Ian, "Party Politics in the Mysterious East", in Hugh G. Thorburn, *Party Politics in Canada* (5th ed., Scarborough, 1985).

Beck, J.M., "An Atlantic Region Political Culture: A Chimera", in D.J. Bercuson and P.A. Buckner, eds., *Eastern and Western Perspectives* (Toronto, 1981), pp. 147-68.

Bellamy, David J., Pammett, Jon H. and Rowat, Donald C., *The Provincial Political Systems: Comparative Essays* (Toronto, 1976).

Brym, R.J., "Political Conservatism in Atlantic Canada", in Brym and J. Sacouman, eds., *Underdevelopment and Social Movements in Atlantic Canada* (Toronto, 1979).

Chandler, Marsha A. and Chandler, William N., *Public Policy and Provincial Politics* (Toronto, 1979).

Clarke, Harold D. *et al.*, *Political Choice in Canada* (Toronto, 1980).

Conley, M.W. and Daborn, G., eds., *Energy Options for Atlantic Canada* (Halifax, 1983).

Elkins, David J. and Simeon, Richard, *Small Worlds: Provinces and Parties in Canadian Political Life* (Toronto, 1980).

Kornberg, Allan, Mishler, William and Clarke, Harold D., *Representative Democracy in the Canadian Provinces* (Scarborough, 1982).

Rawlyk, George, ed., *The Atlantic Provinces and the Problems of Confederation* (St. John's, 1979).

B. *New Brunswick*

Aunger, Edmund, A., *In Search of Political Stability: A Comparative Study of New Brunswick and Northern Ireland* (Montreal, 1980).

Camp, Dalton, *Gentlemen, Players and Politicians* (Toronto, 1982).

Fitzpatrick, P.J., "New Brunswick: The Politics of Pragmatism", in Martin Robin, ed., *Canadian Provincial Politics* (2nd ed., Scarborough, 1978).

Stanley, Della M., *Louis Robichaud, A Decade of Power* (Halifax, 1984).

Thorburn, H.G., *Politics in New Brunswick* (Toronto, 1961).

Woodward, Calvin A., *A History of New Brunswick Provincial Election Campaigns and Platforms, 1866-1974* (Fredericton, 1976).

C. *Nova Scotia*

Akerman, Jeremy, *Black Around the Eyes* (Toronto, 1981).

—————, *What Have You Done for Me Lately? A Politician Explains* (Windsor, 1977).

Antoft, Kell, ed., *A Guide to Local Government in Nova Scotia* (2nd ed., Halifax, 1974).

Atkinson, M.M., "Comparing Legislatures: The Policy Role of Back Benchers in Ontario and Nova Scotia" (French summary), *Canadian Journal of Political Science*, 13 (March 1980), pp. 55-74.

Aucoin, P., "The 1970 Nova Scotia Provincial Election: Some Observations on Recent Party Performances and Electoral Support", *Journal of Canadian Studies*, 7 (August 1972), pp. 25-35.

—————, "The Stanfield Era: A Political Analysis", *Dalhousie Review*, 47 (Autumn 1967), pp. 400-9.

Beck, J.M., *The Government of Nova Scotia* (Toronto, 1957).

_____, "Elections in the Maritimes: The Votes Against Have it", *Commentator*, 14 (December 1970), pp. 7-9.

_____, "Nova Scotia: Tradition and Conservatism", in Martin Robin, ed., *Canadian Provincial Politics* (Scarborough, 1978).

Davis, M., "Voting Behaviour in Halifax Revisited", *Canadian Journal of Economics and Political Science*, 30 (1964), pp. 538-58.

Jabbra, Joseph and Landes, R., *The Political Orientations of Canadian Adolescents: Political Socialization and Political Culture in Nova Scotia* (Halifax, 1976).

Rawlyk, G., "The Farmer-Labour Movement and the Failure of Socialism in Nova Scotia", in L. LaPierre *et al.*, *Essays on the Left: Essays in Honour of T.C. Douglas* (Toronto, 1971).

_____, "Nova Scotia Regional Protest, 1867-1967", *Queen's Quarterly*, 75 (Spring 1968), pp. 105-23.

Smith, Patrick J. and Conley, Marshall W., "Empty Harbours, Empty Dreams", in J. William Brennan, ed., *Building the Co-operative Commonwealth* (Regina, 1985).

D. *Prince Edward Island*

Clark, Marlene-Russell, "Island Politics", in Francis W.P. Bolger, ed., *Canada's Smallest Province: A History of P.E.I.* (Charlottetown, 1973).

MacKinnon, F.P.T., *The Government of P.E.I.* (Toronto, 1951).

_____, "Prince Edward Island: Big Engine, Little Body", in Martin Robin, ed., *Canadian Provincial Politics* (Scarborough, 1978).

MacKinnon, Wayne E., *The Life of the Party: A History of the Liberal Party in Prince Edward Island* (Charlottetown, 1973).

18

Teaching Politics in the Maritimes: Challenging the Vacuum

Rick Williams

FOR NINE YEARS I HAVE BEEN developing and teaching a course on the Maritimes for social work students at Dalhousie University. We started the "Maritimes Course" because we wanted our social work students to begin to think about more than just the individual, personal problems of their future clients. We wanted to make them more aware of the historical context and of the larger social, political, economic and cultural forces which shape the lives of people in this region.

One of the first things we did in the course, and still do each time it is offered, was to ask the students whether they have ever studied the Maritimes in school before. The great majority say no, although a few will have hazy memories about something to do with fur traders or John Cabot back in grade school. I have concluded from this little informal research study, involving some 200 people who were born and brought up in the Maritimes, that school programmes have had a rather limited impact on the contemporary Maritimer's sense of cultural and historical identity.

I think this is a shame. Perhaps the most exciting thing I have learned from my work is that Maritimers love to discuss and analyse their region and its problems, and that presenting them with meaningful opportunities to do so unleashes the kinds of creative energies that make education a rewarding and exciting process. I find that our students from around the region, particularly those from outside of Halifax, have a keenly felt *need* to develop their identities as Maritimers in positive ways, and to express and act on the frustrations, fears, and hopes that they share. What they have not had is solid opportunities to fill that vacuum with information, new perspectives and more developed understandings of why things are the way they are.

I have often had former students tell me that the Maritimes course was one of the most influential and memorable courses they did in their university years. I believe this success has resulted from both the subject matter and the teaching method. The Maritimes course has been taught as a "problem posing" process. It is not a package of facts and premasticated learning to be consumed, but rather a loose structure in which students identify problems that are important to them and then pursue knowledge about them. Along the way they hear about issues that are important to other people, and are challenged about their assumptions and prejudices. Because of this approach, the participants have been more able to grapple with a fundamental orientation to the subject matter that many bring with them as more or less typical inhabitants of the region — an uneducated cynicism and a passivity that dull the political imagination.

This is the main point I want to make about teaching politics. A fundamentally important element in the political reality of the Maritimes is the distorted political culture. Our students manifest this culture which is so inadequately understood as "Maritime conservatism". They bring it into the classroom as a tangible thing, a block to effective teaching and learning. Teaching about politics in the Maritimes can either reinforce or challenge this problem. If we do not do the latter consciously and directly, I am not sure why we would even make the effort to teach about politics in our Maritime schools.

I want to pose two closely related problems that I have come to see as the most powerful influences on politics in the Maritimes. I could not imagine a politics or social studies course being very relevant if it did not spend a lot of time on these problems, and if it did not engage the students in practical struggles with them.

One I have already mentioned — the problem of the purported conservatism of Maritimers. I will argue that conventional interpretations of this phenomenon are very misleading. We need to stop construing the political culture as an aspect of some mythical Maritime "personality", and begin to analyse it as an identifiable social consciousness which has a history and an internal structure, which is produced by comprehensible social forces, and which changes under particular circumstances.

The second interrelated theme is that of dependence. I will argue that the central fact of the political economy of the region is the dominance of government in general, and of the centralized federal state in particular, and that this more than anything else shapes and animates the contemporary Maritime political culture. I will begin with an examination of this phenomenon, and then return to the issue of the political culture.

In 1983 the federal government spent $5.7 billion more than it collected in all forms of revenues in the three Maritime provinces. This deficit spending was equivalent to 32% of Gross Domestic Expenditure in the region. Roughly 50 cents out of every dollar of provincial government expenditure is a federal government transfer. Transfer payments to persons were equivalent to 20% of GDP compared to a figure of 10% for Ontario.[1] These figures do not adequately tell the story of the extent of government's

---

1   These statistics are drawn from *The Provincial Economic Accounts, 1966-1983*, Statistics Canada Catalogue #13-213 Annual, Ottawa.

role in our regional society. We need only think of situations like coal and steel in Cape Breton, the military bases in Chatham, Summerside, and Halifax, the contributions of the unemployment insurance system to the fishing, tourism and forestry industries, or the value of tax incentives and infrastructural supports in attracting and maintaining the region's limited manufacturing sector, to realize how absolutely essential government policies and fiscal practices are to the continued stability of our population in its current geographical configuration.

No more eloquent support for this view could be found than recent statements by the Atlantic Provinces Economic Council and other spokespersons for the business sector. They are expressing grave misgivings about the federal government's strategy of allowing market forces to resolve regional disparities and unemployment problems. They are particularly concerned about plans to cut back heavily on government's role in the region's economy. They say the private sector is too weak to be the "engine of growth", that indeed it is itself dependent on government business and government's contributions to aggregate demand through wages, salaries and transfers.[2]

We are not comfortable in dealing with these realities. Our dependence on government, an institution which the official ideology tells us is democratically responsive and responsible to the people, is somehow construed in very negative terms, an indication of profound weakness or failure. Sometimes it seems we would feel more comfortable if our fate was more to be determined by the likes of Hawker-Siddley, Noranda Mines, Michelin Corporation, or Shell Oil. At least they provide steady jobs. Some would argue that our fate is in these hands, and government is just there to confuse the matter. Whichever is the case, it is something to think about that the dominance of government in our regional lives does not give us a greater sense of self-determination. Historically, dependency and a broad sense of powerlessness have created an alienation from the political system. We expect little of it, and we demand little of it. We accept that it is part of the structure of control over us, not an instrument of our own will. It works for someone else — central Canada, Halifax (if you're in Cape Breton), the French (if you're English), for lawyers or for political insiders. Rather than try to change it, we try to ignore it on everything except the most immediate, personal matters. And then we make use of patronage channels.

2 This was the main theme at the annual meeting of the Atlantic Provinces Economic Council in Saint John, N.B. in March, 1985. A.P.E.C. Vice President William Belliveau summed up the dilemma in saying"We barely have a private sector". (*Saint John Telegraph Journal*, 16 March 1985.) Other spokespersons have pointed out more recently that government spending in the region is equivalent to some 85% of the Gross Domestic Product.

One can identify two basic types of societies in which government constitutes the dominant and pervasive economic institution. One type would be a socialist state, where the principal means of production are publically owned. The other type would be the classical nineteenth-century colonial dependency.

Although there are examples of socialist societies that we might rather forget about, we still think of socialism in a modernized, democratic society as involving a high level of political participation — Sweden is the relevant model. Socialism also implies public ownership and democratic management of the productive sectors of the economy — not just of weak and failing industries and the welfare system. We do not in the Maritimes conform to that model.

Perhaps then we are indeed a colony. We are administered by federal bureaucrats to fulfill certain functions for the motherland: cheap natural resources, supplies of labour when needed, markets for the motherland's manufactured goods, strategically located military bases, and showing the flag. *A Mari usque ad Mare*, and all that. We have local political elites who are highly skilled at manipulating parochial heartstrings and at doing the local song and dance routines, but even more skilled at scrambling for the crumbs that trickle-down from the imperial table. They make sure that things go fine for foreign investors, and they educate, organize and discipline the labour force so that it is always available when and if it is needed, at home or abroad. The local economic elite is well-adapted to colonial life as well. Despite substantial accumulated surpluses ($7 billion in banks and trust companies in Nova Scotia alone in 1983), they rarely take it upon themselves to challenge the external control of our regional economy. Foreign companies control 54 per cent of manufacturing in Nova Scotia compared to 43 per cent for Canada as a whole.[3]

If I am being perhaps a little too dramatic, it is to make a point. How are we in this region to make sense of the fact that the government that we depend upon both for maintenance of the current social and economic status quo, and for any hope of progressive change in the future, is broadly perceived as impotent on the local level, and as an instrument of external control by the ubiquitous Other on the provincial or regional level? In dealing with this question, we see where the issues arising from the region's dependent political and economic structures lead into the problem of political culture.

The purported conservatism of the Maritimes is a cliché whose life I do

---

3 See R.K. Semple, "Regional Analysis of Corporate Decision Making Within the Canadian Economy", a paper presented to "Still Living Together", a conference held at Dalhousie University, Dept. of Public Administration, October 1985. Prof. Semple teaches in the Dept. of Geography, University of Saskatchewan.

not wish to perpetuate. Political studies in the region need to go much deeper to get at the real meaning and historical development of the political culture. We have to stop attributing it to some kind of vaguely defined regional "personality" or ethnic character. This approach at best blames the victim, and, at worst, is tantamount to racism.

There is, in fact, no basis in reality for suggesting that Maritimers are more committed to an articulated, identifiable small "c" conservative ideology than other Canadians. They are no more conservative than other Canadians on most economic and social policy issues — often less so — according to the polls. Bob Brym has established that there is no more basis for assuming that Maritimers are deeply satisfied with the political status quo, or that they want and deserve the governments they get, more than other Canadians.[4]

Is it meaningful, then, to speak of a distinct Maritimes political culture, and to see it as in some sense "conservative"? If, as I have argued, the structure of our regional society, the economic, political and social frameworks of life in the region, increasingly resembles that of a colonial dependency, does it not follow that our political culture should increasingly resemble that of a colony as well?

One of the most salient characteristics of such a political culture is that the process of governing is essentially one of *administering* or *managing* people and their activities. To do this effectively, it is necessary to consult them and take their attitudes and ideas into account. However local and provincial governments have little fiscal autonomy. They do what they can with what they are given. As they are given less, they have to do less. A fundamental antagonism thus grows between government and the people. Government forces us to make do, to adjust, to tighten our belts, to expect less. Political leaders accomplish this by divide and rule. They separate out each group of citizens (who are now known as "clients"), make a policy for them, and encourage the rest of the community to agree that that particular group has really been asking too much. One month it is nursing home residents, the next it is unwed teenage mothers, the next it is local school boards, the next it is hospital workers. Each group is too small to mount effective protest. The Community is gradually broken into isolated, competing interest groups.

Government of this type is hostile to its citizens. To achieve its goals it must exploit their weaknesses and divisions, attack their integrity and their good will towards the social totality. These are harsh words, but think for

4 See R.J. Brym, "Political Conservatism in Atlantic Canada" in Brym and R.J. Sacouman, eds., *Underdevelopment and Social Movements in Atlantic Canada*, (Toronto, 1979) and the articles by Brym and Ornstein in Brym, ed., *Regionalism in Canada* (Toronto, 1986).

a moment about how our government is going about budget cuts and restraints. Think about the idea of cutting off U.I. benefits and forcing people to emigrate as a form of "adjustment". Think of the MacDonald Commission's position (or non-position) on regional disparities.

When you are administering people and forcing them to adapt to what you, the people in power, perceive as "reality", you do not go to them in an honest and authentically open manner and say: "Look, we have a problem. How are we going to solve it together? How can we achieve the greatest good for the greatest number, and with the least pain in the transition?" You do not ask people whether, in the light of a changing world, they really want to stick to the same goals for our economy and the same ways of distributing benefits and making decisions. You fear open debate and controversy about basic social values and economic or political directions. Instead you look for every means to increase your administrative leverage and control. Thus we see the preoccupation of government, particularly at the provincial level, with "efficiency", "productivity", and the adaptation of new management methods.

Similarly party politics takes on a particular flavour. We have an image of patronage as one kind of hold-over from the past. I suspect that this perception is very wrong. I suspect that patronage has taken on new and greater functions in the current era as a means of garnering political leverage from the distribution of increasingly scarce benefits.[5] As people in general are under greater stress, they rely more and more on what works. The citizens too become "pragmatic " and "realistic". As they get less, they expect and demand less.

The post war era in Canada brought the welfare state. For the Maritimes that meant two things: a significant improvement in the material standard of living, and a profound centralization of economic and political power both within and away from the region. The political culture that took root in that era was shaped by the fact of dependency, of remoteness from real decision making. For a while the trade-offs seemed to be acceptable. Now, however, the welfare state is too expensive and the center is calling in its political debts. Now the shadow of dependency becomes apparent. The people do not have a government that represents them, that leads them, that mobilizes them. They have a set of administrators.

The challenge in the Maritimes in the coming period will be to create a new politics, one which is open, democratic and creative, and which draws more and more people into struggles to understand their history, to articulate their feelings, to identify new goals. There is a clear link between

5   This theme was developed by James Petras in his paper "The State in the Caribbean" delivered at the conference "Perspectives from the Caribbean and Atlantic Canada", Saint Mary's University, October 1984.

the development of a new politics and the development of effective political studies. If we do not wish to become propaganda machines, purveyors of the new unreality, then we will have to involve ourselves in opening up the reality to critical examination with our students. As in other colonial societies, to be a real educator will mean in some basic sense to be in opposition, to challenge the status quo openly and systematically.

For those who withdraw in horror from the very idea, I ask you to think again about the "conservative" political culture of the Maritimes. Are we afraid of debate on basic issues? Do we see opposition and intellectual challenge as somehow threatening? What terrible things would happen if a few more of our students ended up as critics of the system, or as advocates of different political values? Are we afraid to allow our students to see the reality of the political system, or even to consider alternatives to the orthodox interpretations? If so, then the education system is obviously part of the problem, part of the system of intellectual control and denial. Is that the kind of education system we want? Is that the kind of educator we wish to be?

19

Teaching and Research in Maritime Politics: Old Stereotypes and New Directions*

R.A. Young

THE TEACHING AND STUDY OF politics in the Maritime provinces make many people feel slightly queasy. Probing the structure of partisan allegiances, the operation of party systems, and the distribution of patronage and payoffs often arouses a distaste rather like that caused when rocks are overturned to see what mouldy items and wriggly beasts lie underneath. While some individuals are clearly fascinated by this, and spend a lot of time being involved closely on the ground, their efforts have broad appeal to that facet of everyone's character which leads us, occasionally, to flip through the *National Enquirer* at the check-out counter or to watch C-grade horror movies. There can also be comfort in the old images of politics in the Maritimes — the snake-oil salesmanship, the rival cliques fighting for the spoils of office, and the politicians who stride across small stages like petty princelings — for these images elicit, especially among Upper Canadians and the more jaded elements of the regional society, that soothing sense of bemused condescension so gratifying to those who can afford to be above the fray. These common attitudes of distaste, fascination, and disdain make teaching about Maritimes politics hard. From outside, it all seems a bit like *opera bouffe*. Within the region, if students are politically unaware, they see the subject as irrelevant or rotten or stupidly futile; if involved, they know it all already and they tend to suspect their instructors of naïveté or, worse, of partisan bias.

This paper is not concerned only with teaching, though I do want to emphasize ultimately that students should and can see how vital politics is, and that they can be led to see their own partisan sympathies and activities in a broader context. My larger purpose is to argue that the old images of politics in the Maritimes are overdrawn and deceptive. Research on the region's politics has concentrated far too heavily on political attitudes and party competition. We know a lot about political participation, but little about other causes of state action, and we know so little about government policies that it is hard to say whether participation in electoral politics

* This paper is reprinted, in abridged form, from the *Journal of Canadian Studies*, 21 (1986), pp. 133-56.

makes much difference in outcomes. It seems to me that the study of Maritimes politics should begin with finding out what governments in the region actually do. In short, my plea is that we start with *policy*, not politics.

The traditional view of Maritimes politics is one which emphasizes parties, elections, and patronage. This image was focussed and spread by the trio of standard works about the region in the Canadian Government Series of the University of Toronto Press. Writing about New Brunswick politics, Hugh Thorburn discussed little beyond the demographic makeup of the electorate, party organization, and elections. The party system, he maintained, "rests more on tradition than on ideas", and the established parties are so similar that "a change of government involves no striking change of policy — mainly a change of personalities in the cabinet and some shifts in the distribution of patronage". Although horizons were widening because of the mass media, politicians still spent "most of their time promoting local, and often inconsequential, projects".[1] Frank MacKinnon's approach to Prince Edward Island was more historical and institutional, his scope was far broader, and his scholarship more restraining of simple judgements. He did argue discreetly, though, that

> The characteristics of party politics on the Island are partially explained by the dominance of political patronage in such a small province. The same factors which bring the Cabinet, the Legislature and the party so close to the people encourage the relentless pressure of influential individuals and powerful groups. In many ways this pressure facilitates the democratic process, but in others it results in unwise decisions, political appointments, and patronage of the worst type. The 'pork barrel' is, of course, an institution of some importance in most governments, but in Prince Edward Island, Ministers and other party leaders require more than the usual amount of political courage to keep it in its place.[2]

In his treatment of Nova Scotia, J.M. Beck also described carefully the evolution of government institutions, but conveyed far less about the province's changing social and economic forces. He argued, for instance, that "Although the purposes to which provincial moneys are now applied have altered markedly over the years, the considerations which guide any cabinet in their distribution remain basically the same". And his summary comments on election practices are typical of those that retain so much attention today: he wrote of a "two-hundred-year-old tradition that any-

---

1 Hugh G. Thorburn, *Politics in New Brunswick* (Toronto, 1961), pp. 83, 181, 184.
2 Frank MacKinnon, *The Government of Prince Edward Island* (Toronto, 1951), p. 249.

thing goes in politics", and claimed that "Normally the parties behave as if an agreement existed which permitted their workers to break every section of the law relating to corrupt practices short of arousing complete public disgust".[3]

Of course, these works were written almost thirty years ago and they were informed by contemporary theoretical concerns, as is evident particularly in the careful and historical description of institutions, which has not, in the cases of MacKinnon and Beck, been surpassed. But they remain widely used works, and a flip through the copies in most libraries will show what has been retained over the years by generations of readers: the juicy bits have been copiously underlined by students who are still learning that Maritimes politics is about parties, elections and patronage.

Martin Robin's *Canadian Provincial Politics* captured some of political science's changing emphasis in the 1960s by focussing on political attitudes and electoral behaviour rather than institutions; indeed, the book's subtitle was "The Party Systems of the Ten Provinces", as though politics were coterminous with parties. In any event, the contributions on the Maritimes recount the standard tales and perpetuate the old images. MacKinnon, on P.E.I., lets loose his gentle irony about politics in the tiny province, going so far as to quote Gilbert and Sullivan:

> And Party Leaders you might meet
> In twos and threes in every street
> Maintaining, with no little heat,
> Their various opinions.[4]

P.J. Fitzpatrick, treating New Brunswick, says in his first paragraph that "The Liberal and Progressive Conservative parties dominate the political environment without fear of challenge or stimulation by third parties, sustained by gerrymandering, patronage, and constituencies with hereditary political loyalties kept intact by ancient religious and ethnic antagonisms". While his essay does deal with the Equal Opportunity program, the treatment is highly personalized, centering on Charles Van Horne and Louis Robichaud, and despite the debates both passionate and intellectual that the E.O. policies aroused, we are still told at the conclusion that "politicians are less concerned with issues than with the parish pump", and we are informed — in the face of overwhelming survey evidence showing high levels of cynicism and political alienation in the province — that "this may

---

3   J. Murray Beck, *The Government of Nova Scotia* (Toronto, 1957), pp. 205, 265.

4   Frank MacKinnon, "Big Engine, Little Body", in Martin Robin, ed., *Canadian Provincial Politics* (Scarborough, 1972), p. 247.

be what the electorate wants".[5]

More recent works continue to pick up these themes. A standard study of Island politics trots out all the hoary old stories about pavement and personation, and aloofly describes the colourful electoral spectacle. The author, declining even to attempt analysis of complex current issues like the Development Plan and the University question or of phenomena like the burgeoning civil service, concludes that politics is much the same as ever: "And yet, even as government moves into novel programs and extended regulatory control over its individual citizens, one wonders if the basic character and essence of Island politics has altered all that much throughout these intervening years. Or does a ghostly presence consider the last two centuries with the confident assertion, 'I was right; it was a damn queer Parliament'".[6] Other examples abound in more widely used texts. In his contribution to *The Provincial Political Systems*, David Bellamy paints the picture impressed upon thousands of students in the region and in the rest of Canada. He describes the Maritimes' conservatism, rural virtues, lack of ideology, pragmatism, cynicism about politics, and ritualistic electoral participation. Then he completes the circle (and reinforces his findings) by arguing that "It may well be that the conservative nature of the societies of Atlantic Canada has conditioned the population to believe that the social change and the impact of the individual upon politics are of negligable significance".[7] Equally noteworthy is the influential text *Party Politics in Canada*, the most recent edition of which finally has an essay on the Atlantic region. Here we are informed that "In other sections of the country, politics is a part of life to be endured, but in Atlantic Canada, it might be called the bread of life. Nowhere else in Canada are politics followed literally from the cradle to the grave as they are in these four provinces". The authors describe a political culture of traditionalism and cynicism, with participation channelled ritualistically through two stable parties, and with patronage providing the motivation: "In short, elections in Atlantic Canada have changed surprisingly little since the premier of Prince Edward Island, Donald Farqharson, observed in 1900 that 'it is simply a matter now of who will buy the most votes and the man who works hardest and is prepared to use means fair or foul will get in'".[8]

5 P.J. Fitzpatrick, "The Politics of Pragmatism", in *ibid.*, pp. 116, 133.

6 Marlene-Russell Clark, "Island Politics", in Francis P. Bolger, ed., *Canada's Smallest Province* (Charlottetown, 1973), p. 327.

7 David J. Bellamy, "The Atlantic Provinces", in David J. Bellamy, Jon H. Pammett and Donald C. Rowat, eds., *The Provincial Political Systems: Comparative Essays* (Toronto, 1976), p. 17.

8 Agar Adamson and Ian Stewart, "Party Politics in the Mysterious East", in Hugh G. Thorburn, ed., *Party Politics in Canada* (5th ed., Scarborough, 1985), pp. 329-30.

Now I certainly do not want to suggest that all these are not worthwhile studies; nor that parties do not sometimes operate as is so often described; nor yet that elections are irrelevant. But is this the whole story? I think not. First, although this old image of regional politics is strong and widespread, its substantiation rests not on thorough and systematic research but on oft-repeated anecdotes and occasional scandal. Second, even were the old stereotype true, it is incomplete as an account of contemporary politics. Provincial governments in the Maritimes have grown large, complex and active. They spend a lot of money, regulate new activities, run enterprises and raise taxes, and their activities cannot be fully accounted for by a vision of 'politics' which is confined to leaders, elections and patronage. To understand government in the Maritimes, one must move far beyond the received images, and the essential first step is to focus on what governments actually do; that is, to study public policy in the region.

This is a matter of more than scholarly significance. Whether Maritimers are engaged in electoral politics as participants, or follow it as a spectator sport, or ignore it altogether, their lives are deeply affected by state policy. These policies should be understood. One obstacle to this is the lack of available material, even of a descriptive nature, about state action in the region. This is due not only to the small number of political scientists in the Maritimes but also to analysts' longstanding concentration on parties and elections. If there were as many pages available on the way government debt is financed, or on Crown Lands policy, or on how Cabinet committees now work, or even on how landlords' and tenants' organizations pressure municipal governments, as there now exist recounting the same old stories of the election-day bottles of rum and the two-dollar bills, then we would be better off. But these gaps can be filled, and they will be filled, as the focus of research shifts towards the nature and sources of policies, and the real impact on citizens of governments' actions. I believe it is time to re-direct our efforts, to stop repeating cosy homilies and funny stories, and to take up the task of clearly analyzing what governments are doing and how and why they do it. This is what studying Maritimes politics now should be about.

The received image of politics in the Maritimes leads researchers to emphasize the distribution of attitudes towards government (which are usually portrayed as conservative and cynical), the organization and orientations of parties (which are hierarchical and pragmatic), the mobilization of partisanship (which is intense but personal rather than programmatic), and the distribution of the post-electoral spoils (which, apart from the love of spectacle and the psychic rewards of belonging to a team, is presumed to motivate the participants).[9] In some respects this image remains accurate.

9 There are some differences in the francophone literature on regional politics, and

But it was far more relevant during the long period of economic stagnation between 1873 and the 1950s. Despite the good efforts of regional historians, it is easy to forget now how underdeveloped and peripheral the Maritimes were. Only a limited response had been possible to the manufacturing opportunities opened by the National Policy.[10] The principal industries served local markets, processed local primary products, or were maintained by cheap labour or tax concessions or both. The exceptions were coal and steel in Cape Breton and pulp and paper in New Brunswick. But in 1941, in Nova Scotia, manufacturing still accounted for only 11.8 per cent of male employment; the rural areas of New Brunswick held 69 per cent of the population; and 59 per cent of PEI wage earners took home less than $450 a year (equivalent to about $2800 in 1981). In the whole region, 62 per cent of the population lived on the 77,000 farms, and of gross farm revenues of $57,600,000, over 20 per cent was accounted for by the value of home consumption.[11] Out-migration, which began around the turn of the century, became chronic, averaging 96 people per 1000 per decade between 1921 and 1961 (and twice that for the 20-34 age group).[12] As it had been for decades, the regional society was highly stable, predominantly rural, and organized around local centres of manufacture and primary-product trade. And political activity meshed with these local economic structures.

The political counterpart of the rural, raw-material exporting economy

especially in that treating New Brunswick. One strong element is the depiction (and reinforcement) of ethnic-group coherence: see Philippe Doucet, "La Politique et les Acadiens", in Jean Daigle, ed., *Les Acadiens des Maritimes: Études Thématiques* (Moncton, 1980), pp. 235-92. Another is the gaining of political power appropriate to Acadian population strength: see, for instance, Léon Thériault, *La Question du Pouvoir en Acadie* (2nd ed., Moncton, 1982). Yet central to both concerns are the issues of participation and of inputs to the political process, rather than concrete analyses of the effects on the Acadian community of public policies. There has also been considerable work on the grand options open to Acadian society: see Thériault, *Pouvoir en Acadie*, and also Jean-Paul Hautecoeur, *L'Acadie du discours* (Québec, 1975). The latter also provides a fascinating treatment of the vehiculing of various ideologies by major Acadian organisations. Still, among these scholars, the emphasis is upon group coherence, grand collective objectives, and political mobilization. And what is perhaps the most widely cited work on Acadian politics stresses how the Acadians were integrated into Liberal partisanship through the distribution of patronage: see Jean-Guy Finn, "Tentative d'Explication du Vote Ethnique Acadien", *Revue de l'Université de Moncton*, 6 (1975), pp. 215-24.

10 T.W. Acheson, "The National Policy and the Industrialization of the Maritimes, 1880-1910", *Acadiensis*, I/2 (Spring 1972), pp. 3-28.

11 Canada, *Census of Canada 1941* (Ottawa, 1950 and 1947), I, pp. 766-71, 349; VIII, pp. 20-1, 24-5.

12 Isabel S. Anderson, *Internal Migration in Canada 1921-1961* (Ottawa, 1966), p. 22; D.C. Curtis, "Outmigration from New Brunswick, 1921-1961" (MA thesis, Queen's University, 1966), Table 13.

in the Maritimes took the form of clientele networks. These are composed of personal relationships through which individuals unequal in status, wealth, and influence exchange goods — generally material favours for loyalty and political support.[13] Such links were forged especially strongly in the lumber trade. At the peak of hierarchies were exporters who owned saw-mills, held timber limits, and conducted their own cutting operations as well as buying from small operators. The latter might run small sawmills, cut freehold land or small limits, and buy wood from farmers. Either operation could be combined with a store (which often operated on credit). Next were farmers and smallholders, who cut their own woodlots for sale up the chain and sometimes worked for others. Last were landless rural labourers and part-time fishermen who worked wherever wages could be made.[14] In agriculture and the fishery were similar but shallower structures of hierarchical interdependence, headed by processors and merchants, and with the most economically vulnerable at the bottom. The operations of patrons were regional, and so were these networks. They permeated politics.

Party systems in the Maritimes coalesced and became identified with their federal counterparts at different rates. In the minds of many in PEI and New Brunswick especially, the parties remained Government and Opposition or, more popularly, Ins and Outs, well into this century. But the coalescing parties in the region were superimposed on clientele networks; indeed, the extension of manhood suffrage deepened these structures by providing the poorest with a vote to be exchanged for favours from patrons upon whom they were economically dependent. In the parties, complex regional networks came together to form great teams of 'friends' fighting for power.

The interlocking of economic and political relations was tightest in rural areas. Local merchants and owners of sawmills and fish plants often were elected representatives to Legislative Assemblies. Their control of leases and licenses and of funds for local road works could reward political supporters and also extend their business contacts and influence. The rural party networks directly incorporated business allies and dependents. In the towns, however, the clientele structures were less coherent and stable. Economic and partisan alliances were not so clearcut as in the country.[15] In

13 J.D. Powell, "Peasant Society and Clientelist Politics", in J. Finkle and R. Gable, eds., *Political Development and Social Change* (2nd ed., Toronto, 1971), pp. 519-37.

14 See, for instance, Graeme Wynn, *Timber Colony* (Toronto, 1981), esp. pp. 113-37.

15 A nice example is provided by W.F. Todd, M.P. for Charlotte County, New Brunswick, between 1908 and 1911. Todd's rural party network was based squarely on the wood trade, but his canvas book for bustling St. Stephen and Milltown divided voters into three main categories — "straight Conservatives", "straight Liberals", and "Liberals you have to pay". See MTO, III/A/1 (especially P.J. Anderson to Todd, 18/9/08) and III/C/1, Provincial Archives of New Brunswick.

urban areas, it was common for political 'brokers' to mobilize support for regional magnates who attended to business. Entrepreneurs provided financing to glue the system, and they could also deliver some employees' votes; in return such benefits as the state could dispense were directed towards them.[16]

These clientele systems permeated politics, and in several notable ways the activities of the state were congruent with them. From this conjunction arose many of the stories about regional politics which have become legend. Inefficiency was one obvious characteristic of government action, as clientelism led to post-election changes in the provincial civil services of Jacksonian proportions. When the Liberals took office in New Brunswick in 1917, for instance, 81 per cent of the 700 permanent government employees left within four months, and road supervisors, game wardens, and Justices of the Peace were also replaced wholesale.[17] Most appointments in the Maritime provinces were arranged by county-level patronage committees, and power was sufficiently localized that new governments could be instructed pretty bluntly about favoured job-seekers. Even skilled positions like medical inspector and highway engineer were claimed on the basis of loyalty to patron and party. Sheer waste was another result, as the system led state spending to be devoted to items particularly valuable to local businessmen but useless to others.[18] Finally, simple graft was inevitable, as money was necessary to fight elections and to maintain the party organizations. Lumbermen often paid political levies for timber berths, and railway and road construction offered rich opportunities for bribe-collecting.

Another, less noted feature of state activity was that spending tended to be highly divisible. This was essential to clientelist politics, for large networks of supporters had to be rewarded selectively and in proportion to their contributions. One fine example is a tourism display mounted in Boston by the New Brunswick Department of Lands and Mines in 1930. The display was of game animals, and the total cost was $5,260, a sum which the *Public Accounts* show to have been spread among no fewer than 66 people: the payments ranged from $274 to cover the minister's expenses in Boston for three days, to $200 for an individual who spent a few weeks in the bush catching animals, to $2 for another person's "Services, Loading Moose". But it was public works, and especially road-building, which best fit the requirement of divisibility, since precise regional and individual

---

16 One should not suggest that this pattern was unique to the Maritimes: see S.J.R. Noel, "Patrons and Clients in Canadian Politics", presented to the Canadian Political Science Association, 1976.

17 Arthur T. Doyle, *Front Benches & Back Rooms* (Toronto, 1976), p. 142.

18 See *ibid.*, pp. 88-90, 191-207 on the Patriotic Potato Gift.

allocations were possible. During the 1930s, over 1,000 New Brunswickers received funds each year for road maintenance, and with their $500 or $1000 they in turn hired many others. Roadwork in PEI was even more finely divided: 50 highway foremen each administered a section of Prince County, and in 1937, section #5 received $274.02 for bridges (spread among 48 people) and $268.37 for roads (dispensed in 55 payments ranging from 84¢ to $21.12).

State spending tended to filter through established political and economic networks well into the 1940s. This assisted businessmen directly, and defused resentment by providing economic elites with supplementary benefits for them to distribute to those with more limited opportunities. It helped sustain clientele structures based in the economy, and it reinforced political relationships which were hierarchical, particularistic and diffuse.[19] For most people, then, electoral politics was part of this system: the teams were known, the leaders were established, and the benefits were clear. But the socio-economic bases of this kind of politics have eroded. Much political commentary continues to be devoted to patronage in the region, and graft — that pale and unhealthy shade of clientelist politics — may persist; yet the conditions that supported clientele structures have largely disappeared, and with them have gone both the traditional basis of party competition and the centrality of electoral politics in political participation. The state does new things in the Maritimes, it does them for new reasons, and people try to influence it in new ways. The old images of Maritime politics are increasingly irrelevant.

Clientele systems, and the old party structures which paralleled them, were based on face-to-face relationships. These were most surely built within the primary industries in stable, rural areas. But urbanization has been rapid in the region, and rural areas have gained odd new urbanites who commute to anonymous white-collar jobs. All primary-sector employment has declined sharply since 1950: more Nova Scotians now work as scientists and engineers and mathematicians (*excluding* teachers and health professionals) than are engaged in either farming or fishing. Moreover, many primary enterprises have grown in scale, making close relationships impossible even where control still rests with local businessmen, which it often does not. The pulp and paper industry, for instance, now totally dominates lumbering, and its interests lie in efficient and rational state spending (according to its definition, naturally), rather than in the transient advantages to be gained from having special friends in office — which were important to lumbermen and exporters as late as the 1950s.

Economic dependency, a mainstay of the system at the lower echelons,

19 R.R. Kaufman, "The Patron-Client Relationship and Macro-Politics", *Comparative Studies in Society and History*, 16 (1974), pp. 284-308.

has also been reduced. Clientelism was challenged from below, by organizations of farmers, fishermen and workers in the early decades of the century, and more certainly since World War II. Industrialists were never quite 'patrons' to many of their workers, and the shallow structures of hierarchical interdependence in agriculture and the fishery proved pretty transparent to hard analyses of the relative flows of benefits through them. Economic bargaining in these sectors has become collective, not individualistic. Lower-class security has also weakened the old link between economic favours and political support. Even were construction contracts awarded to party supporters, for example, it is hard to see how this could secure the votes of unionized construction workers. Dependency has also been weakened by universal social security programs, many of which, like pensions, were extended by the central government. Of course, this transition is not complete: there is some evidence that the non-unionized rural working class was still organized around partisan networks in the 1960s, and the Marginal Work World study in Nova Scotia reminds us that this is still an significant segment in the region.[20] But it is a shrinking one. Patronage is being cut off from the grass roots.

Moreover, the scale of state spending and its mode of distribution have changed. If there once were party patronage systems operating as complementary administrative machinery to that of the state, they now have only weak control over selective incentives (that is, benefits which can be dispensed to supporters and withheld from others). Large bureaucracies, with security bolstered by public-service unions as well as Civil Service Acts, now allocate many benefits according to criteria which are largely determined by non-partisan considerations. Social welfare payments,for example, no longer depend on the discretion of local party chiefs. Loans to companies are scrutinized according to standards laid down by officials in departments of economic growth. If some assistance and contracts are still awarded to 'friends' of the government, politicians nevertheless find it hard to withhold ordinary kinds of support from other firms. While elected representatives can act as ombudsmen for constituents, showing that cases have been neglected or rules misapplied, they cannot easily secure selective benefits for individual supporters: civil servants control the application of rules and often also their content. Of course, new fields of patronage, like lotteries, can be opened up, but they, in turn, are gradually regularized; while clientelism may survive in the "traditionalistic interstices of the

---

20 Peter Leslie, "The Role of Constituency Party Organizations in Representing the Interests of Ethnic Minorities and Other Groups" (PhD thesis, Queen's University, 1967); Peter M. Butler, "Earnings and Transfers: income sources in Atlantic Canada and their relationship to work settings", *Canadian Review of Sociology and Anthropology* (1976), pp. 32-46.

modernizing polity", these eventually close.[21]

The specialization and scale of new state activities also reduce the scope for patronage. Permanent government posts are protected, and unskilled and temporary jobs have limited appeal. As state spending becomes more concentrated, the divisibility of goods diminishes and their selective allocation is impeded. In 1949, for instance, the New Brunswick Electric Power Commission purchased over 39,000 wooden poles and it hired hundreds of men for its rural electrification program; now its employees are protected by union contract and whole power lines are bought at once. When electric-power lines reach the 345 KV league, they are not re-routed to provide a supporter with a profitable expropriation of his back pasture, and when snowplows are designed to clear inter-regional highway systems they cannot be diverted to particular driveways. Electoral politics is still based on geographic constituencies, and the regional distribution of benefits remains very important in political calculation, but traditional clientele structures have largely disappeared, and state spending, which now is primarily at the service of general economic growth, is not easily directed down to individual voters through selective, partisan channels.

All of this is not to argue that electoral politics are insignificant. On the contrary, there is every sign that they are becoming more important, precisely as their content shifts towards greater ideological coherence (though, as will be argued below, participation in organized groups is far more important in shaping policy). The purpose here has simply been to show the inadequacy of the received image of Maritimes politics — one in which political parties continue to incorporate the bulk of the population into competing teams, with the motivational mainspring being their ability to distribute benefits selectively through patronage systems, and with state action being explained by the drives of partisan and clientelist politics. The socio-economic structures which underlay this pattern have very much eroded, and the image is now deceptive, if not wrong.

Of course, there are analysts who do not subscribe to this received view.[22] But the old image predominates, and it continues to have serious effects. It focusses attention on elections, so obscuring other forms of political activity. It stresses 'high politics' and the role of political leadership in shaping policy, and neglects the influence of external actors, the bureaucracy, and the institutional structures of government. It emphasizes the spectacular failures and the scandals and personalities — the Bricklins,

21 L. Lemarchand and K. Legg, "Political Clientelism and Development: A Preliminary Analysis", *Comparative Politics*, 4 (1972), pp. 149-78.

22 See, for instance, the fine essay by David A. Milne, "Politics in a Beleaguered Garden", in Verner Smitheram, David Milne and Satadal Dasgupta, eds., *The Garden Transformed: Prince Edward Island, 1945-1980* (Charlottetown, 1982), pp. 39-72.

the Georgetown Shipyards, the phone calls to Mrs. Buchanan — rather than the quiet, day-to-day evolution of policy within states which have grown very large, complex, and influential. Finally, and critically, it concentrates on policy execution rather than policy impact. A decision about road locations or construction contracts, for example, may well be less important than a decision about the standards of road construction or one setting the criteria of policy evaluation which favour roads over railways. It may be interesting, and highly 'political' in the old sense, that Tourism advertising contracts are let without tender to party supporters; yet decisions with greater impact on the region are whether advertising should appeal to bus tours or backpackers, whether to spend on tourism or manufacturing. Such questions have arisen as Maritimes governments have undertaken to provide a measure of social security and to plan positively economic development, and they entirely overshadow those attached to the remnants of a patronage system formed when the state rented resource rights and helped maintain a road network.

Suggesting that more attention should be devoted to the study of public policy in the Maritimes does not mean that we should neglect the old questions about political participation — about how opinions and interests are conveyed to government. But it does imply that much more effort should be spent on the output side — on discovering what the provincial governments are doing in the region (and also what the central government and local governments are doing). In recent years, the discipline of political science in Canada has shifted in this direction, and useful journals like *Canadian Public Policy* and *Policy Options* have emerged to join the growing space allocated to policy questions in other journals.[23] The growth of policy studies has also produced a number of general texts which academics and practitioners alike find useful.[24] At the provincial level, the opportunities for comparative studies offered by ten disparate systems have been understood; from the viewpoint of the Maritimes, however, they have not been grasped, as most works have little to say about government operations and policies here.[25] Still, the questions posed suggest fruitful

23 This trend is especially notable in *Canadian Public Administration* and the *Canadian Journal of Political Science*, but see also the *Canadian Journal of Economics* and the *Canadian Journal of Regional Economics*, as well as the *Journal of Canadian Studies*. To this must be added the new research flowing from organizations like the Institute for Research on Public Policy, the Fraser Institute, and the Canadian Centre for Policy Alternatives.

24 G. Bruce Doern and Peter Aucoin, eds., *Public Policy in Canada* (Toronto, 1979); Michael M. Atkinson and Marsha A. Chandler, eds., *The Politics of Canadian Public Policy* (Toronto, 1983).

25 Marsha A. Chandler and William M. Chandler, *Public Policy and Provincial Politics*

avenues of work in the region. At the national level, a series of collections dealing with specific government departments and with new policy initiatives has proven very useful, though there is little regional interest in them.[26] Happily, however, this last effort has recently been matched by a group in Halifax which has published *Governing Nova Scotia*.[27] This volume is noteworthy for the serious questions raised, the careful research, and the generally high quality of the contributions, which cover the budgetary processes, the deficit, tax incentives, energy policy, the fishery, housing policy, elementary and secondary education, health expenditures, federal-provincial development policy, post-secondary education, and municipal finance. The collection is a landmark in studies of the region.

These existing works provide useful guides, and suggest several starting points for policy studies. One place to begin is with the awareness that governments have a great many means at their disposal to realize policy objectives. They have many policy instruments. Direct spending, lending, taxation (and tax expenditures), administrative regulation, Crown corporations, regulatory commissions and agencies, and even exhortation and advertising are all means used by governments to attain their ends.[28] There is a huge variety of government actions, and we should not restrict the scope of study too narrowly — to spending, for instance.

But even thorough examinations of provincial expenditures would be useful, especially if conducted historically, and there is a dearth of information about and analysis of municipal spending. Good guides are available for such efforts, and there are data at hand on both spending and taxation from Statistics Canada and the Canadian Tax Foundation (as well as from the provincial *Public Accounts*).[29] Taxation deserves a great deal of study: even simple propositions, such as that governments tend to introduce tax increases in the early years of their mandates, have not been

(Toronto, 1979); Donald C. Rowat, ed., *Provincial Policy-Making: Comparative Essays* (Ottawa, 1981).

26 G. Bruce Doern, ed., *How Ottawa Spends Your Tax Dollars* (Toronto, 1981), *How Ottawa Spends Your Tax Dollars 1982* (Toronto, 1982) and *How Ottawa Spends* (Toronto, 1983); Allan M. Maslove, ed., *How Ottawa Spends 1984: The New Agenda* (Toronto, 1984) and *How Ottawa Spends 1985: Sharing the Pie* (Toronto, 1985).

27 Barbara Jamieson, ed., *Governing Nova Scotia: Policies, Priorities and the 1984-85 Budget* (Halifax, 1985).

28 M.J. Trebilcock *et al.*, *The Choice of Governing Instrument*, prepared for the Economic Council of Canada (Ottawa, 1982); Kenneth Woodside, "Tax Incentives vs. Subsidies", *Canadian Public Policy*, 5 (1979), pp. 248-56.

29 Richard M. Bird, *The Growth of Government Spending in Canada* (Toronto, 1970) and *Financing Canadian Government: A Quantitative Overview* (Toronto, 1979). See also *Provincial and Municipal Finances*, published every two years by the Canadian Tax Foundation.

subjected to systematic investigation.

Regulatory agencies are harder nuts to crack. Often the researcher is limited to case studies (though Maritimes governments, here as elsewhere, offer opportunities for nice, limited comparisons about the treatment of matters like pollution and electricity rate-setting). But there is a vast literature on regulation in Canada, much of it generated by the Economic Council's Regulation Reference of the late 1970s.[30] This exercise provided detailed information about individual regulatory agencies, and more is obtainable from the Law Reform Commission and other sources.[31]

The direct implementation of policy through normal government departments is a standard tool of states, and the issues it raises are at the core of the discipline of public administration[32] Interesting work can be done here simply by using annual reports to chart changes in departmental structures, for the creation of new administrative units is often a signal of policy initiatives. Basic description of departmental organization allows much probing of the relations between the state and its environment. As well, the manner in which policies are actually delivered on the ground, as opposed to the form they take when announced from on high, is a topic of some interest in public policy.[33] Implementation analysis, though, requires detailed investigations and usually inside information, and this may daunt most researchers; yet it is quite feasible at the local level. Crown corporations also offer rich opportunities for research. There are many case studies available, and some of them cover regional firms like Devco, Georgetown Shipyards, and the New Brunswick Electric Power Commission. But much more remains to be done, especially in a comparative perspective.[34]

---

30 For an introduction to this material, some of which concerns the region, see W.T. Stanbury and Fred Thompson, *Regulatory Reform in Canada* (Montreal, 1982). See also G. Bruce Doern, *The Atomic Energy Control Board* (Ottawa, 1977) and Richard J. Schultz, *Federalism, Bureaucracy and Public Policy* (Montreal, 1980).

31 C. Lloyd Brown-John, *Canadian Regulatory Agencies* (Toronto, 1981).

32 Robert F. Adie and Paul G. Thomas, *Canadian Public Administration* (Scarborough, 1982); Marsha A. Chandler and William M. Chandler, "Public Administration in Canada's Provinces", *Canadian Public Administration*, 25 (1982), pp. 580-602.

33 J.I. Pressman and A. Wildavsky, *Implementation* (Berkeley, 1973); Robert W. Rycroft, "Bureaucratic Performance in Energy Policy Making", *Public Policy*, 26 (1978), pp. 599-627; P. Sabatier and D. Mazmanian, "The Conditions of Effective Implementation", *Policy Analysis*, 5 (1979), pp. 481-504.

34 Roy George, *The Life and Times of Industrial Estates Limited* (Halifax, 1974); Roy George, "Cape Breton Development Corporation", in Allan Tupper and G. Bruce Doern, eds., *Public Corporations and Public Policy in Canada* (Montreal, 1981), pp. 365-88; Philip Mathias, *Forced Growth* (Toronto, 1971); R.A. Young, "Planning for Power: The New Brunswick Electric Power Commission in the 1950s", *Acadiensis*, 12 (1982), pp. 73-99. See also Marsha A. Chandler, "The Politics of Public Enterprise", in J.R.S.

Another general approach to the study of policy is that of substance. Here the focus is on particular policy fields, and the analyst is concerned with the whole range of instruments and policies affecting them. The normal starting point is with a distinction between economic policy, social policy, and policy towards the structures and processes of government themselves. It is impossible here to do more than skip lightly over these fields: in the sources cited elsewhere can be found a host of questions and many examples of concrete policy studies.[35] But it is clear that a great deal remains to be done on policy in the Maritimes. On the natural resources front, agricultural policy has been subject to some study, but the administration of Crown Lands has been relatively neglected. Fisheries policies have been well described, but gaps remain in areas like Fishermen's Loan Boards, and issues surrounding the allocation of power to fishing and farming co-operatives, marketing boards, and woodlot owners' organizations constitute a fairly open field. Industrial policy has been the subject of many studies, mostly of spectacular failures, but not too much is known of the day-to-day operation of industrial assistance programs and procurement policies. Energy policy has attracted much attention, especially in Nova Scotia, but many other aspects of development policy, such as tourism, remain to be examined.[36]

On the social policy side, less seems to have been done in the region, at least by non-governmental researchers. As at the national level, much of the running here has been made by Royal Commissions and Task Forces (which can be valuable sources on many policy fields). The useful recent surveys of the whole area contain little specifically regional content.[37] Health policy in itself has elicited fine studies, often built around federal-provincial relations, and a start has been made in *Governing Nova Scotia* on the kind of careful analysis of provincial policies which is needed. Maritimes labour policy is very much understudied, though the historical journals like *Acadiensis* have featured many relevant articles. Education policy, on the other hand, has received some thorough academic attention in the recent collections. On the whole social policy field, though, there is certainly nothing in any of the three provinces like the recent angry analy-

Prichard, ed., *Crown Corporations in Canada: The Calculus of Instrument Choice* (Toronto, 1983), pp. 185-218.

35 See especially the *How Ottawa Spends* series; Chandler and Chandler, *Public Policy and Provincial Politics*; Smitheram, Milne and Dodgupta, eds., *The Garden Transformed*; and especially Jamieson, ed., *Governing Nova Scotia*.

36 Roger Voyer, *Offshore Oil* (Toronto, 1983); M.W. Conley and Graham R. Daborn, eds., *Energy Options for Atlantic Canada* (Halifax, 1983).

37 Shanker A. Yelaja, ed., *Canadian Social Policy* (Waterloo, 1978); Jacqueline S. Ismael, ed., *Canadian Social Welfare Policy* (Montreal, 1985).

sis of the impact on social programs of the B.C. restraint program.[38]

Much information is available about the policies which have shaped institutional structures. A huge literature exists both on how federal policy affects the region and on the impact of federal-provincial negotiating processes. Good recent studies of industrial, energy, and income-maintenance policies provide contrasting cases of federal-provincial discord and harmony, and on regional policy *per se*, a new survey by Donald Savoie should form the starting point for study and discussion.[39] (The current debates concern whether central-government initiatives have been economically inefficient and wasteful or whether they constitute a sop which either assuages the worst effects of Ottawa's neglect, or, more strongly, which helps perpetuate a system in which richer regions actually require poor, peripheral hinterlands.)[40] On the more institutional side, very full accounts are available about the provincial responses which federal development initiatives have provoked, and about the negotiation and implementation of the recent General Development Agreements and sub-agreements.[41] These suggest that federal-provincial policy formulation has constrained the influence of provincial politicians and interest groups, while enhancing the power of civil servants. At the provincial level, efforts at provincial-municipal reorganization — the Byrne and Graham Commissions — spawned much research, as well as some serious commentary.[42] Although

38 Warren Magnusson *et al.*, *The New Reality: The Politics of Restraint in British Columbia* (Vancouver, 1984).

39 Michael Jenkin, *The Challenge of Diversity: Industrial Policy in the Canadian Federation*, Science Council of Canada, Background Study No. 50 (Ottawa, 1983); G. Bruce Doern and Glen Toner, *The Politics of Energy* (Toronto, 1985); Keith G. Banting, *The Welfare State and Canadian Federalism* (Kingston, 1982). See also Donald J. Savoie, *Regional Economic Development: Canada's Search for Solutions* (Toronto, 1986); and Clyde Weaver and Thomas L. Gunton, "From Drought Assistance to Magaprojects: Fifty Years of Regional Theory and Policy in Canada", in Donald J. Savoie, ed., *The Canadian Economy: A Regional Perspective* (Toronto, 1986), pp. 190-224.

40 Thomas J. Courchene, "A Market Perspective on Regional Disparities", *Canadian Public Policy*, 7 (1981), pp. 506-18; Ralph Matthews, *The Creation of Regional Dependency* (Toronto, 1983); Robert J. Brym and R. James Sacouman, eds., *Underdevelopment and Social Movements in Atlantic Canada* (Toronto, 1979). James B. Cannon has provided a useful review of this debate in "Explaining Regional Development in Atlantic Canada: A Review Essay", *Journal of Canadian Studies*, 19 (1984), pp. 65-86.

41 Anthony Careless, *Initiative and Response* (Montreal, 1977); Donald J. Savoie, *Federal-Provincial Collaboration* (Montreal, 1981). Donald Nemetz, "Managing Development", in Smitheram *et al.*, eds., *The Garden Transformed*, pp. 155-175; Mike Cleland, "The General Development Agreement and Provincial Economic Development", in Jamieson, ed., *Governing Nova Scotia*, pp. 163-79.

42 New Brunswick, Royal Commission on Finance and Municipal Taxation in New Brunswick, *Report* (Fredericton, 1963); Nova Scotia, Royal Commission on Education, Public Services and Provincial-Municipal Relations, *Report* (Halifax, 1974); R. Kreuger, "The

the careful historical analysis of scholars of the generation and stature of Beck and MacKinnon has not been replicated, some comparative studies of certain administrative structures are available, and provincial legislatures have drawn some attention.[43]

Finally, at the local level, while there is much material available about structural reform, there is little on how municipal governments in the region actually exercise their powers. General Canadian texts tend to make polite bows in the direction of the Maritimes, though an important recent survey does include a study of Halifax.[44] This gap is unfortunate, but it suggests opportunities for research into areas as diverse as property taxation, parking, snow removal, zoning, industrial parks, recreation, and education. These topics can be tackled at the local level, as an introduction to policy in general, and given the huge regional interest in local histories, perhaps this is a good place to start.

This brief literature review has omitted much. Government publications have hardly been mentioned, though they are accessible and very useful.[45] There has been no attempt to cite more than a few relevant articles from the policy journals. More journalistic sources like *L'Acayen*, *Atlantic Insight*, and *The New Maritimes* have not been covered. Non-specialized journals like the *Dalhousie Review* and *La revue de l'Université de Moncton* have been largely omitted, as have more technical and professional publications like the legal journals. Also neglected is much of the output of institutes like the Gorsebrook Research Insitute, Dalhousie's Institute of Public Affairs, and the Canadian Institute for Research on Regional Development. But the Maritimes is a big place and much is happening.

I have tried, however faultily, to provide some starting points for those

---

Provincial-Municipal Government Revolution in New Brunswick", *Canadian Public Administration*, 13 (1970), pp. 50-99.

43 Bellamy, Pammett and Rowat, eds., *The Provincial Political Systems*; M. Atkinson, "Reform and Inertia in the Nova Scotia Assembly", *Journal of Canadian Studies*, 14 (1979), pp. 133-41. See also Peter Aucoin, "The Expenditure Budget Process: Management Systems and Political Priorities", in Jamieson, ed., *Governing Nova Scotia*, pp. 9-19.

44 C.R. Tindal and S. Nobes Tindal, *Local Government in Canada* (2nd ed., Toronto, 1984); Donald J. Higgins, *Urban Canada: Its Government and Politics* (Toronto, 1977); David M. Cameron and Peter Aucoin, "Halifax", in Warren Magnusson and Andrew F. Sancton, eds., *City Politics in Canada* (Toronto, 1983), pp. 166-88.

45 See New Brunswick, Legislative Library, *New Brunswick Government Documents: A Checklist of Government Documents Received at the Legislative Library*, published annually since 1956 (now to appear quarterly); Nova Scotia, Legislative Library, *Publications of the Province of Nova Scotia: Quarterly Checklist*, published since 1980; and Prince Edward Island, Island Information Service, *PEI Provincial Government Publications Checklist*, published monthly since 1976.

interested in particular policy fields or questions. And I have tried also to show how much can still be done. This need not be done by professionals. If one pedagogical plea may be inserted here, it is that students be encouraged to find out for themselves about government policy, either by reading secondary sources or, preferably, by going out to conduct interviews and gather data and read government documents. In my experience, nothing is so stimulating as coming to grips with primary material, and in teaching I have found both that students learn most when discovering things themselves and that they are quite capable of conducting limited research projects. Those with an historical dimension — even if it is something as simple as reading two departmental annual reports separated by 20 years, or of seeing how tax revenues have changed over a decade — are especially thought-provoking. And research, as other teachers well know, is not beyond students' capacities. If they can learn how doctors and hospitals cure people, they can learn where the money comes from to support health care. Naturally, some ingenuity in choosing topics is needed to overcome apathy. I know this well because my classes contain football players and video-game fanatics and rock music lovers. But it is possible: let them find out where the amateur sport funding comes from, or ask whether rock music should be censored, or investigate the zoning bylaws governing video-arcade location. They can do it.

The final policy studies issue to be addressed is perhaps the hardest one — how to make sense of policy. How do we integrate information about the multifarious activities of modern governments? With respect to the central argument here, this is not just the hardest but also the *least* important issue. What counts is to get started, to look at 'politics' in the broad sense as being about what communities and governments decide to do collectively, and to begin finding out what is actually being done. Large theories which tie together disparate policies and ascribe general causes to state action are highly contestable and inherently ideological. Worrying about them may make us hesitate to start looking around, and to take the easy route of confining our attention to the party system, to electoral politics, and to the dry study of institutions as though they were immutable rather than creations of policy themselves. For the theoretically inclined, nevertheless, there do exist some short, insightful Canadian discussions of public-policy theory, and an excellent overview of theories of the modern state has appeared recently.[46]

---

46 Peter Aucoin, "Public-Policy Theory and Analysis", in G. Bruce Doern and Peter Aucoin, eds., *Public Policy in Canada*, pp. 1-26; Michael M. Atkinson and Marsha A. Chandler, "Strategies for Policy Analysis", in their *Politics of Canadian Public Policy*, pp. 3-19; Robert R. Alford and Roger Friedland, *Powers of Theory: Capitalism, the State, and Democracy* (New York, 1985).

There are at hand two less ambitious frameworks for analyzing provincial public policy. The first centres on the notion of 'province-building', an all-encompassing label for a process through which provincial states seek and obtain increased resources, adopt aggressive positions towards the central government, defend areas of provincial jurisdiction, increasingly regulate and manage provincial societies, and become more active in shaping provincial industrial structures, acting through an expanded, co-ordinated and expert bureaucracy. This concept emerged in the 1960s, and gained much currency as federal-provincial conflict rose through the 1970s.[47] The notion has been thoroughly criticized for its over-generality and neglect of the long history of provincial activism, and the Maritime provinces are unlikely candidates for its full application; nevertheless, writings about province-building contain some important themes that may help organize our thinking about provincial states and particular policy fields.[48]

The other framework which is useful for comprehending public policy in the Maritimes focusses upon the causes of state action. Broadly stated, it is possible to isolate five kinds of factors which explain what governments do. Arranged in decreasing order of immediacy, these factors are the environment within which policy is made, the institutions through which it is formed, the ideas current in the policy, the relations of power existing in the society, and, last, the processes of decision-making.[49] This checklist of causes has the merit of leading us away from simplistic explanations based on public attitudes ("the people wanted it that way") or on the personal inclinations of policy-makers ("the minister was repaying his old debts"). In accounting for state action, we must also consider the environmental features, like foreign markets and federal policy, which set limits on what Maritimes governments can do, the institutional constraints within which they operate, and the relations of power which exist among different groups in the region.

This last is often a touchy topic, but power is central to politics, and it does suggest one fruitful approach to policy studies — the investigation of interest groups. If the electoral process is a flamboyant spectacle which

47 Edwin R. Black and Alan C. Cairns, "A Different Perspective on Canadian Federalism", *Canadian Public Administration*, 9 (1966), 27-44; Alan C. Cairns, "The Governments and Societies of Canadian Federalism", *Canadian Journal of Political Science*, 10 (1977), pp. 695-725; Garth Stevenson, *Unfulfilled Union* (Toronto, 1979).

48 R.A. Young, Philippe Faucher and André Blais, "The Concept of Province-Building: A Critique", *Canadian Journal of Political Science*, 17 (1984), pp. 783-818; R.A. Young, "L'Édification de l'état provincial et le développement régional au Nouveau-Brunswick", *égalité*, 13-14 (1984-85), pp. 125-52.

49 Richard Simeon, "Studying Public Policy", *Canadian Journal of Political Science*, 9 (1976), pp. 555-80.

functions to select the incumbents of state offices, to feed the remnants of a patronage system, and occasionally to resolve highly divisive issues, its efficient counterpart in policy formation is the process through which organized groups present particular demands to state actors. Here is where the day-to-day articulation and resolution of political conflict occurs, and it is through studying the positions taken on issues by various organized interests, and comparing them with real policy outputs, that the analyst can decide who won and so ascribe power.

This point is important in several respects. First, although the study of interest groups abroad and in Canada has attracted much attention, there has been little systematic work published about organized interests in the Maritimes.[50] This is despite the fact that voluntary associations of all kinds have been proliferating in the region. As in other relatively modern societies, these interest groups represent their members in the arenas where state policy is formed. They are in contact with government and are ready to defend their members or to get involved in political competition to get what their members want. Though they have not attracted much attention, organized groups are easy and interesting to study. They are readily identifiable; they are fairly forthcoming about the positions they take on issues, with briefs and presentations at least often being available; and their leaders will usually discuss how satisfied they are with policy outcomes. A glance through local telephone books will reveal all sorts of these groups — fish and game associations, real estate boards, associations for the handicapped, farmers' organizations, sports groups, the Women's Institute — and most will have been politically active, in the non-partisan sense of expressing the membership's position on certain public issues. This universe of organizations, which is the efficient mechanism for the representation of interests and the formation of policy, deserves far more of the attention that has been lavished in the Maritimes on the party system and the hoopla of elections.

This paper has set forth an argument about what the study of Maritimes politics should involve. In doing so, I have overdrawn, perhaps, and have certainly simplified what has been the traditional approach to the topic in the region — the close study of parties and electoral politics and patronage. But this is because the standard image has deflected attention from the study of what these active and influential governments are really doing, much of which is only mildly influenced by the pressures of partisan politics. Yet is is here, with policy, that the study of Maritime politics should begin.

---

50 A. Paul Pross, ed., *Pressure Group Behaviour in Canadian Politics* (Toronto, 1975); William D. Coleman, "Analyzing the Associative Action of Business", *Canadian Public Administration*, 28 (1985), pp. 413-33.

The conditions which supported the old system, and which rendered accurate the image of regional politics which so many still retain, have changed. Scholars and educators should not simply perpetuate that image, but instead should take a fresh look at state activity. I have tried here to introduce some of the work which has been done along these new lines, and to indicate some avenues for research. In so doing I have smuggled in a plea that students be turned loose to do some of that research, especially into interest groups: then they can find a lot more to politics in the region than they are often told exists.

It has always seemed odd that many analysts who so closely describe the parties, the electoral struggles, and the rewards of patronage also find this game repugnant. And even its fans cannot ignore the cynicism about politics which study after study shows prevails in the region. Yet, despite the erosion of the conditions which supported the old system, the rise of big active states, and the emergence of different processes of making public policy, there is still a lot of concentration on this fascinating yet also repellent aspect of regional politics. And so the old image is perpetuated. But as educators we cannot avoid some responsibility for forming students' views. The approach advocated here would largely neglect the features so central in the old image of regional politics. If it had the long-run effect of helping citizens to become more aware of issues and interests, and to conceive of politics more broadly, realistically, and perhaps even uncynically, then much, I think, would be gained.

20 Studying The Maritimes: A Plea for An Interpretive Framework

T.W. Acheson

ONCE UPON A TIME THE post-confederation story of the economic history of the Maritimes appeared to be simple, tiresome and brutish. In the mid-nineteenth century there had been a golden age based on the harvesting, processing and export of a few basic staples, notably timber, ships and fish. As the age of wood, wind and sail gave way to that of iron and steam, natural advantage passed from the region, and it went into a decline which, with occasional interruptions, continues to the present. By the late nineteenth century the Maritimes had become the sick man of Confederation, a rather quaint and unchanging backwater untouched by progressive thought or modernity.

This perception was accepted even by those disputatious regionalists of the World War I period who looked back on a half century in Canada and found the problem to be the Confederation itself, an act, they argued, which had forced the region into an unnatural marriage with an interior continental state.[1] The natural alliance of eastern seaboard and Atlantic Ocean which might have seen the fulfillment of the true destiny of the Maritimes had been abandoned. Their view that the region had prospered with Reciprocity and declined under Confederation and the national policy emphasized the picture of collapse beginning with the end of the wooden ship.

The answer to these regionalists was given by Alexander Saunders in his classic economic history of the Maritimes prepared for the Rowell-Sirois Commission in 1939.[2] He propounded an interpretation of Maritime development which became the economic orthodoxy of the mid-twentieth century, an orthodoxy the outlines of which were repeated in every major text-

---

1 See H.S. Congdon, *The Maritime Provinces Claim Their Rights Under the Act of Confederation: The Right of Maritime Ports to the Trans-Atlantic Trade of Canada* (Dartmouth, 1923); A.P. Paterson, *The True Story of Confederation* (Fredericton, 1926) and *The Problems of the Maritimes Within Confederation* (Saint John, 1930); F.B. McCurdy, *A Statement of Nova Scotia's Position Before the Canadian Club of Toronto April, 1925* (Halifax, 1925).

2 S.A. Saunders, *The Economic History of the Maritime Provinces: A Study Prepared for the Royal Commission on Dominion-Provincial Relations in 1939* (Fredericton, 1984).

book of the period. Like his mentor, Harold Innis, Saunders argued that the economic backwardness of the region relative to the rest of the country was caused by geography and by the mismanagement of natural resources. Saunders argued that free trade with the New England states would have done little to improve the regional economy, that neither Confederation nor the national policy adversely effected the regional economy, that the consolidation of industry in Central Canada was a natural evolution that of itself demonstrated the superiority of central Canadian industry over that of the Maritimes. Most important, everything that had happened between 1867 and 1939 had been the result of natural laws against which no force of human will or endeavour could have prevailed. The economic fate of the region, Saunders argued, was to return to its early nineteenth century roots, and using external capital, produce a few staples for international markets. All other economic activity was and could be of little significance.

Modifications of this bleak and deterministic interpretation began about 1970. At one end of the time period a number of output studies demonstrated that in 1870 the *per capita* industrial output of manufactures in the Maritimes, but especially in New Brunswick, was not markedly different from that in Central Canada. Studying the Nova Scotian economy of 1970, Roy George argued that cost differences of factor inputs could not explain the shortage of new plants in the province.[3]

Examining the century between these two events, several historians and historical geographers challenged the assumptions of the traditional orthodoxy that had been accepted by both Saunders and his 1920s regionalist opponents.[4] They discovered, in fact, that a number of communities in

---

3 Gordon Bertram, "Historical Statistics on Growth and Structure of Manufacturing in Canada 1870-1957", Canadian Political Science Association Conference on Statistics 1962 and 1963, *Report*, p. 122; Roy George, *A Leader and A Laggard* (Toronto, 1970), ch. 9.

4 See T.W. Acheson, "The National Policy and the Industrialization of the Maritimes 1880-1910", *Acadiensis*, I/1 (Spring 1972), pp. 3-28; E.R. Forbes, "Misguided Symmetry" in D. Bercuson, ed., *Canada and the Burden of Unity* (Toronto, 1977), pp. 3-34; David Frank, "The Cape Breton Coal Industry and the Rise and Fall of the British Empire Steel Corporation", *Acadiensis*, VII/1 (Autumn 1977), pp. 3-34; David Alexander, *Atlantic Canada and Confederation: Essays in Canadian Political Economy* (Toronto, 1983); Gerry Panting, "Cradle of Enterprise: Yarmouth, Nova Scotia, 1840-1889" in Lewis Fischer and Eric Sager, eds., *The Enterprising Canadians: Entrepreneurs and Economic Development in Eastern Canada 1820-1914* (St. John's, 1979), pp. 253-72; R.H. Babcock, "Economic Development in Portland (Me.) and Saint John (N.B.) during the Age of Iron and Steam 1850-1914", *The American Review of Canadian Studies*, IX (Spring 1979), pp. 3-37; Henry Veltmeyer, "The Capitalist Underdevelopment of Atlantic Canada" in R.J. Brym and R.J. Sacouman, eds., *Underdevelopment and Social Movements in Atlantic Canada* (Toronto, 1979), pp. 17-35; L.D. McCann,

the region had developed a significant industrial base in the generation following Confederation. Part of this was a continuation of trends which had pre-Confederation roots; much of it directly resulted from the national tariff and transportation policies. The decline of the older staples economy was paralleled by the rise of a substantial industrial economy shaped around textiles, iron, steel and coal. The region already possessed its own financial institutions and soon controlled its own railway link with central Canada. Maritime entrepreneurs and communities, these scholars argued, responded to the new opportunities offered by the national policies just as effectively as had those of central Canada. By 1900 we can speak of two Maritimes — one based on the traditional staples and the other on the continental-oriented industrial base. The consolidation process which occurred early in the twentieth century removed control of much of this new industry from the region but did not effectively diminish its industrial base.

The collapse that critically crippled the economy, the revisionists argue, occurred not in the 1870s but in the post World War I period. The collapse was not the natural ending of a technologically irrelevant wooden ship building activity, but the destruction of an already-developed industrial economy.[5] And that collapse was as much the result of political decisions taken in Ottawa between 1915 and 1922 as it was the operation of any iron law of economics or geography. The broken society of the 1920s was forced to return to the development of staples industry based on the exploitation of timber and fish. Paper making helped the economy but basically the increased significance of primary industry in the region after 1920 reflects the general industrial collapse.[6]

The Great Depression, of course, was a common denominator spreading its miserable effects through North America. It was only in the post World War II period that some feeble efforts to rejuvenate the Maritime economy are obvious. They began with transfer payments to governments and individuals. They continued with shared cost arrangements in education, health and welfare. They culminated in efforts to create a regional industry

"Staples and New Industries in the Growth of Post-Confederation Halifax", *Acadiensis*, VIII/2 (Spring 1979), pp. 47-97, and "The Mercantile — Industrial Transition in the Metal Towns of Pictou County 1857-1931", *ibid.*, X/2 (Spring 1981), pp. 29-64; Eric Sager and Lewis J. Fischer, "Atlantic Canada and the Age of Sail Revisited", *Canadian Historical Review*, LXIII (1982), pp. 125-50; James D. Frost, "The Nationalization of the Bank of Nova Scotia 1880-1910", *Acadiensis*, XII/1 (Autumn 1982), pp. 3-38, and Ian McKay, "Industry, Work and Community in the Cumberland Coalfields 1848-1927" (PhD thesis, Dalhousie University, 1983).

5   E.R. Forbes, *The Maritime Rights Movement* (Montreal, 1979).

6   T.W. Acheson, "The Maritimes and Empire Canada" in *Canada and the Burden of Unity.*

through the development of power grids, transportation systems and, finally, the controversial incentive payments to entrepreneurs. This federal intervention played a considerable role in the development of a substantial service sector in the regional economy after 1950, one which eventually provided employment for a substantial majority of the regional work force. Many private and public figures deplore the scale of this intervention, its costs and its effects; others justify it as a proper response to the experience which has brought us to where we are.

But what significance do these arcane controversies have for students involved in the study of the region? Considerable, I would suggest. For one thing the question can be examined at several levels. At the first level, simply told, the newer interpretations provide an interesting story; indeed, for residents of the area it is a compelling story. For some classes it may not be possible to go much beyond this level. For most students, a move to the second level is to deal with the intellectual challenges offered in the often conflicting interpretations. Finally, for the few, one might raise the challenge of the larger issues of determinism and the capacity of human endeavour.

Above all, the study of these issues provide the opportunity for development of the most important intellectual skills that any social studies can inculcate: the capacity for critical thinking. Among these skills one of the most useful is the examination of levels of ambiguity inherent in any situation. Students must be taught not to accept any opinion easily, must be brought to understand the elements of opinion inherent in any explanation of social events. They should be taught to examine critically the explanations of Maritime romantics like the early regionalists and Andrew Macphail who offer unambiguous explanations of a rejuvenation of the regional economy by returning to the land, or building canoes, or what seems to be a preposterous industrial development. But also they should be taught to look critically at the equally unambiguous explanations of social scientists like Saunders who pronounce on cause by appeal to a general theory, which has as many exceptions as there are in the declension of French verbs, and who can not explain why resourceless Japan is arguably the world's major industrial economy, Switzerland has the highest standard of living in Europe, and Sweden, with only 7,000,000 people, has a major automobile industry. (I, too, laughed at the idea of marketing a Bricklin from New Brunswick until Michelin proved they could market tires from Nova Scotia.)

Unfortunately you will not have the opportunity to deal with any of the issues raised here. Despite the fact that most of the literature relating to the Maritime economy deals with the pre-1945 period, the people responsible for the structure of the new course have decreed that it will begin in 1945. The same faceless experts have also decreed that emphasis shall be placed on the enterprise of Maritimers, thus minimizing the role of federal intervention. You and your students will, therefore, be the victims of another form of unambiguity, this one based upon the interpretive vaccuum. The lack of a proper interpretive framework will be a major problem in New Brunswick where this course will comprise much of the grade 10 academic programme and it will require additional materials and further curriculum development to overcome these weaknesses and give respectability to that programme.

21 *Regional Economic Development*

Roy George

IF THERE IS ONE ECONOMIC topic that preoccupies the minds of people living in the Maritimes, it is regional economic development. It may not be of much comfort to them to point out that their region is not unique. Every country has regions that are poor relative to other regions. The USA has its relatively poor areas in Appalachia and the South. Scotland, Wales and Northern England are economically worse off than London and the South-East. In France residents of the northeastern part of the country are not on average as well off as those who live in Paris. The Mezzogiorno in the south of Italy is much worse off than northern Italy. And much the same situation can be found in other countries, both developed and developing.

So called "depressed areas" are nearly always areas that have seen better days. In earlier periods, they were relatively prosperous, but they relied on industries that have fallen into decline. The traditional textile and coal mining areas are depressed in almost all Western countries and agriculture and fishing tend to be the main support of many relatively poor communities. And as proximity to markets has become more and more important, economic activity has been drawn away from outlying areas.

The Canadian scene is familiar to eastern Canadians. According to Statistics Canada (Catalog 13-201), personal income per capita in the Atlantic Provinces in 1984 was $10,815 (Newfoundland $9,702, Nova Scotia $11,693, Prince Edward Island $10,310, and New Brunswick $10,734), and was thus only 75 percent of that of Canada as a whole ($14,414). Even this relatively lowly position was maintained only because of large transfer payments from the federal government to the region. The Atlantic Region is the economic Cinderella of Canada; technological developments and improvements in transportation since the mid-nineteenth century have undermined its shipbuilding, coal, steel, agriculture, and small manufacturing industries, and made Quebec and Ontario the undisputed centre of the country's economic activity.

Two qualifications of this statement should be noted. First, comparisons of standards of living are usually done on the basis of money income per head of the population. Though this is probably as good as any other measure available, it ignores non-monetary factors which are important to living standards. For instance, many people in the Atlantic Region value highly their relatively stress-free, unpolluted way of life, but this is difficult to evaluate and is seldom included in calculations. And, second, though people in the Atlantic Provinces are economically worse off than other Canadians, they are fabulously rich compared with most of the world's population, and they are much better off than their forebears. It is just that the region has not developed as quickly as other parts of Canada.

Nevertheless, many eastern Canadians are resentful that they should be the poor relations. They tend to blame it on Confederation, which obstructed the north-south flow of commerce, and on subsequent government policies, particularly the Macdonald tariff policy that benefited the manufacturing centres of the country. Such blame is justified only to a minor degree, since the signs of relative decline are traceable to pre-Confederation times.

The general explanation of regional unevenness of development is based upon the location of markets and the cost of production. The Atlantic market is only about 2 million people; the main Canadian markets are 800-1000 miles away; and the costs of production are inflated by the absence of some materials and the small scale of operation (which in turn is partly the result of remoteness from the large markets). And, when development is retarded, there tends to be an outflow of entrepreneurs, capital funds and skilled labour, and the environment and morale of people who remain tend to deteriorate. The downward spiral eventually leads to a low plateau from which recovery is difficult.

During the post-war period, many governments took the position that regional disparities on the existing scale were unacceptable. In Canada in the 1960s, the official philosophy was that Canadians should have similar opportunities and standards of living, wherever they lived. Based upon this philosophy, strategies were put in place to stimulate the development of the country's relatively poor areas, of which the Atlantic Region was the clearest example. The weapons used in Canada have been similar to those used in other developed countries; indeed, they were in many cases copied directly from those used elsewhere. The best known have been the regional industrial incentives offered for new and expanded activities (usually manufacturing) in the designated areas. There have also been tax incentives for the same purpose, and subsidies for transportation, the upgrading of the economic environment, and industrial parks, and estates. And there have been direct fiscal transfers from federal to provincial governments to raise the standard of social services (health, education, welfare and the like) and to finance provincial administration.

It would be nice to be able to report that these strategies have been successful. But there is little evidence in any developed country that regional economic disparities have been significantly reduced. It may be that government strategies have prevented further deterioration, but of that one cannot be sure. Certainly, regional disparities are little different from what they were in the 1960s, even though, out of desperation, governments have heaped incentive onto incentive until a bewildering array now exists. Poor regions in western countries have enjoyed development, but rich regions have developed at the same or higher rates, and so the disparities have stayed the same or increased. Enthusiasm throughout the world for strategies to stimulate regional development has waned — partly because of their seeming futility, and partly because the general economic malaise that descended on western countries in the late 1970s has diverted governments' attention to national rather than regional development.

Students of regional development as part of a high school course in Maritime studies could, with profit, be led to an understanding of the region's present economic situation and of how this situation arose, and encouraged to examine remedies. Topics that should be interesting and helpful to them would include:

A. *The Population of the Maritimes*
— The growth of the region's population over the last century or two; the contribution of immigration to this growth; the immigration patterns: the origins of immigrants, why they left their homelands, where they settled and what economic activity they created; the loss through outmigration: why migrants left and where they went; the contribution of natural increase to population growth: how birthrates have changed over the years and the reasons for such changes; how deathrates have altered, and the role of economic conditions in reducing them; and the future impact on economic growth of a static or declining population.
— The age distribution of the population of the region; the present pattern and how it developed; and the implications of changing age structures in the future — an increasing burden on the working population, changing patterns of demand and production and the possible lowering of the vitality of the population.

B. *Incomes in the Maritimes*
— Historical trends and fluctuations of real and money incomes; comparisons of the region's income per capita with that of the rest of Canada and other countries; reasons for the disparity between the region and Canada; and government policies to reduce disparities; their nature and effectiveness.
— Distribution within the Maritimes: by economic groups and location; reasons for the uneven distribution.

C. *Economic Activity in the Maritimes*
   — The geographical distribution in the region: the present pattern and historical changes, and the reasons for this pattern (why certain industries are located in particular towns).
   — The size distribution of economic units by numbers of workers and value of output: why some industries have grown while others have remained small.

D. *Economic Links*
   — The region's trade with other parts of Canada and other countries, by commodity and destination.
   — Patterns and modes of the transportation activities which carry the region's trade.

In the short time available, it would be impossible to cover this ground in any detail. No doubt, the course would be most interesting if teachers selected topics with which they were most comfortable and explored them in some depth, rather than risking smothering students with factual information about the whole range of relevant topics.

Teachers are unlikely to discover texts or other books suitable for students which cover the selected topics. Introductory economic textbooks would be quite inappropriate. Stories about early immigrants, tales of adventure of seamen of the region, accounts of life in various parts of the region and in various industries, and other books which give a flavour of economic activities in the past and present and quicken students' interest in economic development, would seem appropriate.

The success of this course, as with all other courses, will depend on the knowledge of the teacher and how the material is presented. Again, no introductory textbook is likely to help much. The single source which is most likely to be useful to the teacher is Statistics Canada's *Canada Year Book*; it provides most of the factual information required (though its statistics tend to be a little stale) and gives commentaries on most of the topics suggested above. Other publications which might prove helpful are listed in the bibliography.

To mount a course of a few weeks' duration, which is meaningful and interesting to grade 9 students, will be a difficult and challenging task calling for much preparation and ingenuity on the part of the teachers concerned.

SELECTED BIBLIOGRAPHY

Atlantic development, a socio-economic perspective, a seminar presented by the Maritime School of Social Work of Dalhousie University and the Atlantic Provinces Economic Council, 4, 5 April 1974 (Halifax, 1974).

Buckner, P.A. and Frank, D., eds., *Atlantic Canada after Confederation: the Acadiensis Reader, Volume two* (Fredericton, 1985).

Chapin, M., *Atlantic Canada* (Toronto, 1956).

Economic Council of Canada, *Living together: a study of regional disparities* (Ottawa, 1977),

Fischer, L.R. and Sager, E.W., eds., *Atlantic Canada Shipping Project Conference* (5th : 1981) (St. John's, Newfoundland, 1982).

George, R.E., *A leader and a laggard: Manufacturing Industry in Nova Scotia, Quebec and Ontario* (Toronto 1970).

—————, *The life and times of Industrial Estates Limited* (Halifax, 1974).

Lithwick, N.H., *Regional economic policy: the Canadian experience* (Toronto, 1978).

Ridler, N.B., ed., *Issues in regional/urban development of Atlantic Canada* (Saint John, 1978).

Saunders, S.A., *The economic history of the Maritime Provinces* (Fredericton, 1984).

Woodfine, W., "Regional Economic Disparities — Once Again", *Canadian Public Policy*, I (1983), pp. 499-505.

22 *Folklore and Social History*

Georges Arsenault

FOLKLORE IS VERY MUCH A PART of our culture and of our history. Many people see folklore mainly as something quaint and entertaining; therefore not as a serious subject of research and study. Fortunately, that attitude is gradually waning and more and more scholars are recognizing that the study of the folklore and folklife of a people can contribute substantially to social history and to the history of mentalities. The study of folklore is especially important when studying the common people — the folk — that is to say the main segment of population that traditional history books have taught us to ignore. It is true that those people were not our great political history makers; however they are those who are at the basis of our culture, who are at the root of our distinctiveness as Maritimers. Webster's definition of the word "folk" reminds us clearly of that: "the great proportion of the members of a people that determines the group character and that tends to preserve its characteristic form of civilization and its customs, arts and crafts, legends, traditions, and superstitions from generation to generation".

In my paper I shall try to illustrate some ways by which folklore can contribute to the study of the social history of the Maritimes. I shall limit myself to two genres, namely to the folksong and folktale traditions. My examples will be taken from my area of research which is Acadian folklore, and more specifically, Acadian folklore from Prince Edward Island.

Studying social history through the folksong tradition can be a very fruitful experience. By a close examination of the folksong repertoire, one can get an insight into the mentality and the values of the common people. Not all the songs of the Acadian repertoire can lead to such a discovery. The Acadian folksong repertoire is made up of over 80 per cent of French traditionals, which are songs composed in France and brought over to North America by the pioneers. These constitute a very rich inheritance and it is well known that the French folksong tradition has been better preserved in French Canada, and particularly in the Acadian community, than it has been in the mother country. Unfortunately, these songs, many of which were composed in the Middle Ages, tell us little of the culture and way of life of the nineteenth- and twentieth-century Acadian. For such information one has to examine the locally made songs which make up some 15 to 20 per cent of the traditional repertoire. Most of these local songs can be grouped into three categories: 1) "complaintes" — or ballads; 2) humorous and satirical songs; and 3) songs composed about special events. They were the works of mainly illiterate men and women whose preoccupation was not to promote Acadian nationalism — as was the case with the men of letters — but to "document" the daily life of their community with its qualities and its faults. Through these songs, one gets a sense of values and priorities of those communities.

The "complaintes" are long narrative and plaintive songs composed to remember tragic events such as drownings. A number of preoccupations come out clearly in these songs, the main one being the importance of their religious beliefs. The song-makers were constantly worried about the faith of the victim: would he make it to heaven even if he died before going to confession or without receiving the last sacrament? At the end of their laments, the authors usually asked their audience to pray for the salvation of the soul of the deceased. The following example is from the ballad composed on Francois Richard, from Mont-Carmel (P.E.I.), who was the victim of an accident while working in a quarry in Rumford Falls, Maine in 1892:

> Celle qui fit cette chanson
> Engage tous pour ce jeune garçon
> De dire un Pater et un Ave
> Pour lui aider à se sauver
> La Sainte Vierge faut tous prier
> (Pour) que son âme soit pardonnée.

> (The author of this song
> Urges you all, on behalf of this young lad,
> To say a Pater and an Ave
> To help him save his soul.
> The Blessed Virgin we shall all pray
> So that his soul will be pardoned.)

The "complaintes" also tell us a great deal of the people's belief in fatalism and their resignation in the face of it, of the importance of community solidarity and of the people's attachment to their community.

In the humorous and satirical songs, the preoccupations are of another order. Here the fundamental value was the importance of respecting the local customs and traditions. The traditional social structure was not to be broken and social values such as integrity, uprightness and honesty were highly prized. Individuals who broke those social values could be publicly disgraced through a song. That is what happened to Sylvain Caissie who had stolen and killed his boss' dog. Caissie was severely reprehended by a fellow worker, Thomas Arsenault, better known as Tom Madgitte, the song-maker. This song, composed around 1890, became well known in the community:

Le Chien à Paneau (free translation)

1.   Listen to the story
Of a man called Sylvain Pichi
He played a dirty trick
He stole Paneau's dog.
Some say he shot the animal
Tied down in his basement

2.   It was at noontime, on a Thursday,
Pichi arrived at the factory.
He said he had come
To fetch a vessel he needed for tarring.
But what he had in his mind
Was to take Calbé away.

3.   Pichi, if you had been cautious
You would have taken him by night
Then nobody would have suspected
That you had kidnapped him.
Now everybody says:
That's another of Pichi's tricks.

4.   Pichi, if you received
The sacrements more often
You'd live more happily
With your wife and children,
You wouldn't always have in mind
To kill all the Calbés.

5.   When you'll go to confession
To repair your scandal
The good curé will tell you:
Go pay for that dog,
You will pay "hotly"
For Joe Paneau's nice dog.

6. If you go to Paradise
    Without paying the full price
    Good St. Peter will tell you:
    "Go in the hole down below
    You will find that the price is hot
    For Joe Paneau's Calbé".

There are many songs, such as "Le Chien à Paneau", which reveal the force of folk sanction in traditional Acadian society.

Another group of locally composed songs documents family or community happenings deemed worth remembering. Events such as the building of a factory, a rug-hooking frolic, the birth of twins, and even the mysterious appearance of a ghost (such as the Richibouctou ghost of 1932), have all been celebrated in songs. In those compositions, song-makers remind us that there is indeed a good side to life, that life can in fact be fun. They also sing the pride that they have in belonging to their family and community.

The "complaintes", the humorous and satirical songs, and those songs composed about special local events tell us much about the people's values and mentalities. They offer, however, much more. They also hand down a great deal of information about the activities and traditions of specific communities and of important events which unfolded at the local level. Briefly, these songs offer a broad variety of themes dealing with such things as economic life, community recreation, election practices, tragedies, wedding customs, religious beliefs, and so on.

A study of the song tradition does imply more than a study of the texts. It also implies that we examine the role of singing, that is to say that we look at the various functions which it played in society. We have to consider the role which the singer and the song-maker had in the community. That role was in many ways similar to the one played by the story-teller in the folktale tradition which I would now like to discuss briefly.

Folktales make up an interesting and exciting subject of study. Like folksongs, they have been transmitted orally for many centuries, easily crossing political and linguistic borders to the extent that most folktales are universal. In other words, versions of one specific tale can be found in many countries of the Western World and even beyond. Although this phenomenon is fascinating and the contents of the tales appealing, the study of the folktale tradition should go beyond this when studying the local tradition, especially in the classroom. In my opinion, it is important for a student to come to understand the social function which the folktale and especially the "conteur" or story-teller had in a community. The art of story-telling was a most appreciated form of entertainment prior to the advent of modern forms of entertainment such as radio, cinema, television, organized sports and, of course, bingo. Story-telling was a primitive form of theatre which is still very much alive in traditional communities around the world.

If story-telling were such an important entertainment in a community, then the "conteur" was a member of the community who was highly esteemed. This story-teller was a true actor who was sought not only in his home community but also in the surrounding districts. One indication of his popularity was the mention of his name in local news columns. For example, on 20 January 1898, it was mentioned in *L'Impartial*, a French-language newspaper published in Tignish, P.E.I., that Monsieur Charles Richard, renowned as a "conteur", entertained the guests at a silver wedding anniversary party. On 22 March 1923, the Abram's Village notes, published in *L'Evangéline*, mentioned the visit of a story-teller in the district:

M. André Gallant, from St-Chrysostome, was visiting Abram's Village last week. M. Gallant, who always has interesting stories to yarn, and who knows very well how to entertain, has made himself a great number of friends who are always glad to show him hospitality.

Story-telling was done in a number of informal contexts. The "conteur" would yarn for a group of people of different ages, mostly neighbours gathered in a kitchen. He could also perform in the lumbercamps or in the living quarters of a lobster factory. Mme Florence Bernard remembers vividly as a child, in the 1920s, attending some of those evenings of story-telling. Her stepfather, Ferdinand, a story-teller, and his friend Jack Maxime, a conteur from the neighbouring district, sometimes got together to tell stories. Neighbours, adults and children alike, looked forward to those fall and winter evenings of entertainment which started at about 7 or 8 o'clock in the evening. The kitchen was usually packed with avid listeners, children sitting directly on the floor and keeping a perfect silence as the "actors" unfolded their wonderful stories.

Story-tellers were not always such public figures. In fact, most families had at least one member who could readily assume the role of story-teller for the children. The repertoire was passed down orally from generation to generation. The tales were usually told as bedtime stories. Today, story books have somewhat modified the tradition, although published versions of folktales are still seemingly the most popular bedtime stories for children.

At a time when we are constantly being exposed to cultural influences coming to us from outside our region, and more often from outside our country, it is important, I feel, that Maritimers be made more aware of their identity by exposing themselves more to their cultural heritage. The schools are indeed an area where this sensitizing can be attempted. My belief is that when students are made aware of the folklore of their community and ethnic background, they will carry this knowledge with them throughout their lives. It will serve as a source of inspiration and it will, in many ways, enhance and enrich the cultural life of the Maritimes. May I mention, in closing, that some of the artists who have most contributed to Acadian and Québécois culture are individuals who did study their folklore quite seriously. Antonine Maillet, Edith Butler, Angèle Arsenault, Gilles Vigneault and Pierre Perreault are examples that can be pointed out.

23 The Foxfire Approach: Oral History In The Classroom

Edward D. Ives

IN OUR INSTRUCTIONS FOR this particular program, Phil Buckner told us not to use a "how-to" approach. He did not want us to talk about methods but about problems in Maritime studies. In what I want to talk about today it is really impossible to separate out method from content; they are one. The material gathered and the experience of gathering it are essentially equal in their educational benefits. The approach has had several different names, but the one that seems to be most often used now is cultural journalism, and, I'll settle for that. I have used, in the title, the phrase "Foxfire Approach", because certainly *Foxfire* and the series of Foxfire books emanating from it is the most famous example; but let's call it cultural journalism.

What it comes to is that students create their own subject matter by interviewing members of their own community; then they work these interviews up into some coherent form, ultimately publishing the results in a magazine or a booklet or something like that. I say *their* community, but while it is physically located in a familiar place, it turns out to be almost an "other" community, because frequently young people of high school age and younger don't really have any contact with or any knowledge of the community that their grandparents grew up in and experienced. So for them, it is a truly anthropological sort of discovery. One of the nicest parts about it is, of course, that they discover in this process that their grandfather or grandmother faced and had to solve many of the very problems that they themselves have to face today.

I have often thought of this as kind of a Ptolemaic approach. Carl Becker said somewhere that all history starts with the question, "Who am I?" Its next extension is, "Who are we?" What gives the community, town, province, or nation we live in its particular identity? And of course, coming along with all of this is "Who are they?" That is, we get into the question of "us" as opposed to "others". But we start with the questions, "Who am I? Where did I come from? How am I different from the other people around me, and how am I the same?" So this is where we start, where oral history starts, and the oral history approach gives the student a very alive and dynamic sense of the search for roots, if you want to call it that, or for identity, if you want to call it *that*.

There is no question that the material that is gathered in this way is useful. That is, the students, if they do their work well, go out and interview people who have had experiences in which they are interested. They interview someone who used to be a lumberman, a woodsman, a river driver, a sailor, a longshoreman, a farmer, or a midwife. Those interviews are useful not only to the student directly but also to others, especially if the material is put where it can be used by other people. But the point I wish to emphasize is the the *process* of gathering the material is just as valuable a learning experience for the student as is the material so gathered.

One of the first things the student gets is some idea of what historical documentation actually amounts to. By creating their *own* document, which is what you do in oral history work, they really come to know how tenuous any historical document can be. So they learn to question sources.

There is a tendency in our culture to believe that if something is in writing it is authoritative. An oral history interview transcribed looks much more authoritative, much more trustworthy, than that same interview when it was simply on tape and not written down. Nonetheless, it is the same document either way, and either way it has the same problems that any other historical document has. That is, all documents must be tested in the light of how they were created and how they have been preserved. Knowing how trustworthy the document he or she created is, the student learns to question documents created by others, be they state papers or diaries or public records.

Let me give a couple of examples here. Not too long ago, one of my classes was working on the experiences of women during the Great Depression, particularly during the 1930s. In order to prepare them for this, the other teacher who was presenting the course with me, a historian, gave a series of lectures on what happened during the Depression; and of course she showed pictures of bread lines and soup kitchens and men out of work — the typical pictures one sees in history books representing that particular period. After being given this historical background, the students went out interviewing women here in Maine on what the Depression was like for them, and they were terribly disappointed. Rather than hearing stories about soup kitchens and massive unemployment, what they heard was "Oh, it wasn't so bad.....We always had enough to eat....My husband had a job....We didn't have a lot of money, but it wasn't so bad". And, as I say, they were rather disappointed. They felt cheated, because they had been led to expect reports of soup kitchens and they did not get them.

What, then, were they to believe? Were the experiences of the people they were talking to atypical? Or were the reports that they read in the history books wrong? It brought up questions of the reliability of what they read, how things must be qualified, and how different parts of the country certainly experienced the Depression differently. I think that that was a very important lesson; and I think that many students learned it through the interviewing process.

Another example. A student wanted to do a series of interviews with his grandfather, someone he had been very close to. I said, "Okay John, go to it". He remembered his grandfather as a wonderful storyteller, someone he used to enjoy listening to a great deal. So he went ahead and had a series of interviews with him — I guess he had five or six hours of interview with him altogether. Then unfortunately his grandfather died. There was John, left without really any way to complete his project. Well, we changed the project. I said, "Okay John, why don't you start interviewing other people in the family *about* your grandfather?" So he started doing that, and he also started checking out documentary sources on his grandfather as well. That is, birth and death records, employment records, all this sort of thing, and comparing them with what his grandfather had said.

That led to a real shocker. One of the stories he had asked his grandfather to tell, and that his grandfather had told him many times, was the story of his experiences in World War I — how he went to France, and how in the battle of Guinea Ridge he lost the use of several fingers on his left hand. John discovered through documentary records that his grandfather had never been to France. His grandfather had been in the service for a grand total of about seven days, and then he was discharged. So John had caught his grandfather in what looked like a bald-faced lie. But that led him to think about the whole thing. John finally discovered that his grandfather told that story about his experiences in France only when he had been pushed to tell it, either by John or by his brother. John finally decided that the man was only doing what he thought his grandchildren expected of him, which was kind of an interesting conclusion. John has now finished this work, and it's a fine job. But it has been a tremendous experience for John, not only the experience of putting that thing together but of coming to understand his grandfather's motivations. It has brought him closer to his grandfather than he had ever been before.

Thus there is a sort of age-to-age bonding that frequently comes out of this process. Students may have never experienced talking to an older person for any length of time, and I find that they often become very fond of the person they are interviewing. And, if it is a relative, that person may become, as it happened with John and his grandfather, even more important to them than he was before.

I can give examples from my own experiences, my own interviewing. I had about forty hours of interviews with one man, and he became a very close friend and a very important person in my life. I certainly am a different person because I interviewed Ernest. Another student, Wayne Bean, one of those people who as a child simply loved to sit down and listen to old people tell their stories, developed a very close relationship with his grandfather's best friend, a man named Ralph Thornton. Ultimately, Wayne took my oral history field work course and continued his interviews with Ralph on a more formal basis. He compiled many hours of interviews, from which he put together a little book known as *Me and Fannie*.[1] He and Ralph became very close. Another student had twenty or thirty hours of interviews with a former game warden. Once again, the two became fast friends, and they still are fast friends, a good eight or ten years after the interviews took place. They still correspond, and when Bill comes back to this part of the country, one of the people he always goes to see is Dave the game warden. That is certainly one of the reasons I can recommend this process to you as a learning experience. Wayne and Bill's worlds were enlarged by it. So has mine been, and I think your students' worlds will be too.

Now I can suggest two slightly different classroom approaches that you can use in working with oral history. The first we will call biographical; that is, the student decides that he or she is going to write a biography of some one person. Therefore, he or she has a series of interviews with that one person and puts this biography together from things that the particular person said in the interviews. When I have used this approach with students, I have always insisted on two things. First, the biography must be as honest and forthright a presentation of the subject's life as the student can make it. It must, that is, satisfy the student. Second, it has to be acceptable to the subject as well. That person has to read it and say, "Yes, I am willing to have this published". Now those are two different problems, quite different, and, as you can imagine, it is a tough assignment for students to reconcile them. They find that sometimes the person they are interviewing does not want them to say certain things, while they feel it is necessary to say them in order to present the subject accurately. All biographers of living people face these problems, and there is no reason why high school students should not attempt to face them too.

A second approach is to make a topical assignment, in which you choose one subject and everyone works on that. Let us say that there is a mill in town that is no longer in operation. You get the students to talk to the people who used to work in that mill and who remember what it was like. They can also talk to women whose husbands used to work in that mill, in order to get them to tell what it was like from their point of view. If the whole class is working on one particular subject, they begin to get all kinds

---

1   Wayne Bean, ed., *Me and Fannie: The Oral Autobiography of Ralph Thornton of Topsfield, Maine* (Orono: *Northeast Folklore* XIV, 1973).

of different perspectives on it — how this person saw it, how that one, etc. They can then learn how to pull out those things that all of the interviews have in common and weigh them against those about which there is a difference of opinion.

I have had excellent luck with this approach. We at the Northeast Archives have brought out several books based on such student assignments. For instance there was *Argyle Boom*, a description of how logs were sorted out at the end of the river drive on the Penobscot River. The Boom went out of operation in the 1930s, but we interviewed eighteen men who had worked there, and we were able to take those interviews and, by digesting and synthesizing them, produce a book that described the whole operation.[2]

Just this past year, students worked on the subject of how Halloween is and was celebrated here in Maine. They talked to all kinds of people — not only to older people but also to young people, and even to children. They asked such questions as, "What did you do last Halloween? Did you go trick-or-treating? At what age did you stop going out on Halloween, and why?" We also gathered information on carving pumpkins, not only on how does one carve a pumpkin and what should a proper jack-o-lantern look like but also on who in the family did the carving. In my own family, for instance, I, the father, always did that. I did not want the children carving them, partly out of fear they might "cut themselves", partly out of pure selfishness, I'm afraid. Under the guise of "helping" I indulged myself. I was interested to see how typical this turned out to be, as the interviews progressed.

Let me go back for a moment to the biographical approach. One of the things I would suggest is that you try and get the students away from the idea that they have to interview an "old" person or someone whose experiences were out of the ordinary. Have them interview all kinds of people. Let them interview a member of their own family; they will find out how difficult that can be, because of all the shared assumptions, the things you don't *need* to talk about. Let them interview the local grocer — if there still are local grocers in this day of supermarkets! Let them talk to an automobile mechanic or a druggist. There are many ways for them to discover the common man and learn by so doing that no man is common.

I might say in closing that Eliot Wigginton, who founded *Foxfire* and who is sort of the high priest of the whole movement, has pointed out several times that this particular approach is not necessarily the answer for your "good" student, the one who has the system figured out and who is certainly going on to college. That student may profit from it, no question, but it is interesting how often it benfits the "poor" student, the one

---

2   Edward Ives, ed., *Argyle Boom* (Orono: *Northeast Folklore* XVII, 1976).

who doesn't have the system all figured, the student who is something of an academic "problem". I have heard these students say, "I was ready to drop out of school, I had had enough. Then I got into this course and I really got turned on by it". It does work in that way.

I have not said anything about technique or about necessary equipment. Some of the books in the Bibliography will tell you all you need to know about that, and all I can do at this point I suppose is thank you for listening, and wish you the best of luck.

SELECTED BIBLIOGRAPHY

Allen, Barbara and Montell, Lynwood, *From Memory to History: Using Oral Sources in Local Historical Research* (Nashville, 1981).

Bishop, John Melville and Bishop, Naomi Hawes, *Making Home Video: How to Get the Most from your Videocassette Recording Equipment* (n.p., Wideview Books, 1980).

Gebhard, Krzysztof M., *Community as Classroom: A Teacher's Practical Guide to Oral History* (Regina and Saskatoon, 1985).

Hands On: Newsletter for Cultural Journalism (Published Quarterly by Foxfire, Rabun Gap, Georgia 30568).

Ives, Edward D., *The Tape-Recorded Interview* (Knoxville, 1981).

Sitton, Thad, Mohalfy, George L., and Davis Jr., O.L., *Oral History: A Guide for Teachers (and Others)* (Austin, 1983).

Wigginton, Eliot, *Sometimes a Shining Moment: Twenty Years in a High School Classroom — The Foxfire Experience* (New York, 1985).

Wood, Pamela, *You and Aunt Arie* (Boulder, 1975).

Zeitlin, Steven J., Kotkin, Amy J., and Baker, Holly Cutting, *A Celebration of American Family Folklore* (New York, 1982).

24 Offering New Lamps for Old Ones: The Study of Acadian Folklore Today

Ronald Labelle

WHEN I BEGAN PREPARING THIS TALK, I was thinking about ways in which to explain the usefulness of studying folklore. I was reflecting on the fact that folklorists often find themselves defending the very nature of their study against those who still believe that folklore should be discarded as a remnant of past ignorance. This thought reminded me of the folktale in which an old lamp possessing magic powers is left in the hands of a person who is unaware of its value. It is then foolishly traded away to a clever villain who comes offering new lamps in exchange for old ones. In Acadian society today, people have a tendency to trade away their old lamps without thinking they may in fact be precious. In wanting to get away from the old "Evangéline" stereotype, the Acadian educated class is concentrating its efforts in promoting a modern view of their people by studying contemporary phenomena. This approach implies a rejection of cultural traits which reflect the past. Not that they are trying to forget their past in general: it is more a question of getting away from the disadvantaged position the Acadians used to hold in the Maritimes. To put it simply, because folklore thrives among illiterate peasants, it has become taboo.

Whatever the exact causes of this situation, it is a fact that the unique cultural heritage of the Acadians is sadly being ignored today. What we can do to change this is to show that a lot of traditional beliefs and practices are still relevant in today's society and that they do tell us something about who we are and not only about what our ancestors were like. In other words, have a close look at that old lamp before trading it for a new one.

I will not try to list what should be taught in Acadian folklore because people have had too much of a tendency to make lists of items of folk tradition, as if the elements it was comprised of could be isolated and placed in a neat order. Early folklore studies, and this includes most of the research carried out in Acadia before the 1960s, consisted of collections of folksongs or folktales, where field workers tried to gather as much material as possible, without examining the place folklore had in local society. The publication of Father Anselme's *Chéticamp — Histoire et traditions acadiennes* marked the beginning of the study of Acadian folklore in its social and cultural context. Among authors who have pursued the lead set by Father Anselme, the most noteworthy are Georges Arsenault, Jean-Claude Dupont and Lauraine Léger. Not every aspect of folklore in Acadian society can be explored by a handful of scholars, but the few publications that have been produced so far are very informative.

There are a number of themes that can be examined in the teaching of Acadian folklore. One theme that seems very important to me is that of folk religion. We can learn a great deal about the religious mentality and religious attitudes of the Acadians by knowing about their traditional beliefs. Since religion had an influence on most aspects of Acadian traditional life, one can not set folk religion completely apart from official Catholic practices. In fact, folk religion is manifested whenever people give their own interpretation to what is sacred. Holy water, for example, is a sacred substance that has some uses that are prescribed by the Church. But popular belief comes into play when it is used as a means of protection; for instance, at the beginning of a thunderstorm, when it is sprinkled in the windows all around the house. The connection between popular belief and religion is sometimes tenuous, as in the case of "la neige de mai" or May snow. It is thought that the snow that falls in early May has the power of healing eye problems. This comes from the association between the month of May as the month of the Virgin Mary and the white snow, a symbol of purity. However, people who gather the snow and use it in liquid form to treat eye ailments do not necessarily make this connection. For them, it is just a matter of faith.

There are many beliefs also about the supernatural virtues of statues, images, blessed candles, palms, crosses, medallions and other religious articles. Some of the beliefs were actually encouraged by religious authorities, who saw nothing wrong with practices that were in line with Christian principles. The whole question of folk belief is therefore a complex one. The most important fact to consider is the belief in manifestations of both the will of God and the evil influence of the devil in the world, as well as the ambivalent, and always disturbing, manifestations of the dead.

Among the hundreds of themes found in Acadian legends, most can be related to religious beliefs. Fear of the dead is reflected in many legends where deceased persons whose souls are in Purgatory return to earth to correct a wrongdoing or to ask for prayers. The devil often manifests his presence to claim souls that have been offered to him or to tempt people, as in the story of the devil at the dance. In these legends, the link with Catholic beliefs is even more pronounced, because a priest is usually called upon to come and chase away the devil or to exorcise a person who has fallen under evil influence. Then there is the well known story of the parish priest who rushes to the scene of a fire and recites prayers, after which the wind dies down and the fire is quickly put out. The supernatural power of the priest is also expressed in sorcery legends, where he tries to rid his parish of the influence of a sorcerer who uses a magic book to cast spells. Legends such as these used to be taken very seriously. If they are to be used in an educational forum today, they should be considered as a reflection of deep beliefs and as a way of transmitting values and codes of conduct.

Folk custom is another field where religion and folklore are linked. In Acadian folklore, this is probably the field that contains the most ancient elements. Most feast days such as Christmas, Candlemas Day, Easter, Mid Summer's Day and All Saints Day have a pagan origin and were gradually blended into the calendar of Christian holidays. These originally marked moments of transition in the yearly cycle. The transitions are expressed symbolically in many traditional acts. In early November, the beginning of the season when nature is dormant, sombre ceremonies were held in cemeteries. In May, when nature is reborn, outdoor altars were decked with flowers and young girls wore white dresses during processions. There is also a symbolic opposition between summer and winter at another level. During the growing season, most festivals had a solemn nature. Early in the season, offerings were made similar to pagan sacrifices, in the hope that harvests would be successful. Towards the end of the season, the celebrations were mostly thanksgiving ceremonies.

During the dark winter season, on the other hand, there is a reversal in nature's order which is paralleled by a reversal in social activities. No longer having to centre their attention on work activities, people could devote more time to singing, dancing and storytelling. It is no coincidence that the most highly celebrated Acadian feast of all, Candlemas Day, happens on February second. The Candlemas Day celebrations provide a good illustration of how social organization can be studied through folk customs. In eastern New Brunswick, the sharing of food with poverty stricken members of the community was an important part of Candlemas Day. A big feast and dance took place in one of the houses of the village, but most of the food that was collected before the feast was set apart for a needy family. This is one example of a social custom that reflects people's concern about their fellow villagers. Similarly, when it was time to organize a frolic to do the yearly chores such as chopping wood, if a family head was absent or unable to work, his neighbours would pitch in and quickly get the work done.

It is also possible to explore the relationship between inhabitants of a rural area and their environment by studying subjects like folk medicine. This is a topic which can easily be approached in a classroom, because medicinal plants grow wild everywhere and can thus be gathered and examined. Some of the plants such as gold thread and Labrador tea are native to North America and were used by the Indian population from whom the Acadians learned of them. Others, such as plantain and tansy, were brought over from Europe. So here we have an Acadian tradition which is partly of European background and was partly developed in North America. Folk medicine was used in everyday situations whenever needed. And it is precisely the everyday folk practices which tend to last through time and adapt themselves to modern settings. Many folk remedies are still popular today and the same can be said about other traditions in areas such as weather predictions and gardening activities. In the latter case, the influence of the moon is thought to be great and gardeners still plan their work according to the lunar cycle.

The very persistence of traditions is one of the most important facts to consider when studying folklore. In the case of folk remedies and weather lore, it can be observed that there is still a need for traditional knowledge where scientific developments have not been able to answer every question. In the field of folk belief, one can also observe the persistence of certain phenomena because the supernatural is still as mysterious as ever, while human beings remain as irrational as ever.

Acadian folklore contains a diversity of interrelated elements. These elements, however, are not found in the same combinations everywhere. In fact, folklore in Acadian society is characterized by regional variation. In an introductory folklore class with students from different Acadian areas, it is almost impossible to mention a tradition that all students will be familiar with. A certain custom may be familiar to students from southern New Brunswick and Cape Breton, and be unheard of in northern New Brunswick. In some areas, not enough fieldwork has taken place for us to obtain an accurate view of traditional life. But it is often possible to compare the traditions of different areas, examining at the same time the way of life and the cultural influences present in each one. Thus, it has been observed that legends are more prevalent in coastal areas where people live from fishing than inland where agriculture predominates.

Contacts with other cultural groups also affect the transmission of folklore. The Micmac Indian influence has already been mentioned. One finds Scottish customs among Cape Breton Acadians, as well as Scottish fiddle music. Elsewhere in the Maritimes, German traditional recipes have entered into Acadian foodways, while Irish folktales have been translated into French by Acadian storytellers. There is little unity in Acadian folklore, but the total picture that all the diverse elements make up does reflect the characteristics of the Acadian people, such as their adaptability.

There is one final approach to the matter that I would like to mention here, and that is to recognize that folklore, wherever it is found, is part of the life experience of ordinary individuals. Most folklore research consists of oral interviews where the interviewees speak from their personal viewpoint. It is tempting to consider a few informants as representatives of the Acadian culture of a province or a region. But it is much more realistic to consider the individual nature of each oral testimony and to try to collect the life history of the informants at the same time as their folk culture. A life history provides background information which tells us about the context in which folklore was transmitted. It is also easier to interpret people's attitudes towards folklore when we know what type of economic conditions they lived in and what their family and community life was like. This new emphasis on life history in folklore studies has focussed more attention on oral testimony than ever before. For example, the local study I published entitled *Au Village-du-Bois* is filled with quotes where informants not only describe their folk culture, but give their own views and opinions of the facts. This study involved interviews of about forty inhabitants of a village in the Memramcook area.

It is also possible for a folklore study to concentrate on one or a few individuals. It is amazing how much information can be gathered from a single life history. Professor Sandy Ives's works have demonstrated this. In my own experience, I could metion the interviews I have conducted with Mr. and Mrs. Allan Kelly of Newcastle, New Brunswick. I interviewed the Kellys at first to collect their vast repertoire of Acadian folk songs, but then, when I began to record their life story, I realized there was scarcely an aspect of folklore they didn't know about. Having lived in both fishing and farming communities in eastern New Brunswick, they told me about calendar customs, religious beliefs, folk medicine, weather lore, legends, dances, games and also about material conditions where they lived. There is no better way to get a realistic view of past folk culture than to have it described by people who actually experienced it such as the Kellys. It is of course not necessary to concentrate entirely on the past in folklore research. Children's folklore, for example, has remained just as dynamic now as it was in the past. With their songs, their skipping rhymes, their string games and what have you, it seems to me that children have continued to transmit folklore much more than anyone else in today's society.

So there are several paths to follow if one wants to use folklore in an educational context. Each generation has its own folklore and there are regional variants in each area where Acadians live. As far as finding the material to use is concerned, there are three basic sources. One is to go out and collect it yourself. This is often more feasible than people think. In the classroom, family folklore projects may be organized, where students interview their parents or grandparents. There are several methodological guides available for beginners in folklore research.

Another source of information is the folklore archive. The Centre d'Études acadiennes archive is used much less than it could be at present, partly because people do not know that our extensive collections of recordings are catalogued and indexed in a way that facilitates their consultation.

An inventory was published in 1984 to present our holdings and also to indicate centres where other collections of Acadian folklore may be found. The inventory also contains a bibliography with over 1,300 entries. And this brings me to the last source of information: printed works. In compiling the bibliography for the *Inventaire des sources en folklore acadien*, I tried to include many publications which were indirectly related to folklore, such as reports on agricultural settlements in the nineteenth century, tourist guides and literary works. These compensate in part for the small number of actual folklore studies. In certain areas, such as popular beliefs and children's folklore, very little has been published, while we have many collections of folk songs and folk tales, but few in depth studies of these traditions. Only one series of publications has been produced especially to be used in a school program in New Brunswick. The series called *Vie de nos ancêtres en Acadie* presents seventh graders with an overview of Acadian folk culture. There is also a collection of songs for school children by Florine Després called *Je chante mon Acadie*, while on Prince Edward Island, Georges Arsenault has produced *La chanson du pays* and *Les contes et la légende du pays*, which may be used in teaching folklore. In New Brunswick, a few high school teachers with a special interest in local history encourage their students to do research on the topic, but the seventh grade program is the only one I know of that deals with folklore on a regular basis.

Acadian folklore is a vast subject, as you have probably noticed from this presentation, and it is a field of study which, judging from contacts I have had with students, becomes a fascinating endeavour for whoever explores it. One realizes very quickly how relevant the study of folklore is to today's society and how fundamentally important it is as a cultural field.

SELECTED BIBLIOGRAPHY

1. *Reference Books*
Labelle, Ronald, *Inventaire des sources en folklore acadien* (Moncton, 1984).

Labrie, Vivian, *Précis de transcription d'archives orales* (Québec, 1982).

2. *Fieldwork Guides*
Bartis, Peter, *Folklife & Fieldwork — A Layman's Introduction to Field Techniques* (Washington, 1979).

Goldstein, Kenneth S., *A Guide for Field Workers in Folklore* (Hatboro, Penn., 1964).

Ives, Edward D., *The Tape Recorded Interview — A Manual for Field Workers in Folklore and Oral History* (Knoxville, Tenn., 1980).

3. *General Studies*

Chiasson, Anselme, cap., *Chéticamp — Histoire et traditions acadiennes* (Moncton, 1961).

—————, *Les îles de la Madeleine — Vie matérielle et sociale de l'en premier* (Montréal, 1981).

Dupont, Jean-Claude, *Héritage d'Acadie* (Montréal, 1977).

Labelle, Ronald, *Au Village-du-Bois — Mémoires d'une communauté acadienne* (Moncton, 1985).

————— and Léger, Lauraine, eds., *En r'montant la tradition — Hommage au Père Anselme Chiasson* (Moncton, 1982).

4. *Folklore in Education*

Arsenault, Georges, *La Chanson du pays* (Summerside, P.E.I., 1983).

—————, *Les contes et la légende du pays* (Summerside, 1983).

Després, Florine, *Je chante mon Acadie* (Moncton, 1979).

Doucet, Paul, dir., *Vie de nos ancêtres en Acadie* (Moncton, 1979-).

No 1: *Coutumes, croyances et religion populaire.*
No 2: *Le vêtement.*
No 3: *L'alimentation.*
No 4: *L'habitat et le mobilier.*
No 5: *La pêche.*
No 6: *La forêt et ses occupations.*
No 7: *L'hygiène et la santé.*
No 8: *L'agriculture.*

Legends and Beliefs

Chiasson, Anselme, cap., *Les légendes des Iles-de-la-Madeleine* (2nd ed., Moncton, 1976).

Creighton, Helen, *Bluenose Magic* (Toronto, 1968).

Doucet, Alain, *La littérature orale de la Baie Sainte-Marie* (Québec, 1965).

Jolicoeur, Catherine, *Les plus belles légendes acadiennes* (Montréal, 1981).

Savoie, Francis, *L'île de Lamèque: anecdotes, tours et légendes* (2nd ed., Moncton, 1981).

6. *Social Life*

Arsenault, Georges, *Coutumes acadiennes de l'Ile-du-Prince-Edouard* (Summerside, 1979).

—————, *Courir la Chandeleur* (Moncton, 1982).

Doyon-Ferland, Madeleine, *Jeux, rythmes, et divertissements traditionnels* (Montréal, 1980).

Léger, Lauraine, *Les sanctions populaires en Acadie: région du comté de Kent* (Montreal, 1978).

7. *Material Culture*
Boudreau, Marielle et Gallant, Melvin, *La cuisine traditionnelle en Acadie* (Moncton, 1975).

Chévrier, Cécile, *Les défricheurs d'eau* (Caraquet, N.B., 1978).

Dupont, Jean-Claude, *Histoire populaire de l'Acadie* (Montréal, 1979).

Equipe Découverte de l'habitation acadienne, *Maison Célestin Bourque* (Moncton, 1976).

——————, *La maison Hélène et Roma Bourgeois* (Moncton, 1977).

Equipe Heritage d'herbages, *Es-tu bâdré de tes vivres? — Médicine traditionnelle en Acadie* (Moncton, 1979).

25 Studying Maritime Folklore in Secondary Schools: Some Suggestions

Neil V. Rosenberg

INTRODUCING FOLKLORE TO SECONDARY school students is not a universal practice, but is taking place now more frequently than ever before. For example, in Newfoundland schools for the past several years an elective two-credit course in folk literature, English 3203, which uses a series of booklets on various folklore subjects edited and written by my colleagues and published by Breakwater Press, has been available to grade 12 students. We are seeing positive results from this at Memorial as students familiar with the basic literature and theories of folklore are now beginning to enroll in our undergraduate introductory folklore courses. In a discipline which has yet to receive academic recognition at many Canadian universities, we clearly perceive the usefulness of communicating our perspective to potential students as early as possible. No doubt those of you from other disciplines can appreciate the value of making high school students aware of one's disciplinary viewpoint, particularly when one has some say in the process. Moreover, because the structure of the contemporary university, with its departments, faculties and professional associations, can lead to rifts between what ought to be intellectual allies, we all sometimes behave like religious sects, seeking converts among the young. Perhaps as specialized knowledge and new perspectives on human behavior proliferate, it is to be expected that competition should exist. But it is our obligation to find strength in our diversity through the interdiciplinary bridging of rifts through forums such as this meeting. It is my argument and that of my colleagues that folklore can contribute to the study of Maritime culture knowledge unique but complementary to that offered by other more widely established disciplines, and that folklore can play an important part in interdisciplinary education of the kind that occurs in secondary schools. Indeed, perusal of the various topics of sessions at this conference leads me to suggest that folkloristic contributions can be envisioned for virtually every other subject at this meeting: from ethnicity to economics.

A contemporary definition of folklore is perhaps useful at this point. Earlier definitions describe the lore in terms of oral tradition and customary example, stressing the continuity and variation of such material through time and space. In them, folk culture is the property of isolated, economically marginal, rural people. Today we define folklore in more holistic terms, as processes of patterned artistic expression which are part of the informal dimension of culture among members of groups having some common focus. Everyone belongs to folk groups; for example, the family is one such group. Everyone has folklore; for example, we all use proverbs. Folklore can be verbal, behavioral or material culture. Frequently it is a combination of all of these. For example there was a specific time and place for Maritime lumberwoods song traditions within the context of the traditionally designed and constructed lumbercamp building as well as within the matrix of a traditional daily and weekly timetable of work and leisure.[1]

A basic problem for folklorists is to communicate this viewpoint of our subject to teachers and students who are likely to think of folklore (if they think about it at all) as a collection of songs, stories, or superstitions in a book, collected from some quaint group far away, or from someone very old and old-fashioned. When I spent a year living just South of here near Queenstown doing field research I was constantly told that I could collect folklore up in the Miramichi; but a lively folk dance tradition existed right down the road from me at the Queenstown Orangeman's Hall. In fact, folklore can be collected from anyone, even members of the august group gathered here today. It is a challenge to communicate this perspective to young students in a way which will enhance their understanding of their own culture and that of their neighbors and forebears. In facing this challenge I believe two contrasting themes must be taught.

The first theme is the existence of "classic" folklore collections and studies. While modern scholars define folklore somewhat differently than those of the past, this does not lessen the importance of the great works which shaped the discipline. Just as teachers of literature expect young people to know of Shakespeare and Molière, so we folklorists want students to be aware of the international classics — works like Francis James Child's *The English and Scottish Popular Ballads* and the Grimms' *Fairy Tales (Kinder und Hausmärchen)*. Such works and others like them are introduced and discussed in the university-level textbooks like Richard M. Dorson's *Folklore and Folklife* and Alan Dundes' *The Study of Folklore*. Teachers should be aware of the international classics, and brief introductions to them and descriptions of their contents should be part of the basic education of students to folklore.

---

1 A textbook which is based on the process model definition of folklore is Barre Toelken's *The Dynamics of Folklore* (New York, 1979). Included as examples of a folk group are loggers (52-72). For a discussion of lumbercamp singing, see Edward D. Ives' *Joe Scott* (Urbana, 1978), pp. 371-402.

Other classics are best thought of as national. For Canada we think immediately of the vast and wide-ranging body of materials collected and published by scholars like Marius Barbeau and Edith Fowke — works which have done much to shape the consciousness of folklore in Canada. We are fortunate to have Carole Henderson Carpenter's history of folklore activities in Canada, *Many Voices*, and Fowke and Carpenter's *Bibliography of Canadian Folklore in English*. These works are invaluable aids to the teachers attempting to place Maritime folklore studies in the context of Canadian folklore.

Finally, there are important regional classics which ought to be recognized as such — like the works of W. Roy MacKenzie, Helen Creighton, Anselme Chiasson, and Catherine Jolicoeur. Richard Tallman's review article in *Acadiensis* discusses the major works to that date, but unfortunately only in English.[2] It is particularly important to note the present activity in Acadian folklore which has produced a number of important works in recent years.

These three levels of classic works are essential not only for introducing students and teachers to the ideas and materials that have shaped the discipline but also because examples of the materials these works contain can, in many instances, still be found *by students* here in the Maritimes. This leads me to the second of my two contrasting themes: namely, that, books notwithstanding, folklore has existed and still exists primarily as informal but patterned artistic expression and is in one form or another part of the life of every individual today.

Hence a folklore component in the schools properly involves a twofold organization combining selected readings from the classics with a scheme of planned activities in which students collect folklore — first from themselves, then from their family, and finally within their own community. Such collection is, in my experience, easily taught and is generally accepted by students as an entertaining and challenging novelty. Here is a realm in which every individual can be an expert. All that is needed is some training. To this end a number of useful fieldwork guides are available, and teachers can be shown how to supervise such activity with little difficulty.

The selection of readings for a folklore section as part of Maritime

---

2   MacKenzie and Creighton's work are discussed by Tallman, in "Folklore Research in Atlantic Canada: An Overview", *Acadiensis*, VIII/2 (Spring 1979), pp. 118-30. With regard to Chiasson and Jolicoeur, I am thinking in particular of two major works: père Anselme Chiasson's *Chéticamp: Histoire et Traditions acadiennes* (Moncton, 1961) and Catherine Jolicoeur's *Le vaisseau fantôme: légend étiologique* (Québec, 1970). A useful reference source for other works by these influential Acadian researchers is Laurel Doucette and Gerald Thomas' typescript *French Folklore in North America: Bibliography* (St. John's, 1980).

studies entails another set of contrasts. Folklore plays an important role in a culturally diverse region such as the Maritimes by serving as a symbol for distinctive aspects of ethnic, local, and other group identities. We can point to the Scots fiddle traditons of Cape Breton, or the Acadian calendar custom of Mi-Carême, for example, as folklore associated with specific groups in the region.[3] But certain forms which seem specific to one cultural group within the Maritimes sometimes turn out to have close affinities with those of another group. For example, the English-language ballads and the French-language *complaintes* of Prince Edward Island can be shown to share much in terms of theme, plot, structure, and music.[4] Other Maritime folklore is shared by members of every group: the legend of the burning ship, for example. And certain economic activities which brought together Maritimers from many groups and communities had a social dimension which created a context conducive to the sharing and exchanging of traditions — the Harvest Excursion, for instance.[5]

Folklore is both universal and unique; by stressing this point teachers can relate it to other aspects of literary and social studies, as well as to other approaches to Maritime studies.

---

3 For examples of these two traditions see: Allister MacGillivray, *The Cape Breton Fiddler* (Sydney, 1981) and Georges Arsenault, "La Mi-Carême", *The Island Magazine*, 9 (Spring-Summer 1981), pp. 8-11.

4 Two collections of English-language song which include ballads are Edward D. Ives' "Twenty-one Folksongs from Prince Edward Island", *Northeast Folklore*, 5 (1963), pp. 1-87, and Randall and Dorothy Dibblee's *Folksongs from Prince Edward Island* (Summerside, 1973). For complaintes, see Georges Arsenault, *Complaintes Acadiennes de L'Île du Prince Èdouard* (Montreal, 1980).

5 See Susan Hornby, "Memories of a Golden Land: The Harvest Excursions", *The Island Magazine*, 7 (Fall-Winter 1979), pp. 12-8.

SELECTED BIBLIOGRAPHY

Arsenault, Georges, *Complaintes Acadiennes de L'Île du Prince Édouard* (Montreal, 1980).

_____, "La Mi-Carême", *The Island Magazine*, 9 (Spring-Summer 1981), pp. 8-11.

Carpenter, Carole Henderson, *Many Voices: A Study of Folklore Activities in Canada and their Role in Canadian Culture* (Ottawa, 1979).

Chiasson, père Anselme, *Chéticamp: Histoire et Traditions acadiennes* (Moncton, 1961).

Child, Francis James, *The English and Scottish Popular Ballads* (Boston, 1882-1895).

Dibblee, Randall and Dorothy, *Folksongs from Prince Edward Island* (Summerside, 1973).

Dorson, Richard M., ed., *Folklore and Folklife: An Introduction* (Chicago, 1972).

Doucette, Laurel, and Thomas, Gerald, *French Folklore in North America: A Bibliography* (St. John's, 1980).

Dundes, Alan, *The Study of Folklore* (Englewood Cliffs, NJ, 1965).

Fowke, Edith, and Carpenter, Carole, *A Bibliography of Canadian Folklore in English* (Toronto, 1981).

Grimm, Jacob and Wilhelm, *Kinder und Hausmärchen* (Leipzig, 1856). There are many translations; the English one most often cited by folklorists is Margaret Hunt, *Household Tales* (London, 1884).

Hornby, Susan, "Memories of a Golden Land: The Harvest Excursions", *The Island Magazine*, 7 (Fall-Winter 1979), pp. 12-8.

Ives, Edward D., *Joe Scott* (Urbana, 1978).

_____, "Twenty-one Folksongs from Prince Edward Island", *Northeast Folklore*, 5 (1963), pp. 1-87.

Jolicoeur, Catherine, *Le vaisseau fantôme: légende étiologique* (Québec, 1970).

MacGillivray, Allister, *The Cape Breton Fiddler* (Sydney, 1981).

Small, Lawrence G., ed., *Folk Literature Series* (St. John's, 1983).

Tallman, Richard S., "Folklore Research in Atlantic Canada: An Overview", *Acadiensis*, VIII/2 (Spring 1979), pp. 118-30.

Toelken, Barre, *The Dynamics of Folklore* (New York 1979).

26 Digressions on the K-Mart Bus Teaching Maritime Literature

Gwendolyn Davies

IN THE 1977 MUSICAL revue, "The Rise & Follies of Cape Breton", there is a scene that has become a classic in defining the distinction between the old Maritimes and the new. It takes place at the bus stop for the Ashby-K-Mart bus in Sydney:

Man: Did the Alexandra Street bus go by yet?

Girl : No, I don't think it went by. I've been here for about fifteen minutes now and I didn't see it go by. Probably didn't go by.

M. : Thank you.

G. : You're welcome.

M. : Are you waiting for a bus?

G. : Uh-huh! I'm waiting for the Ashby-K-Mart bus. It's late tonight.

M. : [*Pause*] What's your father's name?

G. : Gillis. Donald Gillis.

M. : What's *your* name?

G. : Donna. I was named after my father.

M. : That's funny. I didn't think there were any Gillises living out *that* way. Where does your father belong to originally?

G. : I think Dad came from Mira Road.

M. : Oh - h! Donald Gillis from Mira Road. That would be John Peter's cousin married to that MacKinnon woman from up north.

G. : I guess so.

M. : Well that would be your --- your father's cousin, John Peter. Is that right? You *do* have an Uncle John Peter Gillis, don't you?

G. : Yes, I do. [*With a slight lilt of recognition*] He's my father's brother.

M. : That's right.

G. : Yeh.

M. : And your father's cousin on the MacNeil side is my wife's sister's second husband's cousin. That would be Teresa. Teresa John Alec MacNeil. And Teresa's sister Mary is the Mary that married your uncle, John Peter. Mary Gillis.
What's your grandfather's name?

G. : Well, I'm not sure.
M. : [*with incredulity*] Your father's father? You don't know your
      father's father's name?
G. : Well we didn't talk about that stuff too much at home.
      [*Pause*]
      Oh, here comes my bus.
      Goodnight [*Pause. No response from man.*]
      Good*night* . . . [*No response from man.*][1]

What is so striking about this exchange is that the young woman means
well but is totally unreceptive to the kinship-conscious overtures of the
man at the bus-stop. Waiting for the Ashby-K-Mart bus, she is, in a sense,
a product of a K-Mart culture. Her comment — "We didn't talk about
that stuff too much at home" — reinforces the image of her as immune
from the winds of history and highlights the contrast between the man and
herself. There is spoofery here, of course — mainly on the gossipy clan-
nishness of the Maritimer who knows everyone and is related to at least
half the population of Cape Breton — but the empty silence at the end of
the sketch as the bus departs for the K-Mart speaks eloquently of a cultural loss on two levels. The teenager may be called Donna after her
father's traditional Highland name,[2] but she has lost both the sense of
place and the sense of historical continuity that form part of her past. And
for the man with an appreciation of that tradition, there is incomprehen-
sion that something so important to his cultural fabric should be treated
indifferently and insensitively by a new generation. His refusal to answer
the girl at the end of the sketch is a telling measure of his bewilderment
and his sudden feeling of isolation.

The ironic confrontation between the Alexandra Street traditionalist
and the girl waiting for the Ashby-K-Mart bus serves as a fitting illustration of one of the problems facing teachers of Maritime literature today.
Our students often have no historical sense. Like the girl waiting for the
K-Mart bus, they increasingly seem to be the products of a K-Mart culture. They are exposed to videos, ghetto-blasters, Prince, and Remo
Williams. They read Timothy Findley's *Famous Last Words*, as did a
class of mine recently, and think that the Duke and Duchess of Windsor of
1936 abdication fame are fictional characters. Small wonder, then, that
the Loyalists seem more than a planet away, or that Sir Charles G.D.
Roberts does not resonate with relevance in their lives.

All of this creates a tremendous challenge for the person setting up and

---

1   Leon Dubinski and Kenzie MacNeil, prod., "Bus Stop", *The Rise and Follies of Cape
    Breton* (Sydney: Quality Records for College of Cape Breton Press, 1977), band 2.
2   The name "Donald" has traditionally been used to designate a Highlander.

teaching a Maritime literature course, for the reading of literature should be a contextual process, not to be pursued in isolation. To respond to the satirical thrust of "The Rise & Follies of Cape Breton" on an immediate level is to respond to its ironic exploration of contemporary social and economic realities. But to respond to it on a contextual level is also to place "The Rise & Follies of Cape Breton" in the perspective of a satiric tradition in the Maritimes that extends from the eighteenth century to the present. There is nothing new in what "The Rise & Follies" has to tell us. As early as 1821, Thomas McCulloch's Mephibosheth Stepsure was pawkily upbraiding the reasons for outmigration, institutionalized poverty, and Halifax exclusiveness in the literary columns of *The Acadian Recorder.* There has been a continuity in Maritime problems, as there has been a continuity in Maritime culture, from the beginning of our settlement, and any response to a production like "The Rise & Follies" can only be enriched by acknowledging that pattern. To teach our students in an historical vacuum, therefore, is to teach them in blindness. If they are losing their sense of history, their sense of who they are under the influence of ghetto-blasters and videos, it is incumbent upon those who are designing and teaching their courses that we at least give them some sense of the context and continuity that was theirs, and that we address the erosions of a mass-market K-Mart society before they get any worse.

For that reason, I approach the topic today — "Themes and Problems in Teaching Maritime Literature" — with certain predilections. There are so many things to which one could give priority in designing the literary component of a course — writers, genres, regions, time periods, technique — that a process of selection does have to take place. But I would like to suggest four areas which should *not* be forgotten in our Maritime literature courses if we are to do justice not only to the literature itself but also to our consciousness of ourselves as a distinctive region.

The first is that a Maritime literature course should not present literature as a merely contemporary endeavour, as part of a great wave of Canadian writing that has emerged in the past two decades and has marked the so-called emergence of a Canadian consciousness. There was, in fact, a sophisticated body of Canadian literature long before the 1960s, and the contribution of Maritime writers to that canon has been a noteworthy one. It is important that students know this, and that they read contemporary Maritime writing fully aware of the fact that regional writers have always given imaginative treatment to the social and historical realities of their day. The poems and stories of Alden Nowlan take on a new dimension when read in the context of religious fundamentalist pockets in New Brunswick or of famine Irish survival in Nova Scotia. The ironic Bridgetown stories of David Lewis in *A Lover Needs A Guitar* are enriched by a study of Ken Tolmie's portraits of the same town in oils, each painting tested for community response by Tolmie's first displaying it in the local barber shop window. And the sense of dispossession in Alistair MacLeod's "The Boat" is given deeper meaning by a knowledge of Gaelic emigrations from nineteenth-century Scotland to the Maritimes, and by an awareness of the twentieth-century outmigrations which have taken people from the "home place" to the Boston states, Toronto, or Calgary.

All of this points to the importance of the social and cultural context in enriching our reading of a work. There are distinctive literary patterns in the history of Maritime writing, one of the most obvious being the prevalence of satire from the eighteenth century until the beginning of the twentieth century. From the Hudibrastic poetry of Jacob Bailey in the 1790s attacking the rise of Methodism, to the witty early nineteenth-century satires of Sir Alexander Croke on the pretensions of Halifax society, to the wave of caustic newspaper sketches in the 1820s, there has been an on-going exposé of the manners and morals of Maritime society through the imaginative writing of the region. Clever, anonymous writers like T.S.B., Anthony Doodledoo, Little Bird, and The Club added their voices to those of Thomas McCulloch, Thomas Chandler Haliburton, James DeMille, and the anti-Confederation wits to make nineteenth-century writing in this region as vital as it was relevant. There was nothing in our tradition of Maritime writing to parallel Susanna Moodie's wilderness of trees and discontent in *Roughing It In the Bush*.[3] We had no Catherine Parr Traill standing in our forests and lamenting the absence of dryads and nymphs.[4] In short, the literature of the frontier with Mrs. Moodie as totem represents an Upper Canadian phenomenon, not the Maritime literary experience where, from the beginning, the texture of society and man's response to it were of paramount importance. This is a distinction that our students should know, for the difference between nineteenth-century writing in Upper Canada and nineteenth-century literature in the Maritimes says much about the forces that shaped our identity. It also reinforces one of the directions a Maritime literature course will undoubtedly take — the identification of what is unique about our area and ourselves as perceived and defined by our writers.

Of the other characteristics that have made our literature distinctly representative of our experience, two must be mentioned. The first is the large body of folk literature and oral tradition which has been central to our culture since first settlement and which has frequently been integrated into the narrative pattern of our more formal or elite literature. It is important for our students to realize that there have been these two liter-

---

3 Susanna Moodie, *Roughing It in the Bush* (reprinted Toronto, 1962), p. 237.
4 Catherine Parr Traill, "A Matter-of-Fact Country" in Carl Klinck and Reginald Watters, eds., *Canadian Anthology* (Toronto, 1974), p. 26.

ary traditions in the region: the folk tradition in English, French, Micmac, Malecite and Gaelic which has included songs, tales, and sayings, and at least initially, was preserved through oral transmission, and the formal or "elite" tradition which has developed contemporaneously with other literatures written in English in other countries. That this second category, the elite, often finds enrichment or indigeneity by turning to the folk tradition, is well-illustrated by the successful integration of Indian legend and mythology into the work of Moses Perley, Douglas Huyghue, Charles G.D. Roberts, T.G. Roberts, or Susan Jones. Frank Parker Day's novels, *Rockbound* (1928) and *John Paul's Rock* (1932), offer excellent examples of the author's successful use of folktale and superstition as substitutes for the psychological development of character, and in Thomas Raddall's "Blind MacNair'" or Alistair MacLeod's "The Boat", there is ample evidence of the way in which the suspense and characterization of a narrative can be enhanced by a skilful introduction of the ballad tradition. The "Song Fishermen" of the late 1920s like Kenneth Leslie, James D. Gillis, Stuart McCawley, and John Daniel Logan recognized the rhythmic and imagistic possibilities of the Gaelic tradition in framing new songs and poems about Nova Scotia, and Leslie's "The Shanachie Man" still stands as one of the finest poems to come out of the province in this period.[5] Whether in these illustrations or in the integration of actual story-telling conventions into Thomas Chandler Haliburton's "The Clockmaker" series and Frank Parker Day's *Rockbound*, there is ample evidence of a literary relationship between the elite and the folk traditions in Maritime culture, little developed in the literary traditions of other parts of English-speaking Canada until quite recently.

The second feature of our literature which often distinguishes it from that of other regions is its distinctive use of language and idiom. Quoted by Mavor Moore in *The Globe and Mail* on 26 October 1985, Concordia professor Lewis J. Poteet has noted that "People in rural and maritime areas both have inherited and are proud of a certain tradition of speaking which is relatively fixed and from that tradition I believe they inherit a taste for making new words and phrases colorful in the same way as those learned from their grandparents".[6] His observations have been richly illustrated in his own work on the South Shore of Nova Scotia, where from imaginatively-coined phrases like "Lordy ole Cock-Robin Christ" or "going like greased lighnin' thru' a gooseberry bush" to the Tudor word "pleasance" for a rose garden, there is evidence of both continuity and innovation in the language

5 An informally-connected group of Maritime poets (which also included Charles G.D. Roberts, Robert Norwood, and Charles Bruce), the Song Fishermen published regionally-inspired poetry in their "Song Sheet" from 1928 to 1930.

6 Mavor Moore, "Insight Gleaned from the Mail", *Globe and Mail*, 26 October 1985.

of a region settled and sustained by the same few ethnic groups since 1751.[7] The speech rhythms and folk culture of this area were well represented by Frank Parker Day in his 1928 novel, *Rockbound*, which captures not only a sense of everyday speech on the Tancook Islands, but also creates an approximation of Lunenburg dialect. Whether in Day ("Why, dat ghost... were dat audacious he used to whang on de back o' de church at evening meetin"), in David Adams Richards' stylized speech of the Miramichi ("Ya — I may as well"), in Sam Slick's colourful tirades against "gander-gutted" Bluenoses in the 1830s ("There's neither spirit, enterprise, nor patriotism here, but the whole country is as inactive as a bear in winter that does nothin' but scrootch up in his den..."), or in James DeMille's Indian place-names in his poetry ("Where the swift gliding Skoodawab-skoosis / Unites with the Skoodawabskook"), there is vitality in the literary use of language in our regional writing which should not be ignored.

Finally, in any discussion of the themes and problems pertinent to teaching Maritime literature, there arises the question of how to address the concept of regionalism in literary terms. In the geography session during the conference, Dr. Larry McCann spoke of regionalism as representing society's identification with a territorial unit. For the writer of our literature, articulating the nature of that identification is a nebulous and elusive process. Being a Maritimer can be something felt in the nerve and the bone, something which defies easy definition in words. Robertson Davies in his 1985 novel of that name speaks of something "being bred in the bone". "Words", as poet Charles Bruce has written in his collection *The Mulgrave Road*, "are never enough".[8] One must also know the "salt" in one's "blood", and fiction writer Alistair MacLeod has echoed the mystery of this identification in the title of his short story collection, *The Lost Salt Gift of Blood*. Certainly, in the poems, stories, plays, and novels written by native authors like MacLeod and Bruce over the years, there is a cumulative articulation of perception and feeling, much of it fluid over time, which says something of who we are. So too do the elements of language and folk culture already mentioned, many of them connected to our ethnic, social, and geographical past within the region. We have regions within regions, cultures within cultures, even in this small geographical area of the world, but common denominators to all these disparities seem to be the land and the sea. Clichéd as it may sound, we find these as recurring images in our literature from Henry Alline's eighteenth-century hymns to Ernest Buckler's fiction of the Annapolis Valley. If satire, then, was a dominant literary mode in the eighteenth and nineteenth

---

7   Lewis J. Poteet, *The South Shore Phrase Book* (Hantsport, 1983), pp. 35, 45, 51.

8   Charles Bruce, "Words Are Never Enough" in *The Mulgrave Road* (Toronto, 1951), pp. 26-8.

centuries, so it is a consciousness of the landscape, of the home place, that is the dominant literary image running through our work for the past two hundred years. Used politically by Roger Viets and Thomas McCulloch in the early years of our society, nostalgically by Sir Charles G.D. Roberts and L.M. Montgomery in the Victorian-Edwardian period, and psychologically by Frank Parker Day, Ernest Buckler, and David Adams Richards in the twentieth century, our sense of place is a key unifying motif in our literary tradition.[9] "Grand Etang is the village of my father and his father", says Clive Doucet in *The Cape Breton Collection*; "It is a hometown of the mind and heart. For no matter how much it changes or I change, Grand Etang will still be my hometown, which is what I believe hometowns are all about. They are your primary references".[10]

One suspects there are no K-Marts in Grand Etang. One suspects that the old man waiting for the Alexandra Street bus in "The Rise & Follies" could empathize with Clive Doucet. Certainly the image of "the hometown of the mind and heart", the village of one's father and one's grandfather, conjures up the contextual approach with which this presentation began and brings us full circle to the significance of looking at our literature in its cultural context. Only by knowing our past will we understand and control our present. Only then will we know "the salt in our blood".

9   Both Roger Viets in his 1788 poem, "Annapolis Royal", ed. by Thomas Vincent (reprinted Kingston, 1979) and Thomas McCulloch in *The Letters of Mephibosheth Stepsure* (reprinted Toronto, 1960) develop a moral and political message through the interaction of the individual with his environment. Charles G.D. Roberts in his Tantramar poetry and in fiction like *The Heart That Knows* (reprinted Sackville, 1985) portrayed the New Brunswick landscape of his youth as a halycon alternative to reality. Lucy Maud Montgomery's "Anne" books are in the kailyard tradition of Scottish popular fiction and treat the rural landscape of Prince Edward Island in a similar vein. Frank Parker Day in *John Paul's Rock* (New York, 1932), Ernest Buckler in *The Mountain and the Valley* (New York, 1952), and David Adams Richards in *The Coming of Winter* (Ottawa, 1974) all employ the central character's relationship with the land as a device in revealing the psychological tensions faced by the protagonist.

10 Lesley Choyce, ed., *The Cape Breton Collection* (Porters Lake, Nova Scotia, 1984), p. 55.

27

The Study of Acadian Literature: An Overview

Robert Whalen

FOR MANY PEOPLE WHO WORK in English-language institutions and teach in English, the greatest obstacle to the study of the literature of the Acadians may well be the language barrier. If one can read French easily, Acadian writing can be the subject of a rich and rewarding study, but those who must rely on the translations will find that most of what has been written is not yet available in English. Nevertheless, the increasing productivity and dynamism of young Acadian writers and the establishment of such publishing houses as Les Éditions d'Acadie and Les Éditions Perce-Neige, will surely persuade English-language publishers to present a wider sampling of Acadian works to their readers.

The bibliography published with this paper includes a selected list of works by and about Acadian writers in French and also indicates some works which are available in English translation. Two recent publications listed in the bibliography should prove of special interest to English readers. In 1985, the Éditions Perce-Neige (the publishing arm of the Association of Acadian writers) published a bilingual anthology of Acadian poetry, which provides a sampling of the poetry of 15 contemporary Acadian poets, accompanied by English translations. Together with the special number of *Ellipse* on Maritime poetry published in 1974, this anthology provides English readers with a reasonable idea of modern Acadian poetry. The second publication of interest to English readers is *A literary and linguistic history of New Brunswick*. This work includes articles by scholars at Maritime universities on Acadian language, poetry, prose fiction, theatre and folklore. It is a study intended for a general audience and complements similar articles on the Acadian heritage which appeared in 1982 in *The Acadians of the Maritimes*. This bibliography also lists other critical studies in English dealing with Acadian literature, mostly articles on the most celebrated of Acadian writers, Antonine Maillet. Although four of her works have so far appeared in English, Acadian literature still provides ample scope for literary translators and for the government's programme of subsidies for literary translations to attempt to remedy this gap.[1]

I was confirmed in my belief that an overview of Acadian literature might be useful to this group when a previous speaker today used the Eiffel Tower as a symbol of our conference. The tower's four legs, we were told, represented the pillars of the social science disciplines, its two-pronged centre portions were made to symbolize folklore and geography, with the whole edifice capped off by *English* literature. This seemed to indicate that a good number of delegates might not yet be familiar with literature written in French in our region. The following comments, therefore, seek to claim for Acadian writing an appropriate place in programmes of Maritime Studies.

Although the historical presence of the Acadians in the Maritimes dates back to 1604, their tradition of imaginative literature is far more recent. Professor Marguerite Maillet in her history of Acadian literature describes five major chronological divisions in the development of writing in Acadia.[2] The first of these (1606-1755) is termed the pre-Acadian period. With the exception of the poetry and drama of Marc Lescarbot, most of the writings of this period were either voyage literature, diaries or letters by missionaries and visitors from France. During the second period, from the Deportation until the time of the first National Conventions of the Acadians in the 1880s, writing consisted largely of missionary journals, administrative dispatches, briefs to government, financial reports, and — for the first time — the occasional poem. The leit-motif in all this writing was the dispossessed Acadian, the trauma of deportation, the hardship of exile, and the preoccupation with "survivance" — the survival of linguistic and religious traditions.

From the 1880s until the 1930s, writing in Acadia was still mostly comprised of journalism and memoirs, although there were some works of imaginative literature. Nevertheless, after 1880, the folktale began to undergo a transposition into literary form. Once again, the themes turned essentially around national issues: the Acadian Renaissance, the need for the Acadians to accommodate to new conditions, and the affirmation of their collective will to survive by creating appropriate educational, polit-

---

1 Teachers from the school system may be interested in a videotaped slide presentation with English commentary on Acadian culture prepared by Karen Tweedie in partial completion of her requirements for an M.Ed. thesis at the University of New Brunswick, in 1984. This videotape, designed for classes at the junior high-school level, brings alive the customs and traditions of the Acadians as part of the cultural component of the junior high French language curriculum (core programme).

2 M. Maillet, G. LeBlanc et B. Emont, *Anthologie de textes littéraires acadiens* (Moncton, 1979), pp. 7-15. See also Maillet's article in *The Acadians of the Maritimes* (Moncton, 1982), wherein she recounts the history of writing in Acadia under approximately similar divisions.

ical, and religious structures. With the fourth period, from the 1930s to 1960, a real increase in literary expression is noted. Now appeared the principal literary genres which make up imaginative literature (the novel, drama, and poetry). The themes in this writing paralleled those common in much of Quebec literature until the end of World War II, extolling the pastoral virtures and the agrarian myth. Most of the literature of this period discussed the fate of the Acadians during and since the Deportation. The martyr image was perpetuated. Literature remained essentially the hand-maiden of national causes.

Finally, the modern period (after 1960) is characterized by a literature of protest. Most novels, short stories and poetry continued to emphasize Acadian traditions, while at the same time re-examining and redefining them. Moreover, the authors took a critical stance towards those forces they felt to be hostile to the development of Acadian society. There was a deliberate attempt to make literary use of the old language of rural Acadia, a phenomenon similar to the use of "joual" as a literary language by Quebec writers in the 1960s. There was great emphasis on themes of individual and collective freedom, especially during the 1970s.

In 1973, Antonine Maillet was asked what it was like to be an Acadian writer at that time.[3] She answered that Acadia was then only beginning to have a written literature. In her view, imaginative literature in Acadia had, for a long time, been essentially an oral tradition. She described herself, in 1973, as the last of an important oral tradition and one of the first to undertake its written transcription. Since this oral tradition was discussed this morning in a session on "Studying Maritime Folklore" by Mr. Labelle and Professor Arsenault, it only remains for me to emphasize the debt of most Acadian writers to that folk tradition. Antonine Maillet describes herself as "d'abord et avant-tout, une conteuse" — essentially a teller of tales.[4] In her fiction this link between the oral tradition and the tradition of the modern Acadian novel expresses itself both in the narrative manner and in the major themes.

In his study of Acadian prose fiction, Professor Hans Runte states that "a good number of Acadian novels have been inspired by history and folklore" and that these can be divided into two groups. First, there are those written by the early twentieth-century authors who were aware of the decline of the oral tradition, and were trying to preserve the written vestiges of it. These writers were concerned with preserving, in a literary transposition, both the oral folktales and the conservative attitudes towards country, religion and language, characteristic of old Acadia. Nearly

---

3 "Visages: Antonine Maillet", University of Toronto Videotape (Toronto, 1973).
4 Cécile Ouellette, ed., *Antonine Maillet, conteuse: Guide pédagogique* (Fredericton, 1985).

half a century later, however, Runte discerns a second group of novelists who make a determined attempt to adapt this tradition to a modern literary expression in the belief that "to understand the present and imagine the future, one must have understoood, and assimilated the past".[5] Thus folklorists, prose fiction writers, and poets have attempted to reinterpret their past and create a new awareness among their fellow Acadians of their potential for the future. This afternoon, in the session on "Studying Maritime Politics", Rick Williams suggested that, when alienated by the all pervasive role of the State and faced by the problems posed by bringing about change, contemporary Maritimers in general have a tendency to try to ignore the problem. Certainly Acadian writers of the 1970s did not do so. In fact, one of Professor Williams' proposals, to view Maritime society as a colony in which our citizens are seen as cut off from avenues of power, was part of the world-view of writers like Maillet (in *La Sagouine*), Leblanc (in *Cri de Terre*), and Guy Arsenault (in *Acadie Rock*).

One of the means by which the contemporary writer set about this task was the rejection or reinterpretation of major myths of the historical and literary past of Acadia. For example, probably no fictional character better than Longfellow's heroine, Evangeline, has symbolized the traditional view of Acadia as a martyred people characterized as long-suffering and passive. The French translation of Longfellow's romanticized view of the Deportation was widely read in Acadia and it became a central motif in the Acadian Renaissance following the 1880s. Scholars have looked at the Evangeline myth and analyzed it in terms of its importance as part of the ideology which favoured Acadian survival; historian Naomi Griffiths speaks of "the adoption and use of their own myths".[6] In an article entitled "Evangeline Qui es-tu?" the poet and film-maker Léonard Forest explains how the Evangeline myth came to be accepted:

> The situation of the Acadians...a century after the "great expulsion" was only the sorrowful continuation of the deportation itself. Literally, the nation had been dispersed into small islands of population each of which lived in isolation and often in fear. ...the Acadian could not bear to look his neighbour in the face: his poverty humiliated him, since it only confirmed his inferiority and his lack of worth. The Acadian lived the deportation not as a victim but as the guilty party.
>
> Consequently, when *Evangeline* burst forth on the American literary

5 Hans Runte, "From Yesterday's Novel to Tomorrow's", in R. Gair, gen. ed., *A Literary and Linguistic History of New Brunswick* (Fredericton, 1986), p. 204.

6 Naomi Griffiths, "Longfellow's *Evangeline*: The Birth and Acceptance of a Legend", *Acadiensis*, XI/2 (Spring, 1982), p. 35.

scene, it spread... like great pacifying music.... The Acadian can finally look his neighbour in the face and it is for this reason that *Evangeline*, written by a foreigner, becomes for the Acadian a historical event. A rallying cry. A hope.[7]

Contemporary Acadian writers, however, have rejected the Evangeline myth (as well as many other formerly cherished symbols) by writing works of fiction which refute it or replace it with alternate versions. In the same article Forest is of the opinion that for Acadians of the 1960s Evangeline is a symbol to be rejected, arguing that contemporary Acadia is casting aside its pose of modesty which reflected a mixture of patience, fear and passivity. This new Acadia, he believes, has cast in doubt its own faithfulness to tradition, and while Evangeline is the very image of the Acadian faithfulness to tradition, today's Acadia no longer reveres this image.

Forest's statement that Acadians no longer accept the Evangeline myth is typical of the protest against and reinterpretation of the past which was one of the major concerns of the generation of Acadian writers in the 1970s. No author exemplifies this better than Antonine Maillet who has described her famous fictional character la Sagouine as "my version of what Evangeline would have been if an Acadian had written Longfellow's poem".[8] The only literary history of Acadia, *Histoire de la littérature acadienne: de rêve en rêve*, sees in Maillet's fiction "the steady succession of heroines — ever the same — all bent upon dethroning Longfellow's Evangeline".[9]

Despite the definite polemical intention of much of modern Acadian writing, the writers themselves reject any attempt to reduce their work to a literature of protest. When asked if it were only a coincidence that the success of her play *La Sagouine* coincided with the rise of new forces among French-speaking Maritimers as shown by the foundation of the *Parti Acadien* in New Brunswick, the making of Perrault's protest film *Acadie, Acadie*, and the establishment of the University of Moncton, Antonine Maillet answered in this way:

> There is a coincidence and at the same time there is a reciprocal influence. The time was ripe for the Acadians to really take stock of themselves and it so happens that this stock-taking was going on at one and the same time at different levels of society.... Both Acadian fiction and film-making bore witness to all of this, so there is,

---

7 Léonard Forest, "Evangéline, Qui es-tu?", *Liberté*, 11/5 (1969), pp. 139-40.

8 "Visages: Antonine Maillet".

9 Marguerite Maillet, *Histoire de la littérature acadienne: de rêve en rêve* (Moncton, 1983), p. 183.

undoubtedly, an interaction between literature and politics but the protest is not merely political. It is also humanistic. It is a protest every man must make.

If you ask me whether I write my books to defend this or that cause, I would have to answer "no". If my books are political it is because the world is like that. I situated *La Sagouine* in Acadia because it was necessary for my heroine to be situated in a particular place and because it was there I had known her.... The Sagouine is the minority figure *par excellence* because she is a woman, because she is Acadian, because she is francophone in North America and because she is poor. She has no identity because Acadia is not a country. She speaks an old archaïc language which is no longer recognized anywhere. In this way she is the perfect example of the minority personality and it is perhaps because of this that she has attracted popular interest. In my version we have Acadia seen from the inside, talking about itself, expressing, studying and discovering itself.[10]

It is obvious, then that Maillet and the Acadian writers of the 1970s speak of problems that reflect both their milieu and contemporary society.

Poets, as well as novelists and dramatists, have turned away from their traditional past, preferring to reinterpret myths and invent new metaphors more in tune with the mood of present-day society. One of the most important of these contemporary poets is Herménégilde Chiasson. Chiasson holds a doctorate in Aesthetics from the Sorbonne, has been a university professor, painter, dramatist and artistic director for radio productions. He is perhaps the most eloquent representative of the Acadian poets today. His published poetry speaks of Acadia as a country of uncertain frontiers, whose territory is essentially a moral one, and whose homeland is only of the soul. It reveals the Acadians' sense of alienation from the wider Maritime community around them and their feelings of frustration and despair. No where is this more clear than in a prose poem written by Chiasson entitled *Jaune*. Although the volume from which this poem is taken is published in French, this particular poem is written largely in English, a strategy whereby the poet suggests the powerful tendency on the part of the Acadians to assimilate to the dominant English milieu.

> ...nous savons dire please a minute please
> pardon me please thank you so very much
> please don't bother please I don't mind

10 "Visages: Antonine Maillet".

> please et encore you're welcome please
> come again please anytime please don't
> mention it please PLEASE PLEASE PLEASE
> please kill us please draw the curtain
> please laugh at us please treat us like
> shit please, le premier mot que nous
> apprenons a leur dire et le dernier que
> nous leur dirons please. Please, make
> us a beautiful ghetto, not in a territory,
> no, no, right in us, make each of us a
> ghetto, take your time please. . .[11]

Despite the late blooming of fiction and poetry in Acadia (a phenomenon largely explained by economic and social factors), you will have
noted from these brief comments some constant themes over time in their
literature. First and foremost has been the preoccupation of Acadian
writers with the collective survival of Acadia as a people. In the early literature this theme was essentially an exercise in consciousness-raising, which
presented the Acadians as martyrs of the deportation, whose salvation lay
in allegiance to the traditional values of language, religion and race. Later
on this preoccupation with collective survival was to change. Most writers,
until the 1970s, sought the survival of their ethnic group by fighting for the
salvation of language and the maintenance of as large a measure of autonomy for Acadians as the Maritime context would allow. Obviously, in
New Brunswick, where the Acadian population was larger (and where the
majority of the writers were based), their demands were more insistent.
But, until the 1970s, these demands were essentially those of the cultural
conservationists who wished to maintain the status quo. In the 1960s and
1970s less conservative writers like Maillet and Chiasson appeared, who
felt that the legitimate ambition of the Acadians was not merely to survive,
but to be more responsible for their own destiny. Acadian writers from
New Brunswick wrote polemical fiction which sought a social system
which would guarantee the greatest degree of growth and expansion for the
Acadian group. Here too the parallels are obvious with similar themes in
Quebec fiction at approximately the same time.

To a large extent what sets Acadian writing apart from the English-
Canadian literature of the Maritime Provinces is that it has so long been
polarized around the polemic of nationalism. As such it has been a literature linked inextricably to a historical group and to serving the perceived
needs of that group in terms of its cultural survival. The literature of the
1970s made Acadians aware of the assimilating forces around them and

---

11 Herménégilde Chiasson, *Mourir à Scoudouc* (Moncon, 1974), p. 44.

promoted a new consciousness of these forces and a new militancy among its readers. Increasingly, however, over the last half-decade the stance of the committed writer is giving away to preoccupation with problems more literary than social. Even those contemporary authors who still lean heavily on the tradition of the *conteur* (the folk narrative) use this device for the purposes of light satire or social comedy, as in the three novels of Laurier Melanson.

Speaking in Fredericton in February 1985, Herménégilde Chiasson, whose early poetry revealed themes of alienation and social protest, declared that his interests no longer lean toward national issues but turn more around the problems of poetic form. Equally associated with the poetry of alienation in the 1970s was the name of Raymond LeBlanc whose volume *Cri de Terre* was the first publication of the Éditions d'Acadie in 1972. Yet he, too, feels that polemical themes are now of diminished concern in Acadian writing. Speaking in 1983 in Montreal to the French Canadian Academy's colloquium on contemporary writing, LeBlanc had this to say:

> Our poetry is more personal, more sincere, more anchored in the physical environment and hides less and less under neo-nationalist slogans. It is also more urban, more linked to daily life, and has more real imaginative power.... It is less tense, more at ease with other writings, seeks more than ever its autonomy, likes to play, to be a little crazy, has become in some sense a performance.... We have dug our roots underground, under the level of speech-making.... We are no longer a standard-bearer of an old society.[12]

It would appear that Acadian writers now deem personal vision, a fresh view of the world, more important than polemics.

What value does the study of the literature of the Acadians have for English-language educational institutions in the Maritimes? Aside from the enjoyment it provides in its own right, it allows us not only to see Acadians as they see themselves, but also to discover their perceptions of us, their English-speaking neighbours. Obviously, literature cannot replace social history but in Acadia it has been an eloquent witness to the workings of the heart and mind of this segment of Maritime society. In the late 1880s, a Quebec writer, Narcisse Faucher de Saint-Maurice, in searching for a symbol to illustrate his view of Canada as two cultural solitudes, hit upon the famous stairway at Chambord Castle in France's Loire Valley. Built as a hunting castle in the fifteenth century for Francis I,

---

12 Raymond LeBlanc, "La jeune poésie acadienne", *Ecrits du Canada français*, 52 (1984), p. 108.

Chambord's main architectural feature is its double stairway so constructed that a person going up, never need meet face to face those on their way down. In this way, the lesser nobles and the King's entourage never needed to meet. Such a compartmentalized existence, Faucher felt, was typical of the relations between the English and French in the Quebec of his time, a situation he felt quite inappropriate for two peoples destined to share common space and common social and political structures. This divisiveness which Faucher perceived in the Quebec of the late nineteenth century was sensed and described in a different metaphor by a former president of the University of New Brunswick who was fond of describing the North and the South (or the English and the French) sections of New Brunswick as divided by a pine-tree curtain. I mention these two images since it seems to me that the study of Acadian writing in Maritime educational institutions can help bridge our compartmentalized lives by drawing apart that curtain and building links of understanding between the different segments of our society.

SELECTED BIBLIOGRAPHY

A. *Bibliographies, Anthologies and Literary History*

Boivin, Henri-Bernard, *Littérature acadienne 1960-1980: bibliographie* (Montréal, 1981).

Cogswell, Fred, and Maillet, Marguerite, *et al.*, *New Brunswick Authors/Écrivains du Nouveau Brunswick* (Ottawa, 1984).

Daigle, J., ed., *The Acadians of the Maritime Provinces* (Moncton, 1982).

Desjardins, Bérnard, *Bibliographie des auteurs acadiens du Nouveau Brunswick, 1946-1972* (Ottawa, 1972).

Doiron, Jean *et al.*, *Bibliographie acadienne* (Halifax, 1984).

Ellipse 16: La Poésie acadienne/Maritime Poetry (Sherbrooke, 1974).

Gair, R., gen.ed., *A Literary and Linguistic History of New Brunswick* (Fredericton, 1986).

Gallant, Melvin et Gould, Ginette, *Portraits d'Écrivains* (Moncton, 1982).

Maillet, Marguerite *et al.*, *Anthologie de textes littéraires acadiens* (Moncton, 1979).

_____, *Histoire de la littérature acadienne: de rêve en rêve* (Moncton, 1983).

Paratte, H.D., ed., *Poésie acadienne contemporaine/Acadian Poetry Now* (Moncton, 1985).

B. *Poetry*

Arsenault, Guy, *Acadie Rock* (Moncton, 1973).

Breau, Raymond, *Chanson poêmes et photos* (Moncton, 1962).

Chiasson, Herménégilde, *Mourir à Scoudouc* (Moncton, 1979).

Comeau, Clarence, *Entre amours et silences* (Moncton, 1980).

Cogswell, Fred, "Modern Acadian Poetry", *Canadian Literature*, 68-69 (Summer 1976), pp. 62-5.

Depres, Ronald, *Paysages en contrebande* (Moncton, 1974).

Duguay, Calixte, *Les Stigmates du silence* (Moncton, 1975).

Forest, Léonard, *Comme en Florence* (Moncton, 1979).

Landry, Napoléon-P., *Poèmes acadiens* (Montréal, 1955).

Langford, Georges, *Arrangez-vous pour qu'il fasse beau* (Montréal, 1972).

LeBlanc, Raymond, *Cri de Terre* (Moncton, 1972).

Longfellow, Henry Wadsworth, *Evangeline* (Toronto, 1982).

Roy, Albert, *Fouillis d'un Brayon* (Moncton, 1980).

C. *Prose Fiction*

Branch, James, *Whose Fault Is It?* (Moncton, 1929).

Brun, Regis, *La Mariecomo* (Montréal, 1974).

Carbonneau, Hector, *Gabriel et Geneviève* (Moncton, 1974).

D'Entremont, Laurent, *Golden farm memories: more rural acadian humor by the author of "The Two acre farm"* (Yarmouth, 1975).

——————, *The Two acre farm: a humorous outlook on the small acadian farms of Nova Scotia in the late 1940's* (Yarmouth, 1973).

Deveau, J.-Alphonse, *Journal de Cécile Murat* (Montréal, 1963).

——————, *Le chef des Acadiens* (Yarmouth, 1980).

Ferron, Jacques, *Les Roses sauvages: petit roman suivi d'une lettre d'amour soigneusement présentée* (Montréal, 1971).

Fitzpatrick, Marjorie A. and Maillet, Antonine, "The Search for a Narrative Voice", *Journal of Popular Culture*, 15/3 (1981), pp. 4-13.

Gobin, Pierre, "Space and Time in the Plays of Antonine Maillet", *Modern Drama*, 25/1 (March 1982), pp. 46-59.

Griffiths, Naomi, "Longfellow's *Evangeline*: The Birth and Acceptance of a Legend", *Acadiensis*, XI/2 (Spring 1982), pp. 28-41.

Haché, Louis, *Adieu, p'tit Chipagan* (Moncton, 1978).

_____, *Toubes jersiaises* (Moncton, 1980).

LeBouthiller, Claude, *Isabelle-sur-mer* (Moncton, 1979).

_____, *L'Acadien reprend son pays* (Moncton, 1977).

Légaré, Huguette, *La Conversation entre hommes: roman* (Montréal, 1973).

Levesque, Anne, *Les jongleries* (Moncton, 1980).

Maillet, Antonine, *Christopher Cartier of Hazelnut, Also Known as a Bear/Christophe Cartier de la noisette dit nounours* (Toronto, 1984).

_____, *Pélagie-la-Charette* (Toronto, 1983).

_____, *La Sagouine* (Toronto, 1979).

_____, *The Tale of Don L'Orignal* (Toronto, 1978).

Melanson, Laurier, *Zélika à cochon vert* (Montréal, 1981).

Savoie, Jacques, *Raconte-moi Massabielle* (Moncton, 1979).

_____, *Les Portes tournantes* (Montreal, 1984).

Shek, Ben-Z, "Antonine Maillet and the Prix Goncourt", *Canadian Modern Language Review/La Revue Canadienne de langues vivantes*, 36 (1980), pp. 393-6.

Smith, Donald, "Maillet and the Prix Goncourt", *Canadian Literature*, 88 (Spring 1981), pp. 157-61.

Weiss, Jonathan M., "Acadia Transplanted: The Importance of Evangeline Deusse in the Work of Antonine Maillet", *Colby Library Quarterly*, 13 (1977), pp. 173-85.

D. *Stories and Legends*

D'Eon, Désiré, *Histoire de chez nous: faits et anecdotes d'un temps qui n'est plus* (Yarmouth, 1977).

Gallant, Antoinette, *Le Journal d'une raconteuse* (Summerside, 1979).

_____, *Little Jack an' de Tax-Man* (Bedeque, 1979).

Jolicoeur, Catherine, *Le plus belle légendes acadiennes* (Montréal, 1981).

Maillet, Antonine, *Par derrière chez mon père: recueil de contes* (Montréal, 1972).

Peronnet, Jean, *Pépère Goguen et les ratons-voleurs* (Moncton, 1975).

Thibodeau, Félix E., *Dans notre temps, avec Marc et Philippe* (Yarmouth, 1976).

28 *The Built Environment*
A Heritage Resource

Susan Buggey

PRESERVATION OF MAN-MADE HERITAGE resources is an important component of the continuity of past, present and future in Maritime society. Heritage conservation approaches managing the built environment with a regard for the design preferences, materials, technology and investment of labour that the built past represents. Within this context I am going to look first at some of the trends within heritage conservation and then, recognizing that preservation is — and should be — selective, at some of the types of studies of the built environment that have been carried out to provide the base for conservation decision-making.

In 1960, Canadians asked about architectural heritage would, in all likelihood, have told you about Buckingham Palace, Hampton Court, or perhaps Versailles. In all probability their touchstones would have been both monumental — the grand architectural traditions — and foreign. Travellers attuned to North America might have referred to Colonial Williamsburg or the new initiatives in Old Montreal. How many Maritimers, in speaking of architectural heritage, would have thought of buildings close to home — Port Royal, for example, reconstructed in the 1930s, or the Halifax Waterfront Buildings, derelict among the rubbies of Water Street?

Since 1960 a revolution has occurred in thinking about the built environment. Social scientists have attributed it to changes in society — the anti-elitism of the 1960s, the new interest in the common man, nostalgia associated with the past in face of rapid societal change, and the alienation of brutalism and modernism. Architects and designers have been attracted to heritage by the visual pleasure offered in the play of light and shadow, the irregularities of Gothic and Queen Anne designs, the colour and texture of wood, stone, and terra cotta. Planners have found an appeal of heritage in the concentrations of buildings in central business districts available for commercial revitalization and in the economic attractions of labour-intensive rehabilitation and the cost savings of urban services already in place. The sharpening of environmental awareness, although focussed on the conservation of natural and wilderness resources, has extended to the built environment, such as the impact of acid rain on stone.

What is the nature of this change? Drawing on a combination of the literature and experience, I would identify five components.

First, there has been a significant shift in attitude towards the built environment. Whereas in the 1960s, it was customary to tear down existing buildings and then ask what should be done with the space, there are now both governmental programs and public pressure to preserve substantial existing buildings and seek new uses for them. Before and after views of the Halifax Waterfront Buildings, restored in the mid-1970s, illustrate the point. Urban revitalization now prevails over urban renewal, even if precariously so.

Second, rehabilitation of existing buildings, such as the restoration of the soldiers' barracks in Fredericton as offices for the New Brunswick Heritage Resources Branch, has largely replaced reconstruction, i.e. the replication of buildings which no longer exist. Two village examples demonstrate. At King's Landing, existing buildings about to be flooded by the construction of the Mactaquac Dam were arranged on a new site to simulate nineteenth-century rural New Brunswick. At Louisbourg, by contrast, the site is original but the buildings are reconstructed, beginning in the 1960s, from historical and archaeological evidence.

Third, early preservation efforts focussed on individual monumental buildings, often those associated with significant personages, whose historical importance was seen as at least as relevant to the preservation as the building itself. The Uniacke House is a typical example. In the 1970s, however, preservationists came to recognize that it was streetscapes and districts, not monumental buildings, that gave sense of place. Rehabilitation in Halifax on both Brunswick Street and Granville Street exemplifies this trend.

Fourth, associated with this last shift, from individual buildings to streetscapes and districts, was a redirection from interpreting the past primarily through historic house museums — such as the Ross-Thomson House in Shelburne — to creating an appreciation of the past as part of the contemporary environment, as in the delightful exhibit of Halifax porches at the Mount Saint Vincent Gallery last year.

Finally, the perception of the historic designed landscape has shifted from clean-up and cosmetic landscaping to some recognition of gardens, parks, squares, boulevards and streets as historic environments in their own right. The rehabilitation of King Square in Saint John is an example of this trend.

The two-year controversy surrounding the proposed highrise development on the verge of the Halifax Public Gardens illustrates what heritage has become. It has centred not upon the monumental residence associated with an important personage or a reconstructed historic fabric to commemorate an historic event, but upon the quality of environment in an area — the scale, design, setback, and impact of accommodating an increasing population density in a largely residential neighbourhood. The opponents of the development have called upon scientific evaluations of wind and shadow effect, and they have tested such conventional heritage tools as legislation, municipal plans and planning processes, public good will, and political pressure. The perpetrators of the development against which these weapons have been volleyed are traditional community leaders — doctors and, more distantly, Dalhousie University. Opposition to the project has focused, in fact, not on a building but on a less "useful" element of the community, a garden, although safeguarding the scale of development and its anchor building, Hart House, has been critical. The ultimate defence has been the pleasure that gardens — and this garden in particular — give. Less the antiquity, the integrity, the scientific interest, than the aesthetic transcendence of this picturesque and peaceful retreat amidst the urban hubbub.

Heritage has now matured in Canada sufficiently to have produced not only a wide range of projects — from the Murray Premises in St. John's, Province House in Charlottetown, Thorndean in Halifax, to Prince William Street in Saint John — but also a literature on diverse aspects of the built environment. There is not a large heritage literature specifically for the Maritime provinces. What there is has been approached in various ways. A significant number of studies, carried out on the national scale, incorporate Maritime examples. Only a few of them, however, are analytical and attempt seriously to define and assess the effectiveness of the region's built environment. While everyone is probably most aware of those studies of individual buildings, it is studies which analyze and interpret the historic built environment — in its various forms and foci — that help us most in understanding the architectural past.

Most often studies of individual buildings have been carried out for purposes of local appreciation, historic site designation or preservation. Churches and houses are the most common types. For example, St. George's Church in Halifax, one of the few buildings in Canada depicting the prominent Palladian round design, has recently been studied both for designation and for funding for its preservation. Individual building studies have also formed the basis of a number of volumes. Local heritage organizations, such as the Heritage Trust of Nova Scotia, the PEI Heritage Foundation, and the Newfoundland Historic Trust, have been particularly active in compiling and publishing such collections.

There have also been valuable studies of particular building types, such as churches, court houses, town halls, schools, and houses. A recent study of early Canadian court houses, for example, found that what distinguished those of Nova Scotia and New Brunswick was the prominence they derived from construction by county authorities and the individuality of their designs, materials and siting to meet needs of a specific situation as expressed by a group of local citizens. Examination by Peter Ennals and Deryck Holdsworth of house types in the Maritimes, based on floor plans, construction techniques, roof design and exterior detail, has identified six district patterns of vernacular housing in the region.

Studies of the architecture of specific communities are valuable for both heritage planning and public appreciation. Lunenburg, the most studied of Maritime communities, illustrates the distinctiveness that architectural shapes (such as the "Lunenburg bump") as well as form, colour and detail give to Maritime townscapes. No one familiar with the region would confuse Yarmouth with Pictou or Sherbrooke with St. Andrews, but in only a few communities have the formative influences and discrete adaptations been recorded and analyzed to portray the unique sense of place that characterizes the community.

Inventory is one of the most popular means of obtaining a view on the past. By using a standardized set of questions to collect available data within defined parameters, it establishes a data base of comparable information. This data base can then be used for assessment of which buildings are most important as landmarks; as examples of styles, technologies, or uses; or as structures that create the essential character of place. Municipal, provincial and federal planning and heritage agencies use inventories to priorize preservation efforts within their constituencies. The Canadian Inventory of Historic Building, which emerged out of a series of regional projects launched in the 1960s, has recorded over 30,000 buildings, constructed almost entirely before 1914, in the Maritime provinces.

TABLE I

Canadian Inventory of Historic Building Recording
in the Maritime Provinces.

	TOTAL	URBAN	RURAL
Nova Scotia	14,850	7,867 (53%)	6,983 (47%)
New Brunswick	11,250	5,049 (45%)	6,201 (55%)
Prince Edward Island	5,193	1,551 (30%)	3,642 (70%)

In the past 15 years CIHB has computerized the data collected and made the information retrievable, not only by geographical location but also by feature — size, construction material, roof, window, door, cornice, etc. Inventory can only tell us what has survived — what is out there now — where it is, and what it is like. It cannot tell what it was like originally, though it gives many substantial clues in this regard. Such information permits individual buildings to be put in context — how representative, or typical, or rare is a building; where are areas of concentration of pattern or character sufficient to constitute a district. Harold Kalman has set forth five widely accepted criteria: Architecture (style, construction, age, architect, design, interior); History (association with person or event or illustrative of broad historical patterns); Environment (continuity, setting, landmark); Usability (compatability, adaptability, public need, services, cost); and Integrity (site, alterations, condition). As Kalman points out, "the purpose of an evaluation is to identify the best buildings within the area being surveyed".[1] What "best" means depends on the weighting and interpretation of the evaluation factors. For example, a heavy weighting to architectural factors will usually favour prominent monumental buildings; a heavy weighting to history will favour structures important for their associations which may not, as buildings, be very important either as representative or unique examples; a heavy weighting to environment will favour buildings which contribute to their districts but may not in themselves be particularly significant.

Detailed architectural data accumulated by the Canadian Inventory of Historic Building have been used most significantly in five studies of nineteenth-century architectural styles published by Parks Canada: Palladian, Neo-classical, Picturesque, Gothic, and Second Empire. Each study examines the historic origin of the style in Europe and America and its Canadian, and regional, adaptation. Each contains examples from the Atlantic Provinces. Each refines Alan Gowan's seminal analysis of the architectural character of Canada and affirms the distinctive integration of European and American architectural patterns to create a distinctive Canadian architectural tradition. The question that emerges is whether there is a distinctive style to the architecture of the region. In examining the Palladian style (the so-called Georgian style because of its prevalence during the reigns of the four King Georges), Nathalie Clerk found numerous examples in the Maritimes, especially in urban centres like Halifax and their hinterlands where imperial administration and Anglicanism were strongest; 10 of her 20 examples are Nova Scotian and New Brunswick buildings. She pronounces Province House in Halifax to be "the best example of Palladian architecture to be found in Canada".[2] In contrast, Janet Wright, studying the architecture of the Picturesque, found individual examples in each province but in none did the generally modest expressions of the Picturesque, such as Girvan Bank in Annapolis, "establish any general pattern of building" as it did in the Canadas.[3]

1   Harold Kalman, *The Evaluation of Historic Buildings* (Ottawa, 1979), p. 22.
2   Nathalie Clerk, "Palladian", *Styles in Canadian Architecture* (Ottawa, 1983), p. 6.
3   Janet Wright, *Architecture of the Picturesque in Canada* (Ottawa, 1984), p. 145.

Unfortunately studies of the architects and artisans and of the materials and technologies they used are still few and far between. William Critchlow Harris, the Prince Edward Island architect whose brother was painter Robert Harris, has alone received monograph treatment, although a few, like the Southcotts in St. John's and George Lang in Halifax, have been the subject of essays, while others, like David Stirling, Frank Wills and John Plaw, appear in the *Dictionary of Canadian Biography*. The limited study of the building industry in the Maritimes to date, focused on Halifax, has examined the transformation from traditional artisanal craftsmanship to industrialization in the construction trades. Ian McKay's study of the carpenters of Halifax illustrates the rich potential of this field.

Studies of the use of materials and construction techniques are also in their infancy. The prominent use of wood in Maritime building has been particularly noted in structures where the style has been typically constructed elsewhere in stone. In the Antigonish County Court House, for example, the columns, porticoes and pilasters are all adapted to wood construction. The rebuilding of Granville Street, Halifax in the 1860s with cast iron store fronts and facades from Daniel Badger's Architectural Iron Works in New York was an early Canadian introduction of that prominent nineteenth-century building material. Recognizing its prevalence in Halifax, Thomas Ritchie has described the city as "the New Orleans of Canada".[4]

James Marsden Fitch, the doyen of American historic preservation, subtitled his seminal work on American architecture "The Historical Forces That Shaped It".[5] Of those forces in the Maritimes, besides the adaptation of European and American architectural styles already noted, the greatest impact on urban architecture came from fire. The conflagrations in Saint John and Halifax are well-documented, although the civic efforts to control building through zoning, materials specification and inspection that resulted, are less well-known. Prominent expressions of business confidence following the fires led the way in rebuilding Granville Street in Halifax in the early 1860s and Prince William Street in Saint John in the late 1870s.

I have tried to give you some suggestion of the ways in which the built environment is being studied and preserved today. I do not want to appear too optimistic: a little has been done, a vast amount remains. Intensive local studies are needed across the region that examine the local distinctions in architecture similar to the distinction of cultural landscape that

---

4   Eric Arthur and Thomas Ritchie, *Iron. cast and wrought iron in Canada from the seventeenth century to the present* (Toronto, 1982), p. 85.

5   James Marston Fitch, *American Building The Historical Forces that Shaped It* (2nd ed., New York, 1973).

Larry McCann has remarked upon. Such studies, based on careful reading of the multi-faceted landscape and a nurtured appreciation of its historical, aesthetic and cultural characteristics, are fundamental to understanding and selecting those parts — both representative and unique — that must be preserved at all cost for the future. To conclude from John Steinbeck: "how do we know it's us without our past?"

SELECTED BIBLIOGRAPHY

Arthur, Eric and Ritchie, Thomas, *Iron. cast and wrought iron in Canada from the seventeenth century to the present* (Toronto, 1982).

Brousseau, Mathilde, "Gothic Revival in Canadian Historic Architecture", *Canadian Historic Sites*, no. 25 (Ottawa, 1980).

Buggey, Susan, "Building Halifax 1841-1871", *Acadiensis*, X/1 (Autumn 1980), pp. 90-102.

_____, "Building in Mid-Nineteenth Century Halifax: The Case of George Lang", *Urban History Review*, IX/2 (October 1980), pp. 5-20.

Cameron, Christina and Wright, Janet, "Second Empire Style in Canadian Architecture", *Canadian Historic Sites*, no. 24 (Ottawa, 1980).

Cameron, Christina et al., *Styles in Canadian Architecture* (Ottawa, 1983).

Carter, Margaret, comp., *Early Canadian Court Houses* (Ottawa 1983).

_____, *Researching Heritage Buildings* (Ottawa, 1983).

City of Halifax, *An Evaluation and Protection System for Heritage Resources in Halifax* (Halifax, 1978).

Clerk, Nathalie, *Palladian Style in Canadian Architecture* (Ottawa, 1984).

Duffus, Allan F. et al., *Thy Dwellings Fair Churches of Nova Scotia: 1750-1830* (Hantsport, 1982).

Ennals, Peter and Holdsworth, Deryck, "Vernacular Architecture and the Cultural Landscape of the Maritime Provinces — A Reconnaissance", *Acadiensis*, X/1 (Spring 1981), pp. 86-106.

Heritage Trust of Nova Scotia, *Researching a Building in Nova Scotia* (Halifax, 1984).

_____, *Seasoned Timber* (2 vols., Halifax, 1972, 1974).

Holdsworth, Deryck, ed., *Reviving Main Street* (Toronto, 1985).

Kalman, Harold, *The Evaluation of Historic Buildings* (Ottawa, 1979).

Maitland, Leslie, *Neoclassical Architecture in Canada* (Ottawa, 1984).

234 Teaching Maritime Studies

McAleer, Philip, "St. Paul's, Halifax, Nova Scotia and St. Peter's, Vere Street, London, England", *The Journal of Canadian Art History*, VII/2 (1984), pp. 113-37.

McKay, Ian, *The Craft Transformed. An Essay on The Carpenters of Halifax, 1885-1985* (Halifax, 1985).

Newfoundland Historic Trust, *A Gift of Heritage. Historic Architecture of St. John's* (St. John's, 1975).

O'Dea, Shane, "Architecture and Building History in Atlantic Canada", *Acadiensis*, X/1 (Autumn 1980), pp. 158-63.

Pacey, Elizabeth et al., *More Stately Mansions. Churches of Nova Scotia 1830-1910* (Hantsport, 1983).

Parks Canada, Manuscript Report Series (Ottawa, v.d.), Reports on Selected Buildings: #256 Roger Bill et al., St. John's, Newfoundland (1974); #260 Ronald McDonald, Mahone Bay, Nova Scotia (1977); #262 Sharon Reilly, Yarmouth (1977); #269 Irene Rogers, Charlottetown (1974-76).

_____, Microfiche Report Series (Ottawa, v.d.), Reports on Selected Buildings: #13 C.A. Hale, Fredericton, Moncton and Woodstock, New Brunswick (1973-76); #33 C.A. Hale, Saint John, New Brunswick (1981).

_____, *Research Bulletin* (Ottawa, 1983), #202 C.A. Hale, New Brunswick: Interim Report on Common School Architecture in the 19th Century; #209 C.A. Hale, Newfoundland: Interim Report on School Architecture Before 1930; #210 C.A. Hale, Prince Edward Island: Interim Report on Common School Architecture in the 19th Century; #211 C.A. Hale, Publicly Funded Schools in Nova Scotia, Pre-1930.

Plaskett, Bill, *Understanding Lunenburg's Architecture* (Lunenburg, 1979).

Rogers, Irene, *Charlottetown The Life in Its Buildings* (Charlottetown, 1983).

Tuck, Robert C., *Gothic Dreams. The Life and Times of a Canadian Architect William Critchlow Harris 1854-1913* (Toronto, 1978).

Weaver, John C. and Lottinville, Peter, "The Conflagration and the City: Disaster and Progress in British North America during the Nineteenth Century", *Histoire Sociale/Social History*, XIII (1980), pp. 417-50.

Wilson, Alex, "The Public Gardens of Halifax, Nova Scotia", *Journal of Garden History*, III/3 (July-September 1983), pp. 179-92.

Wright, Janet, *Architecture of the Picturesque in Canada* (Ottawa, 1984).

29 Inside the Front Door: Recent Approaches and Themes for Interpreting Past Housing

Peter Ennals

IN THINKING ABOUT HOW TO prepare my contribution to this conference I have made certain assumptions about how I fit into the panel of speakers in this session. Whatever expertise I have centres on the matter of housing, and therefore I propose to address myself to that segment of the material cultural spectrum. Since I am, I think, the lone contributor of the section entitled "Our Houses" in the proposed text — perhaps it is appropriate that I stake out this territory. However, when I began to think about what I might say, I found myself wrestling over and over again with the fundamental question: what level of material cultural understanding, and what approaches are appropriate to a clientele of grade nine and ten students? More than that I asked myself: why should material cultural elements be taught to grade nine students at all?

There is in this question, I suppose, just the faintest hint of concern that material cultural subject matter could in the wrong hands degenerate into a purposeless form of antiquarianism, or worse, an exercise in sloppy and romantic artifactual piety. The problem is that material cultural study is as yet an emerging field and one that has no clear disciplinary home. It is significant that in this session you are hearing from an historian, a geographer, and two members of the public service who represent agencies charged with preserving and presenting our national material heritage, which can range in scale and substance from a sub-regional expanse of natural habitat to minute objects of human artifice. On the panel one might have included as easily representatives from Folklore, Art History, Cultural Anthropology, or Historians of Science and Technology. The point is that it is not clearly nor widely understood how the insights that can be derived from an examination of material artifacts are to be used in the pursuit of knowledge. We are dealing with an area of enquiry that lacks a well articulated set of guiding principles or theory, or even conventions and terminology, and I suspect but a few teachers will have encountered what passes for rigorous academic analysis of material culture in their own days at university.

Material culture study has become very fashionable of late. The proponents of the Maritime Studies course obviously see it as an exciting "new" element. Those of us in universities have watched as new courses or programs in material culture have sprung to life, even in the midst of financial restraint. Material culture has become the theme for a number of academic conferences and in this region and elsewhere, there has been an explosion in the past two decades in the numbers of museums that dot the landscape — many of them the outdoor, total sensory type. Of course, new and fashionable does not immediately necessitate that this approach or subject matter should be imparted to young students. As someone who almost twenty years ago dared to swim against the tide of another academic fashion sweeping through Geography, I am a little hesitant of popular academic novelties. In my case I was made to suffer the taunts of fellow graduate students and faculty for proposing to study the barn architecture of southern Ontario. This was simply a laughable proposition in the "Geographic" halls of the University of Toronto in those days — Monte Carlo simulations and factorial ecologies of burgeoning metropolitan growth poles were after all the rage. It is hardly surprising that this recent turn of events has left me with a perverse sense of bemusement.

It is no doubt because of this past suffering that I feel a certain proprietary claim to this field of study. I confess to just a little resentment toward many of my former tormentors who, it seems, have recently become converts. Quite apart from pedagogical propriety, I also have a particular anxiety about this form of enquiry trickling down to the schools. I well remember a professor of mine lamenting with some bitterness an earlier case of this process. The case in point was "urban geography" which became the hot topic in the sixties and soon found its way into the school's curriculum. It was not long before my professor, who had pioneered this field, confronted a new generation of high school graduates arriving in his classes and after a lecture or two, they would confidently announce that they had already had this course and were ready for stronger stuff. It seems that many of his former students had become teachers and exercised the newly won curriculum freedom of the late sixties by producing a simplified version of his course using their own college lecture notes. However, although students believed they had the "real goods", it soon became evident that they lacked the intellectual framework for this sub-field, nor did they have the methodological tools for genuine analysis and understanding of this complex process of settlement development. Yet the pressure on the university community to cope with student 'ennui' was real and I think manifestly unfair. It paralyses me to think that students of mine might be taking their notes of my lectures on material culture and reading them to an impressionable lot of grade nine or ten students. It does not, however, fall to me to make the decision as to what shall or shall not be taught or how it shall be treated. I can only hope that those charged with developing the curriculum and particularly those responsible for implementing it in the classroom will address these questions in a serious way.

The task at hand is to attempt an overview of the "state of the art" in understanding the housing traditions of Maritime Canada, or elsewhere for that matter. Let me begin by recognizing that there are two distinct academic camps who engage in architectural analysis. The first is the art history approach, a well developed and long standing line of enquiry which typically seeks to place buildings into one of several formal art traditions or periods, many of which are international in their scope and classical in their inspiration. For example, much of western European art and architecture from the late seventeenth century through the middle of the nineteenth century can be labelled "neo-classical", in that artists and architects of the period returned to the greco-roman civilizations for designs. These motifs became the acceptable canons of style and taste and designers depended upon a number of academic manuals in rendering built forms. Yet it is also true that buildings that truly reflected the spirit and expression of this movement within the North Atlantic world, especially the Maritimes, were but a fraction of what was constructed by our ancestors. In short these forms, or what some call "high style" architecture, were limited to the small colonial elite. While they are clearly of some interest because they document. the attempts by this class to assert metropolitan taste and style on a new landscape, they leave a great deal of our architectural heritage untouched and, I think, untouchable given the methodology and orthodoxies that prevail within the art history academic tradition. In my view there are real risks to trying to understand the great array of what survives as pre-twentieth century housing stock using this approach. To do so is to force buildings into a classificatory mould that is ill fitted to their nature, and more than that, we deny ourselves the opportunity to understand the cultural integrity and the set of nuances that attaches to the greater mass of more prosaic buildings.

The second "camp" is of far more recent genesis and, to some extent, it has emerged to fill the gap left by the limits of the art history focus. However, it is also true that those who have chosen to study "folk" and "vernacular" architecture — as this more frequently encountered domestic form of housing is coming to be called in the literature — have tended to be inspired by various manifestations of the so-called "new" social history. Accordingly, much of the analysis of these artifacts is carried out with a view to exploring the way of life of common people. Put another way, the house becomes another form of cultural data to be evaluated, counted and analysed in the context of broader historical movements and processes. In North America, and certainly in Atlantic Canada, the majority of academic study of past housing in this vein has been carried out by Folklorists and Geographers: both are disciplines having well developed traditions of material cultural and landscape study. Historians have not been quick to jump into this effort. Perhaps it is because historians have not had a fieldwork tradition; most of the buildings we are talking about went unrecorded and hence largely defy analysis by means of archival documents.

It is perhaps worth noting that there is a third category of study which is not to be lightly dismissed, principally because the work of this genre is becoming so abundant and readily available. I refer here to the kind of work that arises from what I will call gifted amateurs, many of whom have a strong heritage and preservationist instinct. It is difficult and perhaps unfair to characterize this body of work with a single broad stroke, but most of it tends to be "genealogical" and anecdotal; that is, the focus is on identifying who built the house and when, and who has occupied it since. Descriptive rather than analytical references to the architecture of the house are common, and many such works do suffer from the kind of artifactual piety that I referred to earlier. The inevitable appeal of this genre to teachers is that it is likely to be very community specific, and I can well envision teachers being drawn to these volumes for class work because they tell about *some* of the houses that can be found close at hand. I stress "some" because more often than not there is again an elitist bias in the selection of the houses that find their way into these volumes. Typically specific houses are included because they are owned by prominent local personages, or because they have been well kept or restored, or simply because more is known about their descent. Rarely do the authors of such inventories make an effort to provide a representative selection of the past society's houses.

Clearly then I believe the body of work likely to yield the most productive insights into our past housing is that focusing on folk and vernacular architecture. Without a lengthy discussion of what folk and vernacular imply conceptually, let me simply offer the following distinctions. Folk buildings are those which replicate an earlier, usually European tradition in some way. Typically they are "peasant" housing forms, the conceptual details of which were transmitted from generation to generation without great change. Buildings of this type can be expected to have been part of the cultural baggage of many groups — the Acadians, the Scots, the Irish, and the English — and while there may have been some adaptation of old ways of building to new climatic imperatives and different and more abundant building materials, the "idea" and useage of the house survived little altered. Vernacular housing on the other hand is the product of new forces. At one level it mimicked the housing of the elite; yet the dwelling was rendered at a much reduced scale and used simpler stylistic and structural techniques. It was, in effect, one of the early manifestations of what we now call popular or mass culture, one which was increasingly produced using industrial processes, resulting in highly standardized forms and designs, and which was promoted by means of mass communication vehicles such as newspapers, and printed "how to" manuals.

In my mind the purpose of studying artifacts such as housing is that they provide another kind of evidence which documents the human condition. Let us be clear that I am not making exaggerated claims for what material culture can tell us. Rather artifacts such as housing present us with a tangible, a familiar and an accessible piece of evidence that serves as a kind of palimpsest of societies' changing attitudes and values on such fundamental matters as the segregation and specialization of household functions. For example, among the actions that can be charted in the transition from folk to vernacular housing practises are the separation of work space from living space, the segregation of sleeping quarters, and the creation of special gender oriented spaces (eg. kitchen, sewing room). within the house. These questions force one to analyse the interior of the dwelling and how life was lived within — this is very much a current focus of study in the field and one that is surprisingly new. Too often, I think, we have been content to evaluate architecture from the outside, especially giving a lot of attention to the facade with the result that the inside has not been adequately considered. This is not to say that current scholars of housing have given up looking at exteriors — far from it. But the folk and vernacular approach is directed more to seeing these externalities not for their artistic niceties and performance, but rather as a register of cultural continuity and/or adaptation in the case of folk houses, or as statements of socio-economic display and popular culture in the case of vernacular houses. The facade thus becomes a kind of signature that tells us much about the world view of the house's creator, and those who have come along after to modify it.

In adopting this approach, it is essential to keep a sense of broader context very much in view. The houses built in the Maritimes cannot be seen in isolation. We can only understand our houses by looking outward at antecedents in New England, France, Scotland, Ireland, and elsewhere. In fact, I think a study of the region's housing emphasizes just how connected the region was to a wider world. But the strength and persistence of folk traditions in housing among some groups and classes also stresses how complex our past society was, and points to some of the strongly conservative cultural forces that have made this region so perceptibly "traditional" in this present age.

Current research on the history of Maritime housing has stressed the need to adopt new methodologies and to ask a broader range of social rather than aesthetic questions about the artifact. Much research remains to be done but there is as good a base of empirical work already in print in this region as exists within the country. Educators seeking to interpret this region to their students have an opportunity to integrate this dimension of its reality into their picture, but it is important to do so with a clear sense of intellectual and pedagogical purpose and propriety.

SELECTED BIBLIOGRAPHY

Bronner, Simon J., ed., *American Material Culture and Folklife — a Prologue and Dialogue* (Ann Arbor, 1985).

Dorson, Richard, ed., *Folklore and Folklife — an Introduction* (Chicago, 1972).

Ennals, Peter and Holdsworth, Deryck, "Vernacular Architecture and the Cultural Landscape of the Maritime Provinces — A Reconnaissance", *Acadiensis*, X/1 (Spring 1981), pp. 86-106.

Ennals, Peter, "The Yankee Origins of Bluenose Vernacular Architecture", *American Review of Canadian Studies*, XII (Summer 1982), pp. 5-22.

_____, "The Folk Legacy in Acadian Domestic Architecture: A Study in Mislaid Self Images", in Shane O'Dea and Gerald Pocius, eds., *Dimensions of Canadian Architecture* (Ottawa, 1984), pp. 8-12.

Glassie, Henry, *Folk Housing in Middle Virginia — a Structural Analysis of Historical Artifacts* (Knoxville, Tenn., 1975).

Hubka, Thomas, *Big House, Little House, Backhouse, Barn* (Hanover, N.H., 1984).

Mannion, John J., *Irish Settlements in Eastern Canada: a Study in Cultural Transfer and Adaptation* (Toronto, 1974).

Pocius, Gerald A., "Architecture on Newfoundland's Southern Shore: Diversity and Emergence of New World Forms", in Camille Wells, ed., *Perspectives in Vernacular Architecture* (Annapolis, Md., 1982), pp. 217-232.

Schlereth, Thomas J., ed., *Material Culture Studies in America* (Nashville, Tenn., 1984).

30 Material Culture and The Teaching of Maritime Studies

D.A. Muise

MATERIAL HISTORY SHOULD BE MORE CENTRAL to our understanding of the Maritime experience. But the region's museums and historic sites — many and varied in capacity — project a backward looking preoccupation with past accomplishments and happier times. The resilience of this image should not surprise us. It is, after all, virtually the only message that our tourist oriented literature presents to the outside world — and everyone knows that public history is designed to be consumed by tourists more than anything else.

Institutions or programs owing their existence to revivals of fading down-town cores, employment programs, or other transitory objectives are always in danger of becoming self-serving. By orienting their stories to attract spenders and please political patrons, they too often fail to develop specific historical consciousness within their own communities. Such tendencies simply reflect the sanitizing of the historical experience that occurs whenever something is prepared for public consumption. Such objectives may not be all bad, but in the process we can anaesthetize ourselves and rob our proper constituency of its own legitimate past. Halifax and Saint John have changed very much for the better as a result of attempts to recapture their historical experience with major redevelopments of their water-fronts. But those projects probably had little "historical" interest for those residents forced out of neighbourhoods in anticipation of the free-spending visitors who now throng their "restored" streets and buildings.

Over the past two decades the notion of "historic resources" being exploited for economic or political profit has become the norm, not just in the Maritimes but throughout Canada. Our history has come to the attention of governments which, in the process of repackaging it for tourists, often alienate and trivialize it. The built-environment, represented by such developments as the Halifax Citadel, Fortress Louisbourg, King's Landing, the Halifax and Saint John water-fronts — or any of dozens of historic houses and sites throughout the region — is universally presented through the material remains of past societies.

Material realities project images, whether one is looking at past accomplishments or present and future prospects. The semiotics of artifact study can encompass a broad-based approach to understanding a society's progress, not only in terms of technological advances and material accumulation but also in terms of cultural traits. Traditional studies of this genre can take a very specific approach as in the study of furniture styles, wearing apparel, architecture, or the successive technologies used to exploit natural resources. They often involve intricate taxonomies to classify and codify artifacts in accord with one or other organizational principle. They are essentially dedicated to documenting groups of artifacts rather than analysing cultural norms. The better material culture studies today get beyond the artifacts themselves, either to look at the impact we have had on our environment or as a way of better understanding the emergence of distinct communities.

Archaeologists and cultural geographers have done this sort of analysis for years. In the Maritimes, where the living past has been preserved for us in so many ways both in and outside institutional frameworks, the opportunities for advanced understanding are great. Community and region can sometimes be quite difficult to fathom within a course of studies attempting to find common denominators. Consciousness of material traditions can help inform us how Maritimers share and have shared common patterns of production and consumption.

Material history, as expressed through most historic resource institutions, is too easily dismissed as irrelevant to any understanding of the contemporary experience. When the heritage value of objects or structures is directed towards outsiders' interests, age and distinctiveness become the catchwords for development. In the end, what is communicated often has more to say about current economic and political considerations than any level of understanding relevant to the immediate concerns of the people of a community. Sites and buildings are commemorated because they have survived — by accident or design. They can also be specific expressions of a past reality with which politically powerful people wish to identify. Whatever the rationale for such activities, they always reflect the preoccupations of political and economic elites, for that is the constituency to whom they are addressed. Public historians can only marginally effect what is contained therein.

Research on artifacts teaches a level of literacy concerning the nature and functions of the material objects that surround us. A somewhat tired debate over the years has concerned the validity of objects as documents: whether or not one can extract meaning from artifacts at the same level possible from documentary evidence. That debate is probably irrelevant to present considerations, save for the fact that it has led to a great deal of theorizing concerning the nature and scope of material history research. For a review of this literature see Thomas Schlereth, ed., *Material*

Culture Studies in America (Nashville, 1982), which samples the field internationally and includes a massive bibliography.

Most curators of artifact collections will argue that expertise in a particular aspect of the material past comes only with intense acquaintance with both formal and socio-cultural aspects of material traditions. Within this frame of reference, artifact literacy has two distinct dimensions. First, we must learn to read accurately the physical properties — components and structures — of particular artifacts. A universal catalogue registering the properties of all man-made artifacts from our past would interrogate those artifacts in very specific ways. Size, shape, texture, markings, movable parts, etc. would all form part of any entry system. In fact the Canadian Inventory of Historic Buildings and the Inventory of Historic Resources — operated respectively by Parks Canada and the National Museums of Canada — attempt to do this for limited classes of objects through massive computer-assisted samplings of buildings and holdings through-out the country. While they remain too administratively centred to be of much immediate use in research design for social historians, the originators of those programmes have assisted greatly in development of new paradigms for the classification of artifacts and buildings. Their utility for the classroom is still some way off.

Related to an object's physical properties is its subjective history. Where and when it originated, how it was made, who owned it and how it came to be preserved are all relevant questions which all curators want answered. Accuracy in such descriptions can emerge from a deep understanding of relationships between artifacts and their creators — an understanding only possible in the context of a broad understanding of historical processes. Such information, essentially the reading of artifacts for their internal meaning, can only come after careful decisions regarding their disposition.

The second stage of artifact research comes from what one is able to read *into* rather than *out of* the artifact — its contextual and symbolic attributes. Artifacts are, after all, creations of organized communities made up of individuals. Continuities and discontinuities can be clearly reflected in a community's material history, if only we can learn to listen to what the artifacts are telling us. What we can know and understand about them is defined by what we can divine regarding their function. They can tell us about community structures basic to the ordering of society and our capacity to understand them.

Both the subjective and objective reality of artifacts reflects our and our ancestors' ingenuity in overcoming physical limits to the material world. When we can ascribe individual artifacts to a particular person within a very specific context they have a subjective reality. But artifacts have a broader objective reality as well. They reflect and illuminate past community behavioral norms that might otherwise be hidden from the clouded eyes of the present. This objective reality can reflect cultural transfer or patterned behavior based on specific historical experience. One thinks immediately of the ground-breaking work of John Mannion's *Irish Settlements in Eastern Canada: A Study of Cultural Transfer and Adaptation* (Toronto, 1974) which is cast partially within a Maritime Provinces' frame of reference. We can learn much about the emergence of the Maritime community from understanding its many patterned ways of doing things, whether reflected in the technology of exploiting natural resources or some other aspect of the human condition.

To expand the utility of material history we have to abandon two major shibboleths. The first is the notion that artifacts are the exclusive terrain of museums and like institutions. No one in such institutions thinks that for a moment. Artifacts often find their way into museums under very eccentric and egocentric conditions. Most public collections are the product of the peculiar political and social contexts in which they were created. Collections-bound material historians too often close themselves off from examining the broader range of material culture surrounding each and every aspect of past society.

A related shibboleth in need of excision is the elitist distinction made between "Museum Quality" objects and more commonplace relics of our past. Such notions underplay the social meaning of our material past by imposing qualitative "connoisseurship" values on artifacts that have chanced to survive by a sometimes very selective process. Museums can be excessively bound by the idea that all artifacts in their collections have to be beautiful or in some way unique to achieve the distinction of being "Museum Pieces". We all share these very elitist preoccupations regarding beauty and distinctiveness. Once abandoned, our interest can easily be directed towards recreating as much of the everyday totality of the material past as possible. If we want to serve the interests and past experiences of as much of our constituency as possible we must enlarge our present scope beyond limited horizons of institutional collections. Unfortunately, the past consumed things just as it consumed people and resources. Accurately reflecting it becomes a process not unlike the problem facing document-bound social historians who must make do with the scraps of the past that have survived the everyday experience of common people.

Material culture studies cannot be pursued in isolation from other sources of understanding. It is just one of several avenues to understanding past experience; its explanatory range often circumscribed by the availability of complementary documentary or oral sources. One pressing need is for increased methodological interaction between academic and institutional historians and between history and its sister disciplines — particularly Geography and Folklore. The main vehicle for this development in Canada at the moment is the *Material History Bulletin/Bulletin d'histoire de la culture materielle*, published by the National Museum of Man in Ottawa. From the same source comes Peter Rider, ed., *The History of Atlantic Canada: Museum Interpretations* (Ottawa, 1981), in which authors from seven leading museum and historic sites in the region explain how history is interpreted in their respective institutions.

Rather than deal with these theoretical questions we will address two approaches appropriate to Maritime experience that are of current interest to historians of the region. The first is the World of Work. In both our more recent and more distant pasts, material conditions defined and reflected power relationships and workers' direct subjugation to capital. These relationships between capital and labour conveyed various levels of symbolic meaning. Museums and historic villages can and do transmit notions about what it was like to live and work in past time. But most such institutions are often content to romanticize the pioneer experience, thus robbing the everyday lives of ordinary people of much of its meaning. Besides much of the past labour of Maritimers was not preoccupied with settling agricultural communities or operating saw-mills but on harsh and brutal resource frontiers and later in more urban communities. Coal miners, lumberers and fishermen all depended on technological extensions to carry out their work and often shared similar relationships to the wealth and power of the region.

Access to necessary technologies and capital to pursue those objectives was normally controlled by a political/economic system that also determined the disposal of their surpluses. Technological change, while central to the freeing of work from its more brutal aspects, was at the same time a determinant of the workers' condition of life, sometimes even an instrument of subjugation. Material history can assist our understanding of the central dynamic of these work processes. The cumulative study of the material condition of work helps illuminate class relationships and complements ideological perspectives. Discussions of technological aspects of work processes opens the door for consideration of more contemporary problems.

A simple class project would be to have students compose occupational genealogies of their own families and address questions of work patterns and technology from the generational perspective. Visits to any one of the dozens of sites and museums in the region devoted to the pioneer experience, preferably in the company of older people who actually experienced the technologies demonstrated, is a tremendous asset in fostering discussion. Artifacts obviously have to be supplemented in all instances by a variety of other types of sources in order to introduce students to a dynamic notion about the nature of work. Film and photographs can encourage understanding of various conditions of work in the past from a material perspective. Many examples of this sort of treatment are available from the National Film Board of Canada's extensive lists of media products.

The second approach relevant to Maritime experience focuses on the debate over the "Development and Underdevelopment" of the Maritime economy. This debate revolves around a set of assumptions concerning metropolitan-hinterland relations during periods of subordination. The material condition is a function of such dependencies. Communities, or regions for that matter, move through distinct developmental phases. Material dependencies — both for consuming and producing goods — have corresponded, generally speaking, to political dependencies. In the Maritimes, as with all oceanic territories, such dependencies are compromised by access to alternate trading relationships, either legally or extra-legally.

During the era of French domination, for instance, material realities associated with French cultural norms were constantly compromised by the proximity and free access enjoyed by New England traders. Acadian farmers were regularly supplied by the neighbouring colonies, thus breaking the dependence chain. The British century of dominance, from the founding of Halifax through to Confederation, featured massive transfers of British material traditions and technologies. But it also witnessed gradual emergence of locally-based material culture and ready adaptation to neighbouring technologies appropriate to the Maritime condition. The presence of artifacts from the far corners of the world reflected the maritime orientations of the community. Architecture and work implements featured adaptation to the realities of a North American environment where differing conditions and materials frequently imposed a different set of modalities. Finally, maturing Maritime communities produced a rich indigenous material culture during the last half of the nineteenth century, though almost before it took hold it began to succumb to the superior strength of central Canadian competitors within the larger economic system brought into existence by Confederation.

It is always difficult to acclimatize adolescents to a detailed theoretical understanding of the imperatives of metropolitan dominance as revealed in transfers of ideologies and technological realities. On the other hand, we can build upon their interest in more immediate surroundings by a relatively simple exercise in material culture studies. Students might be asked to inventory parts of their homes, say a single room to start. Emphasis in recording would focus on the place of origin and place of purchase of everything found. That would immediately raise a consciousness of our interdependencies for much of what surrounds us on an everyday basis. That understanding of the origins of material life for today's Maritimers should lead directly to consideration of our present economic dependencies and raise questions about how we got to where we are, perhaps even to why. By contrasting present material conditions with historical experience, which can be obtained from exposure to museums and other sites, students could be led to examine the stages of community change. Material consciousness would be heightened and the nature of past and present community illuminated.

Consciousness concerning material conditions can be raised in a variety of ways, but generally has to be nurtured through understanding of present conditions before being extended into past experience. While this should lead to an understanding of the process of change, it need not be exclusively preoccupied with those factors. This exercise presumes access to basic precepts of material culture studies. Extending it to consider ways of doing everyday tasks within communities would have to vary. Tasks within the home might be contrasted over time, or students could be asked to consider their own material possessions in relation to the possessions members of their age cohort might have had in previous times.

If material culture studies are to escape their preoccupation with the "Quaint" ways of the past and become more central to our understanding of the experience and condition of life in our varied communities, we have to become conscious of the ways in which our community experience is taught in the schools. Adolescents have an immediate capacity to understand material realities, but are much less adept in areas requiring high levels of abstraction. Material culture can provide the bridge between the two, reinforcing the central thrust of much of our current intellectual ferment. Experimentation with collective approaches to learning can offer tremendous opportunities for cultural study. Frequently neophyte collectors of one sort of another, students are conscious of style and content in their immediate surroundings. One can take advantage of that natural tendency to evolve a deeper appreciation of larger realities. Advancing a raised consciousness about the centrality of material culture in understanding the basics tenets of community structure and progress can be central to that achievement.

31 Maritime Material Culture Studies in Heritage Resource Institutions

Peter E. Rider

PIERRE TRUDEAU, AS MINISTER OF Justice, once proclaimed that the state had no business in the bedrooms of the nation. As he spoke, scores of government sleuths were examining every aspect of bedrooms, from their furnishings to their design and the activities that occurred within their discreet confines. Of course these researchers were concerned with the bedrooms of yesteryear, and this interest was only a sample of the publicly-funded effort to preserve and to explain the physical remains of our past. No area of Maritime studies attracts greater governmental involvement than material culture. Moreover, this is not surprising in a region possessing greater resources of this kind than most parts of the country.

At least two incentives can be identified as encouraging the study of our physical heritage. The first is that cultural remains are found everywhere and are known to everyone. They provoke curiosity among all, from the child rummaging through the family junk box to the avid collector building the ultimate assemblage of match safes. Because of this almost universal response, things are natural teaching devices. Young minds, particularly, can grapple with them more easily than with abstract ideas. A second motivation for material culture studies comes from the utility that objects have in interpreting the past. Just how useful artifacts are depends upon the item itself, its physical condition and the extent of its contextual information. There is some debate on the degree to which material evidence from more recent times can tell us anything new, but generally objects are most frequently useful in two historical processes, the embodiment of personal or group memories and the documentation of cultural traits within the broader flow of history. In other words, our material heritage serves as icons and/or benchmarks for measuring change.

Teachers will find the world of material culture studies relatively easy to enter. Their passage will be assisted by the numerous museums, art galleries and historical parks which dot the region. Charged with the role of collecting, displaying and interpreting our heritage, these institutions provide several avenues by which the field may be approached. The first of these, exhibits, is the most obvious service, but it is supplemented by increasingly elaborate animation and outreach programmes and by research activities undertaken by a number of larger organizations. Each has its own utility for classroom purposes, so the following comments are designed to assist in the use and assessment of each kind of service.

At first glance museum exhibits, either permanently housed in specialized display facilities or temporarily located in anything from National Exhibition Centres to shopping malls, are straight forward. They address a topic through a selection of artifacts usually accompanied by brief explanatory notes. The appearance of direct and factual impartiality is often misleading. Exhibits bear an overlay of interpretation which should command the viewer's awareness. The first of these is that the subject is important, worthy of the interest of the curators and of the financial investment required to complete the work and, of course, of public attention. Some pretty obscure topics have been brought forth as matters of significance by museums, and a few of them have, in a small fashion, changed the way we think of ourselves. An exhibit is also moulded by one or two additional factors, the storyline and the use of the objects. The storyline contains the statement which the presentation wishes to make and is influenced by a curator's knowledge and bias and the availability of display items, while the treatment of those items reflects a determination of whether they are examples of something or unique pieces of documentary evidence. For the viewer the storyline is of greatest concern.

These examples will amplify this point. At the New Brunswick Museum several years ago, a major reinterpretation of the province's maritime history was offered in "On the Turn of the Tide: Ships and Shipbuilders 1769-1900". Clearly the exhibition wanted to redress the myth of the golden age of sail by portraying shipping and shipbuilding as a localized, financially risky and physically punishing business. The message was direct and obvious to the viewer. Sometimes messages are less apparent. In the permanent exhibit, "Thirty Acres of Snow", at the National Museum of Man in Ottawa, the settlement and development of Canada from colonial to recent times is portrayed. Underlying the presentation is another theme, that of our past as one of exploitation in which man exploited nature and some men, or nations, exploited others. This often manifests itself in a less direct fashion. In one display case, for instance, a baroque clock is set out to be admired as a witness to a former age of elegance and ease. Behind it is an enlarged photograph of a slum taken about the time the clock graced a rich man's house. The message is there, but many miss it, seeing only the clock or occasionally the picture. Even more subtle are hidden messages reflecting assumptions projected upon the exhibit's subject-matter by its creators. A case in point is the British Columbia Provincial Museum which also presents the image of an emerging society. Hardship and struggle are acknowledged, but stout hearts and honest labour are depicted as at last making everything right. Progress is clearly apparent, spurred on by the initiative of a citizenry which, it seems, shares the virtues of the corporate sponsors whose names are listed above the door. Thus exhibits require intelligent viewing and some effort if they are to be appreciated at all their possible levels.

The essence of the artifact is not of great relevance to the average museum visitor but may be of interest to some. It certainly affects the nature of a display. Objects can be perceived as unique records of style or historical information or as examples of some aspect of past reality. Those who see the artifact as a piece of documentary evidence respond to the cry, "The object speaks for itself", and tend to inhabit art galleries or traditional institutions favouring typological exhibitions. Articles are displayed because of their individual beauty or interest or because they show variety or changes within a class of item. When artifacts are regarded as illustrative support for a message developed independently of them, the exhibits often bear a "tell them what they need to know" overtone. Examples of technology, such as saw mills or agricultural implements, or reconstructions along the line of Fortress Louisbourg fall within this tradition.

Regardless of the role assigned to an artifact, its essence is not influenced by its size. Objects may mean small items of material culture, historic houses, site reconstructions and, in the case of ecomuseums, even chunks of landscape. This lack of significance of size stems from the generally consistent impulses which societies bring to the things they create. The city, the shops and the merchandise found therein were produced and consumed by persons sharing similar intellectual attitudes and values. One of the chief merits in studying material culture comes from the development of analytical skills permitting greater sensitivity to immediate environments. Because of the riches that may be packed into a small area, museum exhibits are especially effective vehicles for the improvement of these abilities.

Categorization of museums and related institutions in the Maritimes is difficult because of their number and diversity. Overall, however, they seem to treat artifacts as examples and present explicit but benign messages. Art galleries fall outside of this tradition as do a number of small museums which tend to set out community heirlooms and curiosities. Another interesting departure, in part at least, from the above generalization is the New Brunswick Museum, once the strongest institutional proponent of analytical storylines in the region. Several recent exhibits have been composed of a selection of outstanding pieces grouped according to theme and presented with a minimum of labels. Viewers are left to learn or to be baffled by their encounter with the objects. Teachers, of course, may approach any exhibit in this way, ignoring the interpretative text and focusing their attention on items relevant to a topic selected by themselves. Indeed, most major museum exhibits anticipate a demand for this and have prepared suggestions of alternate themes for educational purposes.

In recent years museums, particularly fine art museums, have been accused of being elitist. Although some demonstrably courted broad visitor support, competition with centres of popular entertainment was difficult and expensive. There gradually emerged a philosophy which sought the mid-course, that of "public programming", broadening the clientele of heritage institutions without entering the world of show business. A variety of products and services have been developed, and some of these can be very helpful in the classroom. Each province has its own selection of resources, but they tend to fall into several distinct categories. The most useful of these types of resources will be described in subsequent paragraphs, and reference will be made to a product emanating from one source, by way of example. Teachers from other jurisdictions may consult their provincial institutions or the federal agencies active in the region for comparable products. Such enquiries are welcome. The Nova Scotia Museum, for instance, has prepared a brochure, *Learning Resources Catalogue*, which provides details on a wide range of services.

Museum Kits are mini-exhibitions in compact boxes. They have been specifically designed for circulation to schools, and they address topics relating to established curricula. In Nova Scotia subjects include pioneer life, early man, and barrel-making. A typical kit contains artifacts, an assortment of slides, booklets, and a teacher's manual. Users are expected to handle the materials with care and to return them promptly, but the contents are durable, replaceable or are replicas. Handling is encouraged. The Nova Scotia Museum makes this clear by informing teachers that "the objects in the kits are not just for display purposes but for your students to touch and feel and use". Rare or fragile items are represented by slides or photographs. This limits the effectiveness of the kits somewhat and restricts the range of possible subject-matter. In an attempt to broaden the base of available objects, some museums have created special loans collections containing artifacts that can be provided for study outside the institutions. The Nova Scotia Museum makes these items known through "The Museum Wishbook" containing their pictures.

Slide sets are another effective vehicle for the presentation of material culture which museums have exploited extensively. Although a natural tendency would be the development of packages which show museum objects or their use, many sets focus on the historical context in which our material heritage is found. They, therefore, cover topics that appear to be only distantly related to museological interests. An example is *Saint John, the City and Its Poor, 1783-1877* by T.W. Acheson, one volume in Canada's Visual History, a joint project of the National Museum of Man and the National Film Board. An early result of the research which eventually produced Professor Acheson's landmark study of Saint John, the set contains thirty slides of original photographs and paintings and a booklet with a brief text, substantial captions for the slides, a bibliography and suggestions for classroom activities. Designed for a national audience, Canada's Visual History unfortunately has committed only ten per cent of its volumes to the Maritimes, and only one-third of that number deal with material culture. The topics are, however, diverse, ranging from furniture to clothing and loyalist architecture.

Publishing represents the mother-lode of information on material culture. Museums turned to publications early as an outlet for research and reference material on subjects falling within their domain. As the need to broaden audiences increased, the published offerings have become increasingly attractive to the general public. Coffee table volumes, popular monographs, thematic studies for collectors, gallery guides, comic books and other emissions in every imaginable printed format represent a wealth of opportunities for the student of material culture. They also involve some hurdles. Well suited to the preparation of textual matter, museums and other heritage agencies are poorly adapted to marketing and distributing their wares. Much of what they offer is unknown to the public and resources are too scarce to maintain large order service operations. Lack of continuity in publishing programmes and a reputation for selecting esoteric or trivial topics have also tarnished the reputation of publications coming from heritage organizations. Institutions regularly issue lists of available titles, but what is really needed is an educational resources co-ordinating group to advertise and assist in the distribution of material from all three provinces plus relevant federal institutions. The rewards for tapping these resources, however, are even now well worth the investment of effort in finding them.

Each provincial museum, plus the National Museum of Man, has a flagship journal which deals with material culture studies. *The Occasional* from the Nova Scotia Museum appears, as the title suggests, occasionally and is sent free to those requesting it. The contents include short articles, news items, and announcements of events. A recent number featured a brief history of the plough in Nova Scotia and a discussion of gravestones. Three indices facilitate reference to back issues. *The Island Magazine*, published by the Prince Edward Museum and Heritage Foundation, seeks to reach a wider audience interested generally in P.E.I. history. It appears semi-annually and costs $3.50 a copy. The range of topics makes it less specifically related to material culture, but generally each issue has an article in the field, an example of which is "Mr. Hall's Machine's" found in number 8 (1980). *NBM News* is produced by the New Brunswick Museum and is a relative newcomer. It appears bi-monthly and is distributed to museum members. Initially a newsheet concerned with events and people in the museum world, its pages are open to experts involved with material culture. Recently an article on Chinese court clothing stressed the international concerns of its sponsor. From the National Museum of Man, persons interested in more detailed articles may obtain a subscription to *Material History Bulletin* for $10.00. Semi-annual issues cater to all parts of the country, but about ten per cent of the contents focus on the Maritimes and even more is relevant to regional interests.

Behind these journals are found an array of other helpful offerings. One standard form of museum publication is the gallery guide, a volume listing the items on display and providing some details about them. An explanatory text may also be found in some. One outstanding example of the genre is *Elitekey*, written by Ruth Holmes Whitehead and published by the Nova Scotia Museum. It was prepared to complement an exhibit of the same name on Micmac material culture from 1600 and is an attractive, authoritative and liberally-illustrated work which does not require the exhibit to be meaningful. The New Brunswick Museum offers its readers thematic catalogues focussing on strong elements within their collection. A brief introduction establishes the significance of the topic and is followed by excellent photographs of the artifacts with identifying captions. These catalogues provide access to parts of the museum's holdings which are not on display and for those who are unable to visit Saint John. Two fine samples are *The Loyalists* by A. Gregg Finley and *Women's Attire* by Valerie Simpson. The P.E.I. Museum and Heritage Foundation acts as a major Island publisher and undertakes the production of substantial monographs. A recent volume, *Charlottetown: The life in Its Buildings* by Irene L. Rogers is the result of painstaking labour in which the biographies of individual houses are knitted together into an effective community history. Excellent illustrations make it an irreplaceable work for anyone interested in Island history or architecture. These few citations represent only a small portion of the titles from which teachers of Maritime material culture may draw.

Perhaps the most eulogized and least practised activity within a heritage agency is research. Few dispute that identification of the nature and significance of objects in a collection and the provision of information on their context are essential to the development of exhibits and public programmes, but such work often fails to pay immediate dividends, and budget cutters are quick to identify anything not showing prompt returns as fat. Teachers, too, may wonder what use thorough investigations of material culture may have for them, although, in this, a surprise may await them. The Nova Scotia Museum, for example, publishes a series, *Info*, which responds to detailed questions about the province's social and natural histories. One sample brochure on tanning takes the reader through the whole process from skinning the animal to making buckskin.

Parks Canada issues an excellent series of pamphlets called "Research

Bulletins" which provide ready access to research under way. To cite an example, number 210, *Prince Edward Island: Interim Report on Common Architecture in the 19th Century* by C.A. Hale, provides an overview of the development of the educational system as well as photographs of a selection of small rural schools. Both Parks Canada and the National Museum of Man have series in which manuscripts of greater length are made available to the public. The Manuscript Report Series from Parks Canada records the research papers prepared by staff and contractors in support of the development of historic sites. Earlier reports seemed to focus on specific subjects relating to one site, such as *Table Glass at Fort Beauséjour*, number 21, but current works tend to be more general, addressing topics like architecture. One interest found throughout the series is Fortress Louisbourg, although the Maritimes, generally, have been well handled. A recent index listed 430 reports, of which 116 dealt with this region. Unfortunately these reports are not widely distributed and must be consulted in provincial archives or the offices of Parks Canada in Halifax. Volumes from the Mercury Series, issued by the National Museum of Man, are more readily available since they are distributed free upon request while supplies last. Topics range across museum disciplines from archaeology and ethnology to folk culture and history. One title that is relevant to the subject of this paper is *The History of Atlantic Canada: Museum Interpretations*, History paper number 32. When volumes go out of print, they may still be found at many libraries since the series is part of a large library exchange programme. Needless to say written and oral enquiries about concerns not reflected in published research findings will generally elicit a helpful response from most large institutions.

Since money and personnel are not available to support wide-ranging research programmes in most museums, allocation of the slender resources which do exist is of some importance. Sheila Stevenson compiled a list of projects in the field of Maritime material culture studies several years ago (*Material History Bulletin*, No. 14) which, while currently somewhat out of date, still provides a general indication of the thrust of research in the region. An attempt to categorize Stevenson's findings follows. The classification of various research approaches is abstracted from an analysis by Thomas Schlereth in his *Material Culture Studies in America* (Nashville, 1982). Schlereth proposed a model for the American situation featuring nine traditions of material culture studies, including art history focussing on masterworks and masters contributing to the development of exquisite taste, symbolism in which popular emotions are depicted in public monuments, and cultural history which attempts to reconstruct precisely past human surroundings. There are also environmentalists who show how our physical heritage reflects cultural migration, functionalists interested in depicting technological change as reflected in man's imple-ments, and structuralists who study material self expression as reflecting former general modes of thought. Behaviourists examine the social controls evidenced by traditions and material remains while social historians attempt to document past shared ordinary experiences. Finally the national character school of investigators creates an image of a collective personality as revealed by a culture's material by-products.

Approximately 68 projects are listed in Stevenson's compilation of which 19 were at the data collecting stage in which the research methodology was not established and eight were insufficiently described to warrant assignment to any category. The table which follows is, therefore, based on a sample of 41 projects and must be regarded as tentative because of the general nature of the descriptions offered in Stevenson's list. To provide a frame of reference, the table also includes a similar breakdown of 38 articles appearing in the first 16 regular issues of *Material History Bulletin*, reflecting national trends in research (see *Material History Bulletin*, No. 20).

RESEARCH PROJECTS BY CLASSIFICATIONS

Classification	% Maritimes	% National
Art History	0	18
Symbolist	0	0
Cultural History	39	45
Environmentalist	7	13
Functionalist	27	16
Structuralist	5	0
Behaviouristic	10	3
National Character	7	0
Social History	5	5
Total	100	100

Sources: For Maritimes, Stevenson; for National, *Material History Bulletin*.

The differences between regional and national research interests are revealing. Of greatest significance is the low rating for art history, all the more remarkable because of the significant galleries in several major centres. No Maritime art museums responded to Stevenson's survey, and this may reflect the absence of research programmes, lack of interest in Stevenson's survey, flawed survey techniques, or a combination of these factors. Nevertheless, the data is likely indicative of general existing conditions. Extra emphasis on the functionalist approach reflects the significance of primary industries and transportation in the Maritimes and the interest heritage agencies have in documenting the technology which supports these activities. Folk culture studies, a regional specialty usually excluded from the *Material History Bulletin* upon which the national sample is based, is well suited to the interpretative approaches espoused by structuralists, behaviourists and students of national, or regional, identity. The mutually high rating for cultural history is not surprising but is, in part, regrettable. This methodology is subject to abuse by collectors who, like geneologists, are anxious to nail down every detail of their subject matter and loath to explain what it all means. Frequently material culture studies exhaust topics descriptively and stop short of the analysis required to give the work meaning and importance.

Researchers in material culture studies must, of course, come to some conclusions about the nature of the items with which they are concerned. One step in this process is the definition of what constitutes an "object", and it might be useful to offer the following statement which helps explain some of the disparate work being done within the field. "Object" is interpreted to mean "an act of culture or nature, either materialized or not materialized". A materialized act of culture could be a table and of nature a cod, while an act of culture which is not materialized is a folk tale, with a birdsong being a similar act of nature. A strict reading of the name of the field "material culture studies" would exclude non-physical attainments, but researchers use evidence, such as folk dances and linguistic analyses, in their work, often as replacements for the material objects themselves. Equally as helpful is written documentary evidence of illustrative matter which can assist in the interpretation of our material heritage.

Properly viewed, material culture studies have the same goal as other fields of regional studies, the understanding of the world view of the people living in these provinces. The task of the folklorist or material historian is thus similar to that of the student of literature or of society. Confusion often exists between the means and the goal. The object is studied not for its own sake, once the identification process is completed, but because it is a fragment of an intellect, a fragment which when placed beside other extant fragments permits an understanding of an individual's or a society's world view. A well developed understanding covers time, thereby permitting a sense of change. The distinction between *studying the object* and *using the object for study* often marks the watershed between those who engage in material culture studies for reasons of curiosity and others who attempt to analyse our physical heritage. The distinction is analogous to the difference between the chronicler and the historian. In the Maritimes much has been accomplished in study of the object, less has been achieved in using that knowledge to explain the past or why Maritimers are what they are today. The challenge and the lure of the field is to harvest the bounty of documentation which has been, and is currently being, assembled.

How can this integrated approach be useful in the classroom? Perhaps a brief example may suggest some opportunities. Just in front of the main gates of the Halifax Public Gardens stands a small monument featuring a bust of Sir Walter Scott. Study it! On the back of the monument are the words: "This bust a replica of the Chantrey bust in the library at Abbotsford was erected by the North British Society of Halifax and was unveiled by the Hon. J.A. Chisholm, Chief Justice of Nova Scotia on Sep. 21, 1932". Who was Chief Justice Chisholm? Why was he a member of the North British Society? What did this organization seek to achieve in Halifax? How was this monument seen as reflecting or encouraging the development of Halifax society? Answers to these questions may be provided by examination of newspapers, especially around the time of the unveiling, by study of the works of Scott, by investigation of any records of the society, Chief Justice Chisholm, and other members and by scrutiny of the monument itself. The monument thus becomes a testament to a set of attitudes which, in turn, constitute evidence from the past. Similar windows of knowledge are to be found all about us. The Prologue of the Rule of St. Benedict cautions us to "listen...with the ear of your heart"; material culture studies requires us to look with the eye of our intellect.

SELECTED BIBLIOGRAPHY

Baglole, Harry, ed., *Exploring Island History. A Guide to the Historical Resources of Prince Edward Island* (Charlottetown, 1977).

Beckow, Steven M., "Culture, History, and Artifact", Canadian Museums Association *Gazette*, No. 8 (Fall 1975), pp. 13-5 and "On the Nature of the Artifact", *ibid.*, No. 9 (Winter 1976), pp. 24-7.

Crépeau, Andrée, "An Inventory of Persons Working on the Material Culture of Eighteenth-Century Louisbourg", *Material History Bulletin*, No. 18 (Fall 1983), pp. 49-50.

Finley, A. Gregg, "The Museum and the Historian: Toward a New Partnership", *Journal of the New Brunswick Museum* (1978), pp. 131-7.

Hamilton, W.B., *Local History in Atlantic Canada* (Toronto, 1974).

"Index" to *The Occasional*, Vol. 1-4 (1973-77); Vol. 5-6 (1978-81); Vol. 7-8 (1981-84).

Rider, Peter E., ed., *The History of Atlantic Canada: Museum Interpretations* (Ottawa 1981).

Riley, Barbara, ed., *Canada's Material History: A Forum, Material History Bulletin*, No. 8 (Ottawa, 1979).

Rosenberg, Neil V., and O'Dea, Shane, eds., *Interiors: Cultural Patterns in the Atlantic Canadian Home, Material History Bulletin*, No. 15 (Ottawa, 1982).

Stevenson, Sheila, "An Inventory of Research and Researchers concerned with Atlantic Canadian Culture", *Material History Bulletin*, No. 14 (Spring 1982), pp. 70-90.

Taylor, C.J., "Parks Canada Manuscript Report Series", *Archiveria*, No. 12 (Summer 1981), pp. 65-119.

32   *Risks, Benefits and Maritime Environmental Issues*

Raymond P. Côté

IN CONTRAST WITH MANY OF THE disciplines represented on the panels at the Conference, there are few, if any, academic or scholarly texts focussing on the analysis and resolution of environmental issues in the Maritime Provinces or Atlantic Canada generally. To my knowledge, only one textbook aimed at senior elementary or junior high school grades has been published with an environmental orientation. The book produced by the ill-fated Atlantic Institute of Education in 1976 is titled *Salar: The Story of Atlantic Salmon*. Salar was an attempt to integrate several subject areas, history, anthropology, geography, biology, resource management, economics and political science, around a central theme, the Atlantic salmon. By following a thread through these subjects, students were able to relate theory and practice.

Many academic and scientific papers have been published by Maritime researchers but these are generally telescopic. Government reports, either from politicians serving on select committees such as those which addressed acid rain and soil erosion, or from government scientists investigating problems in the Baie des Chaleurs, Passamaquoddy Bay or Sydney Harbour also provide valuable sources of information on the environmental implications of development. Royal Commissions and inquiries, such as those which investigated forest management and uranium mining respectively in Nova Scotia, generally receive a broad range of presentations. To some degree, their reports should represent a distillation of the views presented to them. In addition to an analysis of the content of these weighty documents, it may be worthwhile to evaluate different methods of gathering public or interest group opinions. Two other sources of information are also available to students and teachers. Interest groups like the Conservation Council of New Brunswick and the Ecology Action Centre of Nova Scotia have resource collections of their own on environmental issues and publish reports and booklets. The former has recently published the *Dump Dilemma: Waste Management Alternatives for New Brunswick*, while the latter published *Pathways*, a resource manual for teachers on current environmental issues. Popular books do exist. *Budworm Battles* by Elizabeth May, a well known environmentalist, describes the fight to prevent the spraying of insecticides in Nova Scotia's forests. *The Sea of Slaughter* by Farley Mowat is a strong condemnation of our destructive harvesting practices for marine life. Finally, the judgment in at least one court case gives valuable insights into the perspective of the judiciary on environment risks. The court case involved Cape Breton landowners and the owners of the pulp mill in Port Hawkesbury, Nova Scotia.

It is likely that teachers will have to rely on materials written elsewhere and extrapolate the findings to the situation in the Maritimes. If the intent is to teach process rather than detail, the use of those materials should not present unreasonable obstacles. There are two different perspectives that must be considered when teaching and studying the maritime environment. The first perspective is the influence that people have on the environment. The second perspective is the influence, especially of the biophysical environment, on the social and economic development of the region. That perspective is often seen as the sphere of the geographer. In respect of the latter, I trust it is clear to all of us that we have a maritime or marine influenced environment. That marine influence has been a determinant of our major economic sectors: our fishery and our forestry as well as tourism and agriculture, not to mention our culture. Where else do people talk about the weather so much? You all know the old saying, "If you don't like the weather, stay around for a few minutes, it will change!"

The ocean plays a major role in our weather and our climate. It also has had and will continue to have an influence on major energy developments, some of which are also environmental issues. In some cases, the combination of ocean and weather and climate create serious even disastrous problems. In other cases, the ocean provides opportunities. The physical environment, off the East Coast and especially on the Labrador Shelf and the Grand Banks, has already demonstrated its power and the risks faced by those who drill for oil and gas. The Ocean Ranger served to remind us that Mother Nature carries much destructive power. The Vinland blowout, near Sable Island, served to remind us that we do not know as much as we should, and both incidents told us that we had not planned and designed properly.

Generally, the overall probability of a blowout or major spill is considered low. Animals at greatest risk on the Grand Banks are seabirds, particularly the two million thick billed murres. These are flightless for most of their journey from Hudson Strait until they reach the Banks in the fall. In winter the Newfoundland offshore is the single most important feeding area for marine birds in the Northwestern Atlantic. A large spill at the wrong time and in the wrong place could have serious consequences for a substantial portion of these seabirds. Due to weather conditions, ice and bird populations, the risks to the environment during the period from January to March are considered high by the experts. This will focus the discussion on the manner in which we should deal with low probability — high consequence events. Exploration activities can also have some economic impacts linked to environmental hazards. The most significant risk of this nature may relate to the tainting of fish flesh and perceptions of the public linked to a major spill which in turn may affect the marketability of the product. Other aspects include contamination and fouling of fishing gear, fishing exclusion zones, and loss of seabirds as a food source, a small but important part of the local economy of some communities. Many of these impacts can be mitigated by financial compensation.

Environmental impact assessment panels are asked to advise governments, both federal and provincial, on the magnitude and acceptability of those impacts and risks. The question is not whether hydrocarbon exploration and production should proceed but under what conditions. Only in a situation wherein the risks were considered totally unacceptable would governments be forced to question whether that energy source should be utilized and to reassess the most appropriate energy mix for the Maritimes. Such a discussion is a useful one for classrooms at junior high school levels because it brings several disciplines to bear on the question.

We now use several sources of energy in the Maritimes: coal, oil, nuclear, wood, hydro, tides with a little solar and wind power. There are risks and benefits in each case. For example, coal provides us with a locally controlled source of raw material. Mining this coal generates employment and other economic benefits. But our coal is dirty, that is, it is high in sulfur and other contaminants. That sulfur as sulfur dioxide contributes to our regional acid rain problem. Acid rain imposes costs on society and the environment. The acidification of lakes and rivers causes declines in fish populations; historic buildings and statues are slowly eroded. In addition, forest productivity may be affected as indicated by laboratory experiments and the findings of scientists in Germany's Black Forest. However, we can also reduce sulfur emissions in ways that create employment. Coal can be washed before it is used and scrubbers can be added to the stacks of thermal electric generating stations. This, in turn, raises the cost of the coal. What is the appropriate balance of risks and benefits? What is the consumer willing to pay?

Fundy tidal power, oft discussed as a Maritimes energy megaproject, also has its risks and benefits. The benefits include the creation of thousands of jobs for the period of the construction of the facilities and the ripple effect of that money through the Maritime economy. In addition, the export and sale of the power, from a truly renewable resource, will generate millions of dollars. However, there are environmental risks that at this time are difficult to measure in monetary terms. At least one mathematical model has predicted a rise of six inches in the high tide as far

262 Teaching Maritime Studies

away as Boston. Other effects include disruption of the migration of the shad populations, salt water intrusion into ground water and changes in the climate behind the barrage. Because the energy sector is so important, the environmental issues linked to it provide very good examples for the presentation and discussion of the concept of risks and benefits. A good reference book for teachers is *Energy Options for Atlantic Canada.*

The climate and geomorphology of the region have also influenced land-based sectors. We may have a more diverse ecological spectrum than is found in any similar sized land mass in Canada. It has been said that the manner of development of the region is as much tied to the nature of the land as it is to the historical paths the people of the region have followed. Our soils and climate are such that rotation periods for trees are longer than many of our competitors. That longer rotation in turn means more opportunities for insect pests, diseases, and infestations. This creates pressures for the use of pesticides to protect valuable timber. The use of pesticides in forests, whether herbicides or insecticides, has been debated at length in the Maritimes. Political pressures brought to bear on a previous Liberal government in Nova Scotia resulted in a decision against spraying the Cape Breton Highlands. That spruce and fir forest has now been devastated by the budworm. In turn, significant socio-economic impacts have been noted. Concern over ecological and public health effects of pesticide formulations have resulted in major demonstrations, letter writing campaigns, political battles and court cases. Even though major epidemiological studies have been conducted in New Brunswick to evaluate the relationship between spraying and cancer and spraying and birth defects, the proof expected by the opponents of the program remains elusive. Absolute safety is not a reasonable goal but establishing an acceptable or tolerable level of risk can be an onerous task. One could provide more examples of the impact of the environment, the biophysical environment, on our social and economic development.

The second perspective emphasizes people's influence on the natural environment and how that, in turn, affects our social, cultural and economic environments. This is the traditional perspective that we routinely see in activities of our governmental, environmental protection agencies and reflected in the press. These issues include hazardous waste disposal such as the Sydney Tar Pond, ground water contamination from fertilizers, acid rain, and pollution in shellfish growing areas. In the Maritimes, our natural resources and resource industries have been the focus of our attention, notably forestry and the fishery. In the classroom two kinds of impacts or influence provide opportunities to explore such issues. Emphasis could be placed on the ways we have mismanaged our forests and fish populations by mining them rather than managing them to allow for sustainable development. You may disagree with Farley Mowat in the

Sea of Slaughter but the book provides good material for a classroom debate. The other emphasis deals with the disposal of wastes and the detrimental effect this practice has had on our coastal fisheries and to some degree, through air emissions, on our forests. There is at least some evidence, from the laboratory and circumstantially from Germany's Black Forest, that acid rain, if it continues at present levels and intensifies, could have a measurable long-term impact on forest productivity. Given some of the natural limitations on productivity, man-made contributions of a detrimental nature are not welcomed by foresters. Being unable to quantify the risks, though the costs may be very high, decision-makers in North America have been reluctant to use this argument as a basis for regulatory action.

One could easily list a number of examples of the effects of liquid waste discharges on coastal environments but perhaps the most striking is shown in a map produced by the federal Department of Environment and the Department of Fisheries and Oceans. The map depicts some 250 bays and inlets around the Maritimes that are closed to the direct harvesting of clams, oysters and mussels. The cause is bacterial and viral contamination from sewage, municipal and agricultural runoff. In some cases these closures have direct economic impacts on local fishermen and tourist use of shellfish. Risks, while low, have occasionally been manifested in cases of gastroenteritis. In 1972, 500 people in Montreal and Quebec City were treated for the illness after consuming oysters from Caraquet Bay, N.B.

These issues demonstrate that in analyzing environmental issues, there are always risks and benefits. The situations or issues can almost never be resolved in terms of black or white, absolute safety or no risk. From a teaching perspective and for that matter, for an improvement in environmental management in the future, fostering a better understanding of the risks and benefits of actions that we may take, is a very important contribution. The problem of pollution is essentially a problem of economic externalities. Again from a teaching perspective, the concept of externalities is a very important one to impart to students. We are slowly reaching a point where a lack of attention to our natural environment is coming back to haunt us. We are beginning to realize that the disposal of wastes has costs beyond the direct costs of the disposal practices, that air emissions have costs beyond those attributed to the polluter's control equipment. It is becoming clearer that a good quality natural environment is actually a prerequisite to a productive resource-based economy.

This concern is slowly emerging as an area of public policy. The formulation of public policy is based on several factors, notably economic, employment, legal and political considerations. The economic considerations revolve around questions of regional disparity, international trade and costs to industry. At a time of economic restraint, job creation and stability become important factors, particularly in government planning. Legal considerations such as the ability to enforce regulations and deregulation have now been augmented by questions regarding rights of the individual as enshrined in the new Constitution. The synthesis of these considerations by individuals results in the generation of public opinion, which through the political process, influences the formulation of public policy. That opinion is based on the understanding and perceptions of individuals about particular subjects. From the media, one knows that these subjects range from abortion, nuclear weapons, free trade, South Africa to hazardous wastes, forest management and acid rain. The basic question to be answered by politicians and government regulators is: i.e. what level of risk will be acceptable to the public? Answering that question is giving decision-makers increasing difficulty in the formulation of public policy. The process of assessing risk is seen by some as a scientific task and by others as a socio-economic exercise. This leads to concerns of decision-makers about addressing real as opposed to perceived risks.

Class exercises can be organized to permit students to gain a better appreciation of risk perception. A random canvass can be done of classmates or of the neighborhood, using lists of activities ranging from riding a motorcycle or an ATV, chopping wood, flying an airplane, smoking, working in a coal mine, consuming food additives, spraying pesticides to mining uranium. Tabulation of the results by various categories, such as age, sex, education and employment, provides some understanding of the perceptions of different groups in society. While we all have our own biases, better decisions on environmental issues should be made if we at least undertake to compare the risks and benefits in combination with some effort to understand the perceptions of different groups at risk from an activity or gaining some benefit from it.

It should now be clear that, contrary to the perceptions of many, the study and resolution of environmental issues in the Maritimes as elsewhere is not a scientific exercise. The toxicological and ecological components are scientific in nature but the environmental issue is a product of the biophysical, social, cultural and economic factors. Our perception and understanding of those factors have a large influence on the resolution of those issues. An integrated approach is necessary. But, environmental issues, especially those linked to primary resource sectors which are so important to our society, culture and economy, can be a very useful vehicle for studying the Maritimes.

SELECTED BIBLIOGRAPHY

Anderson, G.J. and Brimer, A.E., *Salar: The Story of the Atlantic Salmon* (Halifax, 1976).

Brown, R.G.B., et al, *Atlas of Eastern Canadian Seabirds* (Ottawa, 1975).

Conservation Council of New Brunswick, *The Dump Dilemma: Waste management alternatives for New Brunswick* (Fredericton, 1985).

Côté, R.P. and Wiseman, R.D., eds., *Environmental Risks From Offshore Exploration — An overview prepared for the Ocean Ranger Commission* (Ottawa, 1984).

Ecology Action Centre, *Pathways: A resource and teaching manual about current environmental issues affecting Nova Scotia and the world* (Halifax, 1981).

Emond, P., *Stop it: A guide to citizen action to protect the environment of Nova Scotia* (Halifax, 1976).

Environment Canada, *Coal and the Inland Water Environment of Atlantic Canada* (Halifax, 1979).

——————, *The Atlantic Region of Canada: An ecological perspective* (Halifax, 1974).

——————, *Public Perceptions of Environmental Quality in Atlantic Canada* (Halifax, 1984).

Freedman, W., *An overview of the environmental impacts of forestry, with particular reference to the Atlantic Provinces* (Halifax, 1982).

Gordon, D.C. and Dadswell, M.J., *Update on the marine environmental consequences of tidal power development in the upper reaches of the Bay of Fundy* (Halifax, 1984).

Guppy, S., Fern, Y. and Wildsmith, B., eds., *Water and Environmental Law* (Halifax, 1981).

Hildebrand, L.P., *An Assessment of the Environmental Quality in the Baie des Chaleurs. Environmental Protection Service* (Halifax, 1984).

Hirvonen, H.E., *Terrain Sensitivity to Acid Precipitation in Nova Scotia* (Halifax, 1984).

Keachie, P.M. and Côté, R.P., *Toxic Pollutants in the Saint John River Basin. The Saint John River Basin Board* (Fredericton, 1973).

Lamson, C. and Hanson, A.J., eds., *Atlantic Fisheries and Coastal Communities: Fisheries decision-making case studies* (Halifax, 1984).

Longhurst, A., *Consultation on the Consequences of Offshore Oil Production on Offshore Fish Stocks and Fishing Operations* (Ottawa, 1982).

May, E., *Budworm Battles* (Halifax, 1982).

McLeave, R.J., *Report of the Commission of Inquiry on Uranium to the Province of Nova Scotia* (Halifax, 1985).

Mowat, F., *Sea of Slaughter* (Toronto, 1984).

NORDCO, *Study of the potential socio-economic effects on the Newfoundland fishing industry from offshore petroleum development* (St. John's, 1982).

Nova Scotia Royal Commission on Forestry, *Report* (Halifax, 1984).

Sable Island Environmental Assessment Panel, *Venture Development Project: Report of the Sable Island Environmental Assessment Panel* (Ottawa, 1983).

Socio Economic Review Panel, *The Socio Economic Implication of the Venture Development Project Offshore Nova Scotia* (Halifax, 1984).

Taschereau, P.M., *The Status of Ecological Reserves in Canada* (Halifax, 1985).

Vandermeulen, J.H. and Scarratt, O.J., "Impact of Oil Spills on Living National Resources and Resource-based Industry", in D.J. Scarrat, ed., *Evaluation of Recent Data Relative to Potential Oil Spills in the Passamaquoddy Area* (Dartmouth, 1979).

Varty, I.W., *Environmental Surveillance in New Brunswick. Effects of Spray Operations for Forest Protection Against Spruce Budworm* (Fredericton, 1980).

Versteeg, H., *Handbook on Environmental Law for New Brunswick* (Fredericton, 1983).

Victoria Palmer et al. vs Stora Kopparbergs Bergslags Aktiebolag, Nova Scotia Supreme Court Trial Division. SN No. 02555 (Halifax, 1982).

Whyte, A.V. and Burton, I., eds., *Environmental risk assessment* (Toronto, 1980).

Wilson, R.C.H. and Addison, R.F., eds., *Health of the Northwest Atlantic* (Halifax, 1984).

Wilson, R.C.H., Eaton, P.B., Hall, S.E. and Stone, H.H., *The Quality of the Environment in the Atlantic Provinces* (Halifax, 1979).

33   *Urbanization And Maritime Society*

Peter McGahan

THERE ARE MANY POSSIBLE approaches to the study of Maritime society, to the exploration of social change in the region. As with Canadian society as a whole, a stress on the process of urbanization is a fruitful way to "capture" many significant social processes and patterns. If we adopt the geographers' concept of a "cone of resolution", this focus on urbanization entails three levels. At the "broad" end of the cone, the macro level, we must consider urbanization of the region as a whole, the evolution and general characteristics of the Maritime urban system, as a subsystem indeed within the national system of cities. Moving down the "cone", at the meso or intermediate level, we focus on more specific features of metropolitan and urban communities — the relationship, for example, between changes in employment opportunities, housing supply and inter-urban migration flows. At the narrowest end of the "cone", the micro level, our focus is most intense — as on perceptions by urban residents of the quality of life in their communities. Research on urbanization in the region is not yet extensive. Our knowledge of the dynamics of urbanization at each of these levels is still quite incomplete. We may, nonetheless, identify patterns or questions that are worthy of further thought.

Canada is an urban nation. In the Maritimes Nova Scotia reflects this status more than its two neighbors. Whereas New Brunswick's population is almost evenly split between rural and urban, and P.E.I.'s is primarily rural, a majority of Nova Scotia's residents live in urban centres. Yet a new trend is occurring that demographers have found intriguing. The past decade has represented the first time in a hundred years in Canada that the proportion of the population classified as urban declined (from 76.1 per cent in 1971 to 75.7 per cent in 1981). The rate of population growth between 1976 and 1981 in rural areas has been greater than that in urban areas. This is the case in all parts of the country, with the exception of the Prairies and the Yukon. It is especially true in the Maritimes. The provinces with the largest declines in rate of urban growth are P.E.I. and New Brunswick. This trend has been termed "counterurbanization", and a similar pattern has appeared in the United States, Europe, and even in some underdeveloped countries. It is a process of population deconcentration that is markedly changing North American settlement patterns. Since much of this rural growth occurred in the fringe areas of urban centres, the attractiveness of rural environments in proximity to a city may account for part of this trend.

Consistent with the counterurbanization trend, the rate of metropolitan growth in Canada has declined significantly over the last three decades. Between 1976 and 1981 the non-metropolitan population actually increased slightly more than did the metropolitan. The two Maritime metropolitan areas grew only slightly between 1976 and 1981, Halifax by 3.6 per cent and Saint John by 1 per cent, half or less than the average (6.2 per cent) for Canada's major urban centres. All of those metropolitan areas with central cities losing population are in the East. Saint John's central city showed the second greatest loss of population (-8.4 per cent) of any in the country. Halifax, with a loss of -3.5 per cent, experienced approximately the same level of population decline as St. John's, Newfoundland. Surrounding rural non-farm areas have, in contrast, grown rapidly, underscoring again the trend toward deconcentration. The questions this trend raises are numerous. What are the economic and social causes of deconcentration? What are the demographic and socioeconomic characteristics of those moving to rural non-farm areas? What implications will this emerging settlement pattern have for transportation, housing and economic policies at both the provincial and federal levels?

The demographic and socioeconomic characteristics of the Maritime urban population mirror, to a degree, those that are found elsewhere in Canada. For example, average household income is lowest in this region (Table 1). Yet, in each of the three Maritime provinces, household income of urban areas is greater than that in rural areas, as it is in the rest of Canada. Average income increases with size of community, although here differences exist among metropolitan areas. Average household income is lower in Saint John ($22,948) than in Halifax ($23,807). Reflecting this difference, a higher proportion of Haligonians (12.1 per cent) have a University degree in comparison to residents of Saint John (6.7 per cent). How does this contrast relate to the mix of economic activities, the industrial structure, and the "quality of life" in each centre? Halifax, at least demographically, is more "dominant" in its province: one out of every three (32.8 per cent) Nova Scotians resides in the Halifax metropolitan area. In contrast, fewer than one out of every five (16.4 per cent) New Brunswickers lives in Saint John. The point here is that, when we move down the "cone of resolution", we find intriguing variations among urban areas even in the same region. Between 1971 and 1981 the employment growth rates in the financial/real estate/insurance and service sectors — the tertiary area — were much higher in Halifax than in Saint John. On the other

Table 1

Average Household Income by Urban Size Group, Urban/Rural, and Province, 1981.

Province	Urban-Total	Size Group 500,000+	100,000-499,999	30,000-99,999	Under 30,000
Total	$25,060	$26,519	$23,824	23,434	$22,698
Newfoundland	23,251	-	25,694	-	21,928
Prince Edward Island	20,277	-	-	-	20,277
Nova Scotia	21,563	-	23,776	20,289	19,246
New Brunswick	21,359	-	-	22,320	19,817
Quebec	23,309	23,960	21,494	22,069	21,933
Ontario	25,869	27,994	23,962	23,484	22,444
Manitoba	22,648	23,100	-	20,535	21,177
Saskatchewan	23,482	-	24,868	22,301	21,489
Alberta	28,580	29,575	-	26,891	25,973
British Columbia	26,350	27,694	23,857	24,832	25,202

Province	Rural-Total	Rural-Non-farm	Rural Farm	Total
Total	$22,259	$21,769	$24,962	24,460
Newfoundland	18,029	18,022	-	21,198
Prince Edward Island	18,721	18,278	-	19,338
Nova Scotia	19,011	18,888	22,011	20,476
New Brunswick	18,633	18,565	20,349	20,112
Quebec	21,035	20,748	23,556	22,869
Ontario	24,091	23,764	25,885	25,577
Manitoba	18,879	18,423	20,040	21,721
Saskatchewan	21,272	18,811	25,000	22,637
Alberta	25,484	24,809	26,798	27,969
British Columbia	25,442	25,147	28,671	26,171

Source: Statistics Canada: 1981 Census: Catalogue 92-934. Reproduced with permission of the Minister of Supply and Services Canada.

hand, manufacturing employment growth in Saint John, 15.5 per cent
from 1971 to 1981, exceeded the average for Canadian metropolitan areas.

Going back to the "broad" end of the cone, and disregarding these
intra-regional differences, we must recall that overall the urban Maritimes
form part of the "hinterland", subordinate to the industrial heartland
within the Canadian national system of cities. Historians have traced
through the evolution of this division in the late nineteenth century. Core-
periphery contrasts in economic diversification, secondary manufacturing
and access to national markets were well established by 1911. When we
look to the present, the potential impact of free-trade agreements and new
regional resource development on this heartland-hinterland division
remains unclear. Its possible erosion matches counterurbanization in
latent influence on the nation's settlement pattern.

Linked to this settlement pattern, more recent trends show interesting
changes in the direction of Canada's migratory movements. Comparing
the periods 1970-75 and 1975-80, the Maritimes have begun to experience
net inflows of migrants (Table 2). And, as in the rest of Canada, this is
characteristically mobility from one urban centre to another. Migration

Table 2

Net Interprovincial Migration: A Static Comparison for the Periods
1970-75 and 1975-80.

Province	1970-75	1975-80
Newfoundland	-6,152	-6,306
Prince Edward Island	3,327	2,913
Nova Scotia	3,587	5,024
New Brunswick	9,820	12,829
Quebec	-102,963	-145,945
Ontario	29,887	-46,751
Manitoba	-29,940	-42,400
Saskatchewan	-70,774	15,938
Alberta	40,854	137,018
British Columbia	116,847	72,899
Yukon and North West Territories	5,508	-5,217

Source: Jeanine Perreault and Ronald Raby, "Recent Developments in
Interprovincial Migration in Canada and Possible Scenarios for
the 1980s", *Demographic Trends and Their Impact on the Canadian Labour Market* (Ottawa, 1981), p. 102.

generally tends to occur within well-defined streams. One such stream is inter-metropolitan migration. In each province, including Nova Scotia and New Brunswick, at least half of the in-migrants to metropolitan areas had moved from other census metropolitan areas in Canada (Table 3). This, of course, partly reflects the variation in employment opportunities. Whether such a "flow" continues as counterurbanization proceeds remains to be seen.

Metropolitan communities differ in the strength of their attraction to out-of-province migrants. A higher proportion of in-migrants (67.0 per cent) come to Halifax from a different province than is the case for Saint John (55.5 per cent). Both pale next to Calgary, where during the period 1976-1981 four of every five persons moving there came from outside Alberta. Differences in Maritime metropolitan out-migration are also worthy of note. Haligonians when they leave are more likely to depart from the province entirely than are residents of Saint John. We know that long-distance migration is more common among the better educated, those with higher socioeconomic status. Does this difference in provincial out-migration reflect the socioeconomic characteristics of Halifax and

Table 3

Total In-migrants to CMA by Province, CMA vs. Non-CMA Origin, 1981 (%).

Province	1976 Residence of CMA In-migrants	
	CMA	Non-CMA
Newfoundland	73.6	26.4
Nova Scotia	57.2	42.8
New Brunswick	63.6	36.4
Quebec	66.5	33.5
Ontario	73.6	26.4
Manitoba	64.6	35.4
Saskatchewan	63.4	36.6
Alberta	58.2	41.9
British Columbia	75.1	24.9

(Prince Edward Island is excluded because it has no CMA.)
Source: Statistics Canada: 1981 Census: Catalogue 92-907, p. 2-1f. Reproduced with permission of the Minister of Supply and Services Canada.

Saint John noted earlier? More refined data are needed before we can answer this question.

When we study migration, especially rural-urban migration, as a social and cultural process, two points are especially relevant to Maritime society. For one thing, too often attention has been given simply to individual characteristics of migrants — their educational and occupational levels, for example — without adequate focus on the organization of the community of destination. The latter's stratification system, economic structure, and patterns of ethnic segregation may have a profound effect on the extent to which contact is possible with native residents, and the degree to which participation in its institutions can occur. For example, migrants in Northeastern New Brunswick move to urban centres physically and culturally not very distant from their rural communities of origin. At these points of destination they experience little improvement in their housing or in employment opportunities, reflecting the low level of economic growth in the region's urban areas. The structure of opportunities in such communities is restricted regardless of migrants' skills, ambitions, or experience.

Frequently in the past, the process of migration has been interpreted as a function of "push-pull" factors. This presents too rationalistic a picture of the migration decision, and ignores the social and normative context. One study of Northeastern New Brunswick showed that the poorer a community, the less likely are its residents to leave: "Welfare and other mechanisms had served to reduce the forces compelling out-migration to the point where the ties of community could act as an almost decisive counter-force in discouraging such an out-migration".[1] Despite economic deprivation, residents live in a rent-free community, receive at least some unemployment insurance and welfare payments, and feel some attachment to their daily routines; this inhibits rates of departures. Consideration should certainly be given to push-pull factors — economic decline in the community of origin and the presence of employment opportunities in the centre of destination. But the effects of these "objective" factors are not automatic. An important intervening variable is the normative system. It is this which determines how situations of economic disparities in communities will be perceived, whether migration is seen as permissible to enhance life chances, and which categories of people are prohibited from moving. Those who leave the rural communities of Northeastern New Brunswick are economically not very successful. Migration is thus perceived by remaining groups of residents as not necessarily offering a viable alternative to conditions at home. For some at least it is defined as a less legitimate channel for advancement, and this perception discourages

1 S.D. Clark, *The New Urban Poor* (Toronto, 1978), pp. 53-4.

Table 4

Population Born Outside Canada by Province, 1981

	% of Total Population Born Outside Canada
Newfoundland	0.3
Prince Edwward Island	0.1
Nova Scotia	1.1
New Brunswick	0.7
Quebec	13.6
Ontario	52.4
Manitoba	3.8
Saskatchewan	2.2
Alberta	9.2
British Columbia	16.3
Yukon	0.1
Northwest Territories	0.1

Source: Statistics Canada: 1981 Census: Catalogue 92-913, Table 1B. Reproduced with permission of the Minister of Supply and Services Canada.

movement out of the community.

Urbanization, in the demographic sense, represents partly a process of population concentration. Contributing to this process, especially in the past several decades, has been the clustering of immigrants in Canada's major cities. One out of every two immigrants today lives in either Toronto, Montreal, or Vancouver. The Maritime urban system is distinctive in that it has not been the recipient of these "streams" (Table 4). Only 7.3 per cent of the population of Halifax and 5.1 per cent of Saint John's residents are foreign-born. This fact has both influenced and reflected the level of urban growth in the region. We must also recognize the impact that immigrant clustering, or the lack of it, has on the destination of successive "streams". As with migration, social and cultural forces have shaped the location of urban immigrants. Immigrants choose to go to particular cities and not to others for a variety of reasons. The greater the average earnings in a city and the lower its unemployment rate, the more likely will it be attractive to immigrants. Nevertheless, we must recognize the importance of other factors, such as the extent to which the city already contains a large proportion of foreign-born. One study found that relating "immigrant supply" variations among cities only to average earning differentials is not adequate. The presence of friends and relatives is actually the most important factor attracting an immigrant to work in a particular city. The direction in which urban immigration "streams" go is thus self-sustaining through the impact which "chain-migration" has. In short, "immigrants go not so much where the money is, but also go where other immigrants are".[2]

The result of immigration to Canada over time is the creation of an urban ethnic mosaic. Here again the Maritime metropolises are distinctive in that this mosaic is less defined than elsewhere. Comparatively few residents of either Halifax (20.9 per cent) or Saint John (17.7 per cent) claim an ethnic origin that is other than British. Obviously the proportion of French rises elsewhere in the region. The point is, however, that our cities are not marked by intense ethnic mixtures. This is not to deny the importance of ethnicity in the lives of particular groups nor of issues relating to Francophone-Anglophone divisions. Yet the impact of ethnicity, as a multicultural phenomenon, is not of the scale we see in other parts of urban Canada.

The contemporary urban and metropolitan community consists of a set of subareas differentiated in terms of population and land-use types. With urban growth this differentiation or spatial distribution becomes more evident. An analysis of differences among neighbourhoods within each Canadian metropolitan area reveals a "widely known fact that, in most cities, age differences in the population are distributed in a concentric zonal pattern. Peripheral areas tend to be dominated by families in the early stages of child-bearing and child-rearing; inner suburbs tend to have a somewhat older age profile which approximates that of the city as a whole; and inner-city areas are less family-oriented and have a disproportionate share of the city's elderly population, young singles who have left their parental home and childless couples".[3] This is evident when we examine the distribution of the 1981 population 65 years and over in Halifax in varying census tracts. In most of Canada's metropolitan areas, low socioeconomic status groups tend to be concentrated near the central business district. Again, the 1981 distribution of low-income families in Halifax confirms this pattern.

Spatial distributions are created by a sifting and sorting through residential mobility: "an orderly social geography results as like individuals

---

2   Frederick L. Reid, "The Supply of Immigrants to Canadian Cities: 1921-1961" (MA thesis, Queen's University, 1973), p. 47.

3   Frederick Hill, *Canadian Urban Trends. Volume 2. Metropolitan Perspective* (Toronto, 1976), p. 31.

make like choices, in response to regularities in the operation of the land and housing markets and the collaboration of similar individuals who act to exclude dissimilar people from their neighbourhood or to restrict minority groups to particular areas".[4] The decision of where to live is a product of the interaction of such factors as price of the dwelling unit, and the type and location of residence as well as such individual attributes as housing needs reflecting stage of the family life cycle, income, and particular life-style preferences. Certain spatial regularities emerge from that interaction. For example, as households move through the family cycle, their requirements for space change. As the number of children in the family increases, the demand for greater space also increases. This need can best be met by relocating at greater distances from the city centre. A gradient pattern is thus produced. Households in the child-bearing and child-rearing stages more commonly reside in the periphery; pre-child or post-child households are more attracted to core or inner zone areas.

One important characteristic of urban ecological structure is the manner in which social classes are segregated, especially groups at the extremes of the socioeconomic scale. Residential mobility tends to sustain this pattern of segregation, as a recent study comparing Moncton, Halifax, and Saint John has shown. Different socioeconomic groups move within "distinct migration channels, as expressed in the similar status categories of the origin and destination area".[5] This is a function both of choice (desire among the more affluent to live in a neighbourhood that forms an appropriate symbol of their status) and constraint (the less affluent are unable to afford the housing and commuting costs associated with living in a particular neighbourhood). Residential mobility within the urban community maintains the spatial separation characteristic of groups at the opposite ends of the socioeconomic scale. Urban spatial and social differentiation are closely intertwined.

One central feature of Canada's urban spatial mosaic is ethnic residential segregation. In Maritime cities we cannot explore this as intensely as elsewhere because of the previously noted trend of relatively low levels of immigration to this region. As Hill has documented, Saint John and Halifax have among the lowest levels of ethnic segregation of any metropolitan centre in Canada. The ethnic mosaic is spatially as well not keenly evident.

One intriguing question that taps the social psychological or micro

---

4   Philip H. Rees, "Concepts of Social Space: Toward an Urban Social Geography", in B.J. Berry and F.E. Horton, eds., *Geographic Perspective on Urban Systems* (Englewood Cliffs, N.J., 1970), p. 313.

5   John Short, "Residential Mobility", in L.S. Bourne, ed., *Internal Structure of the City: Readings on Urban Form, Growth and Policy* (New York 1982), p. 199.

dimension of urbanization is whether the "quality of life" — however that is defined — systematically varies among types of cities. Is the quality of life significantly "better" in one urban community than in another? This is an extremely difficult question to answer; we cannot devise one single overall measure of quality of life, nor even a set of unambiguous measures. One recent attempt to examine quality of life variations within the Canadian and Maritime urban systems is a survey conducted of "concerns" that residents have in 23 urban areas, including Halifax, Charlottetown and Saint John. An index of city liking was used, derived from such items as perception of the city as an ideal place to live. A high positive score indicates high liking. This is a subjective and indirect measure of quality of life. Nevertheless, the results are interesting. Size of urban centre is not easily correlated with assessment of the city, since Charlottetown and Halifax rank in the top half, Saint John in the bottom half. Least satisfaction with their city is found among residents of Regina, Saint John, Calgary and Edmonton. "Given their privileged economic position and their status as the capitals of the land of opportunity", the negative view of the Albertan cities is perhaps surprising.[6] Those attributes of cities negatively assessed most frequently are road and traffic conditions, pollution, and local government. Although more specific assessments of services and facilities also are not clearly related to size of city, there is a tendency for cultural and entertainment facilities and public transportation to be rated more positively by those living in the largest cities. Nonetheless, "urban size, in and of itself, does not result in the development of particular problem syndromes. Instead the difficulties experienced by specific cities appear to be more closely related to their economic, political and social histories than to their size".[7] Indeed, urbanites' perceptions of quality of life may be related as much to the location and type of their neighbourhoods as to the characteristics of their cities. Residents of inner-city areas in the largest metropolises, for example, evidence greater anxiety about crimes against the person than do urbanites living elsewhere.

As in other industrialized and urbanized societies, the crime rate has risen steadily in Canada. Break and entries tripled between 1962 and 1980. Between the late nineteenth century and mid-twentieth century, whereas the relative proportion of violent crimes against the person declined, the relative proportion of crime against property increased substantially. Any major structural change in a society — such as industrialization or urbanization — tends to be associated with rising crime rates. Perhaps partly reflecting the lower level of urbanization in this region, crime rates in Eastern Canada fall below the national average, as Table 5 indicates. Yet

6 Tom Atkinson, *A Study of Urban Concerns* (Toronto, 1982), p. 11.

7 *Ibid.*, p. 14.

Table 5

Five-year Average of Selected Crimes per 100,000 Population (1977-1981).

Jurisdiction	All Criminal[1] Offences	Criminal Code[2] Offences	Provincial[3] Statutes	Municipal[4] By-laws	Crimes of[5] Violence	Property[6] Offences
Canada (excluding Atlantic Region)	8,709.8	8,230.3	1,743.9	307.1	639.3	5,341.0
Newfoundland	5,558.1	5,162.6	1,427.5	56.2	453.1	2,952.2
P.E.I.	5,582.8	5,197.8	3,649.9	28.6	344.3	2,820.6
Nova Scotia	6,972.1	6,408.8	3,682.3	173.9	530.0	3,605.4
New Brunswick	6,055.5	5,669.1	1,752.6	197.0	450.5	3,177.9
Atlantic	6,250.7	5,245.6	2,470.4	126.3	475.5	3,263.0

1 All Crimes — includes all Criminal Code offences, and Federal Statutes (e.g. Bankruptcy Act, FDA, NCA).

2 Criminal Code Offences — All Criminal Code offences exclusive of drugs and criminal driving offences.

3 Provincial Statutes — Does not include driving offences.

4 Municipal By-laws — Municipal By-laws.

5 Crimes of Violence — includes homocides, attempted homocides, manslaughter, sexual assaults (male and female), robberies, and all assaults.

6 Property Offences — all property-related crimes (Break and enter, thefts, frauds).

Source: Robert C. Kaill and Paul Smith, *Atlantic Crime Profile* (Halifax, 1984).

278 Teaching Maritime Studies

Table 6

Police Zone of Occurrence by General Type of Call, 1982, Saint John (%).

Type of Call	Central	East	West	Total
Crimes against the Person	70.6	23.5	5.9	100.0 (68)
Crimes against Property	67.8	19.0	13.2	100.0 (584)
Domestic Dispute	62.3	26.4	11.3	100.0 (106)
General Disturbance	72.1	16.9	10.9	100.0 (183)
Public Drunkenness	83.1	9.2	7.7	100.0 (65)

Source: Peter McGahan, *Patterns of Crime in Saint John and Fredericton* (Ottawa, 1983).

even within the region, criminal code offences are more likely to occur in urban areas. Robbery and break and entry are increasing, reflecting the trend toward 24-hour convenience stores. Theft of motor vehicles is a relatively common occurrence near the region's metropolitan areas. The rate of vandalism, in contrast, is higher than the national average in rural P.E.I. In all three Maritime Provinces arson is more common, on a per capita basis, than in the rest of Canada as a whole. Why this is so is unclear. We expect, in general, the crime rate in the years ahead to increase in the region — especially crimes against property.

There has been some initial research recently on the spatial distribution of crime *within* the region's cities — termed the ecology of crime. Central areas of cities frequently show the highest concentration of crime, with lower rates occurring in outlying residential areas, as Table 6 suggests for Saint John. However, the spatial distribution of crime may vary according to the category of offence. Whereas violent crime is more apt to occur in low-income areas, robbery appears more dispersed throughout the city. The spatial distribution of crime must be linked to analyses of demographic, socioeconomic, and land-use variations within an urban community.

Indeed, that is the key to regional urban studies. Whereas our research may be conducted at different levels of the "cone of resolution", it is still *one* cone. We are — in urban migration, urban crime, urban residential segregation, counterurbanization — not dealing with an assortment of discrete social phenomena. Our object is a sociospatial *system*; our objective ultimately is to better understand how these aspects of urban and metropolitan life are linked, how they mesh together.

SELECTED BIBLIOGRAPHY

A. *General Patterns of Urban Growth*

Berry, Brian J., "The Counterurbanization Process: How General?", in Niles M. Hansen, ed., *Human Settlement Systems* (Cambridge, Mass., 1978), pp. 25-49.

McGahan, Peter, *Urban Sociology in Canada* (2nd ed., Toronto, 1986).

Robinson, Ira M., *Canadian Urban Growth Trends: Implications for a National Settlement Policy* (Vancouver, 1981).

Statistics Canada, *Canada's Cities* (Ottawa, 1980).

—————, *Canada's Changing Population Distribution* (Ottawa, 1984).

—————, *Urban Growth in Canada* (Ottawa, 1984).

B. *Selected Characteristics of Maritime Urban Population*

Abramson, Jane A., *Barriers to Population Mobility: Four Economically Lagging Areas in Atlantic Provinces and Quebec* (Saskatoon, 1968).

Careless, J.M.S., "Frontierism, Metropolitanism, and Canadian History", in Ramsay Cook, ed., *Approaches to Canadian History* (Toronto, 1967), pp. 63-83.

Clark, S.D., *The New Urban Poor* (Toronto, 1978).

Gertler, L.O. and Crowley, Ron, *Changing Canadian Cities: The Next 25 Years* (Toronto, 1977).

Grant, E. Kenneth and Joseph, Alun E., "The Spatial Aspects and Regularities of Multiple Interregional Migration Within Canada: Evidence and Implications", *Canadian Journal of Regional Science*, 6/1 (1983), pp. 75-95.

Kalbach, Warren, *The Effect of Immigration on Population* (Ottawa, 1974).

Macdonald, John S. and Macdonald, Leatrice D., "Chain Migration, Ethnic Neighborhood Formation, and Social Networks", *Milbank Memorial Fund Quarterly*, 42 (1964), pp. 82-97.

McCann, L.D. "Staples and the New Industrialism in the Growth of Post-Confederation Halifax", *Acadiensis*, VIII/2 (Spring, 1979), pp. 47-9.

Nader, George A., *Cities of Canada. Volume One: Theoretical, Historical and Planning Perspectives* (Toronto, 1975).

Perreault, Jeanine, and Raby, Ronald, "Recent Developments in Interprovincial Migration in Canada and Possible Scenarios for the 1980s", *Demographic Trends and Their Impact on the Canadian Labour Market* (Ottawa, 1981), pp. 93-111.

Ray, D. Michael, *Canadian Urban Trends* (Toronto, 1976).

Reid, Frederick, "The Supply of Immigrants to Canadian Cities: 1921-1961" (MA thesis, Queen's University, 1973).

Reitz, Jeffrey G., *The Survival of Ethnic Groups* (Toronto, 1980).

Shannon, Lyle W., and Shannon, Magdaline, "The Assimilation of Migrants to Cities", in Leo F. Schnore, ed., *Social Science and the City: A Survey of Urban Research* (New York, 1968), pp. 49-75.

Simmons, James W., *Canada as an Urban System: A Conceptual Framework* (Toronto, 1974).

Stone, Leroy, *Migration in Canada: Some Regional Aspects* (Ottawa, 1969).

_____, "What We Know About Migration Within Canada — A Selective Review and Agenda for Future Research", *International Migration Review*, 8 (Summer 1974), pp. 267-78.

C. *Urban Spatial Structure*

Abdul-Karim, Yusuf, "The Ecological Structure of Halifax 1971-1976" (MA thesis, University of New Brunswick, 1981).

Balakrishnan, T.R. and Jarvis, George K., "Socioeconomic Differentiation in Urban Canada", *Canadian Review of Sociology and Anthropology*, 13 (1976), pp. 204-16.

Darroch, A. Gordon and Marston, Wilfred G., "Patterns of Urban Ethnicity", in Noel Iverson, ed., *Urbanism and Urbanization: Views, Aspects and Dimensions* (Leiden, 1984), pp. 127-55.

Hicks, Jacquelyn A., "The Development of Moncton: An Ecological Perspective, From 1938" (MA thesis, University of New Brunswick, 1980).

Hill, Frederick, *Canadian Urban Trends. Volume 2. Metropolitan Perspective* (Toronto, 1976).

Mensah, Ernest, "The Demographic and Ecological Perspectives of Spatial Distribution in Fredericton and Saint John, 1971-1976" (MA thesis, University of New Brunswick, 1982).

Rees, Philip H., "Concepts of Social Space: Toward an Urban Social Geography", in B.J. Berry and F.E. Horton, eds., *Geographic Perspectives on Urban Systems* (Englewood Cliffs, N.J., 1970).

Salins, Peter D., "Household Location Patterns in American Metropolitan Areas", *Economic Geography*, 47 (1971), pp. 234-47.

Short, John, "Residential Mobility", in L.S. Bourne, ed., *Internal Structure of the City: Readings on Urban Form, Growth and Policy* (New York, 1982).

D. *Quality of Life Variations Among Cities*

Atkinson, Tom, *A Study of Urban Concerns* (Toronto, 1982).

Stewart, John N., *et al.*, *Urban Indicators: Quality of Life Comparisons for Canadian Cities* (Ottawa, 1976).

E. *Urbanization and Crime*

Brantingham, Paul and Brantingham, Patricia, *Patterns in Crime* (New York, 1984).

Harries, Keith D., *Crime and the Environment* (Springfield, Illinois, 1980).

Kaill, Robert C. and Smith, Paul, *Atlantic Crime Profile* (Halifax, 1984).

McGahan, Peter, "Criminogenesis and the Urban Environment: A Case Study", *Canadian Police College Journal*, 6/4 (1982), pp. 209-25.

————, *Patterns of Crime in Saint John, 1915-1959* (Halifax, 1984).

————, *Police Images of a City* (New York, 1984).

Pyle, Gerald, *et al.*, *The Spatial Dynamics of Crime* (Chicago, 1974).

34

Secondary Sources for Maritime Studies: A Bibliographical Guide

Eric L. Swanick

CENTRAL TO CURRENT national bibliography is *Canadiana*. Published by the National Library of Canada, it appears eleven times per year in print and in microfiche formats with annual cumulations. It is a classified catalogue, classified by the Dewey Decimal system. Under the National Library Act, by law materials are to be deposited with the National Library of Canada and these materials will be cited in *Canadiana*. Unfortunately, there is a great deal of material that does not make its way to Ottawa. This material is published privately, often in limited quantity, often sold by word of mouth and often better collected by local institutions with a local or regional focus. If we can obtain bibliographies on local materials from these local collecting institutions, we will all benefit.

One such regional bibliography is "Recent Publications Relating to the History of the Atlantic Region", which has appeared in each issue of the semi-annual *Acadiensis* since 1975. It has, I think, been quite successful in bringing under control a large body of Maritime material. Although the term "history" appears in the title, this term has been abused with a great deal of regularity. The bibliography always contains references on current social, economic and political matters. As well it contains references to archaeology and anthropology, although it does omit both current literary material and current scientific subjects. It includes references to books, government publications, articles, theses and sections or chapters of books which deal with Atlantic Canada, arranged under a geographical classification. One section deals with two or more provinces and the remaining entries appear under the appropriate province. A number of serial bibliographies which appear on a regular basis in other publications, such as, *Canadian Ethnic Studies*, *Histoire sociale/Social History*, *Urban History Review*, *Study Sessions* of the Canadian Catholic Historical Association, and *La Revue d'histoire de l'Amérique française* are searched regularly and the material of local interest added to the *Acadiensis* bibliography. As a test of its adequacy I checked several of the bibliographies prepared for the "Teaching Maritime Studies" Conference and found only two Atlantic Canada references not previously cited in the *Acadiensis* bibliography. (This will be rectified in the next listing.)

Another current regional bibliography appears in *The Fiddlehead*. Entitled "A Checklist of Recent Literary Publications in Atlantic Canada", it has appeared three times to date and plans are for it to appear in every third issue of *The Fiddlehead*. This checklist includes references to anthologies/collections, bibliographies, drama, juvenile literature, poetry and prose. Whenever possible these listings contain ISBNs or ISSNs and prices of the items concerned. The New Brunswick Legislative Library also publishes on a bi-monthly basis *Selected Accessions = Liste sélective d'acquisitions*. A supplement to each issue cites newly acquired New Brunswick material. Your name can be added to the mailing list at no cost by writing to the Legislative Library.

Of the three provinces the only one with a fairly developed bibliography is that of New Brunswick. *New Brunswick History: A Checklist of Secondary Sources = Guide en histoire du Nouveau-Brunswick: une liste de contrôle des sources secondaires*, published in 1971, and the two supplements are again much more than strictly 'history'. The 7000+ references include material on literature, politics, environment, housing and much more. Unfortunately, the original work and the first supplement of 1974 are both out of print; only the 1984 supplement is still available. For Prince Edward Island, Harry Baglole compiled *Exploring Island History: A Guide to the Historical Resources of Prince Edward Island* (1977) and Alison Kemshead *Prince Edward Island: A Bibliography of Social, Economic and Political Conditions* (1980). In Nova Scotia Robert Vaison has compiled two bibliographical guides to the province, *Nova Scotia Past and Present, a Bibliography* (1976) and *Studying Nova Scotia Its History and Present State, Its Politics and Economy: A Bibliography and Guide* (1974), and Brian Tennyson *Cape Breton: A Bibliography* (1974). The most promising news from the region is the SSHRCC funded bibliography of Prince Edward Island. Work has progressed steadily in this project for the past two years. It will contain approximately 30,000 items — all monographs, sections of books, journal articles that deal with Prince Edward Island, all Prince Edward Island imprints and monographs written by Prince Edward Islanders.

Most lists are fair game for selection purposes. The important point is whether the selection person knows the selection area. With limited funds available there is a danger of smaller institutions relying on encyclopedias rather than books, especially if only a few books can be purchased. Moreover, timely reviews are often difficult to obtain. One of the best sources is the *Atlantic Provinces Book Review*, which is free, contains good sound book reviews and is timely since new books are reviewed soon after their publication. The reviews in *APBR* are also good because they let the blows fall where they should; just because a book was produced locally, it does not follow that it deserves a good review and the book will not be reviewed that way in the *APBR*. Other reviews are available in *Acadiensis* and *The Fiddlehead*, as well as other regional journals such as *Nova Scotia Historical Review* and *The Island Magazine*. Of course, the checklists appearing in *Acadiensis* and *The Fiddlehead* can be used for selection purposes. They are current and, although they do not provide complete order information, you can always write to the appropriate contributor.

The unrevised CIP entries which will appear in *Canadiana* are also published as a monthly 'Forthcoming Books' insert in *Quill and Quire*. CIP is the initial for the Cataloguing in Publication program coordinated through the National Library of Canada. This program provides author, title and, if appropriate, subject information on books, in advance of the book's physical appearance. *Quill and Quire* also provides a separate publication of publisher's addresses on an annual basis. On a more local scale, the Atlantic Publishers Association has issued an *Atlantic Book and Periodical Publishers Catalogue* (1984), but it includes only the publications of those who are members of this organization. There is a great deal more in the Maritime provinces which is published privately or by those who are not full-time publishers and who are not members of the Atlantic Publishers Association. And, of course, there are publishers' catalogues and notices. It is easy to get on a mailing list for this free information by writing directly to the publisher.

For information about Government publications one can consult *Canadiana*, but it cites only those federal and provincial publications which the National Library of Canada has received. It is much better to use provincial checklists of government publications, since they are more complete, often more timely and more often than not provide sufficient ordering information such as price and an address. Each province publishes a checklist or a listing of its publications — Prince Edward Island, a monthly, Nova Scotia, a quarterly with an annual cumulation, and New Brunswick, an annual. New Brunswick will be issuing a quarterly; it is to start with the first quarter of 1986. There are no costs in having your name added to any of the provincial mailing lists. On the national level, the federal government issues a quarterly checklist of their 'official' publications and a weekly 'pink sheet' of new publications. For addresses of federal departments, agencies, commissions both in Ottawa and in the provinces, you may obtain at no cost a publication entitled *Serving You in Both Official Languages = A votre service dans les deux langues officielles* (1984). In some instances it is possible to be placed on the mailing list for certain departmental, agency publications by writing directly to that government body. I should also like to draw your attention to a work by Catherine Pross entitled *A Guide to the Identification and Acquisition of Canadian Government Publications: Provinces and Territories* (1983), which includes addresses on where to locate government publications and notes on the government structure and bibliographies compiled. Finally, Statistics Canada publishes annual catalogues, a monthly on Atlantic Canada economic statistics, statistical kits, and census material. They have a regional office in Halifax with a toll-free line.

There are a number of useful indexing services such as the *Canadian Periodical Index*. A monthly with annual cumulations, it indexes several Maritime periodicals, including *Acadiensis, Atlantic Advocate, Atlantic Insight*, and *Dalhousie Review*. However, a number of significant Maritime periodicals are not indexed in *CPI*, such as *Atlantis, New Maritimes* and *Nova Scotia Historical Review*. In 1981 the Council of Head Librarians of New Brunswick published *An Inventory of New Brunswick Indexing Projects = Inventaire des projets d'indexation en cours au Nouveau-Brunswick*, which cited completed projects as well as projects in progress. It includes references to the indexes of various New Brunswick newspapers, to certain books and papers, to church records and to other items. Each entry, and there are 73, provides details on who to contact and some content analysis. The Indexing Committee has recently been re-established and hopefully more indexing projects will be undertaken. Dorothy Cooke has completed an index to the first *Acadiensis*, which is available from the Dalhousie School of Library Service. Recently a twelve-year index to the current *Acadiensis* was published and there have been indexes published within the journals themselves for *La Revue de l'Université de Moncton* and *Les Cahiers de la Société historique acadienne*. Some periodicals cumulate their tables of contents at the back of their most recent volume, for example the *Collections of the Nova Scotia Historical Society*.

There will always be a need for more periodical indexing but I do feel quite strongly that there needs to be much more book indexing done in this geographical area, especially material published by local publishers. As concerned individuals, teachers should write to these publishers to inform them that much of a book's contents are lost when the book does not have an index. Every book can become a reference book with an index. Without an index as Malcolm Muggeridge once said a book is similar to a railroad guide without the stations being marked on. Much work also needs to be done in indexing newspapers. Harper for New Brunswick and Pratt for Nova Scotia have compiled lists of newspapers for their respective provinces and there are projects underway within both New Brunswick and Nova Scotia to compile checklists of the newspapers. Generally, however, Maritime newspapers are not well served by subject indexes.

It is especially difficult to locate report or proceedings literature in the Maritimes. Often regional political science, anthropology, economic and other associations move about from year to year. Within each province there are libraries whose priorities are to collect locally or provincially.

286 Teaching Maritime Studies

You should become aware of these, should be in contact with them, try to tour them, and use their staff. Regional academic research in progress is reported through the *Atlantic Canada Research Letter*, although this material is largely of the social sciences and humanities. Some newsletters of regional organizations are especially useful for news on articles/ materials being produced by their discipline. One very good example is the newsletter of the Atlantic Association of Sociologists and Anthropologists.

It is often difficult to find out what research is taking place on regional topics. What the area needs is a database of current and ongoing research dealing with the region. A model for such a project is the Canadian Plains Research Center, which serves as a clearing house for research on the three Western provinces. On a more limited scale, the Gorsebrook Research Institute at St. Mary's University, Halifax, is compiling a bibliography of Atlantic provinces resource industries from confederation to the early 1980s. An annotated bibliography on the New Brunswick worker, 1880-1980, is to appear in the near future; the principal coordinator is David Frank of U.N.B.'s Department of History. The Archaeology Branch of the New Brunswick Department of Tourism, Recreation and Heritage will publish a bibliography on Maritime archaeology early in the new year. L'Institut canadien de recherche sur le développement régional at the Université de Moncton will also publish a major bibliography on regional development early in 1986. There are a number of other projects under way or being planned. Hopefully these will all be successfully completed and assist in regional studies. But teachers must lobby their association and/or department to have reading lists prepared for various levels and to have resource lists prepared in their various areas of interest. Without such lists teachers will not find it easy to come to grips with the new Maritime Studies course.

SELECTED BIBLIOGRAPHY

1. *General*

Atlantic Association of Sociologists and Anthropologists. *Newsletter.* Vol. 1, no. 1 - 1975 - Halifax: Mount St. Vincent University, 1975 -

Atlantic Canada research letter. Vol. 1, no. 1, Fall, 1982 - Halifax: Gorsebrook Research Centre, St. Mary's University, 1982 -

Atlantic Provinces Book Review. Vol. 1, no. 1, 1973 - Halifax: St Mary's University, 1973 -

Bates, Iain and Nevill, Ann, comps. *Atlantic libraries and archives; a directory of special collections.* Halifax: Atlantic Provinces Library Association, 1981. 56 p.

Brown, Barbara E., ed. *Canadian business and economics: a guide to sources of information = Economique et commerce au Canada: sources d'information.* 2d ed. Ottawa: Canadian Library Association, 1984. 469 p.
- a major contribution; classified under topics such as bibliographies, demographic data, directories, communications, consumers, economy, energy, finance, government, labour, manufacturing, primary industries, small business and transportation.

Canadian annual review of politics and public affairs 1960 - Toronto: University of Toronto Press 1961 -
- an annual, among a number of other items it includes a lengthy (10 p.+) account of each province.

Canadian periodical index = Index des périodiques canadiens. Vol. 1, 1938/47 - Ottawa: Canadian Library Association, 1947 -
- indexes a number of Maritime periodicals as well as citing articles from many other periodicals which just might contain Maritime Canada material.

Canadiana. Ottawa: National Library of Canada, 1950 -

Council of Head Librarians of New Brunswick. *Directory of New Brunswick libraries = Répertoire des bibliothèques du Nouveau-Brunswick.* 4th ed. Moncton, 1984. 30 p.

Daigle, Jean, ed. *The Acadians of the Maritimes: thematic studies.* Moncton: Centre d'Etudes acadiennes, 1982. 637 p. ill. - issued also in French.

Hall, Agnez, Ruthven, Patricia, and Swanick, Eric L. *An inventory of New Brunswick indexing projects = Inventaire des projets d'indexation au Nouveau-Brunswick.* Fredericton: Council of Head Librarians of New Brunswick, 1980. 51 p.
- lists 73 indexed sources, a number of which are in-house.

Harper, J. Russell. *Historical directory of New Brunswick newspapers and periodicals.* Fredericton: University of New Brunswick, 1961. 121 p.

Kemshead, Alison. *Prince Edward Island: a bibliography of social, economic and*

288 Teaching Maritime Studies

political conditions. Monticello, IL: Vance Bibliographies, 1980. 16 p. (Public administration series; no. 529).

Lowry, Colleen, comp. *Directory of libraries and archival institutions in Prince Edward Island 1985.* Charlottetown: Provincial Library, 1985. 18 1.

MacDonald, Eric G. and MacDonald, W. Stephen. *Fundy tidal power: a bibliography.* Halifax: Institute of Public Affairs, Dalhousie University, 1979. 82 p. ill.

New Brunswick historical and cultural directory = Répertoire historique et culturel du Nouveau-Brunswick. Saint John: Association Museums New Brunswick, 1984. 52, viii p. ill.

Nova Scotia. Provincial Library. *Directory of Nova Scotia libraries.* Halifax, 197(?) - an annual.

Ryder, Dorothy. *Canadian reference sources: a selective guide.* Ottawa: Canadian Library Association, 1973. 185 p.; first supplement. 1974. 121 p.; second supplement. 1981. 311 p.; excellent annotated source.

Tratt, Gertrude. *A survey and listing of Nova Scotia newspapers, 1752-1957...* Halifax: School of Library Service, Dalhousie University, 1979. 193 p.

University of New Brunswick. Department of Sociology. *Abstracts of master of arts theses, 1960 to 1984, Department of Sociology, University of New Brunswick.* Fredericton, 1984. 136 p.

2. *Acadian*

Arsenault, Georges. *Bibliographie acadienne; bibliographie sélective et commentée préparée à l'intention des enseignants de l'Ile-du-Prince-Edouard.* Summerside: La Société-Saint-Thomas d'Aquin, 1980. 26 p.

Centre d'études acadiennes. *Inventaire général des sources documentaires sur les Acadiens...* Moncton: Les Editions d'Acadie, 1975 - 77. 3t.
- vol. 1 is an inventory of 'sources documentaries'; vol. 2 is a bibliography of books, brochures and theses; vol. 3 is a bibliography of periodical articles.

Contact-Acadie; bulletin du Centre d'études acadiennes. No 1 - déc., 1982 - Moncton, 1982 - useful up-dating service, free.

Lévesque, Paulette, comp. "Dix ans d'ouvrages de référence sur l'Acadie et les Acadiens (1973-1982) = Ten years of reference work on Acadia and the Acadians (1973-1982)", *APLA Bulletin* 47 (July, 1983), pp. 5-7.

Potvin, Claude, comp. *Acadiana, 1980-1982: une bibliographie annotée = an annotated bibliography.* Moncton: Les Editions CRP, 1983. 110 p.

3. *Economy*

Cannon, James B. "Explaining regional development in Atlantic Canada: a review essay". *Journal of Canadian Studies = Revue d'études canadiennes,* 19 (Autumn, 1984), pp. 65-86.

Holland, Charlotte, *Catalogue of development plan reports.* Charlottetown: P.E.I. Department of Development, 1979.

Statistics Canada. *Atlantic provinces monthly economic indicator report...* = *Provinces de l'atlantique rapport mensuel de l'indicateur économique.* August, 1983 - Halifax, 1983 -
- by region and by province this monthly gives details on work force, income, spending and more.

Statistics Canada. *Historical statistics of New Brunswick* = *Statistiques historiques du Nouveau-Brunswick.* Ottawa, 1984. 231 p. ill. (Catalogue; no. 11-X-526).

Swanick, Eric L. *New Brunswick regional development during the '60s and the '70s: an introductory bibliography.* Rev. ed. Monticello, IL: Vance Bibliographies, 1979. 37 p. (Public administration series: bibliography; P-204).

4. *Ethnic*

Canada. Department of Secretary of State. Multiculturalism Directorate. *The Canadian family tree.* Ottawa, 1979. 250 p. ill. - issued also in French.

Canada. Department of Secretary of State. Multiculturalism Directorate. *Cultures Canada* = *Cultures Canada.* Vol. 1, no. 1 - January 1980 - Ottawa, 1980 -
- contains news on the subject of multiculturalism, cites publications. Free.

Canada. Department of Secretary of State. Multiculturalism Directorate. *Publications supported by the Multiculturalism Directorate...* Ottawa, 1981 - occasional.

Morrison, James H. *Common heritage: an annotated bibliography of ethnic groups in Nova Scotia.* Halifax: International Education Centre, St. Mary's University, 1984. 134 p.

5. *Folklore*

Fowke, Edith and Carpenter, Carole Henderson, comps. *A bibliography of Canadian folklore in English.* Toronto: University of Toronto Press, 1981. 272 p.

Halpert, Herbert, ed. *A folklore sampler from the Maritimes, with a bibliographical essay on the folktale in English.* St. John's: Memorial University of Newfoundland, 1982. 273 p.

Labelle, Ronald, éd., *Inventaire des sources en folklore acadien.* Moncton: Centre d'études acadiennes, Université de Moncton, 1984. 194 p.

6. *Geography*

Atlas de l'Acadie: petit atlas des francophones des Maritimes/Samuel P. Arsenault... [et al.]. Moncton: Editions d'Acadie, 1976. 31 f. of plates.

Bérubé, Adrien. "Vers un atlas prospectif de l'Acadie", *Le Brayon*, 7 (oct./déc., 1979), pp. 3-56. ill.

DeGrâce, Eloi. *Noms géographiques de l'Acadie.* Moncton: La Société historique acadienne, 1974. lv. en pagination multiple.

Geomarine Associates Ltd. *Annotated bibliographies, Atlantic region national parks.* Halifax, 1974. 324 p.

Nova Scotia. Public Archives. *Place-names and places of Nova Scotia.* Halifax, 1967. 751 p. ill. — reprinted by Mika Publishing, Belleville, Ont. in 1974.

Rayburn, Alan. *Geographical names of New Brunswick.* Ottawa: Surveys and Mapping Branch, Department of Energy, Mines and Resources, 1975. 304 p. ill. (Toponymy study; 2).

——————. *Geographical names of Prince Edward Island.* Ottawa: Department of Energy, Mines and Resources, 1973. 135 p. ill. (Toponymy study; 1).

Note: gazeteers for each province are available from the federal Department of Energy Mines and Resources; maps are available from the provincial Department of Natural Resources or its equivalent in other provinces and from the Department of Tourism.

7. *Government*

Bishop, Olga B. *Publications of the governments of Nova Scotia, Prince Edward Island, New Brunswick, 1758-1952.* Ottawa: National Library of Canada, 1957. 237 p.

Canada. Treasury Board. *Serving you in both official languages = A votre service dans les deux langues officielles.* Ottawa: Communications Division, Treasury Board, 1984. 99, 103 p.
- gives addresses of federal departments, agencies, commissions, etc., in the provinces as well as in Ottawa.

Government of Canada publications: Quarterly catalogue = Publications du gouvernement du Canada: catalogue trimestriel. Hull: Canada Publishing Centre, vol. 27, 1979-

New Brunswick. Legislative Library. *New Brunswick government documents: a checklist of government documents received at the Legislative Library...1955 = Publications gouvernmentales du Nouveau-Brunswick: liste de contrôle des publications gouvernementales du Nouveau-Brunswick établié à la Bibliothèque de l'Assemblée législative...1955* - Fredericton, 1956 -

Nova Scotia. Department of Government Services. *A guide to the Nova Scotia government.* Halifax, 1983. 230 p. - a useful somewhat dated guide.

Nova Scotia. Legislative Library. *Publications of the province of Nova Scotia: a checklist compiled in the Legislative Library of documents received during the calendar year, 1967* - Halifax, 1968 -

——————. *Publications of the province of Nova Scotia: quarterly checklist.* Vol. 1, no. 1 - June 1980 - Halifax, 1980 -

Pross, Catherine A. *A guide to the identification and acquisition of Canadian government publications: provinces and territories.* 2d ed. Halifax: School of Library Service, Dalhousie University, 1983. 103 p. ill.
- a very useful research tool. It provides information in the government struc-

ture, legislative publications, bibliographical information and details on how to acquire legislative documents.

Prince Edward Island. Island Information Service. *P.E.I. provincial government publications checklist.* Charlottetown, 1976 -

8. *History*

Allen, Robert S. *Loyalist literature: an annotated bibliographic guide to the writings on the loyalists of the American revolution.* Toronto: Dundurn Press Ltd., 1982. 63 p.

Armstrong, Frederick H., Artibise, Allen F.I., and Baker, Melvin. *Bibliography of Canadian urban history - part II: the Atlantic provinces.* Monticello, IL: Vance Bibliographies, 1980. 33 p. (Public administration series; no. 33).

Arsenault, Georges. *Initiation à l'histoire acadienne de l'Ile-du Prince-Edouard.* Summerside: La Société Saint-Thomas d'Aquin, 1984. 110 p. ill.

Baglole, Harry, ed. *Exploring Island history, a guide to the historical resources of Prince Edward Island.* Belfast, P.E.I.: Ragweed Press, 1977. 310 p. ill.

Cooke, Dorothy. *An index to Acadiensis, 1901-1908.* Halifax: School of Library Service, Dalhousie University 1983. [109] p. (Occasional paper; 33).

Godfrey, W.G. " 'A new golden age': recent historical writings on the Maritimes", *Queen's Quarterly* 91 (Summer, 1984), pp. 350-382.

Hamilton, William B. "Atlantic Canada". in *A reader's guide to Canadian history; vol 2, confederation to present*/edited by J.L. Granatstein and Paul Stevens. Toronto: University of Toronto Press, 1982. pp. 277-297.

_____. *Local History in Atlantic Canada.* Toronto: Macmillan, 1974. 241 p. ill.

Muise, D.A. "The Atlantic provinces". in *A reader's guide to Canadian history; Vol. 1, beginnings to confederation*/edited by D.A. Muise. Toronto: University of Toronto Press, 1982. pp. 78-122.

Palmer, Gregory, ed. *A bibliography of Loyalist source material in the United States, Canada and Great Britain.* Westport, Conn.: Mockler Publishing in Association with the American Antiquarian Society, 1982. 1064 p.

Peterson, Jean. *The loyalist guide: Nova Scotia loyalists and their documents.* Halifax: Public Archives of Nova Scotia, 1983. 272 p.

"Recent publications relating to the history of the Atlantic region". *Acadiensis.* Fredericton: Department of History, University of New Brunswick, 1975 -

Smith, Leonard H. *Nova Scotia genealogy and local history; a trial bibliography.* 2d ed. Clearwater, Florida: Owl Books, 1984. 84 p.

Swanick, Eric L. *New Brunswick history: a checklist of secondary sources.* First supplement. Fredericton: Legislative Library, 1974. 96 p.; second supplement. 1984. 214 p.

Swanick, Eric L. and Frank, David. *The Acadiensis index, vols. I-XII (Autumn 1971 to Spring 1983).* Fredericton: Acadiensis Press, 1985. 88 p.

Taylor, Hugh A. *New Brunswick history: a checklist of secondary sources = Guide en histoire du Nouveau-Brunswick: une liste de contrôle des sources secondaires.* Fredericton: Provincial Archives of New Brunswick, 1971. 254 p.

Tennyson, Brian, comp. *Cape Breton: a bibliography.* Halifax: Department of Education, 1978. 114 p.

Vaison, Robert. *Nova Scotia past and present, a bibliography.* Halifax: Department of Education, 1976. 164 p.

9. *Literature*

Aubrey, Irene E. "Canadian children's literature in the Atlantic provinces", *APLA Bulletin* 47 (Sept., 1983), pp. 5-9.

Bauchman, Rosemary. *Scotia story tellers; personal glimpses of 21 Nova Scotia writers.* Hantsport, N.S.: Lancelot Press, 1983. 173 p. ill.

Bibliothèque nationale du Québec. *Littérature acadienne, 1960-1980: bibliographie.* Montréal, 1981. 63 p. ill.

"A checklist of recent literary publications of Atlantic Canada", *The Fiddlehead.* Fredericton: Department of English, University of New Brunswick, 1984 - - has appeared in issues 138 and 141 and to appear in no. 145 and every third issue.

Klinck, Carl F., ed. *Literary history of Canada: Canadian literature in English.* 2d ed. Toronto: University of Toronto Press, 1976. 3v.

Laugher, Charles T., comp. *Atlantic provinces authors of the twentieth century: a bio-bibliographical checklist.* Halifax: School of Library Service, Dalhousie University, 1982. 620 p. (Occasional paper; 29).

Maillet, Marguerite. *Histoire de la littérature acadienne, de rêve en rêve.* Moncton: Editions d'Acadie, 1983. 262 p. (Collection universitaire). - the last several pages of this work are devoted to a chronological history of Acadian literature, very useful.

Melanson, Lloyd J. *Thirty-four Atlantic provinces authors = Trente-quatre auteurs des provinces de l'Atlantique.* Halifax: Atlantic Provinces Library Association, 1979. 38 p. ill.

The Oxford companion to Canadian literature. General editor; William Toye. Toronto: Oxford University Press, 1983. 843 p. - useful sections on the Maritimes and its writers.

10. *Material Culture*

Lebreton, Clarence. "Material culture in Acadia", in *The Acadians of the Maritimes: thematic studies*/edited by Jean Daigle. Moncton: Centre d'Etudes acadiennes, 1982. pp. 429-475. ill.

Material History Bulletin = *Bulletin d'histoire de la culture materielle* No. 3 - 1977 - Ottawa: History Division, National Museum of Man, 1977 - - issue no. 15 is devoted to Atlantic Canada. Book reviews, conference reports and short bibliographies are often regular features in each issue.

Stevenson, Sheila. "An inventory of research and researchers concerned with Atlantic Canada material culture", *Material History Bulletin* = *Bulletin d'histoire de la culture matérielle* no. 14 (Spring, 1982), pp. 78-89.

11. *Native Peoples*

Aboriginal rights research. Fredericton: Association of Non-Status Indians, 1977 (?). 209 1.

Allen, Robert S. *Native studies in Canada: a research guide*. 2d ed. Ottawa: Treaties and Historical Research Centre, Department of Indian Affairs and Northern Development, 1984. 185 p,
- issued also in French; includes short bibliographies.

Canada. Department of Indian Affairs and Northern Development. Research Branch. *Research reports, 1983* - Ottawa, 1983 -
- an annual listing of research reports; issued also in French.

Corley, Nora T. *Resources for native peoples studies* = *Resources sur les études autochtones*. Ottawa: Collections Development Branch, National Library of Canada, 1984. 343, 341 p.
- fold map in pocket: provides details on material in both major and smaller institutions.

Daugherty, Wayne. *A guide to native political associations in Canada*. Ottawa: Treaties and Historical Research Centre, Department of Indian Affairs and Northern Development, 1982. 33 p.

——————. *Selected annotated bibliography on Maritime Indian history*. Ottawa: Treaties and Historical Research Centre, Department of Indian Affairs and Northern Development, 1984. 22 p. - issued also in French.

Hamilton, W.D. and Spray, W.A., comps. *Source materials relating to the New Brunswick Indians*. 2d printing. Fredericton: Hamray Books, 1977. 134 p. ill.

Herisson, M.R.P. *An evaluative ethno-historical bibliography of the Malecite Indians*. Ottawa: National Museums of Canada, 1974. 260 p. (Canada. National Museum of Man. Ethnology Division. Mercury Series: Papers; no. 16).

Note: The U.N.B. Micmac-Maliseet Resource Centre's holdings are part of the university's on-line computerized catalog system. The holdings in two broad categories are (1) Indian curriculum materials from all parts of Canada and the United States, and (2) printed and other resources of practically every description of Micmac and Maliseet history and culture.

12. *Politics*

Elliott, Shirley B., ed. *The Legislative Assembly of Nova Scotia, 1758-1983: a biographical directory.* Halifax: Department of Government Services, 1984. 397 p.

Garland, Robert E. *Promises, promises...an almanac of New Brunswick elections 1870-1980.* Saint John: Division of Social Science, University of New Brunswick at Saint John, 1980. 222 p. ill.

New Brunswick. Legislative Library. *Elections in New Brunswick, 1784-1984 = Les élections au Nouveau-Brunswick, 1784-1984.* Fredericton, 1984. 311 p. ill.

13. *Women*

Conrad, Margaret. "The re-birth of Canada's past: a decade of women's history", *Acadiensis*, 12 (Spring, 1983), pp. 140-162.

Kielly, Marion. "Resources on women's studies - P.E.I.", *APLA Bulletin* 45 (January, 1982), pp. 45, 48, 49.

Lemieux, Thérèse et Caron, Gemma. *Silhouettes acadiennes: biographies de femmes.* Campbellton, N.-B.: Féderation des Dames d'Acadie, 1981. 374 p. ill.

McKee-Allain, Isabelle, Clavette, Hugette. *Portrait socio-économique des femmes du Nouveau-Brunswick: tome 1.* Moncton, N.-B., 1983. 124 f. ill.

Mazur, Carol and Pepper, Sheila, comps. *Women in Canada; a bibliography, 1965-1982.* 3d ed. Toronto: O.I.S.E. Press, 1984. 377 p.
- a classified bibliography, several classifications are sub-divided by geographical area.

Zonta Club of Charlottetown. *Outstanding women of Prince Edward Island.* Charlottetown, 1981. 163 p. ill.

14. *Useful Addresses*

Acadiensis
Campus House
University of New Brunswick
P.O. Box 4400
Fredericton, N.B.   E3B 5A3

Association Museums New Brunswick
277 Douglas Avenue
Saint John, N.B.   E2K 1E5

Atlantic Provinces Library Association
c/o School of Library Service
Dalhousie University
Halifax, N.S.   B3H 4H8

Canadian Library Association
151 Sparks Street
Ottawa, Ontario   K1P 5E3

Centre d'Etudes acadiennes
Université de Moncton
Moncton, N.-B.   E1A 3E9

Conservation Council of New Brunswick
180 St. John Street
Fredericton, N.B.   E3B 4A9

Council of Head Librarians of New Brunswick
New Brunswick Library Service
P.O. Box 6000
Fredericton, N.B.   E3B 5H1

Ecology Action Centre
5th Floor, Roy Building
1657 Barrington Street
Halifax, N.S.   B3J 2A1

The Fiddlehead
The Observatory
University of New Brunswick
P.O. Box 4400
Fredericton, N.B.   E3B 5A3

Island Information Service
Prince Edward Island
P.O. Box 2000
Charlottetown, P.E.I.   C1A 7N8

Research Branch, Corporate Policy
Dept. of Indian and Northern Affairs
Ottawa, Ontario   K1A 0H4

Nova Scotia Dept. of Education
Trade Mart Bldg.
Brunswick at Cogswell
P.O. Box 578
Halifax, N.S.   B3J 2S9

Nova Scotia Legislative Library
Province House
Halifax, N.S.   B3J 2P8

Nova Scotia Provincial Library
6955 Bayers Rd.
Halifax, N.S.   B3L 4S4

Provincial Library
P.O. Box 2000
Charlottetown, P.E.I.   C1A 7N8

Public Archives of Nova Scotia
6016 University Ave.
Halifax, N.S.   B3H 1W4

School of Library Service
Dalhousie University
Halifax, N.S.   B3H 4H8

Information Service
Secretary of State
Ottawa, Ontario   K1A 0M5

Statistics Canada
1256 Barrington St.
Halifax, N.S.   B3J 1Y6

Communications Div.
Treasury Board of Canada
Place Bell Canada
Ottawa, Ontario   K1A 0R5

Vance Bibliographies
P.O. Box 229
Monticello, IL   USA   61856

CONTRIBUTORS

Ernest Forbes teaches courses in the history of the Atlantic Provinces at the University of New Brunswick in Fredericton. He is best known for his work on the Maritime Rights movement.

Colin Howell is a member of the History Department at Saint Mary's University and the author of a number of important articles on the Maritimes.

P.B. Waite has been at Dalhousie University since 1951, where he is now McCulloch Professor of History. His most recent work is *The Man from Halifax: Sir John Thompson, Prime Minister.*

Larry McCann teaches geography at Mount Allison University and edited *Heartland and Hinterland: A Geography of Canada.*

Graeme Wynn is Associate Professor of Geography at the University of British Columbia and the author of *Timber Colony.*

W.D. (Bill) Hamilton is a Professor of Education and Director of the Micmac-Maliseet Institute at the University of New Brunswick in Fredericton.

Harold Franklin McGee Jr. is a Professor of Anthropology at Saint Mary's University. He edited *The Native Peoples of Atlantic Canada* and co-authored with Ruth Whitehead *The Micmac: How Their Ancestors Lived 500 Years ago.*

N.E.S. Griffiths is a Professor of History at Carleton University and the author of many books and articles on Acadian history.

Léon Thériault teaches at the Université de Moncton and has written exclusively about modern Acadia.

J.M. Bumsted is a Fellow of St. John's College and Professor of History at the University of Manitoba. His publications include *Henry Alline* and many articles on the Maritimes.

James H. Morrison is Dean of Arts and Associate Professor of History at Saint Mary's University and the author of a bibliographical guide to ethnic groups in Nova Scotia.

J.A. Mannette is a doctoral candidate in sociology at Carleton University and is writing a dissertation on "Nova Scotia's Black Renaissance, 1968-86". She teaches part-time at Saint Mary's University.

Jim Walker teaches history at the University of Waterloo and has written extensively on Black history in Canada and in the Maritimes.

Margaret Conrad is an Associate Professor of History at Acadia University. She was an editor of *Atlantis* and has written a soon to be released biography of George Nowlan.

Martha MacDonald is an Associate Professor of Economics at St. Mary's University and is currently involved in research on women and development in rural Nova Scotia.

Sheva Medjuck is Associate Professor of Sociology at Mount Saint Vincent University and has written extensively on the implications of nineteenth-century economic and social development in New Brunswick, particularly on the role of women in development.

Ian Stewart teaches at Acadia University and studies Maritime politics.

Rick Williams is an Assistant Professor and teaches political economy at the Maritime School of Social Work at Dalhousie University.

Robert Young is a member of the Political Science Department at the University of Western Ontario and has published several works dealing with the Maritimes.

T.W. Acheson is a Professor of History at the University of New Brunswick in Fredericton and the author of *Saint John: The Making of a Colonial Urban Community.*

Roy George is the Dean, Faculty of Management Studies, Dalhousie University and the author of *A Leader and a Laggard.*

Georges Arsenault holds an M.A. in Folklore from Laval and is Professor of Acadian Studies at the University of P.E.I. He has published numerous books and articles on Acadian history and folklore in P.E.I.

Edward D. (Sandy) Ives is chairman of the Department of Anthropology and Oral History at the University of Maine and the author of several books on the folklore and folklife of Maine and the Maritime Provinces.

Ronald Labelle has an M.A. from Laval and is in charge of the folklore archive at the Centre d'Etudes acadienne. In 1986 he was awarded the Prix France-Acadia for his book, *Au Village-bu-Bois: Memoires d'une communauté acadienne.*

Neil V. Rosenberg is Past President of the Atlantic Canada Institute and Director of the Folklore and Language Archive in the Department of Folklore at Memorial University of Newfoundland. Among his publications are *Folklore and Oral History* and *Bluegrass: A History* and a number of articles about aspects of folk tradition and country music in the Maritimes.

Gwen Davies is in the Department of English at Mount Allison University and has written extensively on Maritime literature.

Robert Whalen is a Professor of French at the University of New Brunswick in Fredericton and a specialist in Acadian literature.

Susan Buggey is Chief, Historical Services, Environment Canada, Parks in Winnipeg, and Adjunct Professor, Department of Landscape Architecture, University of Manitoba. Her research has focussed on the historic built environment and on its application in heritage conservation.

Peter Ennals is an Associate Professor of Geography at Mount Allison University with an interest in Canadian cultural history.

Del Muise is a Cape Bretoner who teaches history at Carleton University and the editor of volume one of *A Reader's Guide to Canadian History.*

Peter E. Rider is Atlantic Provinces Historian at the National Museum of Man.

Raymond P. Côté works at the School of Resource and Environmental Studies at Dalhousie University.

Peter McGahan is Dean of Faculty and Professor of Sociology at the University of New Brunswick in Saint John.

Eric Swanick works at the Legislative Library in Fredericton and is responsible for preparing the bibliographical section of *Acadiensis.*